The Book on Tai-Chi

© 2022: Gail Brubaker - Senior Professor of the Arts

ISBN: 978-0-9769823-9-5

Printed: 2022 - Ft. Lauderdale, Florida USA

ALSO BY THE AUTHOR:

PARROTS OF THE CARIBBEAN
UNDER THE DOUBLE HELIX
THE KILLER APP
NOW IT CAN BE TOLD
NIGHT BLOOMING JAZZMEN

Author

Gail Brubaker

Publisher

EPAKS Publications

Technical Editor

Ken Herman

Cover Design

Gail Brubaker

Ken Herman

Special thanks to:

I would be remiss if I didn't first acknowledge the incomparable Dot Ross for endless patience and support on this project. Next, a needed thank you goes to Ken Herman and EPAKS for editing and invaluable input.

Also I need to acknowledge the people who patiently took the time to educate me through my years in the ways of Tai-Chi and martial arts in general, whether directly or through life's experiences. Some such individuals are included in the Sea Stories section.

A very special thanks and aknowledgement to WikiMedia Commons. The many amazing graphics in this book would not be here without the hard work of collecting such an amazing and open portfolio of images for everyone to use. The endless hours of scanning this trove of images was not only educational and enjoyable, but helped make this book what it is.

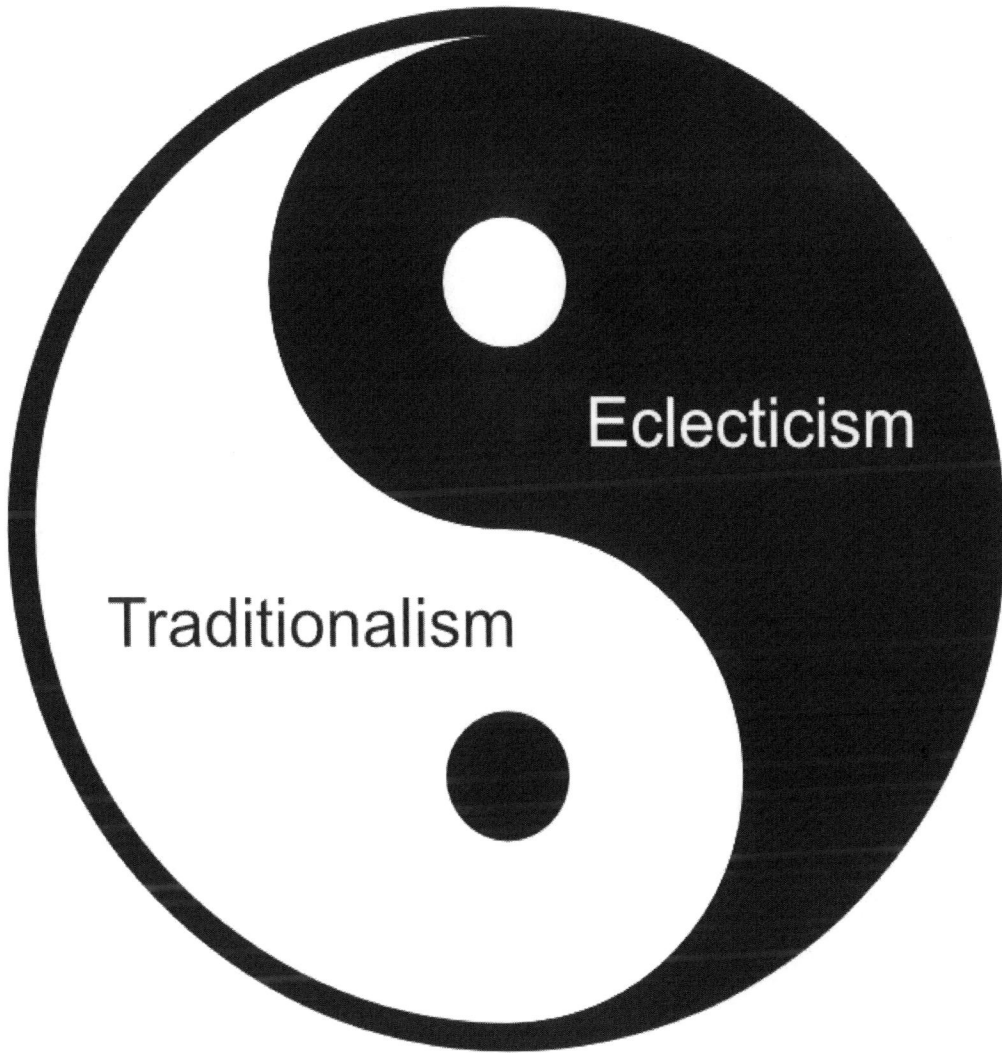

*A project that is neither
feasible nor commendable*

*THERE IS MORE IN HEAVEN
AND EARTH THAN
IS DREAMED OF IN YOUR
PHILOSOPHY
HORATIO*

Table of Contents

Forward   9

How Did This Happen?   10

Tai-Chi Theory and Physiology   13

    Funambulism 14

    Inspiration 19

    Chi 24

    Brain Wave States 29

    The Chemistry of Emotions 34

    Voltage 37

    Structure 41

    Simulacra 43

    Healing Hands 45

    A Word on Healing 50

    Third State of Consciousness 52

    Intestinal Fortitude 55

    Body Energy States 57

    Music 60

    Maxwell's Demon 65

    Synergy 68

    Natural Movement and Health 71

    The Body Makes its Own Medicine 74

    Tai-Chi for Health 77

    Living Waters 79

    Slow Boat from China 85

    Postureality 87

    Postures 90

        Push 92

        Press 94

        Fair Lady 96

        Levitate 98

        Eagle 100

        Snake Creeps Down 102

        Crane Spreads Wings 104

        Single Whip 106

        Play Guitar 108

        Seven Stars 110

Tai-Chi Theory in Action   112

Fighting 113

Thaumaturgy 117

Uweza 120

The Other Kind 124

Batesian Mimicry 128

War Horse 132

Thanatophobia 135

LUM 140

Super Karate Power 145

Ho'o.loli 146

Iron Men 151

Zoomorphism 154

Strategy and Tactics 161

Fighting Styles 164

Weapons 169

Tai-Chi Fighting 174

Options 179

    Monkey 180

    Mantis 182

    Snake 184

    Crane 186

    Tiger 188

Nautiloidea 190

Shuangzizuo 192

Zen-O-Phobia 195

Brubaker's Law 198

Yin/Yang in Tai-Chi Application 200

Tai-Chi Death Touch 203

Applications 207

    Rat's Claw 208

    Eye of Pheonix 211

    Two Finger Sword 214

    Tiger's Mouth 217

    Dragon's Head 220

Tai-Chi Theory and Philosophy   223

Forward 224

Monoceros 229

Phases 233

Time 236

Gravity 242

Themis 247

Manitou 250

Mind Control 253

Mind Intent 256

Meditation 261

Focused Attention 265

Who's Talking 270

Ethereality 275

What's the Point 277

Beginning 280

Two-fer 285

The Long Game 288

Internal Arts 290

Geese, Magnets, and Decoherence 294

Jieshu 300

You Never Know 305

Intermission 307

Why Don't You Just Say So 311

Yin/Yang - Manifestation 314

A Brief History of Rhyme 319

The One and The Other One 324

Quantum Chromodynamics 328

Titivations　　334

Who Says So 335

Tableau 337

What They're Saying 344

    Dr. Bonell 345

    Dr. Burack 346

    Dr. Laura 347

    Dr. Falck 349

What Else They're Saying 350

Sea Stories　　351

Introduction 352

The Boatyard 353

Happy Halloween 355

Johnny B 357

Shattered Expectations 359

Time's Up 361

Merry Christmas 363

Friends 365

Tiger Joe 367

Bill Boggs 369

Big Boyz 372

The Bell Telephone Hour 375

Anchors Away 377

Punch-Pourri 379

Bunch-O-Nuttin' 383

Vastness of the Sea 388

Final Thoughts   390

Fini 391

Laeta Finis 396

The End 399

Epilogue 401

Looking Forward 403

Index   405

Forward

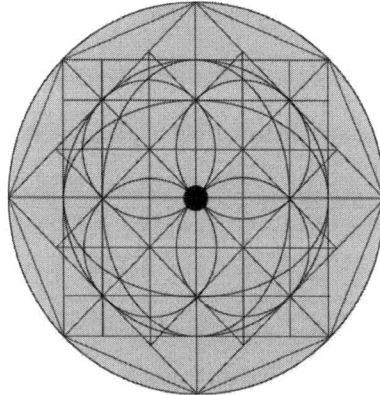

The Kenpo Yantra

EPAKS Publications has been producing high quality American Kenpo specific literature and learning tools for well over a decade. Without question, the author of this book has been an asset to these endeavors. When the idea of branching out into non-Kenpo specific materials arose, the author came up as a natural addition to its catalog. This proposition was only bolstered by the author's familiarity with both Tai-Chi and American Kenpo and with his lengthy tenure in the arts.

Although the information presented in this book took a lifetime to gather, the collaboration of transforming this project from merely a concept to physical form took over two years. In that time, it became apparent that this new book would not only rise to the lofty standards originally anticipated, it would make for a considerable departure from previous works produced by this company as well.

The delicate balance of humor, seriousness, and a clear understanding and presentation of the material is a striking departure from what one would normally come to expect from a work of this nature. It is, at both the same time, a good read and a coherent, structured approach to such a detailed, subtle, and vast subject matter.

Anyone who has attempted to put their thoughts on paper quickly realizes that such an undertaking is not what they expect. It is much harder to make one's thoughts not only organized, but also comprehensible for another's consumption is much harder than one initially believes. Put succinctly, its hard work. And, to further make the resulting product enjoyable to others is truly a labor of love. This project can be described as such.

It is hoped that the reader enjoys this work as much as EPAKS Publications has enjoyed working with the author to make it a reality. It is further hoped that the reader takes the time to muse over the offerings presented in this book, while also enjoying the minute detail decisions that went into its design and layout. Every effort was made to ensure this book was effortless for the reader to understand, appreciate, and spend copious time pouring over its presentation of content. It is a shame that such an ancient and popular art as Tai-Chi is, all so often, mis-understood or overlooked by its reputation from the uninitiated public or equally uninitiated martial artists of other disciplines.

EPAKS Publications

How Did This Happen?

"How did this happen?" is a good question for a detective. And, since I did have a career as a Private Investigator it is very comfortable for me to answer this conundrum from that perspective. As a starting point, let's begin with a premise. It may seem unrelated, but I'm going to answer that question with a statement: The history of policing as a municipal function is only of recent development.

The first organized government mandates regulating police type activities never appeared until Louis the Fourteenth enacted a royal decree, creating a paramilitary force to institute control in Paris in 1667. Prior to that, population centers were brutal, dangerous places. The rest of Europe was slow to catch on, with London waiting until 1820 to create the first recognizable modern police department. This was under the supervision of Robert Pele and is the reason British police came to be known as Bobbies.

In the new world there existed a similar situation, with the first American police department established in Boston in 1838. Canada had departments that predated Boston by a bit, but prior to that...you were on your own. City living was hazardous - merchants and shipping companies hired private protection.

Before the marauding, plundering European invasion; native Americans kept social order through tribal councils administered by village elders. If someone was out of line, everyone knew it and the tribe would enact collectively to maintain order and mete out justice. Most small hamlets and villages throughout the world functioned in the same way. And, rural communities in the east were no different.

There was no constabulary in ancient China. The Imperial Guard was in the magic city protecting the emperor. True, there was from time to time a system of regional magistrates exercising civil authority; but for much of China's history It was every village and literally every man for himself.

Like most municipal functions in China, police services were nonexistent. With Elders maintaining organizational control over family groups. The family unit was ward, precinct and bally-wick. With different family units banding together when necessary to provide for the common defense.

Many villages consisted of just one or two families, and if a band of brigands came to town (like they torched the village in *Platoon*) it was up to the family unit to repel them. If your family possessed a secret technique, like the tiger claw or panther punch, you wanted to keep that occult, hidden within the family. It could mean the difference between keeping your crops and homes; or rape, pillage, and murder.

Most fighting styles were family styles with local champions regarded as regional heroes. Family pride and loyalty to style created an atmosphere of secrecy to protect this important knowledge. Most fighting techniques were "tough-guy" or what came to be known as external styles; featuring power strikes, Dim-Mak vital area attacks, blood chokes, and bone breaking maneuvers.

In Chen village they too practiced a family style. A style so effective that they dared to call it Tai-Chi.

Tai-Chi means "Grand Ultimate" (among other things). Tai-Chi-Chuan translates as "Grand Ultimate Fist". And, in ancient China you didn't go around calling your style Grand Ultimate if you couldn't back it up.

This system took a different tack. Instead of meeting force with force, Tai-chi fighters blended with incoming power. Instead of enduring injury due to collision, they preferred to remain whole; to be able to fight a little longer. As they systematically expanded these ideas, certain principals began to emerge through an ever expanding understanding of physics, psychology and human nature. Along the same path, a knowledge of anatomy and physiology emerged, based on traditional Chinese medicine, including an understanding of circulating fluids and the nervous system; which produced an accurate, in depth science for both fighting and health maintenance.

Because it was a tradition in Chinese culture to only pay your doctor as long as he kept you healthy, most people were very familiar with movement and yogic style treatments as healing modalities. Tai-Chi stylists couldn't help but notice the similarity between Tai-Chi fighting movements and many of the Chi-Kung prescriptions commonly recommended by doctors. The flowing, twisting actions inherent in Tai-Chi fighting movement, provided the internal organ massage recommended as wellness remedies. Combined with yogic breathing techniques and focused attention paradigms, it became an efficient use of time to perform your supplemental health exercise at the same time you practiced your martial art.

There has always been a long running debate about the discrepancy between health, nurturing, movement and proper fighting technique. Some practitioners say correct martial art application equates to precise Chi-Kung health routines. While, many maintain subtle tweaking is required to maximize for one or the other. But, I maintain that in martial art, sometimes one or two degrees can make a vast difference; and any movement is always good for you.

Which is a better exercise: tennis or basketball? I say that 90% of the benefit is just in the fact that you're moving at all. In Tai-Chi, you generate many of the internal benefits whether you employ a specific Chi-Kung or not. Regardless, most practitioners soon realized that they could get a two-for-one by practicing martial arts and performing Chi-Kung, at the same time.

As fame of the martial prowess of Chen fighters spread through the land, many styles began to feature Tai-Chi type movement. The sister arts of Bagua and Tsing Yi were born. Outsiders tried to appropriate the jealously guarded secrets of the Chen family, and there is the famous story of how Yang Lu Shan infiltrated the Chen inner circle by taking a job in the kitchen and watching the Chen train at night.

After a while, Yang challenged Chen fighters and started beating the old man's top students. So, Master Chen accepted Yang as the first non-Chen Tai-Chi student. Eventually, Yang broke away and formulated the Yang style of Tai-Chi. which has become the most practiced Tai-Chi form in the world.

It didn't take long for word of this brilliant martial art to reach the Imperial City, and they dragged some masters up to the palace to perform a demo. As previously stated, keeping the formulas for your Particle Beam weapon and Cobalt Bomb secret was the prime directive.

As stewards of the family art, they did not want the Emperor's court to know that these peasants possessed a devastating fighting style. So, the masters insisted that Tai-Chi is for health only. And, from that day forward Tai-Chi would forever be known as a health maintenance regimen.

Fast forward to the 1960's and Tai-Chi began to grow in popularity in the west. Cheng Man Ch'ing reluctantly pared down the long form to accommodate the short attention span of the western mind. But even in China, Tai-Chi was becoming a dying art, because it was just too long and arduous to learn.

In China during the cultural revolution, Kung-Fu training was oppressed by Government decree. Many martial arts masters were "re-educated" or eliminated outright. Somehow, Cheng Man-Ch'ing made it to this country and taught successfully in New York City. As a matter of record, I received my teaching authorization from one of Ch'ing's students and teach a modified short Yang form.

While well-established today, Tai-Chi is still mostly shrouded in mystery. In the following pages, we will try to present an understanding of why and how it is what it is.

There is a renowned basis for Tai-Chi being known as a healing art. For example, it is taught in many hospitals and often recommended by reputable, progressive doctors. This prescription is not limited to recovering patients, but also for maintaining proper health and well-being. Chi-Kung means "health nurturing". If you have an interest in a holistic approach to health and longevity, it may prove worthwhile to peruse these pages and begin to understand that the body creates its own medicine; and that healing originates from within.

Tai-Chi Theory and Physiology

The Health Implications of Tai-Chi Principles

We are slowed down sound and light waves, a walking bundle of frequencies tuned into the cosmos. We are souls dressed up in sacred biochemical garments and our bodies are the instruments through which our souls play their music.

Albert Einstein

Funambulism

"The good old days" and "things ain't what they used to be" are classic American adages that themselves are relics of the past. The modern world has wrought many distractions and conveniences that have changed our species in some fundamental ways. But, just as the old philosopher observed in the book of changes, there are always tradeoffs; and here too the Yin/Yang of everything prevails.

In 1900 America, nine out of ten jobs were in agriculture. Within fifty years 90% were in industry. The vast majority of factory jobs were less taxing than farm labor; although mill work, for one, was still undeniably a physically demanding endeavor.

The dream these workers held for their children was of prosperity and an easier life. In the sixties, this ideal was exacerbated by the new medium of television, which portrayed a future of sit-down jobs in climate-controlled environments. This prediction, along with many others, proved to be fairly accurate. Even the implausible suggestions of outer space themed programs; which featured robotic assistants and personal mobile communication.

While the promise of this was being promoted, American kids, lucky enough to live in or near a bucolic landscape, could still enjoy the simple youth; not dissimilar from that of their fathers and grandfathers. I, myself, was able to lie face down, gazing into a stream; catch tadpoles; jump from the pump house into a pond; and ride bikes for miles. Real Tom Sawyer stuff. Tree-houses, forts, and sandlot sports were all typical of many American communities. This included the Midwestern enclave I called home during my formative years. Sadly, I believe this is no longer typical.

Five decades ago, as I meandered aimlessly through young adulthood, one detour found me travailing with a small circus. This was fantastical, even then, but not an impossible thing to have happened. Today however, no one can experience this. There are no circuses.

The last great American circus gave its final performance on May 21 2017. Ringling closed the big top forever. The brothers began shows in the late 1800's and combined with Barnum and Bailey in 1907. The original five cent admission initiated a business behemoth, that propelled the Ringlings to become one of the richest families in the country.

In case it seems that this is a tribute to circus life, or a reminiscence of a lost era, it is not. But by way of comparison and explanation, here in Florida, it is currently difficult to take a visitor snorkeling, without lamenting how teaming the reef used to be. Similarly, to reference a high wire act, without at least a passing homage to the circus, seems somehow ungracious. Gentleman, remove your hats please!

Tight wire artists, sky walkers, high wire and slack wire performers are known collectively as Funambulists. Currently, there are no legal or industry standards as to where one designation begins and the other one ends. Customarily, any wire elevated more than twenty-feet is considered high wire. In sky walk, a cable is stretched between rocky precipices or fixed between buildings. The parameters of slack wire are undefinable. An analogue shares the famous jurist's definition of pornography; "I know it when I see it". Regardless, any funambulist relies on a highly cultivated sense of balance to maintain equilibrium.

Supreme confidence and nerves of steel, are required of anyone working high. The soft shoes allow the performer to feel the wire, and position their center-mass directly over the base of support; which is wide in the lateral direction, but narrow in the sagittal.

A high wire artist may extend his arms, or even use a pole to distribute mass away from the pivot point, increasing the moment of inertia. Angular acceleration is reduced, and expanded time sense allows the performer to develop the torque needed to initiate anti-tipping maneuvers. This is in contrast (Yin/Yang) to the figure skater who brings their arms in to accentuate rotation like a spindle, concentrating mass and rotation into their center, increasing spin.

These highly developed skills and the physics underlying them are synonymous with many of the primary principals of Tai-Chi. Principles which stimulate the practitioner into fine tuning their internal gyroscope, improving their overall balance, and acquiring an extremely advanced spatial awareness of their physical body. This is one of the foundational benefits of forms work.

Balance is essential in all athletic endeavors, especially in martial arts. This is specifically so with ones like Tai-Chi, where one is continually shifting from one, one legged stance, to another one-legged stance. A stable base allows the practitioner to deliver spectacular discharges, by being rooted and transferring power into the target. Even when protuberant or eccentric (out of position), balance is the body's ability to return to a stable position or trajectory following a disturbance to equilibrium.

The spatial body awareness developed through the practice of Tai-Chi, creates an awareness of the body's center of gravity. This point is different for everyone. A man's tends to be just above the navel, due to upper body mass. A woman's is usually below the navel, because of the larger hips. A child's tends to be in the mid chest, because of a disproportionately large head compared to their body.

Center of gravity occurs when the mass of an object is distributed in equal directions. The lower the center of gravity, the more stable a body becomes either at rest or during acceleration. Awareness of one's center of gravity is essential for maintaining equilibrium and fall prevention. And, fall prevention is one major factor in preventing needless injury.

Fragility and frailty increase with age. The risk of death from any injury is exponentially increased if the subject is frail. Also, it is highly more likely for one to acquire an injury if they are fragile. Even in situations that may seem incidental to most people. This is a major strength of Tai-Chi. The health benefits derived from Tai-Chi training are a key deterrent to both of these addressable conditions.

Any exercise program a senior can engage in will partially stave off the ravages of aging. However, the systemic internal science of Chi-Kung is appurtenant for these conditions. While resistance training and mild cardio-vascular conditioning can extend both years and quality of life, the focus on improved balance demanded by Tai-Chi specifically addresses a crucial vulnerability of this age group. Improved balance is propitious for persons of any demographic. But, this effect is greatly pronounced in persons in their declining years.

It has always been personally rewarding to witness my students increase stability and improve confidence, especially among the elderly, in and out of a clinical setting. I have both taught and administered Tai-Chi programs at several hospitals, medical centers, and retirement communities. Notable doctors avidly recommend this form of self-improvement to not only to help improve balance, but because if there is one thing an old person cannot afford to do, is take a spill.

Alas, the risk of falling increases with age. One third of people over 65 will fall. Once a senior experience a fall, two-thirds will fall again within six months. More women fall than men. Falls are the leading cause of death for people over 65. 50% of all fatal falls are people over 75. Also, falls frequently result in a hip fracture. Undeniably, training in Tai-Chi will help improve balance and will significantly ameliorate this danger.

When I reference improved balance in Tai-Chi training, I euphemistically say, "fine tune the gyroscope". But how specifically does Tai-Chi affect this basic sense? How does a pianist play faster runs, or a marksman become more accurate? By challenging that behavior. Requiring it perform at a higher level. One that is more demanding than the conditions of ordinary, typical motor functions.

In the case of balance and equilibrium, the internal structure of concern is the vestibular system. A sensory system that detects spatial orientation, motion, and head position. Within the inner ear is the vestibular labyrinth which contains the cochlea and semi-circular canals. There are complex components like the ampulla which contains the stereocilia bathed in endolymph. To complicate things further, there are the otolith organs; which sense forward and backward movements, as well as gravitational forces. In addition, the utricle detects horizontal movements and the saccule senses vertical movements. Also, the crystals called Otoconia that cause so much trouble with vertigo, when displaced.

Information from the vestibular system is coordinated with input from other position detection sensory apparatus. They each collect within the gray matter which comprises the body's administration center. The brain's cerebellum is located at the point where the back of the head meets the spine. Position feedback from the muscles, joints, and eyes transmit information to this part of the brain on the position of the body in relation to the environment. Neurotransmitters signal the muscles to make postural adjustments to maintain balance.

Kinanesthesia, more popularly known as Proprioception, was called a sixth sense by sir Charles Bell, and allows the detection of limb position and joint motion, even in darkness. This differs from neuromuscular control which is the efferent motor response to afferent signals. This requires a properly functioning contralateral cerebral cortex.

This system transmits signals at incredible speeds and has the capacity of being fine-tuned. Learning to ride a bicycle provides a good example of challenging the synergistic capability of these integrated components. When developed over time, they will provide increased balance and finer spatial awareness.

Acrobats who can juggle while riding a unicycle on a high wire is representative of an "impossible" skill I have observed in the circus. This, as well as many other "impossible" feats. Challenges demonstrated by humans who were willing to devote the time and repetition to advancement of the human potential. Before the internet, the circus was the sole repository of spectacular feats of balance. Now, amazing has become routine; proving the incredible human organism is capable of improvement and higher development. Most certainly, the sense of balance and equilibrium required by daily activities is far from one's maximum potential.

How much one will develop balance and equilibrium is solely up to you. Regardless, any improvement will be helpful both in and out of the ring. One can be satisfied with just standing and walking, becoming a master of the Tai-Chi form, or even develop to rival the great Zamboni. Either way, it's Yin/Yang - a question of balance.

Inspiration

Atmospheric pressure at sea level is 14 psi; it is 10 psi at an altitude of 10,000 feet. This is because there are fewer molecules pushing down at 10,000 feet than there are at sea level. Their combined weight is decreased and the pressure that forces the molecules together is reduced. Air molecules spread out as atmospheric pressure decreases, and the air becomes thinner. This translates to fewer molecules by volume.

While oxygen is the big player in in our biology, the most abundant gas, by far, in atmospheric air is nitrogen at 78%. Oxygen only makes up 21%; leaving a 1% mixture of other gasses:

- argon
- carbon dioxide
- neon
- helium
- methane
- krypton
- hydrogen
- nitrous oxide
- xenon
- ozone

There occur other dioxides in minuscule proportions as well as particulate matter, like: dust, spores and pollen. The number of gas molecules per cubed meter differs at varying elevations, however, the mixture contains the same ratio of gasses no matter where or how high a measurement is taken.

When we breathe, we aspirate these various gasses, through the pharynx via the trachea. The gases then pass into bronchial tubes, which are passages that lead into the lungs. The gas mixture is then exposed to the alveolus. The diaphragm and muscles surrounding the ribs allow the bones to move, facilitating deep breath.

The alveolar wall has an average thickness of 0.5 micrometers. This provides for the molecular transfer of gasses. The transaction occurs in the delicate alveoli. Only a few layers of cells separate the pulmonary capillaries from the inhaled air. This allows carbon dioxide and oxygen transport from the bloodstream; this process is known as gas exchange.

Alveoli resemble bunches of grapes. This shape provides for a large surface area for gas exchange, as atmospheric air is exposed to pulmonary capillaries. There are about 450 million alveoli in the lungs of an average human. This represents a surface area 40 times greater than the person's entire epidermis.

The body relies upon hemoglobin to transport oxygen. When oxygen is released by the hemoglobin, it penetrates into the cell. The waste product of this cellular activity is carbon dioxide. This carbon dioxide is captured, cycled back to the lungs and released as exhalation. This final process occurs because it is difficult for oxygen to dissolve in blood. Water molecules bond to carbon dioxide and form carbonic acid, which converts on demand into bicarbonate and frees a hydrogen atom.

The primary role of oxygen, in human physiology, is to provide the body with energy. Organelles called mitochondria generate this energy. They combine oxygen with nutrients supplied by the digestive system, creating a type of energy called adenosinetriphosphate (ATP). This packet of transformed energy can then be used directly by the cell. One molecule of glucose provides 35 units of energy as ATP. Oxygen is an anathema to free radicals and pathogens.

Deep breath can be likened to a fire extinguisher by attacking and purging pathogens, while also removing and expelling other invasive particles. One major reason why athletes are healthier compared to non-athletes is because they take advantage and expose the benefits of the deep breathing process. This process also inspires more oxygen into and throughout the body.

In today's society, chronic stress, either real or imagined, causes many individuals to remain in a constant state of flight or fight. Couple this with the fact that in the western culture, most people breath very shallowly; confining the majority of the breath to the upper third of the lungs. The result of both of these tenancies is shallower and faster breathing.

To observe the palpable outcome of this aberrant breathing condition, watch someone engaged in personal conflict; such as a disagreement. They are almost panting. This is a natural mechanism to prepare the body for action. When the action never comes, the hyperventilation creates a pathological condition known in Chinese medicine as fire energy excess. The prescription, of course, is controlled, slow, deep breathing allowing the bodily systems to function as nature intended.

The sympathetic and parasympathetic nervous systems are antagonistic. When one system is engaged, the other shuts down. When the brain identifies possible danger or to prepare the body for high energy output, and possible injury, the body engages a catalog of systemic adjustments.

Digestion and peristalsis stop and blood is sent to the muscles in preparation for extreme exertion. The entire organism experiences an adrenaline dump to supercharge key systems. Pupils dilate, teeth clench, breathing becomes shallow and rapid to supply a temporary boost of oxygen, to power the muscles for action.

It is easy to see that living in a constant state of anxiety, as described above, produces biological stressors. The process to counter the above scenario, is to engage the parasympathetic system (Yin/Yang), reversing the caustic consequences of neurasthenia that agitate and damage the organism.

The parasympathetic nervous system is the body's rest and recuperating mode. The opposite and reverse (Yin/Yang) of the flight or fight response. It causes a decrease in heart rate, stimulates normal peristaltic smooth muscle movement, and focuses the body's mechanisms toward energy building and repair. It is the body's healing modality.

The body seeks equilibrium. It is constantly making adjustments to maintain homeostasis. One of the design premiums is the ability to engage the parasympathetic response at will. Again, as described above, this is achieved through the simple process of deliberate, slow, deep breathing.

The slowed breathing is then comprehended by the other bodily systems. The result is the automatic engagement of the parasympathetic system. This method is simple and effective. In other words, to promote healing and down regulate the fight or flight response; just transition to slow, methodical breathing.

There are a variety of breathing techniques. Many modern adaptations have been created to try and squeeze just a little extra benefit from the ancient methods. Much medical research has been dedicated to verifying the corollary between breathing patterns and physiological response.

Breathing techniques are quite varied. There are energizing breaths, cleansing breaths, and breaths that synchronize heartbeats. Most of the modern formulas involve some manner of counting. Each have their place and provide amelioration to varying degrees.

This book has a broad scope and is intended to serve only as an introduction to these arcane protocols. Because of this fact, for our purposes, I will advocate only one method. But it's a doozy.

THE COMPLETE BREATH

To begin preparation, one can sit or stand. The following is a simple checklist of addenda that provide a synergistic effect with the breathing technique:

1. Alignment: Make sure the shoulders are over the hips. If standing, your center is between the feet with weight distribution evenly distributed. Whether sitting or standing, next...

2. Relax the external musculature: Take a moment to feel each muscle, and when you think you are completely relaxed; let go some more. Become limp to the point of collapse. Take notice of which muscles are actively involved in holding the body upright. Then relax all others. Next...

3. Cultivate awareness: Feel the energy coursing through your body. Feel the life force circulating inside of you. By tuning your perception to body awareness, you will become cognoscente that you are a vibrating aggregation of bio-energies collaborating harmoniously. In unanimity with the environment. At peace. The pure joy of just being.

Begin a long, slow, deep inhalation. Protrude the lower abdomen as you use the mental imagery of filling up with air below the navel. This is not possible, of course, but it facilitates inverting the diaphragm, so that we can fill the lower lungs.

Once the lower abdomen feels full and you cannot fill it any further, begin to concentrate on filling the mid-chest. There is a strange phenomenon. When concentrating on the lower abdomen, you simply can't take in any more air. The inhalation just stops. But, once the attention is shifted to the mid-chest, more space seems to become available. This bit of self-subterfuge is a fortuitous device to assist in breathing with the whole lung.

Continue the process of filling the mid-chest. At some point, this too will begin to cease as the mid-chest reaches maximum capacity.

Now, shift your attention to the two high lobes under the clavicle. This is a zone that is often a problem area, because the air it is commonly not fully flushed out and can become stagnant. Dead air can accumulate here and the warm, moist environment can foster pathogens. Clearing out this space can prevent mold, spores, and viruses from gaining a forward position against your immune system.

By starting at the lower abdomen and progressively filling each area consecutively, this methodology amounts to packing air on top of each of the preceding regions. Visualize a fountain with three cups. Each cup in-line begins to fill as the preceding one begins to overflow.

Once the entire lung is filled to capacity, retain the breath for three or four seconds. This brief breath retention initiates the dive response, which further initiates cellular respiration. After the desired time period, let the breath be expelled outward with a sigh. Simultaneously with the exhalation, release any tension that may have accumulated in the shoulders and make a conscious gesture to relax the trapezius and deltoids.

The sigh is an integral part of the technique. From one point of view, one can think this as the opposite and reverse of the kiai yell. Along with the breath technique, there are also imaging and hand mudras. These can be used as an adjunct, to enhance the technique energetically. But, the complete breath is a standalone modality, and requires no embellishments.

Complete Breath - QUICK START GUIDE

- ✓ fill the lower abdomen
- ✓ when that feels full
- ✓ fill the mid chest
- ✓ when that feels full
- ✓ fill the two high lobes
- ✓ retain for three of four seconds
- ✓ exhale (with sigh)

Many of the methodologies perceived to be occult or esoteric are also thought to be inscrutable. While it is true that there are abstruse layers of complexity in the secret knowledge; many practices are just nuts and bolts stratagems. No more mystical than eat more vegetables or follow the golden rule. Many Eastern secrets intersect well with functional medicine and universally understood concepts of spirituality.

The ability to affect the Sung state of extreme relaxation is one of the most beneficial therapeutics you can derive from this book. Yet it is ludicrous in its simplicity. Likewise, the complete breath is easily learned and not taxing in any way. But there is a secret: you have to do it.

On the one hand, you can read about a successful diet or a tip about driving safety; recognize its merit; and say: "oh yeah, that sounds like a good idea." But hearing about a profound tip, acknowledging it, and never implementing it is slothful. And, this leaves no one to blame, except yourself. Especially when ignoring the beneficial advice proves to be so costly.

The complete breath is one such practice. You cannot find a more powerful method to inaugurate health and self-discovery than this simple technique. One can be lead to living waters, but only you can take the drink. Stand in wu-ji. Feel the aliveness in your body. Breathe. Feel the joy of just being.

Chi

There are many translations of the word Chi (Qi). In Tai-Chi, there are specific targeted definitions necessary for implementation of energetic protocols. Also, It can be used as a general term for non-specific particulate matter or fluid capable of coursing, cascading, or flowing. Further, as a noun or a verb denoting movement, flow, or particular energies. Chi permeates time, space, and consciousness; and quantifies, yet transcends, a comprehensive definition. One's acquired awareness of Chi can create an all-present background state, and may subtly alter their psyche; sometimes permanently.

Biologically, Chi can refer to the energy found in hormones, neurotransmitters, and A.T.P. On a macro scale, systems of municipal infrastructure, like water and sewage, roads and bridges; while being utilized, enjoy a type of Chi. Intangibles like will, love, vitality, stamina, and life force all possess Chi.

Pragmatically, Chi is often used interchangeably with migration of fluids and kinetic energy. Also, Chi is an analogous concept; inclusive of all things and dependent upon the context of a conversation. Even lifeless things, like rocks, have Chi; due to the flow of electrons in the molecular structure.

Trying to establish a blanket definition of Chi can be likened to the task of penetrating a sphere; it doesn't matter where you begin. So, let's just start with some common meanings.

Air: Something everyone understands, but if asked for a definition, the answer would probably be both nebulous and specific, based upon context. If discussing lift among aeronautical engineers, it's one thing. From an auto safety perspective, the importance of tire pressure is another. And, from a medical and scientific perspective, the effect this mixture of gasses has on the human organism is vital.

Fluids: Again, this is dependent upon context. Chi is often sited when referring to endogenous fluids such as blood or lymph. The same holds true for water or other fluids as they course through the human body. Where biological context is one thing, nautical is another. Ship builders or fishermen would use it in a distinctly different, yet similar way. And still, even granular objects can be thought of as possessing Chi when moving energetically. Situations such as a landslide, nebula clusters, along with other astronomical movements all express a form of Chi.

Energy: This denotes both chemical and kinetic; phenomenal and psychic. It includes energy waves of any description - electrical, vibratory, light, sound, food, thought, and emotion. Each of these possess varying degrees of Chi. Also, the energy itself can be thought of as Chi. This also includes the motility, excitation, and awareness of any type of action.

It would seem obvious for Tai-Chi practitioners to maintain a strong emphasis on Chi, after all it is right in the name. The word Chi in Tai-Chi does and doesn't necessarily fully refer to any energetic aspects of the art, but is more a coincidence of the Chinese lexicon. Be that as it may, there certainly is Chi in Tai-Chi.

Swirling around and through new age mysticism and health practices is the idea of a life force. A universal dynamism that animates all life forms; far beyond just supplying nutrients to living cells. The acknowledgment of this animating energy, as well as physiology, is in keeping with the binary concept of Yin and Yang. This is because Chi may be qualified as either Sheng-Qi; which is positive, or Sha qi; which is negative.

Chi is the vital spirit that animates all living things. And yet, inanimate objects can also possess a type of Chi. In this instance, it would refer to a quality or character. Legitimate foods contain active enzymes and would be said to have Chi (Yin). This is in stark contrast to the dead food that most Americans consume (Yang). Food that is just something that keeps one from being hungry - until the next reload of lifeless goop. There is much sagacity in the maxim - living food for a living body.

The idea of Chi and parana have a long history in the traditions of the east. Both primitive Europe and the Judaeo Christian tradition hint at analogous notions; concepts like the breath of life and spirit. These ideas surely developed because humans innately feel an aliveness attributable to more than chemical reactions.

In ancient China, Chi was regarded commonly as a life force, but among the medical community more often than not, Chi was related to the circulation of blood and other fluids. Specific conditions and treatments apprehended Chi as a circulating humor. But, in mind/body, focused, attention practices; the idea of life force prevailed.

While, at first glance, it would seem clarifying to do a deep dive into the various explanations of Chi, it is probably more instructive to break it up; addressing each aspect of Chi as they occur in familiar analogs. Extensive dissection of each aspect would prove confounding, if taken as one treatise. It is for this reason I will merely supply a list of definitions of Chi. If only to deepen one's understanding, while simultaneously promoting elucidation of this fundamental concept.

- CIRCULATING HUMORS OF ALL TYPES

- BIO-ELECTRICAL IMPULSE

- BRAINWAVE ENERGY

- ANIMATING LIFE FORCE INSIDE THE HUMAN BODY

- MOLECULAR ENERGY THAT BINDS INANIMATE OBJECTS

- ANY NATURAL VIBRATORY PHENOMENON

- PSYCHIC ENERGY

- KINETIC ENERGY

- QUANTUM FIELDS

- CURRENTLY UNKNOWN UNIVERSAL MATRIX

In age-old concepts that presage dark energy and quantum field theory, Chi was generally regarded as the animating matrix that pervaded the universe: A kind of electric, spiritual, psychic intelligence. And the more we as an ever more advanced species learn, the more and more accurate this original theorem seems to be.

チ

For our proposes, to understand this nearly ubiquitous concept is to derive greater benefit from the practice of Tai-Chi. One order of business is to explore the nuts-and-bolts function of Chi in the body as accessed by Tai-Chi practices. Another is to develop an understanding of Chi as an introduction to a way of thinking as it applies to its many integrated subjects.

If it vibrates, binds, or flows, it is Chi. The use of allegorical terms is well established in elocution. This emblematic device is fairly common and not just limited to literary works. For instance, in language, universal or blanket terms are commonly accepted both in the felicitous and slang lexicon. This includes concepts, like: cool, hot, dude, and crazy; as well as adopted terms which are borrowed from other languages. Terns such as: aloha or boss. On the other hand, necessary or critically important terms of many peoples tend to hyper-focus meaning of words. As an example, the indigenous arctic aborigines have many words for snow, which are far more specific and precise.

Being a "straight shooter" and "always doing what you said you would do" are axioms that cover a wide range of distinct life situations. At the same time, they also provide an inclusive blanket of "universality" that is comprehended by almost everyone. Indeed, there are times when minutiae are necessary, but there are also times when this can cloud discernment. In these instances, a general term typically fosters a clearer perceptivity.

If one were trying to imbue a child, early on in their life, with modern adaptive survival skills; it would be expedient to explain ways to avoid trouble with comrades and authority. One could inefficiently cite hundreds of specific examples of ways to avoid suspicion and incarceration. Or, the juvenile could easily be advised to - just be honest.

To say there is only one way to get from Cleveland to Toledo is both imperious and arrogant. And, dependent upon context. There are different "best" routes. There is the fastest way, the scenic way, the accepted way, and/or the way that is easiest on the car - just to name a few. What if the road is blocked or you need to relax and suffuse another type of stimulus? There are main roads, side roads, scenic avenues through bucolic countrysides, and restful visages with farms and woodlots. In essence, by taking an "alternate" route, one can affect a slightly different person. For instance, exposure to a serene milieu, in contrast to a city route, will alter one's biochemistry. One becomes imperceptibly reformed, accepting, contemplative....changed.

For populations where their culture was immersed in an accepted understanding that all things are connected, these peoples intuitively apprehended that fluids and energies were the same. To them, this concept was not stupid nor crazy. And, some of these cultures were extant well prior to the scientific age. Without the facilitation of modern instrumentation, these peoples may not have comprehended voltage-gated ion channels, or the science of gas exchange, but assuming that fluid, chemical, and electric forces were congruous/euphonious is a very intelligent and, dare I say, prescient conclusion.

In other words, to lump together fluids, chemical and electrical energy, brain function, and spirituality are not incongruous in a society that regards all things as interconnected.

Brusque (intense and opinionated, but pertinent) diatribe: It throws people off track and wastes valuable time to attack terms and concepts that are seemingly archaic or incongruous with a narrow cultural prejudice. Intellectual bullies masquerading as arbiters of truth, are just cynics scanning for anything out of place with their rigid worldview.

Where possible, I have tried to present concepts in a manor compatible with the western mindset. There are times, however, when a Chinese ethos proves to be a better architype. After all it is a Chinese art. To properly grasp certain processes may require an adjustment of psyche and behaviorism. To step outside narrow prejudices, release chronic, orthodox thinking, dwell in equanimity, and allow an appreciation of an alternate understanding, and the mind that created it.

Recognizing that Chi is a universal life force is tantamount to osmosing the expansive thinking required to enter the doorway for perceiving commonality, the congruity of Tao, and field theory. Likewise, recognizing the correlation of fluids, breath, and nerve impulse as synergistic; instead of separate and distinct systems or things. Undeniably, these processes are related and cooperate together to make the entire unit function.

Chi, Tao, Yin/Yang, and five element theory are interrelated as each individual concept reveals. Chi as a universal engine is congruent with Tao as a universal energy matrix. Chi is one thing; and many things. For the western trained audience, it may be instructive to reiterate the Born rule: probability density is amplitude squared. So, while there are trillions of energy points in multiple dimensions, there is only one wave function; and that is the wave function of the entire universe.

Brain Wave States

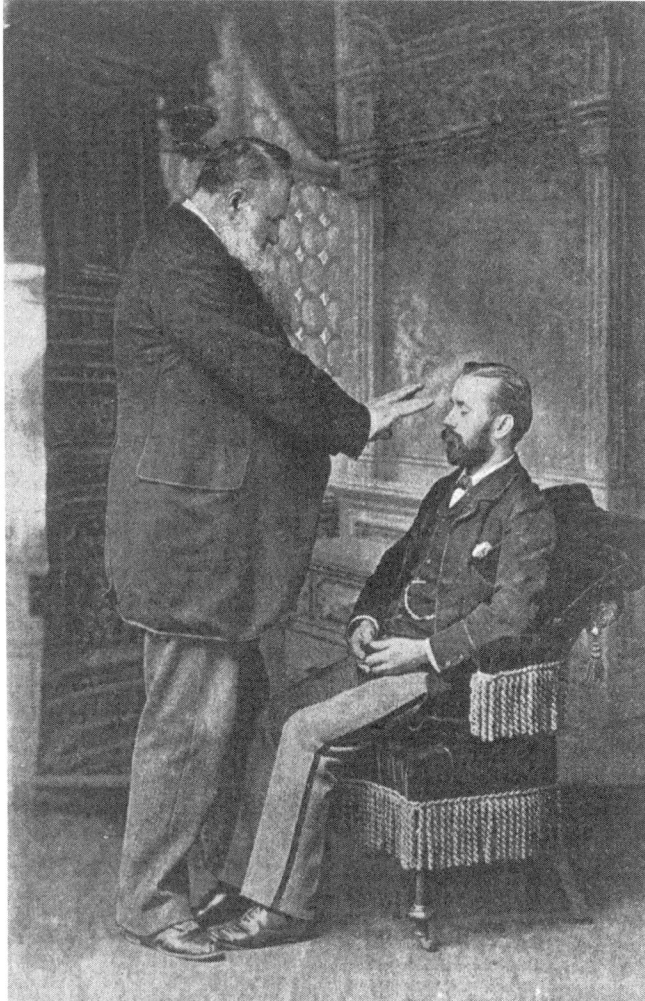

For the purpose of continuity, we will pro tempore regard the brain as a purely physical structure. Just another organ. We will temporarily avoid the pertinent question, *just who is it that looks out through these eyes?* These issues will be addressed in subsequent essays of this book. The different aspects of brain function are many and complex. For now, let's narrow our focus.

The role of the brain in Tai-Chi training transcends any obvious influence on motor function, timing, or spatial awareness. To extract maximum function from this organ, is a delicate dance; since it is the primary role of the brain to function as the control unit and problem solver. Not unlike riding a war elephant, you are technically the commander. But, the powerful beast has a will of its own and can disregard or override direction from an impotent hamout. Collaborating with its idiosyncrasies, gently nudging when necessary, and sometimes just letting it do its own thing.

Neurogenesis is of great interest to most practitioners of Tai-Chi, Chi-Kung, and related arts. This seems a good place to start, because it addresses two important points. What can we do to improve brain function? And, can existing braincells be preserved?

The process by which nervous system cells are generated by neural stem cells is called neurogenesis. Older adults are often told to pursue Tai-Chi because learning a new skill benefits the brain. And, the breathing and movement increases fitness and mediates pathological conditions.

The topic of neurogenesis is germane because production of nervous system cells is paramount to maintaining youthful vitality. It is also pertinent because it illustrates an important point of Tai-Chi training in general - the accuracy and timelessness of Tai-Chi principals. As an illustration, for years respected authorities with letters after their names claimed new brain cells could not be made. But then, new research and discoveries prompted a reversal of the previously iron clad position. A position Tai-Chi has apperceived all along.

In 1928, Santiago Cajal, the father of modern neuroscience declared the adult human brain never makes new neurons. This theory held sway for decades. Research conducted in the 1980's started to disprove this long held conclusion, and as further discoveries were made, the backtracking began. So when it comes to disputes between a mechanism that is still learning and the ancient wisdom, it's good to remember this anecdotal tale.

Brain chemistry will be addressed in another essay. For our purposes let us consider brainwave states. Control and creation, thereof, and how this insight can enhance our practice of Tai-Chi, and the interaction of our perception and the environment.

Anything that alters your perception produces changes in your brainwaves. Psychotropic drugs and plants with psychoactive properties are commonly used in our culture to alter brain function. Brainwave training however has a long history in eastern traditions, like yoga and Chi-Kung. There are newer, somewhat comparable methods, such as brainwave entrainment. However, here we are exploring the well-trod natural path with a reliable and vaunted history of success. Instabilities in brain rhythms create the whole pantheon of emotional and psychiatric problems that plague modern man. Aggression; bipolar disorder; panic attacks; and the other costly, detrimental conditions that are so common and pernicious in our society.

We have discussed how emotions create chemical changes in the body. But what creates our emotions? Or, our thoughts and feelings for that matter. The impetus, the first cause, is communication between neurons. Our actual thoughts are the corporeal manifestation of disturbances in the brain's electric field. Conscious thought produces electrical impulses, which transmit signals to various body systems; often to dramatic effect. Different states of mind produce various clinically verifiable brain wave states.

Brain waves are produced by synchronized electrical pulses from the communication between masses of neurons. A fluctuation of voltage. This electrical activity is referred to as a brain wave. So called because it is cyclic and wavelike in nature.

Brainwaves are divided into 5 different bandwidths that create the entire spectrum of human consciousness. Our thinking, feeling, and emotions; along with other stimuli elicited by our interactions with the environment and other people; result in specific brainwave states. Rock, paper, scissors. Part of a feedback loop.

HUMAN BRAIN WAVES

GAMMA 31 - 100 Hz		Insight Peak focus Expanded consciousness
BETA 16 - 30 Hz		Alertness Concentration Cognition
ALPHA 8 - 15 Hz		Relaxation Visualization Creativity
THETA 4 - 7 Hz		Meditation Intuition Memory
DELTA 0.1 - 3 Hz		Detached awareness Healing Sleep

0.0   0.2   0.4   0.6   0.8   1.0   (Seconds)

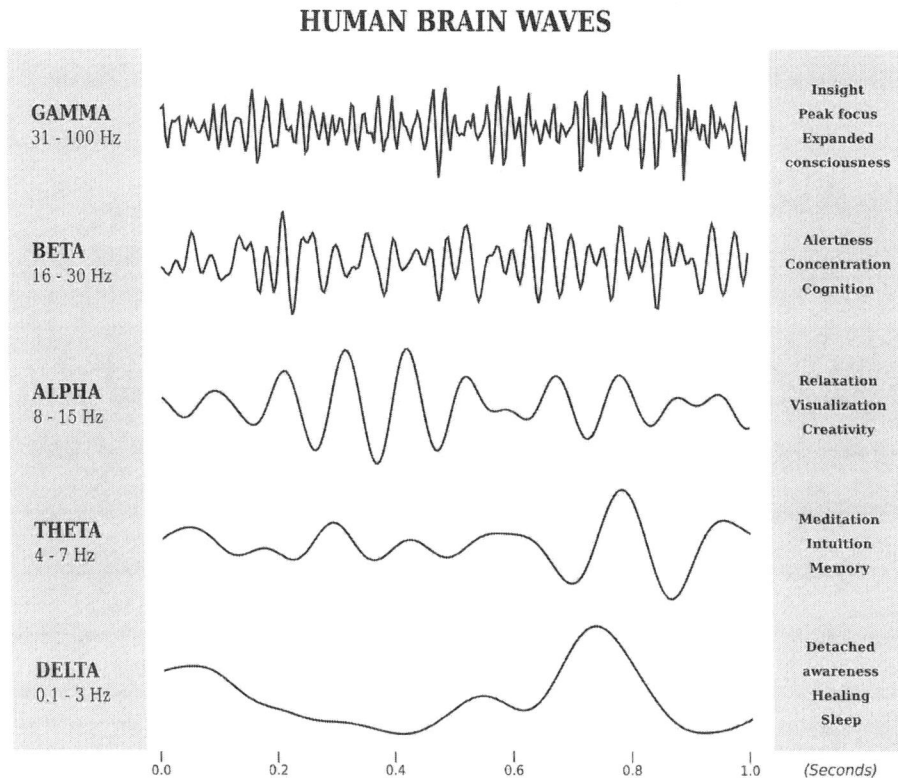

DELTA	Slowest, deep dreamless
THETA	Sleep, Zen meditation
ALPHA	Idling, daydreaming, mindfulness.
BETA	Normal waking consciousness, alert, focused, problem solving.
GAMA	Fastest of all brain wave bandwidths. Allows for the processing of information from different areas of the brain simultaneously. Heightened perception, elevated consciousness.

The brain wave frequency of 8 Hz is the borderline between the alpha and theta frequency ranges. This is the state experienced during meditation and Tai-Chi, when the two hemispheres of our brain are working at peak synchronization. When we command our emotions, we exert conscious control over our body chemistry and brainwave states. Our war elephant carries us through to victory.

Our DNA replicates at a frequency of 8 Hz which is also the nuclear magnetic resonance of hydrogen atoms, A fact which is significant, but deferred for examination later in this book.

The Brain

The Body

The Brain

Brain

Body

Yin

Yang

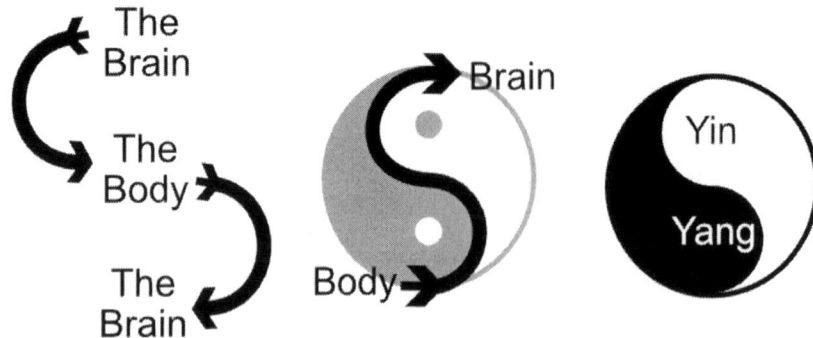

Awareness of brainwave states exercises command over emotions. Emotions influence body energy states. Paper covers rock. Rock breaks scissors. Scissors cut Paper. Which brings us to focused awareness and MIND INTENT

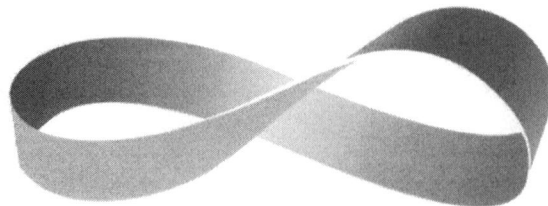

If a brain wave is defined as a rapid fluctuation of voltage between parts of the cerebral cortex, then a look into voltage in the human body is in order. This will require an exploration of wave function, the Lorentz force, and quantized electromagnetic fields; which will ultimately leave us with an Ouroboros like sensation. And, the conclusion that endeavors of this nature are best to be understood viscerally. Which is why traditional teachers and guides speak of the brain metaphorically.

To attempt to write a scientific explanation of "romantic love" would be interesting. But I'm sorry to say, not very helpful. Some things in this world are best processed by the heart. An as-yet undefinable area of human experience, passion is a brain function that; energizes the body, vexes the mind, and disturbs spirituality. A mysterious process that transcends any graph of brainwave function.

The brain contains about 100 billion neurons which are electrically excitable cells. Every neuron has a resting voltage of 70 millivolts. They communicate through both electrical and chemical activity. How the brain processes stimulus is a discussion for another time. Therefore, Sensory transduction is not germane here, as our concern is the influence of the brain on the organism holistically.

Since the brain is a control unit in itself, to derive maximum executive function, one should realize the brain will automatically regulate countless systems, monitor afferent levels, and set parameters on chemical messengers. For superior health and to function optimally, during a crisis situation, it is imperative to develop awareness of brainwave states. In an effort to down regulate problematic mental dilemmas and runaway emotional states, trained methodologies up regulate systems that produce efficaciousness, by bringing them under conscious control.

As unrealizable as this technique may sound, it is possible to train states of mind, precondition mental response, and utilize brainwave states to maximize effectiveness. One learns to engage the parasympathetic system for healing and employ the sympathetic response to enhance combat effectiveness. Conscious control of brainwave states is equally elemental and significant to one's training as is physical conditioning or motor response.

Indeed, thoughts and feelings have their genesis in the brain, transcending a purely clinical explanation. But, this discussion is concerned with how brainwave function influences the systems and organs of the body. And, how the mental aspects of Tai-Chi practice affects chemical messaging and biological processes.

The Chemistry of Emotions

If one fundamental idea of this book is to help you understand that the body makes its own medicine, then it's also essential to understand that it makes its own poison. For instance, if we are trying to down regulate the stress response, then it's easy to see that governing our emotions would be a good place to start. I don't think anyone needs to be told what happens to a person in a fit of rage. Uncontrollable, literally out of their minds. While the chemical result of a mind state like this may allow you to possess super human strength and even help you win some fights; the downside of this condition is that you certainly won't have access to any fine motor skills. Any kind of fight science or technique is utterly out the window. The smooth, even countenance of a skilled fighter who sees everything coming and counters effortlessly is the epitome of the martial artist. While there are times it may be helpful to throw the switch and go psychotic at will, this book is the antithesis of that. It is about Tai-Chi.

Let's address emotions and health. Look at someone in extreme anger - accelerated heart rate, B/P spiked, veins popping. Adrenaline dump. Not healthy. So any process that allows you to never subject your body to that type of stress; would be good to know. Or, even model your life after. People who have formed the habit of living in a constant state of anxiety are micro-dosing themselves with stress chemicals all the time. In Tai-Chi, we start each day by calming the mind and dosing the body with a flood of healing chemicals, triggered by the relaxation response.

One nice thing about this subject is that you don't really need to understand the chemistry to derive its benefits. But, it does help to have a stronger compulsion to be at least partially aware of the science of internal health nurturing.

Within that tone, let's start with the monoanime neurotransmitter system. The neurotransmitters we're mostly concerned with are dopamine, noradrenaline, and serotonin. Each are derived from one amino acid. That's why they are monoanimes. They are produced by neurons in the upper brain stem. The raphe nuclei produces serotonin; the ventral tegmental and substantia produces dopamine, and locus ceruleus for noradrenaline. Nerve cells project axons and release transmitters throughout the cerebral cortex. Monoamines bind to an array of receptors which are excitatory. Monoamine systems are regulating systems.

The amygdala and other limbic structures synthesize information and control emotions, delivering the message to the brain. Different monoamines affect different emotions. For example, depressed people tend to have low levels of serotonin, where noradrenaline is involved in the fight or flight response. In depth research and an abundance of abstracts are readily available on the internet about this topic. This chart summarizes the three most commonly referenced neuotranmiters and the ratios that are involved with each emotion.

EMOTION	SEROTONIN	DOPAMINE	NORADRENALINE
ANGER	LOW	HIGH	HIGH
SHAME	LOW	LOW	LOW
FEAR	LOW	HIGH	LOW
SURPRISE	HIGH	LOW	HIGH
JOY	HIGH	HIGH	LOW
EXCITEMENT	HIGH	HIGH	HIGH

I only include this basic information so you don't forget that the mind / body connection is very real and not some imagined process that no-nonsense people can't be bothered with. Emotions directly affect bio-function. State of mind has consequences. A principle part of Tai-Chi training is developing the ability to control mental states, and in a sense, learning to fashion artificial emotions. To influence the production of the endogenous healing chemistry, while maintaining a focused command center during duress.

A researcher at the university of Colorado named Amy Cuddy observed a phenomenon during her study with animals. What she noticed was that timid animals had high concentrations of cortisol and aggressive animals had high concentrations of testosterone. Further research revealed that aggressive animals, acting timidly, had high cortisol and low testosterone; and timid animals, acting aggressively, had high T and low C.

So, she decided to perform an experiment with her students. What she uncovered was that merely assuming the posture of aggression or timidity affected hormone levels. With this new knowledge, she developed a series of postures to elicit a given chemical balance, as revealed through a series of blood draws. One, hands on hips, menacing stare, she named "wonder woman". Another, was called "the executive", and so on. The conclusion was that by merely assuming the posture of a state, the bio-chemistry changed accordingly. If that's not Tai-Chi, then I don't know what is.

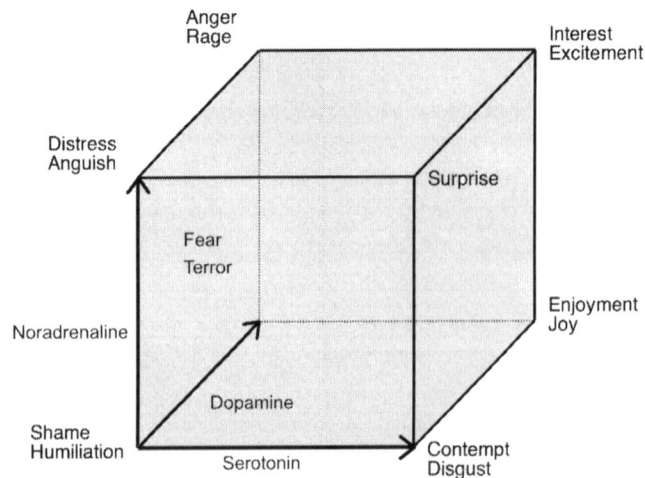

The ability to fine tune your bio-chemistry is not some far-out, mystical hypothesis. It's a nuts and bolts science well known to yogis, therapists, and others familiar with the mind / body connection. Your body is constantly making adjustments to accommodate your changing situation. In the case of physical trauma, it dispatches an array of healing chemicals to the injury and / or affected areas. But, the body / mind also makes chemical adjustments based upon your emotional state. Being startled can cause a heart attack. Being meditative can cause the heart to heal. You don't need to wait for N.A.S.A. to make some break-through discovery, nor have Seimens develop a bio-emotion regulating machine. It's already available. The mind / body techniques perfected by the old masters are the time honored prescription for maintaining hormonal equilibrium. The practice of Tai-Chi down-regulates the stress response and up-regulates the relaxation response. This is the internal alchemy.

Voltage

Movement is good for you. It maintains homeostasis. Too little leads to physiological atrophy, too much and the body breaks down. You need to challenge the muscles, the connective tissue, the bones. Astronauts must work out extra hard in the presence of micro-gravity. We evolved in the presence of 1G gravity and require it's resistance to maintain health. The effect of Tai-Chi on bones, organs, connective and vascular tissue will be addressed in subsequent chapters. For now, let us explore the function of muscles in Tai-Chi. But before we do, let's mix science with history to help assimilate some relevant information.

Beer. I can speak with some authority on the subject, but will only reference it in passing; as it pertains to the development of the modern PH scale. In 1909, Soren Sorenson worked at the Jarlsberg Brewery in Denmark. It was there that he developed understanding for what we now call PH.

PH - the abbreviation for Potential Hydrogen. The PH scale is a way to grade acid/base from 0 to 14. Pure water is considered neutral (at 7). There is more to PH, however, than just the Yin/Yang of acid/alkali. Another example would be chemical and electric. Or, electrochemical.

PH in differing solutions will create voltage. Our bodies are about 65% water. All cells in the body are basically the same in this regard, and cells are designed to run on a PH between 7.35 and 7.45. By measuring the voltage generated by the solutions within our body we can optimize our understanding of the electric nature of our physical vehicles.

PH, however, can be used to explain voltage between liquids. A solution is either an electron donor or an electron stealer. If it is an electron taker it gets a "+" sign. If it's an electron donor it gets a "-". This is because electrons have a negative charge. This phenomenon can be measured by using a voltmeter, which can also be referred to as a PH meter. Most meters are capable of both readouts. Milli-volts in solutions are directly correlated to PH. The voltage is converted on a logarithmic scale which reads out 0 - 14 PH. If cells must run on a PH of 7.35 - 7.45 that would translate to -20 to -25 milli-volts. An electron donor with a PH of 14 would read as -400 MV. An electron stealer with a PH of 0 would read as +400 MV.

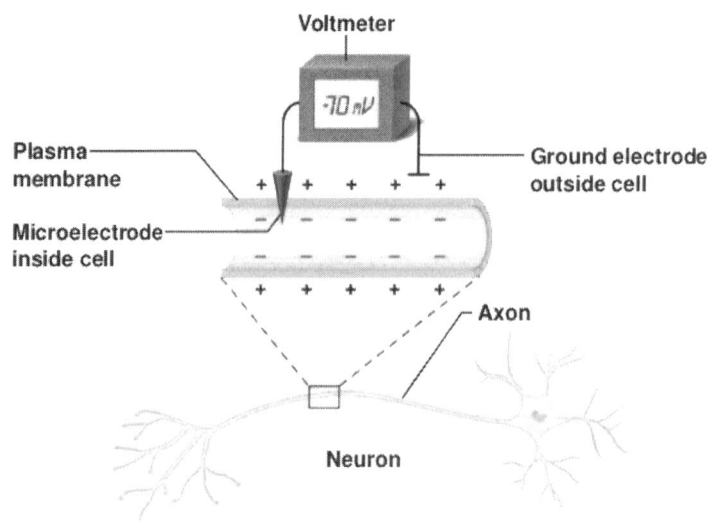

neuron memberane voltage at rest

How do all these voltage revelations work within the human body? Action potential (nerve impulse) travels down an axon, where there is a change in polarity across the membrane of the axon. In response to a signal from another neuron, sodium- (Na+) and potassium- (K+) gated ion channels open and close as the membrane reaches action potential (nerve impulse). This action potential results in an impulse signal traveling down the axon, where there is a change in polarity across the membrane of the axon.

The piezo-electric effect occurs when a substance is stressed and emits electrons. Every time you move your muscles, you generate electricity. Cell membranes and fascia are analogous to capacitors. In contrast, the muscles parallel batteries, being animated by ADP, converting it to ATP for use by the mitochondria. Inside the mitochondria, the citric acid cycle or Krebs cycle, elicits a charge on the cell membrane. The action potentials that travel down connected neurons are based on electric current, generated by the movement of sodium and potassium ions into and out of cells.

Throughout my study of Tai-Chi, I have been told that the energy travels through the fascia. This is true because the fascia functions as a semiconductor. It allows electrical signals to travel at high speed; but only in one direction. The fascia surrounds all body organs. And, it is through the seemingly random, convoluted fascia pathways that we have developed the acupuncture meridian system. Capitalizing on the electrical energy flows. Acupuncture is specifically designed to stimulate electrical responses through the fascia pathways that connect directly to the organs; effecting their function. Through the interplay and support/destruction concept of five element theory, treatment of pathological conditions may be obtained.

Health may be maintained and physiological distress addressed, by maintaining a suitable electrical charge through the muscle battery system and delivering electrical energy through the meridian system.

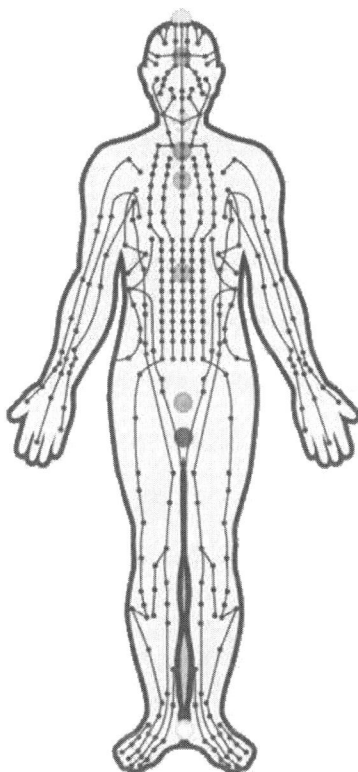

meridian example

Subtlety is the watch word in Tai-Chi. As a practitioner, you are trying to fine tune your perceptions to such tolerances, you begin to develop equilibrium on a microscopic level. This, in point of fact, is where the internal alchemy takes place.

At this point, one would be justified in making the criticism that these brain waves and subtle electric currents are just not strong enough to matter. After all a milli-volt is just 1000th of a volt. Although this amount may seem minute, it is here that the Yin/Yang aspect pervades the universe, by holding sway over the macro; which, in contrast, generally manifests more tangibly and obviously. A lethal dose of cyanide is just 135ppm. It is, however, the tiny fractions that occur on a microscopic level that provides the catalyst for real discernible action in the body universe.

Consider the tiny spark that ignites a volume of dynamite initiating an effect that has tremendous real world results. This errant spark is a prime example of a cascading reaction. How about a match to gasoline? It is, in fact, only the thin layer of emitted vapor that ignites the gasoline. When man uses his intellect to construct an internal combustion engine, a small amount of vapor in the presence of a minuscule electric spark produces real usable mechanical energy. All of this from a diminutive volume of chemical. In the human body, curcumin can produce tangible results, but only because of a catalyst. In the presence of pepperine its effect is enhanced by 2000%.

A vaccine has a life-saving effect on the human organism by causing a reaction within the human body. But, antibodies are by no means the only resultant stimulus the human body produces. Most medicines have no direct action on a pathology, but rather, stimulate the body to produce a reaction that addresses the problem.

A vaccine is an example of an outside agency that causes the body to produce healing. In the Tai-Chi health regimen, we replace a drug catalyst with organ massage, altered breathing patterns, and electric energy stimulated and directed by disciplined mind intent. This is no different than the body's reaction to a chemical. The body's reaction to physical stimulus is why doctors say exercise is good for you.

If I suffer a bruise, the body springs into action by dispatching actinic curatives to the damaged areas, as needed. By twisting and contorting in Tai-Chi, the body also directs chemical envoys to the stimulated sites. Maintaining proper PH (voltage) through Tai-Chi, internal alchemy augments the bio-electric system, which results in vibrant good health.

As described above, the human body is designed to normally function at -20MV to -25MV, compared to healing, which operates at -50MV. The relaxed state created by following proper Tai-Chi protocols, results in the removal of physical stress barriers which retard the flow of Chi; and thus providing the suitable electric field for health maintenance.

The body is many things at the same time. A bag of water and a spiritual vehicle. A collection of chemical reactions and biological plumbing. An awe inspiring study in complexity of whatever system you happen to be focusing on. For the sake of developing an understanding of energy in Tai-Chi, appreciating the electrical aspect of the human organism is a basis for advancement in the art.

All 70 trillion cells in the human body communicate via electromagnetic frequencies. Electromagnetic exchange is foundational to all body functions. In fact, all cells, chemical messengers, and atoms produce electromagnetic fields. Also, muscle tissue and neurons are considered electric tissue. Furthermore, muscles and neurons are actuated by electrolyte activity between extracellular fluid and intracellular humor.

Cellular bio-energetics are enhanced by yogic protocols such as those in Tai-Chi. These dynamics also facilitate production of ATP and mitochondrial enzymes. Maintaining a full charge of the body's electrical system results in vibrant good health. While we tend to think of our biology as primarily chemical processes, it facilitates our understanding of internal energy work to be reminded that without voltage we are dead.

Structure

The first aspect to look at, relative to Tai- Chi, is structure. Obviously, a house without a foundation is not structurally sound, no matter how much fancy gingerbread you plaster on the outside. But, the foundation of a house is more than the main pad and first rows of concrete blocks. Proper structure also applies to the plumbing and wiring. Yes, you can add elaborate lighting fixtures and bidets, but the foundational plumbing and electric must be sound.

Likewise, your foundation, plumbing, and wiring must be robust, yet supple and free flowing, without compromise, to transmit the bio-energy for the ideal, desired results. A common Tai-Chi maxim is to think of the body as tubing, to allow the free flow of the body's fluids, neurological signals, and energy.

The skeletal system, of course, is the body's primary structural foundation. All other body structures either hang onto or are supported by the skeleton. Far from being a dead steel framework, the bones of the human body are living structures, but are medically known as a rigid organ. The bones' key functions are to store minerals, produce red and white blood cells, and protect the other organs.

Osseous tissue, AKA dense connective tissue, is composed mainly of a collagen called ossein and bone minerals. But as living tissue, bone can also contain nerves, blood vessels, endosteum, periosterum, bone marrow, and cartilage. Collagen protein gives bone elasticity, because bones are basically brittle and do not resist sheer stress well without it.

Generally speaking, bone has a compressive strength of about 165 Mpa., a tensile strength of 100-120, and rates a shear stress strength of 50MPa. One can reference the mega-pascal rating compared to common materials used in engineering.

While it is informative for the martial artist to understand the bones' resistance to various types of stress, mostly, we project our power around or through osseous formations to impact the organs they were designed to protect. Much of the pressure point curriculum involves stretching, pinning, or pinching nerves against bone.

Proper structure is the first consideration in Tai-Chi health techniques and martial art application. To facilitate better understanding, it could be clearer to substitute the word structure for alignment. In order to maximize the free flow of all elements vital to life, and target delivery to pathogenic areas, the body's alignment needs to be in accordance with the laws of nature that act upon it. Improper alignment restricts these delivery routes, and over time, the plumbing corrodes and the wiring oxidizes, exposing your house to decomposition, rot and mechanical failure.

If one paints and varnishes, to protect the wood in their home; maintains the roof, sweeps debris outside to prevent the growth of pathogens, or removes decayed organic matter that invite vermin; they would be considered a conscientious home owner. For proper maintenance, one should think of their home as almost a living thing. Let's see...what other living thing warrants such care?

Correct alignment is critical for the proper transfer of energy in martial technique. So true, for the proper circulation of energy in the health maintenance aspects. Which is why, it is commonly said that: whatever is proper Tai-Chi, for martial art, is proper for health.

The Tai-Chi solo sequence mirrors the universe, in that some aspect is always in motion. This is something beginners are told to help them maintain flow. But, the universe is also in perfect synchronous motion, the template for Tai-Chi movement. The joints rotate in proper relationship to each other; coordinating each body part to deliver maxim power to a vulnerable vital area, or to capitalize on an off-balance opponent one has drawn into a compromised position. Proper alignment allows for the maximum transfer of kinetic energy into the target, while not radiating any power back to its source, and creating a power vector that is always primed for delivery.

Celestial structures are never out of position. The entire expansive array of our galactic fabric advances in perfect alignment to maintain the healthy order of the universe. Turning and stirring harmoniously; always in motion. Also good advice for a fighter. Don't pose. Keep moving.

Keep moving is also the best advice for health maintenance. After all my years in these endeavors, It is my considered opinion that exercise is more important than nutrition. Did I mention that the body makes its own medicine?

Simulacra

In a volume compiled in the early first century, many instances of spontaneous healing are attributed to a Nazarene prophet named Joshua Ben Joseph. In the Hellenized translation of these books, he is known as Jesus.

There are three occasions in the bible where Jesus healed people and told them "Your faith has made you whole". For people of faith, that's all you need to know. Jesus had the power to heal, because of his exalted status.

There are, however, miracles of healing throughout all of time where some patients experience rapid, unexplained recoveries and amaze the medical doctors of the day. Faith healing and positive health outcomes, resulting from prayer, are an accepted reality among people of strong religious belief.

What about hard-headed pragmatists who dismiss such happenings as coincidence, a numbers game, or a statistical anomaly? When unexpected conclusions manifest, that confound expected trial results; researchers are quick to invoke the placebo effect, and rebuke the positive outcomes as due to intentional psychological factors. When the symptoms abate, despite having only used a nonactive treatment; we should, instead, celebrate the beneficial influence of an endogenous agency. This apparent "phenomenon", which is frequently and demonstrably observed, definitively demonstrates the power of the mind to manifest a dramatic positive development in the physical organism.

There is much evidence to indicate the efficacy and impact of the brain and central nervous system on the immune system, biologic defense, and rapid recovery from infection and disease. Research into mind / body reciprocity enhance standard treatment, contribute significantly to favorable outcomes, and reinforce the effectiveness of an interdisciplinary approach.

The parietal cortex, and the prefrontal cortex are the higher cognitive processing centers of the brain. The visual association cortex initiates imaging that activates these centers. Actuating these brain centers properly, allows an adept to actually have a perceptual experience in the mind's eye, with no external visual input.

MRI studies have revealed that the lateral geniculate nucleus, and visual cortex activate when engaged in mental imagery. Visualization can evoke analogous cognitive, physiological responses equivalent to an actual, external experience; providing both performance benefits and engaging systems that mediate neuropathic pain.

Also identified by the MRI analysis, were eleven bilateral cortical and subcortical regions that showed increased activity when engaged in visual image manipulation - i.e., the occipital lobe, the posterior parietal cortex, the precuneus lobule, the three frontal regions, the frontal eye fields, the dorsolateral prefrontal cortex, and the prefrontal cortex. And you thought you were just daydreaming.

When reliving some past offense, or imagining a confrontation with someone of differing political opinion, you experience the same physiological effects as if engaged in real conflict. Conversely, when retreating to your mental sanctuary (a.k.a. your happy place), your physiology is flooded with an array of endogenous healing balms.

The placebo effect is simply a conjured medical term to explain one simple aspect of the power of the mind to heal. If trained to higher capacity, or if bequeathed with a certitude of the highest conviction, results can become ...well... miraculous. Bear in mind that the simple carpenter from Nazareth accepted none of the credit for his dramatically, transformative results. He said it plainly, because he wanted you to know: Your faith has made you whole.

Healing Hands

Bioelectrodynamic effects in the optical range of the electromagnetic spectrum have been proven empirically. Living cells produce spontaneous emission of photons with significantly higher intensity than emission by thermal radiation. Experiments, like these, are non-complex and easily verified.

Non-thermal emission of photons from living cells is a well-established phenomenon. Other bio-electric effects exist as well. Acoustic and radio frequencies for example. Depending on a particles dielectric constant, a force effect has been observed where dielectric particles were attracted to some cells and repulsed by others. This has been attributed to dielectriophoresis caused by electromagnetic field of cells. The frequency of this field has been estimated as hundreds of MHz. Also, mechanical vibrations have been proven in a very broad frequency range in cells. Since many structures in cells are electrically polar, they will generate electromagnetic fields if they vibrate.

Modern medicine uses electromagnetic radiation in the intermediate frequency range for the treatment of bone damage and stimulation and regeneration of nerves. This is an approved treatment for tumors utilizing alternating electric fields in the range of 100-300kHZ. Some modalities are electric field centric, while others are magnetic fields that invoke currents in living tissue.

TAI-CHI ENERGY

The Chinese have long held that the Chi generally travels under the skin, but to be more specific, it flows through the connective tissue and sometimes the bone. With our modern understanding of anatomy this can only mean one thing. The energy travels through the fascia.

Deep fascia is a layer or dense, fibrous, connective tissue that surrounds muscles. Visceral fascia suspends the organs. Piezoelectric current flows through the fascia, which acts as a semiconductor. As a side note: you would be a blob of jelly without this type of tissue.

When this type of tissue surrounds vascular tissue it is called perivascular. When it occurs around lymphatic vessels it is called perilymphatic. The fascia that separates muscles is called myofascia. The fascia around the bones is the periosteum. The fascia not only provides cushioning and lubrication between tissues; but serves as an insulator, ensuring proper electrical conductivity in the body. The postures, movement and focused attention employed while executing the Tai-Chi solo sequence utilizes these pathways for energy circulation.

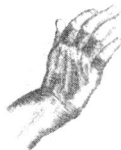

WHERE IT'S AT

Through focused attention techniques, bio-energy can be concentrated and directed to specific areas. But naturally observed, this energy can be easily perceived as collecting in the hands. Cultures throughout the world have known and utilized this phenomenon since ancient times.

In Egypt, hand gestures were performed in prayer rituals and carved in bas-relief on the walls of the pyramids. Greeks, Romans and native Americans all recognized the importance of developing this obvious concentration of energy. Buddhist priests and even Jesus are usually represented displaying stylized hand gestures. An essential part of Ninja training is Hand knitting.

Hindu mystics, however, developed the science of hand mudras to a fine art. Mudra is, in fact, a Sanskrit word meaning seal, and is a high science within the yogic arts. Developed and refined since antiquity, hand mudras are utilized regularly to assist with healing and spiritual development.

I used to touch my thumb sequentially to each of my fingers, and tell my pet coyote: "It would have been you, if only you could do this." The opposable thumb is often cited as the main reason humans came to dominate the planet. With man's huge brain and dexterous appendages no other species could compete. There may be however, more hidden potential in these appendages than mere mechanical advantage.

Hands are revered in all cultures for obvious reasons. My Kenpo instructor when explaining a technique was known to say: "He's been hit so many times, it's impossible to hold all the places that hurt". So, why do your hands cover the place of injury? Why do you scratch your head when you think? Or, cover your face / hold your head when receiving bad news? "They told me, and my head was in my hands".

Folding hands in prayer is so accepted that we never contemplate why one needs to clasp hands in order to communicate with the almighty. This is so established in all traditions that no one questions its purpose. Certainly, people pray if their hands are otherwise engaged; such as with a bilge pump, defibrillator, or M-79. Given a quiet moment, however, in need of ethereal communion and the hands come together. So, what does this process have to do with any of it?

The use of the hands as an instrument of energy has a long history. Chi-Kung, Mudras, and "laying on of hands" are common examples of the manner in which people regard the power inherent in this most dexterous of human appendages.

The hands may be compared with a saw blade, but in order for the saw blade to do its work, there is a complex series of electric and mechanical inner workings on which it relies. The energies amalgamated to project or be perceived in the hands are collectively inherent in the human organism. Efferent and afferent pathways innervate electrical signals in the hands.

It is an electric universe. Our cells run on electricity. Since the inside of a cell is negative relative to the outside, a voltage differential across the membrane results. The plasma membrane voltage of cells in the human body usually runs between -20mV and -200mV. (The negative sign is used to indicate that the inside is negative to the outside.)

When there is a larger differential in charge across the membrane, this creates a higher voltage. Most nerve cells have a resting membrane potential ranging from -40mV to -90mV. The membrane is said to be polarized when the value is around -70mV.

Our cells are influenced by many complex biological factors and are also subject to stimulus from interactions with the external environment. For our purposes, it is sufficient just to know that our cells run on electricity and interact with the electrical make up of most elements on the periodic table.

THINGS TO CONSIDER

NERVE IMPULSE	=	ELECTRIC SIGNAL
PH	=	VOLTAGE
MOVEMENT	=	CREATES PIEZOELECTRICITY
FASCIA	=	CONDUCTOR / RESISTERS
MIND	=	SWITCH-BOX / CONTROLLER / MIXING CONSOLE

At this point, it is fair to ask: "Is directed energy real or even possible?"

If we accept the premise that the body makes its own medicine (as indicated in other chapters), and that the wisdom of the body will direct healing when and where it's needed. Is it then really such a leap that some kind of energy can be transferred from one bio-electric organism to another?

Energy transfer, as a phenomenon, is commonly acknowledged. In this book, and in others, are examples of how to transfer power ballistically when striking the human body. Certainly, when the cue ball strikes the eleven and is driven forward, impacting the seven; that is kinetic energy transfer. Touching a nine volt battery to your tongue or feeling radiation from high voltage electric lines is another type. And, there can be real cell damage caused by the power of solar radiation, while on the beach. As an extreme example from a living source: electric eels can generate over 800 volts! Fun fact: electric eels are not eels at all. They are actually fish.

ENERGETIC SOURCES EXERT INFLUENCE ON ONE ANOTHER WHEN IN PROXIMITY

When you see your old war buddy for the first time in forty years, you are compelled to embrace. Those hearts crave physical proximity. Why place your lips on someone's forehead, pet a dog, or hold hands? Are these phenomenon just social convention? Or is there a perceptible energetic stimulation. To simply say that the dog's fur feels good, or I love my wife, I think is to ignore the manifestation of energy perceived by emotion.

Because we are dealing with incredibly multifaceted energies, which are simultaneously interpreted and amplified by the human mind; results originating from generalized, scientific equipment; that is designed for non-specific purposes, may not fully satiate the ardent skeptic. But, a plethora of affirmative studies are readily available.

This leaves empirical evidence as the prima facie case for the power of energy healing. I have known a great many therapists who work with energy, and their results suggest undeniability. For critics who decry positive results as an illustration of the placebo effect, this only verifies the position suggested in the previous chapter of the power of the mind to heal.

I was initiated into Kria yoga in the early eighties by Hari Harinanda, and it is from him that I received my shaktipat, which is the psychic energy transference. The guru examines and ensures that you have been properly instructed in the technique. He then places his hand on your head and directs a lightning bolt of energy to affect a spiritual jump start, which you are then expected to develop and advance by continuing with the technique. On the day of my initiation over one hundred of us shared this experience.

I used to attend a yearly Tai-Chi convention, which lasted for four days and drew huge crowds. The promoter would always bring in interesting lecturers and instructors each year. On one occasion, the keynote position was held by an elderly teacher from San Francisco, who only spoke Chinese. The situation was fairly comical because the interpreter spoke English only slightly better than the teacher. At the end of his presentation, 2500 of us in the auditorium received a startling, strong, electric shock right in the middle of our chests. Stunned silence is what followed! An impressive demonstration of energy transfer.

We, of course, attributed this demonstration to a very high level of secret knowledge possessed by only a few adepts, like this octogenarian Chi-Kung master. A few years later, while leaving Sunday services with my girlfriend, the Rector was shaking hands as parishioners exited. As we spoke, I mentioned that it was her birthday, and would he give her a special blessing. He uttered a few words, waved his hands, and the same jolt we had received from the Chinese master shot through our sternums.

This is real. This technique may be delivered by adherents of different paths and disciplines, but is an obvious and spectacular instance of energy transfer. In neither case were we expecting nor looking for an electric charge. But, we were recipients none the less. Chi-Kung, Reki, and other methods have a demonstrable high success rates. Cultures without the benefit of E.K.G. machines and P.E.T. scans developed other methods to diagnose and cure disease.

I have witnessed and been helped by energy healers of diverse stripes. Internal energy techniques and hand mudras are an essential part of my personal regime. Although practices such as Reki and cranial sacral therapy are commonly denounced as unverifiable, I would once again question bias and testing methods. But the real judge will ultimately be your own mind and experience. I would wish for you the benefits I have received from energy healing. And if you still need convincing, I hope you encounter a Guru, Chi-Kung adept, or gifted parish priest.

A Word on Healing

We are all fortunate to live in an era of exceptional trauma care. Modern treatments and diagnostics are truly lifesavers. However, there are people all over the planet who exist and even thrive with very little medical intervention. While death rates are high, they don't reach for pharmaceuticals for every little complaint. In counterpoint, to those in the "civilized" world, who are led to believe there is something wrong with them if they are not taking some type of prescription.

If we were to distill this "civilized" understanding of health maintenance by observing television commercials, one would form the opinion that the human body is somehow inadequate to function without administering powerful drugs or nutritional supplements.

One who is steeped in Tao and appreciates the opposites and reverses, as understood by the concept of Yin and Yang, would be wary of the idea that the human body needs to be constantly saturated with chemicals, and is never capable of functioning while consuming only food water and air.

Often times people think of chemical treatments as a neutralizing device, like a fire extinguisher, that conquers and eliminates the offending condition. However, in truth, many drugs work by triggering a reaction within the body to cause natural processes to heal with endogenously produced agents.

In many instances, the body heals itself. There are conditions physicians don't even treat - sprains, broken toes, cracked ribs…tape 'em up. Let the body work. The classic visual of this is the cartoon version of an accident victim in quadruple traction. This is nature functioning as master physician - the wisdom of the body providing the right medicine in the proper amounts. The health care professionals merely administer the proper fluids, monitor, and observe. The body provides the necessary healing agents.

As an eloquent example: while growing up, there was an older couple who lived down the street. One winter they both caught the same cold. She went to the doctor, he bought a bottle of whiskey. They were both better in a week.

If someone plows me in the side, the body immediately responds by dispatching a cascade of healing biochemicals to that area. For a mild impact, it sends a little healing. If it was more a damaging shock, it sends a lot. This is not just for trauma, the same is true of other pathological conditions of the internal organs.

Furthermore, if I receive a blow that mildly injures my liver, the body sends healing to that organ. But what if the trigger wasn't an impact, but a very mild stimulation. The body will still react by sending healing agents to the liver. Except, this time, it won't be a therapeutic dose, but a maintenance dose.

Now, of course, if I had an infection, a growth, or a broken bone; I'm running straight for modern medicine. But we're not talking about a lifesaving procedure or intervention.

Instead, let's suppose there was a highly developed system that would dispatch these biochemicals and other healing elements in a particular sequence for optimal health maintenance. That practice is Tai-Chi. Tai-Chi is highly targeted toward health maintenance. It generally (but not solely) contributes to good health through Internal organ massage, increased respiration, and moving fluids through the tissues.

Well, one might say. Doesn't tennis or golf do that? Yes. Exercise is always good for you. But Tai-Chi defers in that it is a targeted science. Let's take as an extremely elementary example, one element of Tai-Chi movement: waist rotation.

Most core body movements in Tai-Chi are preceded by hip and waist rotation. The waist rotation is key to insuring internal organ massage - aided by proper structure, breathing, and mind intent; influencing its fundamental elementary biology. In short, these physical actions stimulate the body's vitality on a cellular level. There is a direct connection between exercise and longevity; this is partly due to the fact that challenging the body through physical stress directs cellular energy towards maintenance and repair and down regulates apoptosis (cell death).

These subjects will be explored in depth in subsequent dissertations. Suffice it to say, that this practice; developed by geniuses and perfected by application of the scientific process, is a proven formula for healing and health maintenance. The following essays will hopefully provide insights and answers to the most common questions for those inquisitive about this art.

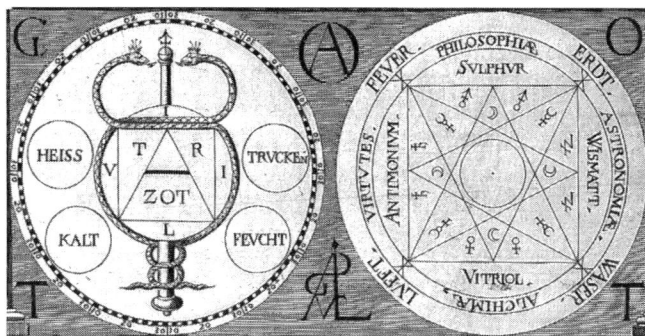

Third State of Consciousness

Looking at the trajectory of mankind, it's easy to get seduced by impressive historic events. To be distracted by monumental occurrences like wars, scientific breakthroughs, and the splendor of cultures; like the roman empire. But it's understandable to wonder, as many anthropologists do: "What were they thinking? How did an ordinary person process events in their own time?"

It would be logical and normal to apply the thought process of modern man to the speculation of the primitive mind. It has always been my guess that despite the lack of technological advancements, people separated from us by time are not much different than we are today.

I offer as testimony the pre-Socratic Greeks, or anything written in the bible. It all sounds intelligent and well thought out, which is why we still reference those sources today. While this serves as evidence of the wisdom of our ancestors, it is not, however, the terminus of this study to ruminate on the mental powers of our predecessors. I would like to take an abrupt turn and offer a personal hypothesis.

Saint Patrick's day is an occasion when society affords the general population the opportunity to drink to excess. And, no one feels restrained from celebrating the drunken Irish. It is here where an astute imbiber would be sure to include the drunken Italians, the drunken French, and the drunken Germans; and just about everyone else who has inherited European customs.

Drunken Musicians, drunken house painters, drunken plumbers, and other occupations are regularly associated with drinking to excess. Throughout Europe and America, intramural sports teams keep many pubs solvent celebrating wins and losses.

In countries without the cultural romance with alcohol; hashish, opium, or any of its derivatives are routinely relied upon for escapism. Where regions that have prohibitions against ch3ch20h and T.H.C. tend to be prayerful or meditative cultures. Which brings me to this proposal and query - why?

Is there something missing that the human organism is incomplete without? A nutritional need? We crave particular foods, because they provide some missing element required for proper biological functioning. When the body needs water we thirst. But, what is this need to get out of ourselves. Why would evolution have provided this desire that diminishes productivity and creates a temporary vulnerable state. Occam's razor states that the most likely answer to any perplexity is the simplest one.

It would seem logical to conclude that man naturally aspires to higher states of consciousness. Owing, however, to his ingenuity and depraved genius to find the easiest way; man discovered biotic chemical placebos in nature as a artifice, simultaneously advancing his abilities but impeding his natural development.

When man encounters a thing of beauty; a flower, a horse, a polished table; he wants to reach out and touch the object, to interact with it, to bring it more completely into his experience. The material world is magnificent and provides complete satisfying sensations of every description. But, man also innately feels the need to connect with higher realms, to bring into his experience that connection that completes his existence.

Humans deplete their fortunes, impact their health, and jeopardize happiness in pursuit of altered awareness. A third state of consciousness. Sleep, awake, and awakening. An astute observer is aware of this and knows this need is filled with religion, meditation, drugs and alcohol. Which of these actually completes this circuit. Makes the connection humans are desperately endeavoring towards. Recognizing this innate incompleteness, religion, and the yogic science of god contact, offer paths to accomplish this essential element of human existence.

Those who feel the need to complete the circle look to the east for formulas and practices that may resolve this part of the human paradox. Or, you may fill the void with mechanistic diversion and chemical sedation. Man should use his powerful intellect to wisely examine just what he is feeling, and choose a path...Cheers.

Third State of Consciousness

Intestinal Fortitude

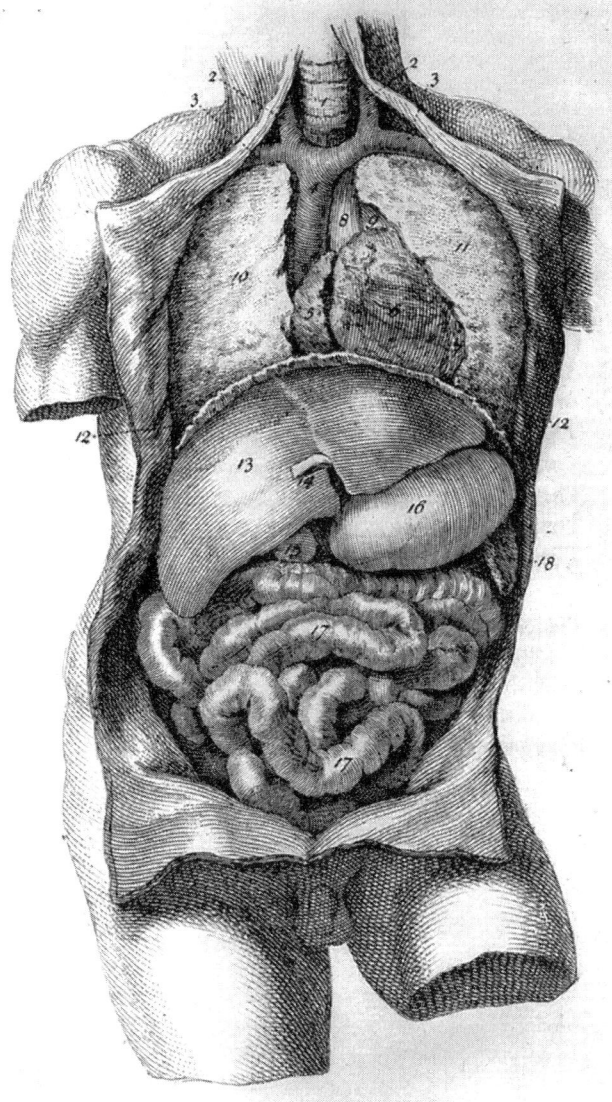

Tai-Chi means grand ultimate. Tai-Chi-Chuan translates as grand ultimate fist. Practitioners of this art should not go around calling the art grand ultimate if they can't back it up. That means you must poses the skill, conditioning, and whatever could be considered as secrets of the art.

No martial art is usable, of course, if one is paralyzed with fear. So, it goes without saying that having guts is the Yin/Yang compliment to having skill. Conversely, it may prove informative to consider the health aspect of guts as compared to the euphemism for courage as used above.

In many respects, guts are of equal importance to skill in the fighting aspect of the art. But expanding this comparison further, the gut is to the brain what the gas tank is to the automobile. Indeed, the gut / brain (vasovagal) connection has received considerable attention in recent years, as research reveals the preeminent importance of this conjunction.

Indeed, much attention has been focused by health enthusiasts on diet and the gut microbiota. New research reveals, however, that movement and exercise alter microbial gut communities as well. Movement downregulates pro-inflammatory cytokines and up-regulates anti-inflammatory cytokines and antioxidant enzymes by altering the gene expression of intraepithelial lymphocytes. Host-microbial homeostasis is dependent on these antimicrobial factors. Studies also suggest that exercise maintains the gut mucus layer, which keeps microbes from adhering to the gut epithelium. Furthermore, exponential growth of evidence supports the role of V.N.S. in the modulation of gastrointestinal functions. The bidirectional interactions between the brain and the gut microbiome integrates the gastrointestinal, immune, and central nervous system.

Likewise, body movement affects the autonomic nervous system and the neuron network that innervates the gut. The abdominal massage created by Tai-Chi movement reduces transit time in the large intestine, increases mixing of intestinal contents, and informs gut motility. The contact between microbes and the gut mucosal immune system are affected by exercise induced heat stress as the core temperature raises during physical activity. In other words, the benefits of the internal organ massage provided by Tai-Chi movement cannot be derived by just sitting in a chair.

Furthermore, the turnover rate of molecules through metabolic pathways is known as metabolic flux. When skeletal muscles contract, metabolites, myokines, and neuroendocrine hormones are released as a result of this stimulation. Twisting, turning, and abdominal compression all contribute to proper functioning of gut processes and maintenance of gut flora. Each organ benefits similarly from the physical stimulation wrought by Tai-Chi movement. And finally, all these illustrations are used to only superficially highlight the impact of mechanical force on the function of gut health.

When acknowledging that exercise is vital to health maintenance, most tend to limit their thinking to primarily cardio vascular fitness or maintaining a strong usable musculature. However, the influence of abdominal massage on gut function cannot be overstated. It may take courage to dominate in a physical confrontation, but it requires intelligence to recognize the merit of the abdominal stimulation garnered by Tai-Chi movement. Mental focus, breath work, and the benefits to abdominal microbial communities are a synergistic enterprise. Full comprehension of the integrated, unitary function of our human vessel begins with the understanding that "as the gut goes, so goes the brain."

WILLIAM WALLACE.

Body Energy States

A primary principal that requires our attention Is body energy states. There are variations and degrees, but in keeping with the binary principal, its most instructive to focus on just two. Let's examine what body energy states mean in the context of Tai-Chi. For health, generally, we want to up regulate the relaxation response and down regulate the stress response. There are other altered states used for fighting and self-defense, but let's make a couple of gross general illustrations and comparisons just so we have an analogous example.

Suppose a very lazy person is relaxing in a hammock. This is a great example of the body enacting the relaxation response, in many respects similar to a Sung state. The body has shut down the stress response, potentially dosing in and out of consciousness. In a theta brain wave state (4-8 cycles per second). His wife speaks to him, informing him that she wants him to mow the grass. He only mumbles. Nothing can make him move.

Now suppose something extraordinary happens. A kid throws a fire cracker into the yard, or he gets stung by a bee. His body energy state changes quickly and dramatically. Brain waves jump into the super-conscious zone (40-80 cycles per second). A flood of stimulants, coagulants, and all the rest. The chemistry of this dramatic change will be more deeply explored in the chapter aptly titled "The Chemistry of Emotions". But, the ability to control, focus, and direct this type of energy is imperative when one is surprised, startled, or filled with righteous rage.

What we're striving for in Tai-Chi is to bring these processes under conscious control (not super-conscious). It does not suit our purpose to be paralyzed by fear, muscles so tight one can't move. Most of all, for health; but also to enhance our martial art. Within this context, it is enormously helpful to be in a more relaxed state. This state provides us with the ability to strike smoothly, evade and think clearly. Personally, I went through a period where I would get winded after a relatively short period of sparring. I was in such a tense state while fighting, I was gasping for air after a few minutes. The answer? It wasn't to do more running and build up my C/V. All I needed to do was relax.

Police training provides another good example. Fun fact: when your heart rate rises above 140 bpm your hands begin to clench. But, if your finger is on the trigger... An officer simply can't make panicked decisions. His team and the subject could suffer dire consequences.

In a crisis situation it is imperative to keep a cool head, and not just life or death situations. Anyone subject to action needs to control their emotions/body energy states for optimal performance. Mountain climbing, water skiing, taking a test. For instance, if you are driving and spill hot coffee in your lap. The consequences of how you react could be far worse than some minor burns. This capacity to influence one's conscious mind is foremost in innumerable situations.

On the surface, it appears like all we're talking about is controlling our emotions. But that is just one, small aspect of this skill. Breath control is another factor in influencing one's body energy state. Again, let's use police training. In my opinion, a required part of their curriculum should be tactical breathing. Some academies do provide this training, some don't. Regardless, this skill is really just yogic breathing. But what macho law enforcement officer wants to rely on Pranayama breathing?

Modern science now confirms what those that have taken the time to incorporate this formula into their activities have always known; taking long deep breaths, slows your heart rate and activates your parasympathetic nervous system. Researchers are now referring to a group of neurons at the base of the brain stem as "the breathing pacemaker".

From one point of view, what we have is really a chicken or egg situation. Or rock, paper, scissors. Or a mobius strip. Or name your own personal poison. This situation is where one element directly influences the other and they are tightly inter-related and cross-influential. Yet, they are both of profound importance. If you use a breathing technique, you slow your heart rate and calm your emotions. If you calm your mind, heart rate and breathing slows. Performance enhanced. Survival optimized.

When one is under stress it's akin to pouring battery acid into their system. It results in a cascade of endogenous chemicals all designed to increase awareness to a heightened level in an attempt to surmount a crisis situation. But, when you live in a constantly heightened state, your stress response is permanently at full throttle. This creates a pathological condition known in Chinese medicine as fire energy excess. Most people living in modern society fall into this level of body energy and are in dire need of some type of yogic or Tai-Chi training. Not just for their health, but also for their longevity.

One other practice that also works hand-in-hand with breath control in engaging the parasympathetic nervous systems is consciously relaxing the external musculature. But, by far, it is our emotions that cause the most dramatic and immediate change in body energy states.

In short, thoughts are energetic cluster bombs that set off bodily reactions that alter health and decision making. Seemingly superfluous techniques like building a mental sanctuary, or retreating to your happy place may seem frivolous and ineffective. It is, however, an example of how state of mind reigns in runaway biological processes.

The opposite/reverse, of course, is also true. For instance, the ability to put on their "mental armor" or even go psychotic at will, flushes out one's fear and floods their body with invincibility. Think of the comparative effectiveness of striking someone paralyzed with fear compared to someone who is "ready to go".

Finally, one's mind creates a narrative and the body reflects back an emotion that directly influences their body energy state. Unfortunately, most individuals usually provide too much negative input. In such instances, the accompanying chemical dump has instantaneous caustic effects, and over time creates chronic pathological conditions. Incorporating Tai-Chi practices such as those presented throughout this book, help one conquer this negative feedback loop and inject the positive aspects of the Yin/Yang.

九

So far, this chapter has only provided a general overview of body energy states. But, this is just as a starting point. We have not discussed directed energy, focused awareness, nor identifying internal energy and moving it around. Energy manipulation, projection, and direction are advanced techniques that all begin with understanding and controlling basic body energy states. It all starts with energy awareness.

Now, onto a practical exercise that may help you understand and internalize these concepts further. To help develop awareness of your body energy state, while also realizing your aliveness. An exercise that is only one of many that one may perform to help in developing the positive, internal energies of your Tai-Chi and self.

Close your eyes. Perform a few cycles of the complete breath. Consciously relax your muscles. Let your shoulders melt down into your hips. Try to affect a Sung state of profound relaxation. Now, imagine a cord pulling your body upward from the top of your head. Feel your body hanging from the cord. Feel your vertebrae separate from the upward pull. Relax your shoulders. Just let everything hang. Subtlety is key here. Forget about sending or receiving energy. Feel your bio energy surging. Just stand there. Just be aware. Be aware of your body functioning. Be aware of the fact that you are alive and you are energy. Also, be aware that of all this is internal, all part of you.

Now, feel the air enter your nostrils. Feel your lungs fill. Be aware of the sun. Be aware of the wind. Be aware of the earth beneath your feet. Be aware of your entire environment. Birds. Trees. Even traffic and miscellaneous sounds. You are part of this environment. You belong to the world. Also, be aware that these are external stimuli.

It all starts here. Feel your body. All your concentration. All your attention... All of your awareness.

Music

EVERYTHING IN LIFE IS VIBRATION Albert Einstein	IF YOU WANT TO FIND THE SECRETS OF THE UNIVERSE THINK IN TERMS OF ENERGY FREQUENCY AND VIBRATION Nikola Tesla
VIBRATION IS BOTH FIRST CAUSE AND SUSTAINER OF ALL TEMPORAL OBJECTS Gail Brubaker	FEEL THE VIBES MAN Jerry Garcia

"You never hear the one that gets you", is a well-worn statement of gallows humor often heard among mercenaries, soldiers, drug runners, and others immersed in death culture activities. The reason, of course, is that bullets travel faster than sound. Anyone who has ever been shot at knows that first the bullet goes by, then you hear the report.

Those whose military service predates the computer age, may recall having been told: "they are nothing without their rifle"; and also learned that the standard issue M14 is a gas operated, semi-automatic, air cooled, magazine fed, shoulder weapon that has a muzzle velocity of 2600 feet per second. This bullet velocity is emblematic of a standard modern firearm. Because of this simple fact, most modern-day ammunition is designed to fire faster than the speed of sound. All, that is, except for the iconic .45, which usually travels around 850-875 fps, but with a light load, can come in well under 800fps. So, watch out!

This is germane because the only real world examples of supersonic speed most people can directly relate to are firearm projectiles and jet aircraft. One comprehending the fact that things can and do move faster than the speed of sound can be expanded to encompass the incomprehensible idea of objects potentially moving faster than the speed of light. But, this expanded conception also opens one's thinking to exotic concepts of energy. And, the subject matters detailed throughout this book are designed to unveil and impart to the reader information about these non-conventional forces.

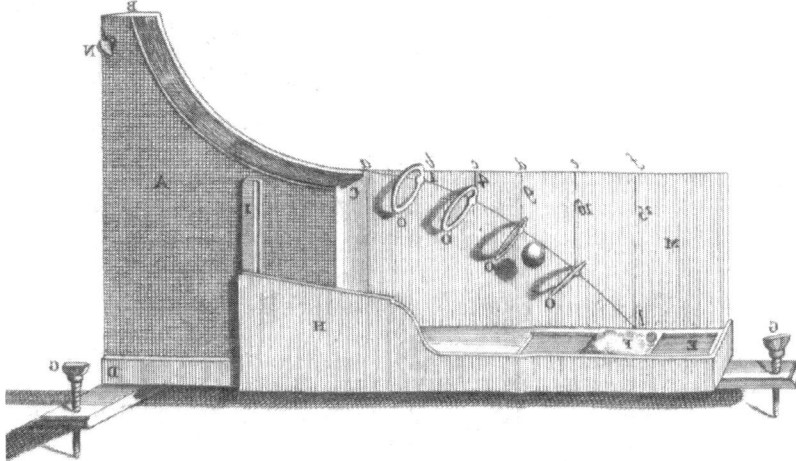

The speed of sound is about 767 mph or 1,125 fps. Sound volume is rated in decibels and the relationship of one sound to another is referred to as an interval, where frequency is the scale used to differentiate between various sound waves. The sine wave diagram is the visual presentation used to represent frequency.

As energy travels through a medium, it produces energy waves. Some common terms used to depict this event are: rumble, vibration, turbulence, or a specific phenomenon such as prop wash. Sound is a specific type of energy. Therefore, it too produces energy waves which occur at various frequencies; some destructive, some remedial. One interesting fact about waves is that at specific frequencies, known as a resonance frequency, they intensify as they propagate through specific media. This is why soldiers must break step when marching across a bridge.

Another interesting fact about sound waves is that when sound is perceived as harmonious by the human ear, the organism responds with a cascade of endogenous chemicals beneficial to the human physiology. This is one reason why all human life, everywhere on the planet, have somehow felt compelled to produce vibrational energy through the air. Some examples of this are: mantras; Gregorian hymns; mission bells; yodeling; calls, and chants - of Buddhists, Native Americans, and Celts, to name a few. They all feel it radiate it into the environment, act upon a distant animate being, layer, and build; reverberating back to its source. Music is vibration.

Music therapy is a recognized treatment for many conditions, such as: physical disabilities, psychiatric disorders, and an array of medical and health related issues. The psychological and physiological response to sound perception is a legitimate branch of science called Psychoacoustics. In that vein, people from all walks of life regularly motivate and self-medicate with stirring anthems, loud driving rock, torch songs, and other forms of music.

What is a crescendo? Harmony? Feedback? Vibration can be very impactful on the human organism. Audible frequencies, overtones, resonance, harmony, and dissonance are all employed to alter or impact human perception and biology. Vibration is both first cause and sustainer of all temporal objects, as well as operations of human biological systems.

Extracorporeal shock wave therapy utilizes high frequency energy in the treatment of bone fractures and has been considered standard treatment for ureter stones for decades. ESWT absorption through bone is an area of study scrutinized by Western researchers in recent times, but well understood by Eastern trained adepts historically.

Sound vibration impacts the human systems in very real ways. Low intensities of ultrasound are frequently used diagnostically. It is well established that bone growth and healing is enhanced by ultrasonic intensities of one to three watts. Improvements in muscle spasm, pain, joint stiffness, and muscular mobility have also been sighted.

Note that the low intensity is purposeful. This for avoiding overheating of tissues, which is a recognized potential negative consequence of sound therapy. Yin/Yang.

The systematic employment of weight transfer that occur during execution of the Tai-Chi form are used to produce similar results. Stress-generated potentials occur when pertinent bones subjected to a bending load become electronegative, concurrently other portions of bone become electropositive. Stress induced vibration. Likewise, this physicality provides the same amelioration achieved through mechanically induced stress provided by the weight bearing aspects of physical labor, resistance training, or activities that were once routine before the modern era.

Electronegative potentials that occur in non-stressed bone express stress-generated potentials when subjected to bending, twisting, and load bearing. Low intensity, pulsed ultrasound is commonly employed by physicians to treat foot and ankle pathology. The pulsed ultrasound works by applying mechanical pressure to the affected area, producing mechanical stress, resulting in the promotion of bone formation. The equivalent principal is demonstrated in the practice of the Tai-Chi form. Like respiratory, organ, and emotional homeostasis, bone integrity is maintained by external (bio-mechanical) and internal (biological) stimuli.

The developers of traditional Chinese medicine and indigenous martial arts were ordained to formulate within the governing precepts of the natural world. A major tenet of the TCM canon is to operate in harmony with the natural environment. Bio-stabilizing and chemistry balancing paradigms such as breathing exercises, and movements that provide internal organ massage, worked synergistically with weight bearing methods that maximized the added dimension of bending and twisting the bones of the supporting structure, producing vital mechanical stress.

This has been verified in our own age by the most sophisticated scientists in the most advanced fields, directing time and resources to developing programs for space travelers to prevent physical atrophy. Astronauts functioning in a microgravity environment can experience up to a twenty percent bone and muscle loss during extended space missions.

Despite critical duties, astronauts still must devote two hours a day to resistance training to combat the effects of zero gravity. Complex machinery has been fabricated to assuage bone and muscle atrophy. Such as the Combined Operational Load Bearing External Resistance Treadmill (COLBERT) and the Advanced Resistance Exercise Device (ARED). Terrestrials fortunate enough to remain earthbound, can simply perform the Tai-Chi sequence.

Everything is vibration. Quantum fields, atomic structure, planets, and music is, most certainly, vibration. Music is vibration, but it is also mathematical. For example, octaves, intervals 5th, 3rd. All beating in accordance with mathematics and the laws of physics - and, of course, geometry. There are even spiritual traditions that refer to this sacred geometry.

Sound vibrations create reactions within the human organism. Some emotional, some via association. Before electricity created a saturation of the visual arts, music was the way most people connected with other human beings. I could tell you a sad, sad story; but if you set it to music...Niagara Falls all around.

The vibration itself, however, affects biology in some very physical ways. Baby shaking can be fatal. Driving repeatedly on a rocky road can damage the kidneys. Microwave ovens cook by vibrating water molecules. Ultrasound is used to break up kidney stones and has served as a template for directed energy weapons. Audible sound, but at a high pitch, is reminiscent of the Kung-Fu technique colloquially know as the lion's roar.

Vibration can be used to hurt (Yang) or to heal (Yin), in the same way that medicine that is beneficial in the right proportions, but ineffective or toxic in the extreme. Vibration in its various guises is utilized advantageously every day. Undulating therapeutic tables in chiropractors' offices, home back massagers, and stress reliving personal vibrators are all examples of exploitation employing this element. Creation of, or limiting vibration in elemental applications is undeniable. From the writhing, jiggle as the sperm fights for entry to implant energy to create the zygote, to the bacteria that will one day decompose your corporeal structure. Wiggling, throbbing, and pulsating; driving every action, from the photon to the avalanche. It is not a static universe.

Music is as effective as any psychoactive drug by inducing profound changes in brain chemistry. Sad music, stirring nationalistic anthems, ominous movie soundtracks; each create moods and attitudes deeply trenchant. Clearly, music has the power to induce or alter behaviors. The obvious aptitude of sound vibration is commonly demonstrated to anyone who has attended a rock concert, or been in proximity to an automobile driven by a hip-hop enthusiast.

Physics defines energy as particles vibrating in fields. A perturbation in a field. Vibrational energy is foundational in all aspects of the universe from the quantum world to the mundane interactions of all functions of terrestrial life.

Recognizing the elemental, basal influence of vibration is the realm of both the occult and prosaic understanding of the building blocks of our world. Advancing understanding of vibrational effects and interactions of all matter is the science of harmonics, interval, and dissonance, which serves as an introduction to the mathematics found in the golden ratio and the Fibonacci scale. If an in-depth dive into these subjects was attempted, it would leave no room for any information on Tai-Chi in this book.

Vibration, as used in fighting technique, will be explored and expanded upon in subsequent chapters. Suffice it to say, vibrating palm and related applications are real, and every bit as valid as the medical procedures verified at the start of this essay.

While the word vibration has taken on a shallow, vapid connotation in recent history, it is often used by the most serious-minded physicists to describe the nature of the sub-atomic universe. Particles vibrating in fields is not occult or mystical, but simply just the way things are.

Einstein said that life without music would be inconceivable. Whenever he reached an impasse, he would listen to Bach or Mozart to spark his creativity. He believed Mozart's music revealed the harmony of the universe. It was also his opinion that Amadeus did not create his music, but discovered it fully formed. These ideas, of course, are related to his stated concept that he did not arrive at his understanding of the laws of the universe through his rational mind: He transcended.

It is felicitous for our purposes that music is a form of vibration that everyone can relate to. Understanding that vibration is nominally the base action of all mater and is expressed by harmony and interval. These characteristics demonstrate the foundational principals of life and the universe as a whole. And, in fact, are the very definition of the word metaphor.

One often hears someone say "music is life". At face value, the statement is taken to infer that the emotional intimacy and emotive qualities of the musical experience, epitomizes existence, This phrase however runs deeper than a simulacrum. It is a serendipitous phenomenon that music not only is easy to understand and empathize with; it is also an apt metaphor for the foundational principals of everything.

Maxwell's Demon

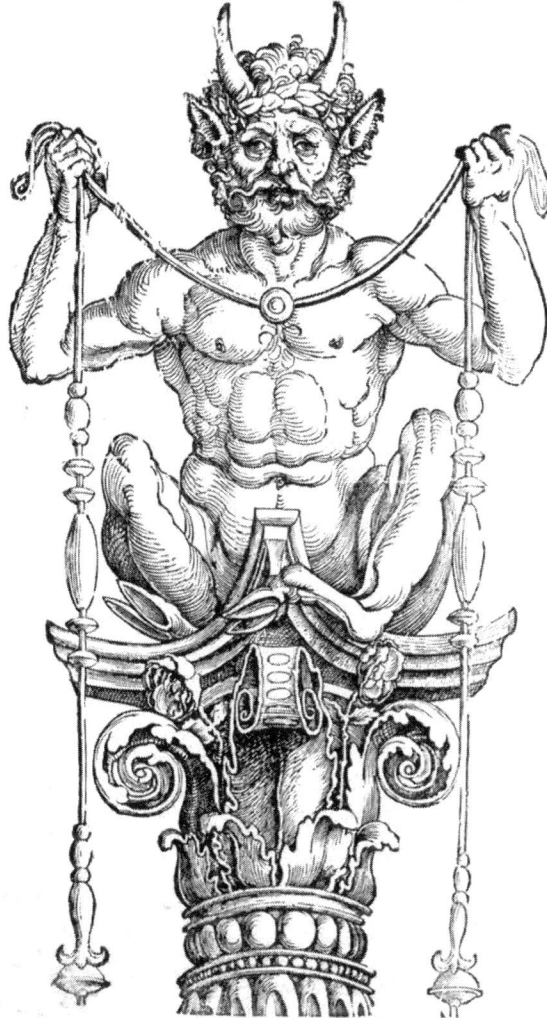

When it was said that Einstein stood on the shoulders of Newton, Einstein retorted that he stood on the shoulders of Maxwell. James Clerk Maxwell was a Scottish physicist and mathematician who lived from 1831 to 1879. He laid the groundwork for many of the revelations developed in physics the 20th century. Despite his multiple of contributions to science, he is probably best known for a thought experiment he posited in 1867.

In Zen monasteries it is common to challenge advanced students by posing unanswerable questions called koans. The most famous, of course, "what is the sound of one hand clapping"? The purpose of the koan is to confound the brain, in a deliberate attempt to short circuit the mind's processes. This short circuit has the effect of bypassing the conscious and unconscious mind, entering it into a state where there is no effective, deductive reasoning, no preconceptions, void of clutter and mind pollution, such as: fantasy, myth or delusion. But, most importantly, you must suspend logic.

The West also has a version of the koan which, superficially, may seem unanswerable. And, this puzzle performs an entirely different purpose. It is called the "thought experiment". In our machine-oriented culture, this purely conceptual proposition is designed to produce an actual result and further scientific advancement: where personal development and awakening are not germane. The intention of Maxwell's paradox was to challenge the second law of thermodynamics, by creating an improbable circumstance that Lord Kelvin later dubbed Maxwell's Demon.

In the conundrum, Maxwell proposed a box with two chambers where molecules of hot and cold flow freely between both chambers. Partitioning the two compartments is a door guarded by a demon who has the ability to identify and allow specific molecules to pass based upon the heat of the molecule.

Every time a cold molecule drifts into the left side, the demon allows it, whereas hot molecules are not permitted to pass. Over time, hot molecules begin to collect in the right chamber, slowly separating from the cold molecules. Ultimately, the left side becomes completely filled with cold molecules, the right with hot; seemingly violating the second law of thermodynamics.

Claude Shannon later came along and, in a contribution that would provide a leap in computational sciences, proposed that the demon required energy to perform his work, and thus balanced out the system. This provided an answer to the problem that lasted over fifty years. But, I maintain that in Maxwell's original proposition "the demon" is a supernatural being who does not require energy. My proposition, however, would demean Shannon's laudable advancement. Later, Von Nuemann introduced the idea of entanglement into the equation, thus introducing the quantum element, furthering development in this field even more.

There is much to be discerned from Maxwell's thought problem, and I have been deliberately obtuse, because the physics lesson is not the point; at least not in this discussion. Of course, these guys are titans of modern science and I am teaching Tai-Chi in the park. I propose, however, that we use Maxwell's famous conundrum to lead us in an entirely different direction. One where the ramifications are more dire.

In a new paradigm, I propose that we too have an area with two divisions, also guarded by a supernatural being, only in this paradigm the wager is table stakes. In this scenario, an angel guards a supernatural realm. He also has the authority to sort individuals, separating them into either the hot place or the cool place. But remember, the door monitor is an artifice. Once authoritative dominance is removed, all returns to ubiquitous equanimity.

Let's not forget the main question in Maxwell's corollary was to the law of entropy; ultimately cycling back to Wu-Chi, depending on if you prefer the word randomness or chaos. The hypothesis of Maxwell's probe was disintegration and the ultimate return to the primeval state. So too in my comparison.

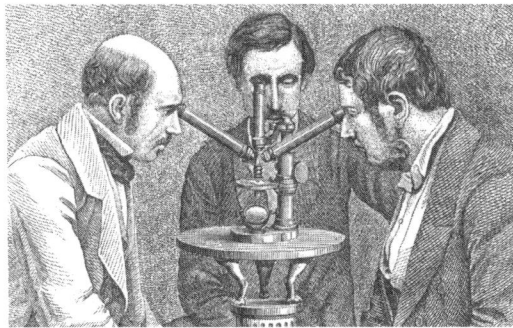

Physicists occasionally use analogies like Maxwell's demon or Schrodinger's cat to offer a mental picture to promote the understanding of a principal. Theses propositions are also referred to as "word experiments" or "thought problems", and are offered alongside an equation to foster clarity. I whole-heartedly agree with their use because it adds some life and color to otherwise daunting math problems. People who are mathematical thinkers excel in the sciences. Most others, however, interpret the world through concepts and visual pictures. And, although Aesop spoke to a primitive audience, it seems no different today - TV is more popular than reading.

Maxwell created an example that would violate the second law of thermodynamics. He had a specific objective regarding kinetic temperature and molecular velocities. But, the analogy also applies to other general theoretical concepts, such as: monitoring energy stores, fighting, or longevity.

Once the break is made from pure math, all rules are off, and everything becomes poetry. By choosing a mental illustration, like the demon, the analogy becomes open to comparisons like my angel proposition variation. Yet, this could be anything in which subjects wear or degrade; or there is a deliberately controlled separation of Yin and Yang. But, how is this germane to our purpose?

Philosophically, our world and the whole universe is winding down. From a fighting perspective, understanding that you possess only a finite store of energy may inform your intent to finish things quickly. For Tai-Chi health relevance, all human cells and systems are endlessly disintegrating. Your will, intellect, spirit, and Shen are the demon monitoring the door.

Your higher mind is at the door….the choice is yours…you little devil!

Synergy

When observing a fast car, one's first thought, understandably, might be, "what's in that thing?"; because our attention is focused on the most obvious source of power, the engine. The owner recites a number, and we respectfully nod our heads in reverence.

This is not misdirection by the owner, nor ignorance on our part. The engine, after all, makes the vehicle move. This attention to the engine is deservedly so, because a well-engineered power plant is crucial for obtaining impressive speeds by terrestrial vehicles. But paramount to attainment of the highest speeds are other contributing factors, such as: total weight, friction, and aerodynamics. The most powerful engine in the world would not achieve its full potential, if the fuselage were a large heavy box with prohibitive wind resistance.

Skilled engineers meticulously craft exterior body dynamics, conduct detailed wind tunnel protocols, and analyze formulas, to enhance results by fractions. Massive resources are dedicated to these adjunct endeavors; all to squeeze just a little more performance from the unit as a whole. Experts labor over every facet of the vehicle, from wheels, to steering, to the drive train, each working together towards a common goal - maximum effectiveness.

Most people are drawn to Tai-Chi for its health benefits. As training progresses, and perceived esoteric elements are introduced, neophytes may become judgmental and judicious in their acceptance of the abstruse contributing aspects of the art.

Pragmatists may reject, as a whole, all elements other than balance and leg strengthening. Others may be more accepting of breathing and organ massage. A smaller minority acknowledge the mind element as a possible component. But like the experts in metallurgy or aerodynamics, that share holistically in motor sports success, the perceived tangential elements of Tai-Chi are rejected as secondary: Something other than just movement.

The goal of previous chapters was to isolate principals, and through documented science and anecdotal messaging, to form a base understanding of the individualized aspects of seemingly extraneous data. In a, practical, real world example: most people understand that a sedentary lifestyle is the unhealthiest; a step-up would be clement, moderate activity, such as walking or gardening; and athleticism is healthier still. But, to best maximize health potentials there are regimes that capitalize on both ancient and contemporary knowledge to augment one's well-being. In the case of yoga and Tai-Chi, research validates the holistic wisdom and bolsters this common knowledge.

The sections Mind Intent and Brain Wave States introduced the brain science that established the premise that one's mind can have a dramatically positive effect on the human organism. Likewise, when one's thought is concentrated on a specific anatomical site, actual neurological influence takes place. The awareness of corporeal impairment results in innate healing energies being directed to the infirm site. Conversely, patients placed on painkillers typically heal at a slower rate than subjects who are permitted to have awareness of the physical distress, because the needed awareness is lessened at the designated bodily region and/or redirected to other locations.

SIX HEALING BREATHS (Liu-Zi-Jue)

There are as many arcane modalities in Eastern healing methodologies as there are people to think them up. Original formulations have been hybridized over the centuries, some additions are true enhancements, where others are personal preferences or just guesses. This same bastardization took place in the fighting arts, with dynamic fighting styles; some becoming watered down shadows of their former selves.

The routine presented here is one version of a widely accepted mode of focused attention and directed energy to maintain homeostasis. It is a powerful technique, but not immediately dramatic. Intravenous administration of Seconal or dextro-amphetamine sulfate, would produce near instantaneous and overpowering results. This is a subtle naturalistic method utilizing minuscule endogenous energies. But like muscle building, results do not appear overnight.

Presented here is a well-established process, variations of which are used regularly throughout the world. Some formulas feature a different sequence for men and women, some have an alternate order. Others assign a particular number of breaths for each organ. Nine seems to be the most prevalent.

I would suggest starting with just three breaths, as frustration and boredom will defeat those with short attention spans. The barbells will do you no good serving as a shoe rack in the corner. So, just stick with three for now. As stated earlier, there are many recognized variances, but this is the practice as I would like to present it.

Begin with a few rounds of the complete breath. Relax the external musculature. Affect a Sung state.

Liver... Start focusing your attention on the liver. Bathe it with a healing green light. Allow the light to express itself. It may radiate from the liver or receive a beam from a nebulous external source. It could be a combination of both. At any rate, the liver should continue to glow green. Draw a long, slow, deep, inhalation into the organ, allowing it to permeate it completely. Exhale while making the healing sound of the liver. Shhhhhhhh.

Heart... move your attention on to the heart. Bathe the heart with a dazzling red light. Bring healing breath into the organ, saturate every molecule with radiant vibratory mental radiation. The heart should continue to glow red. The saturation of light should remain constant while exhaling the healing sound of the heart. Haaaaaaaaa.

Stomach... transfer your attention to the stomach/pancreas. Bathe this area with a radiating yellow light. Let it glow strongly into the region. Bring in the healing breath. The healing sound on the exhale is Whoooo. Almost like a soft whistle.

Lungs... shift your attention to your lungs. Saturate the lungs with a milky opaque light. Draw the healing breath into the entire lung, like in the complete breath. The healing sound for the lung is Sssssssss. Like a serpent.

Kidneys... relocate your attention to your kidneys. Immerse both organs in vivid blue light. Pull the healing breath into the kidneys. Permeate the medulla and renal cortex with breath and light. Include the adrenals. Exhale the healing sound Chooooo.

The final procedure is magisterial, and as such, can be performed individually at the beginning or end of the form; or as demonstrated here as a seal to the cycle of healing breaths.

Bai-Hui... concentrate your attention on your Bai-Hui. Feel this spot intensely. Bring a luminous beam of intense white light into the top of your head from the high, high heavens. Thundering, pounding a fire hose of celestial white light. The brilliance of the light intensely radiates straight down the spine from GV 20 at the fontanel all the way down to GV 1 at the perineum. The column of lustrous energy saturates your entire body, emanating through every pour of your skin. Hold this image for as long as you can. The healing sound for triple warmer is Eeeeeeeee. Almost between an H and an E.

Finally, the light recedes to source. Return to an awareness of the bio-energy coursing through your body. Feel the aliveness of each cell. Perform the complete breath.

Natural Movement and Health

Natural movement is the single most comprehensive type of health maintenance beneficial to the human organism. This is because it evolved globally with the organism to keep fluids moving through the tissues and stimulate peristalsis for proper nutrient absorption. You are designed to move. Movement, challenge and resistance, force biologic systems to pulse; moving fluids through tissues, delivering nutrients and healing compounds. This also stimulates cell division, when necessary, to build muscle and increase strength, in order to meet changing situations and adapt to the demands of survival.

The uniquely specific types of movement that evolved with each animal provides for the exact type of agility and strength to meet challenges found in its environment. A natural gestalt; organisms are also adapted to their specific oxygen levels and temperature ranges, to allow for maximum performance. In order for humans to maintain homeostasis, they evolved to jump, climb, squat, bend, twist and remain active through the day. When modern conveniences almost completely replaced natural challenges from the environment, it may have become easier, but there is a price to be paid; both in wellness and longevity. Our ancestors wisely recognized this, and created systematized exercises to provide a replication of the stressors found naturally in our more primitive, and yet more holistic, environment.

If a gandy dancer is employed by a railroad to lay new sections of track, the body is receiving vigorous exercise that challenges every bodily system to become functionally optimal, meeting the new demands. I think it would be elevating for the reader to take a moment and describe the systems and forces in detail that are taking place with such an example.

First, the traps, pecs, biceps, core, and leg muscles strain to lift the 16-pound sledge hammer. Deep breathing simultaneously occurs as the tool is swung to high elevation. Next, a momentary physical relaxation takes place that coincides with a mental focusing, as the hammer reaches its zenith. This is followed by the deltoids, brachial radials, and muscles of the core contracting in unison as a forceful, yogic breath is expelled. This is more accurately described as a momentary concentration of tension which guides the projectile downward. A state of semi relaxation, if you will, while also maintaining loosened control in body, but a tight control in the mind. One which allows gravity to pull, while judiciously guiding the tool, in concert with this natural force. At last, the hammer impacts the spike. This is a transformative moment. This is where the kinetic energy ceases and other energies are resultant. For instance, vibration radiates through the handle. This new element has the effect of stimulating all body systems. Finally, the hammer is lifted to its original ready position, (port arms), with a breath inspirated to untensed tissues, and a mind now assessing the outcome of the entire action. This catharsis moment allows glucose and oxygen to re-invigorate the entire organism. Breath and mindset re-initiate, primed for action again.

Averaging 15 to 20 strokes per minute is a highly productive rate. Even at only 10 strokes per minute, this translates to 600 strokes per hour. 600 times 16 pounds totals 9600 pounds of lifting per hour. Compare this routine to the regimen of an average gym rat. Although they share many of the same exertions, they are not benefited by the added fresh air, or a sense of accomplishment; not mention the rhythmic yogic breathing and the regulated on/off (Yin/Yang) mantric pattern.

What does this amount to? Our super-fit gandy dancer does not need specific concentrated exercise to make every muscle pop in a convoluted, artificial fantasy of muscular development. The calloused hands and cardio-vascular exercise provided by this intrinsic natural conditioning, creates an entity which eventually functions optimally under the demands of these highly stressful conditions. And, I would guess, making the organism plenty tough as well.

Body builders have never been as mighty as guys who are just big and strong. This is because body shaping is a cosmetic endeavor. Modern gymnasiums that artificially pump a superfluous protuberance unnaturally, are not in keeping with the Tao. And, they certainly are not health clubs. Construction sites or family farms are health clubs. None the less, Zoomba, aerobics, and weight training are a good place to start. They are far better than nothing, yet not nearly optimal; but can indeed improve the health of a sedentary person.

In contrast, the movements endemic to the Tai-Chi form are not confined to being just concentrated, yogic, curative modalities. They are specifically designed to replicate many of the natural movements experienced by someone working on a construction site or small family farm. To only name a few: bending; squatting to pick things up; stretching to pick fruit; hammering, or rotating with a gentile twist, while slinging chicken feed. This list goes on and on.

If your torso movement seldom provides any internal organ massage or your day consists of; transfer of a softened, depleted lump from the automobile cockpit to an ergonomically designed office chair; then a scientific system of movement would be required to replace the benefits lost between how you live now, and how our farm mom, construction or railroad worker lives.

Because of their style of living, these individuals will maintain a naturally robust and healthful state. A state experienced by animals which are still adapted to surviving in their native, demanding environment. For your own health, I implore you to consider the words written here. Consider the proposition and make up your own mind. And, if you come to the conclusion that your health does need a "pick me up", Tai-Chi will definitely fit the bill.

To be sure, we will explore the many facets of exercise science. But, this book will not stop there. It will attempt to justify the time and energy invested to learn, absorb, and internalize the concepts of Tai-Chi. Admittedly, a few of the concepts presented here may seem arcane, while others might require a slight suspension of disbelief, or at least require looking at the proposition from a new point of view. Or, employing a new kind of logic and accepting seemingly disparate connections.

The exercises presented in this chapter are valid, but I am just personally convinced that the vast majority of these non-organic exercises do not even approach the benefits of Tai-Chi. This is because

Tai-Chi leaves the realm of being just an exercise; it can better be described as a targeted, healing modality and a science of concentrated, physical movement.

Ultimately, one must decide if assimilating precepts contrary, foreign, or seemingly fantastic is worth the expenditure of personal effort. But, if you have a curiosity as to why others would eagerly give the precious moments of their life into such a time investment, here in these pages are some of the principals on which this is decision founded.

The Body Makes its Own Medicine

STOP READING NOW

(That's all you really need to know)

So, you've decided to read on. Very well. In short, the body knows how to maintain health and heal injury. It also properly regulates chemical and electrical bio-transmitters. Furthermore, It knows how to properly circulate energy, in the same way it knows how to pump blood or digest food. The human organism does this automatically, and doesn't necessarily need any enhancements. But like the athlete or bodybuilder who voluntarily seeks to enhance their performance and/or musculature (and you who have also decided to read on); what follows are the modalities for maximizing one's internal culture.

For example, If I cut my arm, the doctor doesn't impose a healing on the injury. She provides a suitable field for the body to heal itself. She irrigates, sutures, and bandages the wound and then steps back and allows the body to heal itself. In other words, she attempts to maximize the environment for the body to "do its thing." She also may prophylactically administer unnecessary antibiotics, but mostly, she trusts nature to provide the healing. The classic cartoon image of an accident victim in quadruple traction illustrates that the most advanced treatment we have is to immobilize and rely on the wisdom of the real internal medicine.

When one performs Tai-Chi or other healing modalities, the body experiences a cascade of hormones, enzymes, and neurotransmitters all designed to heal and maintain their tissues and organs. These processes are induced by causing the body to react to both internal and external stimuli, postures, and contrived emotional states, directed by mind intent and focused awareness.

By applying the theory of Yin/Yang (aka opposites and reverses), one should be able to easily deduce that the counter mind/body state would be not only deleterious and potentially injurious to the human organism. When one takes on an angry state or is placed under extreme stress, such as a close personal loss or natural disaster, their body begins to saturate their whole system with caustic chemicals. One's body reacts by imposing extreme measures in an effort to deal with the perceived grave or threatening situation. This is tantamount to pouring naphtha in your gas tank, driving 150 miles an hour, and slamming through the gears. It's very hard on the mechanism.

One primary purpose of this book is to augment your Tai-Chi, by helping you to understand how its practices may be used to enhance the relaxation response; allowing the body to automatically and organically negate the stress response. There are many actions working in symphony to achieve this outcome; both overt and subtle. One begins to develop their understanding of these processes by intrinsically apprehending three major principals.

STRUCTURE

BODY ENERGY STATES

MIND INTENT

One of the primary impetuses of this book is to convey the idea that the body seeks equilibrium and is endowed by nature with an amazing array of mechanisms to maintain homeostasis. Throughout the health sections of this book, one should come to realize that the above three subjects are its primary focus. Other sections of this book will explore some more exotic topics, such as: energy movement, energy projection, and mind intent. This is chiefly because I know these subjects are of significant curiosity for many neophytes, amateurs and even the adroit practitioner.

There are principals which govern Tai-Chi as a martial art, but this will be addressed later in this volume. As a natural path for health maintenance, breathing, movement, and state of mind; all greatly influence the component interaction and overall function of the human organism.

It is laudable that man has developed sophisticated interventions to address extreme anomalies. But, to assault the delicate balances innately occurring within the human body by saturating its balanced system with unnatural, powerful chemicals is as irresponsible as exceeding the design parameters of any complex, mechanical device.

On the other hand, extreme circumstances require extreme countermeasures. In the case of a life-threatening bodily malfunction, surgery and powerful drugs may not only be necessary, but entirely mandated. Conversely, to routinely saturate one's system with harsh chemicals not found in nature, one ultimately disturbs the subtle balance refined by millennia of evolution; destroying the exquisite balance of a natural, efficient, and self-contained configuration.

To maintain homeostasis in accordance with parameters of regulation established as the human organism developed in the natural environment; breath work and discriminating movement may be employed. These methodologies function by gently massaging the internal organs without the further influence of any other outside agencies. A more complete overview of the workings of these techniques is discussed in-depth in other parts of this volume.

The desire to immediately overpower a maligned condition is typical of the "defeat and destroy" mentality that has made our species dominant in our sphere of influence. The mandate of Yin and Yang, as delineated within the art, demands that not every symptom need be met with crushing subjugation. In the absence of life-threatening or traumatic circumstances, a subtle administration is the appropriate prescription.

Developing an enhanced cardio-vascular function and increased musculature certainly contribute to good health, but not every problem is a nail. Geniuses who examined and perceived human biology, utilizing a more inspired method, established a system of health maintenance that requires no equipment nor external modulating chemical activity.

Without question, extreme programs will most certainly produce extreme results. But those radical approaches should be the exception. Preserving the delicate internal processes, however, requires implementing a more subtle approach - an opposite or reverse, if you will. Maintenance of mechanical systems is a far more refined craft than just ripping out parts and revamping the envisioned design. If magic may be defined as: "things aren't always as they appear"; then the healing modalities obtained from the practicing of these natural approaches are truly magical.

The dilemma of presenting material within the stated confines of a beginners guide obfuscates many important motifs. At this juncture, introducing an arbitrary exercise, could prove... revelatory. As a springboard for more expansive thought, I would here suggest an exercise to promote a deeper understanding and prompt further study. Using five element theory as a template, it is portentous to appreciate the Interconnectedness of bodily system. To foster a deeper appreciation of a holistic approach to health, Using the five element theory of the cycle of creation/destruction as a guide, the reader may find it worthwhile investing in research to find the correlation of the following topics:

- Angiogenisis

- Stem cells

- Gut microbiome five element diagram

- DNA

- Immune system

Tai-Chi for Health

The integration of breath, organ massage, movement and mindfulness enhance the efficiency of internal chemical activity. This aggregate creates a cascade of endogenous nutrients, enzymes, hormones, and neurotransmitters. An internal healing balm. The combination of movement, breathing and mind intent work together to produce a synergistic effect that promotes homeostasis throughout the entire organism.

The techniques of Tai-Chi produce benefits on both a macro and micro level. They can address clearly observable organic difficulties, such as: muscle strain or weakness. Also, they incite beneficial therapeutics that address specific issues, like injury and/or compromised tissues. Additionally, they contribute to enhanced organ function, as well as other readily perceived benefits. Benefits, such as; stretching and developing tendon and ligament strength. Furthermore, on a molecular level, these practices help in regulation of systems that retard telomere attrition and promote governance of co-factors of the genetic material.

To facilitate understanding of these concepts, it might prove helpful to quote a respected authority, such as Erwin Schrodinger, who is attributed with saying; "Incredibly small groups of atoms, much too small to display exact statistical laws, do play a dominating role in the very orderly and lawful events within a living organism".

The energies required to initiate and affect catalytic changes within the human biological system are, many times, undetectable under standard laboratory analysis. Regardless, they exist and are capable of producing profound effects. Throughout this manual the word subtle will occur frequently. This word is used to exemplify the statement by Dr. Schrodinger. The concepts and modalities utilized throughout Tai-Chi and Chi-Kung practices are well understood by ancient masters to work at this subtle intensity.

Tai-Chi movement, breathing, and mind intent collaborate to produce healing to damaged or compromised physical structures. The internal massage, increased circulation, accelerated lymph propulsion and dispatch of healing compounds work in concert synergistically. All interacting and cooperating to activate parasympathetic healing neurohormones. Simply speaking, Tai-Chi fosters self-healing. This is real, natural health maintenance.

The concepts summarized above will be explored in greater detail in subsequent pages. Suffice it to say that these practices were developed and fine-tuned by a type of understanding that differs from the mechanistic, instrument-based science that was established in the western world. If one were resistant to objective inquiry, these principals and techniques might appear to be occult and esoteric. But to an open, non-biased individual, they would seem inspired, natural, and practical.

Throughout this book, I offer empirical evidence and some basic science that is hopefully able to circumvent prejudices of the western mind. Not that Tai-Chi needs to defend its concepts or prove anything to anyone. Any enterprise that promotes unity of mind and spirit, and fosters harmony with the environment and fellow creatures is conducive to peace of mind and unanimity. And, not unlike many of the other great truths, many are called but few answer.

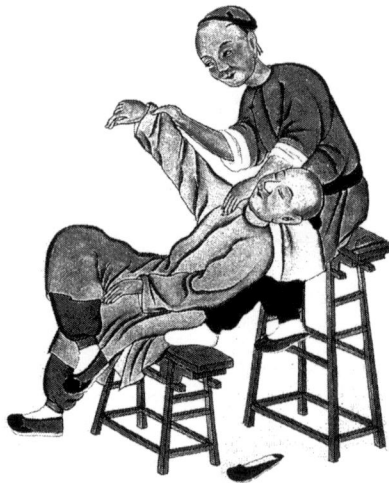

TO THE POINT

Tai-Chi derives many of its health benefits from structural alignment, enhanced fluid circulation, and breathing protocols. However, the importance of overt and incidental stimulation of acupressure points are of paramount importance. While there are accupoint targeted modalities to address specific anomalies used as stand-alone treatments, the therapeutic stimulus of the body's energetic system that occur during proper execution of the form cannot be over-emphasized.

It would be against my nature and Tai-Chi concepts in general to write a book that was preachy or authoritative. I offer this information altruistically. This guide is meant to be joyful and rewarding like an early walk or other morning ablutions. Let us probe together this subject matter and explore the internal alchemy. We're all stuck on this rock together, let's make the best of it.

Living Waters

One important theme of the previous chapters was to introduce the idea that the body makes its own medicine. And, that through specific physical techniques, your body is able to generate, nay, synthesize these healing chemicals endogenously. The Yang to this process would be consciously controlling what you put into your body. To clarify - what is the benefit of developing good mind/body practices if your internal chemistry has to fight to just stay even with the poisons you knowingly put in your body.

As a point of fact, in Chinese medicine all the components consumed and absorbed by the body are collectively referred to as Gu-Chi: food energy.

Nutrition is a complex subject and everyone has their own ideas. Most regrettably, I would rather discuss religion or politics, than nutrition. Diagnostics, while often helpful, add to the strife and confusion. For instance: I once knew an Ironman triathlete who worked as a firefighter/paramedic. His triglycerides were through the roof, because of this he was dismissed from his position. In contrast, there are numerous overweight people with relatively low numbers.

In my case, I've had very high triglyceride numbers for forty plus years. This situation obviously concerned me, so I once paid some crazy, huge amount of money to have a full body scan. The result; my blood vessels were clear. The cardiologist said: "for some reason with you it's just not sticking". He went on to say: "sometimes your body is doing that for a reason. We just don't know what that reason is yet".

The body may be producing cholesterol to address some other, yet undetermined, pertinent need. There is ongoing research that indicates this may be for a certain type of infection control. But, if looked at through one lens, there could be an entire industry that is reaching a skewed conclusion, with a strong conformation bias; not to mention potential financial profit motives.

When someone states authoritatively that a fad diet or supplement regimen is what everyone should be doing, I switch the conversation to sports. Best for whom? If respected, established researchers can succumb to financial inducements and research bias; so can writers, owners, and developers in the health food industry. For those who follow the Tao, the path is simplistic.

水

LIVING FOODS FOR A LIVING BODY

The active enzymes in living foods provide the chemical catalyst to produce homeostasis in the human organism. If you think the human body is a chemistry set that only requires carbs, fat, and protein; try living on sodas, potato chips, and protein isolate and see what happens. The active enzymes in living fruits and vegetables provides the "Chi" that activates the body into absorbing the sustenance effectively into the cells. Even fresh, killed animal flesh is loaded with this active life energy. Nutritionists now admit that the co-factors in living foods are essential for proper utilization of nutrients. Synthesized vitamin C may have some application, but naturally occurring vitamin C, with its complete co-factors, is crucial for maintaining complex operations of the human organism.

If you are a vegetarian, or just someone who has two vegetables with his pot roast, you are allowing your body to construct and repair with organic life energy. I, myself, always start my day with fresh fruit, often yogurt (with live active cultures), and may still have a traditional breakfast. At least I'm giving my body a chance to work with the Tao. And, even though I eat meat, I try to consume as much plant life as I can; because the living organism demands life energy. About the only thing I make sure I always include is mushrooms and garlic. But you find what works best for you. The point here is to not make the body pull nutrients out of the bones and organs because it is not receiving the proper building materials, and that is in living foods.

There is no doubt in my mind that 50% of people's chronic health problems could be cured by a strict vegan diet, as a therapeutic regime. The body is tough. It can take a lot. But, if you ask too much, like never adding any oil to your car's engine, it will eventually seize up.

Like the neurological stimulation produced by the awareness aspects of Tai-Chi, micro-nutrients and living enzymes are a program of subtlety. Get in tune with the Tao.

THE BODY MAKES ITS OWN MEDICINE

but to maintain homeostasis it needs

LIVING FOODS FOR A LIVING BODY

Imagine there were an efficiently run city dump. The community was committed to recycling. Everyone organized on one, focused goal; to have a clean, vigorous, vituperate process that utilized total input; with no waste of resources. Every day, long lines of trucks queued up; were inventoried, inspected, categorized, rated, and qualified. Dedicated employees dispatched truck contents to appropriate areas. Paper and cardboard here - copper there. Glass in this bin - aluminum over there.

For years the refuse processing runs like a military operation. Then, one day, a bunch of gangsters shows up with a load of gunpowder to be disposed of. Everyone goes nuts. Operations grind to a halt to address a foreign threat. Employees scramble. Chaos ensues. The formerly efficient process that was capable of handling wild swings in volume and content are thrown in disarray. Experienced intelligent managers simply can't process a dangerous substance they have never seen before.

Experts often call various biological processes systems. And like our capable city refuse center they will perform as advertised, as long as personnel and equipment can function within design parameters. Try and process a foreign toxin and machinery breaks down; staff and operations erupt into chaos.

Your body evolved processing natural components not polydextrocellulose. Don't court a potential catastrophe, like above, by over challenging the system. The food industry capitalizes on human cravings the same way drug dealers, tobacco companies, and "big pharma" do. Create an unnatural need for their Frankenstein products. Give yourself a chance by developing a desire for things of this earth.

Suppose someone worked in a shop. He used a paper cup to hold nuts and bolts. Every day fasteners in and out. Eventually, there is a material failure. The paper tears and the bottom falls out. The demands exceed the design capabilities. The cup was soundly manufactured, but was never made to withstand unreasonable expectations. Across the room, another worker uses the same cup only for drinking water. His cup ultimately fails also. After all, it's only a paper cup. But lasts much longer, because the demands placed on it did not exceed design parameters.

Don't ask your body to process more than it is capable of. Health is in your hands. Survival however goes to the slick, the fast, and the wise. Take phyto-chemicals for example: the healing properties of deeply colored fruits and coniferous vegetables are well vetted.

I know a promoter who has made a great living conducting seminars touting the benefits of incorporating phyto-chemicals in the diet. His choice of delivery system is the smoothy. He sells high-end blenders and shows charts and graphs about the nutrient content of his recipes. It's all beneficial and valid; except consuming emulsified produce, bypasses a vital biological process; and drinking vegetables in this form only delivers a fraction of their nutrient content, when liquefied.

Digestion begins in the mouth. Enzymes in saliva, that act as catalysts, begin the digestive process while masticating. The emulsified food must spend a reasonable amount of time being "pretreated" before being passed along to the next stage. Without the enzymes provided by the initial stage of processing, the remainder of the cycle is incomplete. Yes, the phyto-chemicals are there, but unavailable to the body for utilization.

This is just one example of how you must be proactive and fully educate yourself in food and nutrition. The same is true of yoga and Chi-Kung health practices. If there are missing elements, or you have received incomplete or improper instruction, you are cheating yourself out of the benefits that can be derived by these proven techniques.

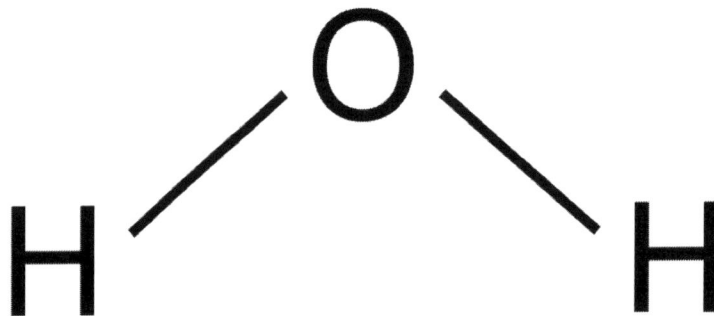

$$H \diagup O \diagdown H$$

Living foods have a vibrational frequency which can be interpreted in electrical terms. Analysis of various items consumed by the human organism are rated in megahertz (MHz). Here are two lists. On the left, the human body in various states of vitality. On the right, some common food items.

GOOD HEALTH	60-70 MHz	COOKED MEAT	3-5 MHz
CELLS MUTATE	BELOW 60 MHz	NUTS / SEEDS	50 MHz
COLD/FLU	58 MHz	LIVING GREENS	70 MHz
CANCER	42 MHz	OLFACTORY STIMULATION (FROM A ROSE)	300 MHz
NEAR DEATH	20 MHz		

Measurable electrical values are important to foster understanding. Electrical stimulation and signaling is vital to the human body. But living enzymes, Chi, life force energy, or any other image you wish to visualize adds unnecessary complexity to a very simple equation: Only living foods can impart life. Regard the body as a chemistry experiment at your own peril.

Read, study, cross reference. Improper training can be a waste of time or even dangerous. The health industry is fraught with shysters and used car salesmen. 4 color brochures and slick websites are no guarantee of validity of content. Nutritional supplements are not regulated by the FDA. These supplements may contain ingredients which are ineffective or even dangerous. "Big bad" Campbell soup is regulated, verified and inspected. A supplement manufacturer is totally unregulated, and often times foreign produced.

My Guru said: "any food that is healthful and life giving which is normal to your culture, is good food. Who am I to come over here and tell you what to eat". It was statements like that, and his tolerance for carnivores and alcoholics in general, that made me acknowledge that this is the guy for me. He did close however by quietly adding: "It is best to be vegetarian." For chemical and vibratory reasons, it is obvious that this is the case.

But also as you develop a sense of oneness and unity with all things, it becomes undeniable that the hog and the chicken are your brothers, and also deserving of life. If you've ever known a sad eyed, old cow; you would consider it monstrous to plunge a knife into her, while standing face to face.

I, however, do not have that problem. In our mechanized industrial culture, I can pay someone else to do my killing for me. I may partake of flavorful, complete proteins attractively displayed at my local super market. I can peruse the refrigerated counter labeled "beef" and see, not a dismembered bovine, but a food item called "Delmomico" or "Porterhouse", which absolves me from any direct culpability. My mother had to wring the chicken's neck and pluck it's feathers. I enjoy an unrelated item, called K.F.C.

Your body has to work hard to remove the toxins and additives from the "normal" American diet. There is no doubt in my mind that many of the chronic pathologies which now plague modern people, could easily be reversed, by adhering to a strict vegetarian diet. The human organism is capable of reversing disease, in many cases, but you have to give it a chance.

The obscene drug advertisements, that now clog our airwaves, are testimony to the idea that it is "normal" for everybody to have something wrong with them. It is not "normal" for everyone over the age of 50 to have diabetes. The body seeks equilibrium and can achieve it, if you just get out of the way. You can try diet fads and assault your body with engineered supplements, or heed the simple advise of Hari Harananda - It is best to be vegetarian.

EPILOGUE

one more word about animals

There was a golf course I played many times (in either Wisconsin or Minnesota) that had two unusual natural hazards. On the eighth tee was an old graveyard, no larger than a small front yard; with very old, weather-worn headstones from the sixteen and seventeen hundreds. I lost my ball there a couple of times.

On the fourteenth fairway was a Holstein cow, She always seemed to be in the same place. Don't know whether it was the sun or the grass, but she seemed to like it right there in the middle. Hilarious! One time I had to make a chip shot from between her legs. My ball rolled directly between all four hooves. I placed one hand on her back and hacked with my eight iron one handed. I got to know her pretty well and always regarded cattle differently from then on.

In America, if you were to propose making coats from family cats or having dog steak for dinner, the villagers would come for you with pitchforks. Sheep, goats, and pigs all have personalities and often bond with their co-residents on family farms. I knew someone who named his turkeys...then ate them.

Indigenous peoples often pray for the souls of game animals, and refer to fellow animal travelers as "brother otter" or "wolf people." If it is unthinkable to slaughter an elephant, how much less a lamb. There are many nutritional reasons to consume plants exclusively; perhaps also, empathy and compassion.

Slow Boat from China

One of the most common questions new practitioners have, is: "Why is Tai-Chi execution is so slow?" There are, of course (Yin/Yang), two answers to this question.

First, for fighting application. Movements simply can not be practiced full speed due to the strikes being thrown with so much power that muscle tearing and joint damage would be the typical result.

Second, regarding healing aspects of the art. This answer requires a more in-depth explanation. To implement proper internal organ massage, circulation, and enhanced lymph propulsion, the degree of stimulation must fall into a "Goldilocks Zone" of acceptability.

By way (Bi-Hui) of example, if a student were to receive a penetrating impact to the forearm: one that would most assuredly result in a bruise; a prudent, experienced instructor would usually start the immediate application of massage to the affected area. The goal of this therapeutic action is to spread out the occult blood, allowing the body to ameliorate swelling and increase circulation to the injury. Ultimately, the treatment is for the purpose of expediting healing to the affected area, marshaling one's endogenous healing compounds. In essence "jump starting" the recovery process.

If, however, the administrator of the massage was insensate and overzealous, grinding callously, this action would not only further injure the area, but be treated by the body as a further damage to the area in question. Conversely, lightly stroking the trauma field would prove inadequate to provide any stimulation of the natural healing response. Instead, only the proper, appropriate degree of compression is felicitous.

Similar to above example, the self-administered provocation provided by the prescribed twisting, bending movements, those inherent throughout the Tai-Chi sequence, also initiate the production of the appropriate endogenous healing compounds. These compounds are aptly dispatched to areas of concern. These areas of interest are dictated by reaction to environmental encounters or internal functional requirements, as commanded by the wisdom of the body.

Although the form is usually practiced at "Tai-Chi" speed, it may be executed at a variety of speeds; all for different reasons. For instance, training slow cultivates applicable alignments and perfect balance; application speed is used to facilitate Fa-Jin energy release; or, as originally stated, "Tai-Chi" (Goldilocks) speed is to enhance internal function. The stimulation provided by this intermediate speed and rhythm induces the release of a cascade of hormones, enzymes and neurotransmitters, strategically discharging them throughout the body.

Knowing what one is doing, and why, is paramount when one chooses at which speed the sequence is performed. Over time, one gains experience in the art and begins to acquire the requisite skills to determine which speed is appropriate for the need. And, while extremes in appliance may be occasionally required at either end of the spectrum; walking the razors edge of corporeal benefaction requires the wisdom of understanding of the middle path.

Here again, Tai-Chi provides a metaphor for many other temporal incidences - extremes are useful, when required or necessary, but usually the most favorable trajectory of one's journey is the measured one. Like learning the skills of celestial guidance on a slow boat from China, one should be able to intuitively find the right course and speed.

Postureality

There is an old adage that says, "a fool who persists in his folly shall become wise." There exists an undeniable poignancy with this observation and it would be easy to smile at this trifle and move on to the next distraction. But, since we know there is Yin/Yang in everything, let's flip this musing and explore it's opposite/reverse - "A sage who persists in his wisdom shall become foolish."

This proposal isn't just flippant nor iconoclastic. Or, recreants pursuing appetent giant slaying. Rather it is a reasonable exercise pursuant to a functional perspective. Put succinctly, all things have a tipping point. For example, creatures and entities approach a state of evolutionary perfection, then decline. Furthermore, all natural phenomena and processes germinate, bloom, ripen then rot. In reality, nothing just keeps improving forever. Put another way, organisms and collections of individuals can indeed become too big for their britches. The universe seeks equanimity through chaos, The exquisite organization that is your cellular structure, shall return to disorder, regulation through dispersion - so says the second law of thermodynamics.

As expounded in a preceding essay, the observation was raised of just how small things are on the quantum scale. Turns out this may well be the Yin/Yang tipping point. Things that we find useful on a macro scale are literally rendered academic, when examined microcosmically. So for practical purposes, operations on small scales are meaningless. Consequently, not just matter, but space itself prefers an atomic structure for our current reality. This observable phenomenon is recognizable in all human endeavors.

Apparent within this omnipresent structure is that balance is also preeminent in all things, even devotion to our creator. Yet mavens, fanatics, and those with a predilection for religious zealotry, are impassioned to the extremes. Some religious cranks crave only to worship god, not do anything else, not even work, just pray.

So too of our other great religion, science. Taken to a fanatical excess, it becomes ostensible that pragmatism itself, is a form of zealotry. It is my considered opinion, that we have now reached that tipping point. Further elaborations on this observation will appear in subsequent articles. But for now, it is congruous and poignant to consider the deeper principals and higher aspects of the subject at hand.

I want you to get the most from your Tai-Chi, and like many other examples in the human endeavor, that may mean, not looking too closely. This is germane because, as repeatedly stated throughout this tome, only results matter. A luthier may have high level knowledge of woods, glues and acoustics, but a deep understanding of quarks and the electromagnetic force in that wood is meaningless to his customers or those who appreciate the music emitted by his creations.

This Doesn't mean that up is down, black is white, or right is wrong, it only means that every inside has an outside and every crest has a trough. This is an important distinction, and one of the key elements of this book.

买前

It is for this reason that there has been little or no focus on subtle energies, as expressed and postulated by transmission through the twelve meridians or eight extraordinary channels. I believe this subject is both important and viable, but their relevance to our specific pursuit is, at best, tenuous. In fact, researchers are not sure that they even exist. But, since these pathways figure prominently into Tai-Chi theory and practice, it is unavoidable to not make mention of these arcane conduits or how they relate to five element theory. So, to accelerate progress and promote a functional understanding of Tai-Chi practice, I have strenuously avoided references to these topics beyond the tipping point of practicality.

My Pai-Lum instructor told me, "Don't even tell them about internal, because they get the benefits whether they know what they're doing or not". I mention this quote because of its sagacity and humble truthfulness. Much of the internal benefits are simply inevitable, they are inherent in the movement. The subtle internal alchemy occurs automatically, just by virtue of proper execution. For this reason I will only include a highly condensed description of the postures and hints at the martial art application. Besides, more in-depth analysis of these can be found in just about any book on the subject.

As repeatedly stated in this volume, the magic is in the movement. For maximum efficiency, just having an awareness of this fact is sufficient. A deep comprehension of the minutia is unnecessary and may be distracting. But, if after comprehensive study and intensive training, you believe that the subtle actions occurring in the twelve meridians and eight extraordinary channels are decisive, then you write that book. This one is a field manual, and as such its primary focus is efficiency and practicality. Tai-Chi survival if you will.

What follows are illustrations of some of the common postures from the form. Since proper structure is paramount for both energy flow and self-defense, several visual angles of each have been provided to facilitate correct physical positioning. And, once the correct alignments are affected, the wisdom of the body circulates humors, and produces appropriate chemical cascades as dictated by the demands of the postures. The postures themselves provide the parameters for the applicable biological processes. In short, the body knows how to produce and circulate healing the same way it commands over peristalsis or lymph propulsion. Further enhancements provided by breathing and mind intent, are addressed in subsequent chapters.

After all of this discussion, I believe I can wrap this whole thing up in just four words - just do the form.

Postures

During the fifty years I thought about writing this book, one thought was consistent: there would be no graphics and no pictures. I felt it was far too important to communicate concepts and ideas, while wasting precious space with virtually meaningless static examples of a fluid art.

Pictures in the martial arts books of my day ware always grainy and indistinct. Advancements in graphic reproduction didn't seem to improve this situation to any degree in my modern era. Then, when my hard working collaborator and I stumbled upon the compelling and masterful line drawings and woodcuts from previous centuries, it was decided that the images from European history may serve as a type of visual translator. These fascinating images could help to bridge the gap between known references from the Western world, and Eastern art; where every line and spatial orientation has significance.

Advancements in computer technology and three dimensional modeling has allowed me to produce images capable of a type of representation that actually illustrates proper Tai-Chi postures. Images that are a close facsimile to an actual human, with body alignments and visual representations that are truly helpful. It is my hope that one can actually analyze the images in detail. One can examine the proper posture, stance and foot positioning, along with arm, elbow, and hand alignments: Literally allowing the reader to see proper shape and angle of the entire posture. This is something I thought would never be possible. I encourage the reader to use the images of this section, mimicking the alignments and position, in an effort affect correct execution.

Historically, my resistance to including any illustrations revolved around the fact that they simply never seemed helpful. Most books on the subject, prompt the question, "a graphic of what"? At what point of the execution has the action been "stop framed"? Tai-Chi postures don't necessarily have this same problem, as there is a well-established protocol, with many of the postures serving as static stances for breathing routines and leg strengthening.

I finally came to the conclusion that, if a picture is worth a thousand words, then it is certainly advantageous to include them. Never the less, I believe that the bulk of the important information is presented in the text and not the images. And, that it is far more effective to communicate conceptually; by building images in the mind. So these images are included to serve as an adjunct to the written word. Hopefully, these images will enhance one's perspective and understanding. But, one should not just skip the text and rely soley upon the images as their reference. Even if they are awesome.

Push

Key Elements

- ROOT: push into the earth while effecting discharge

- UNITARY BODY MOTION: anatomical synergy

- TARGET: liver 14, bladder/Illiac crest, kidneys

- HEALTH FORM BENEFITS: kidneys - a band of muscle provides an undulating massage improving renal function

Push is the hallmark technique of all Tai-Chi styles. Bump, shove, butt, and redirect are all variations of the idea of push. Often initiated with an initial shove followed with an immediate ballistic, explosive, driving penetration. (push/punch). This of course can be reversed (Yin/Yang) by initial shock wave penetration, followed by a surging thrusting discharge. (punch/push).

back obliques, bottom, and top views of posture

Push

Press

Key Elements

- ROOT: structurally strong stance assures all power is directed into the target; without radiating back to source

- HANDS: power triangle multiplies energy transfer mathematically - note how press may flow into snake option

- TARGET: gb24 - lv13 - cv14 - vc15 - bl45

- HEALTH FORM BENEFITS: due to its similarity to the posture "push" this movement is also beneficial to the kidneys

Press emphasizes the importance of reinforced block and reinforced strike. Due to the geometry of the "power triangle", the impetus of the core and stability of the stance contribute synergisticly to deliver force through structural integrity, contributing to a impact greater than the sum of its parts.

back obliques, side, and top views of posture

Fair Lady

Key Elements

- ROOT: may be delivered as a single or double strike, and in one application, it allows kinetic energy from an overhand to convert to Peng

- HANDS: Lead hand arcs like the blade of a saber, curving uniformly from pinky tip to medial edge of scapula, while rear hand is delivered with a grinding, twisting penetration

- TARGET: varied; dependent on delivery from front, back or side: lv14 – gb25/26 – tw17 – gv14 – cv17 - st9/10

- HEALTH FORM BENEFITS: while tradition maintains that this posture is beneficial to the chest area and the lungs (which seems to be often overlooked in some texts), and it is also purported to relieve cramps

- EXECUTION: the posture, famously depicted, is not full execution; rather is usually shown at the moment of interface, and then often immediately transforms into a spiraling energy which is delivered with a snapping twist and commonly aided by a shuffling back-up mass; while the lower hand and elbow are simultaneously repositioned to be properly aligned with the rear hip (forming a continuous line from back to front)

Also know as the bow and arrow stance (directly translated from gong jian bu) and is the most commonly used stance in Tai-Chi.

back obliques, side, and top views of posture

Levitate

Key Elements

- ROOT: the name says it all

- HANDS: uniform; as if resting on a tabletop: slung in a loose "dead hand' manor

- TARGET: raking motion to gb1, with retreating energy; also provides the opposite/reverse opportunity to effect shoulder strike

- HEALTH FORM BENEFITS: traditionally purported to promote proper function of internal organs

If this movement could be properly executed within the form, one would be truly levitating. Subtle weight shift, balance, and theatrics are required to properly perform the transition at the required pace. This fact ensures that the form can never be perfected, while simultaneously providing a lofty beacon to strive toward.

back obliques, bottom, and top views of posture

Eagle

Key Elements

- ROOT: a low strong cat stance is required to properly affect this posture

- HANDS: pointing the hands diagonally at a 45 degree angle opens the chest, allowing for a full and complete breath

- EXECUTION: considered an "A" or "B" move in forms competition

- HEALTH FORM BENEFITS: addresses Yin weakness; activates Yang energy

Fluidity through transition contributes to both health maintenance and martial prowess. Great control and grace are needed for equitable appliance of this stance.

back obliques, front, and top views of posture

Snake Creeps Down

Key Elements

- ROOT: great body awareness and leg strength is required to affect this posture

- HANDS: a pulling sensation should be felt in the chest as the rear hook hand separates from the front threading hand

- EXECUTION: the low posture allows the practitioner to weave the lead hand around the legs, preparatory to the shoulder throw

- HEALTH FORM BENEFITS: The classics state that this posture tonifies the kidneys and contributes to general vitality

In form's work, maintaining continuity and consistency of speed can be challenging.

back obliques, front, and top views of posture

Crane Spreads Wings

Key Elements

- DIRECTION: centrifugal; explodes outward from center

- ENERGY FLOW: direct or spiral

- EXECUTION: nerve launch

- HEALTH FORM BENEFITS: heart, central nervous system - the full length of the spine

Exploding from center with a snapping whip, reminiscent of the powerful Fukian white crane. The loose heavy wings are launched with a twitch, then transforms into a blasting pounding type of power (Yin/Yang) on impact. A Pelican taking flight, or a catapult may be more familiar. Adaptable as a block or a strike, Inner gate or outer gate. Offense or defense.

back obliques, bottom, and top views of posture

Single Whip

Key Elements

- DIRECTION: cardinal points of the Bagua

- ENERGY FLOW: multi-energetic

- EXECUTION: whip - Hua

- HEALTH BENEFITS: liver - digestion

The iconic Tai-Chi posture. Single whip has myriad applications. Quintessential for energy work, after Wu-Chi. Seminal for Chi-Kung. This paradigmatic pose offers many yogic health benefits and martial arts applications. As a static posture, used frequently in other routines.

back obliques, front, and top views of posture

Play Guitar

Key Elements

- DIRECTION: compressing / oppositional

- ENERGY FLOW: inward / downward

- EXECUTION: close the circle

- HEALTH BENEFITS: digestive

This position teaches a squeezing, compressing kind of energy. Although seemingly a sister technique to Lift Hands, differing energies and application. Excellent for reading energy, and flowing while waiting for a change.

back obliques, bottom, and top views of posture

Seven Stars

Key Elements

- Direction: spiral or looping, low to high

- ENERGY FLOW: brute to whipping

- EXECUTION: crosses center, but returns

- HEALTH FORM BENEFITS: blood circulation, and small intestine

The opposite/reverse of crane spreads wings, this movement utilizes centripetal force. Initiated with a raw brute power, the penetration is delivered with a sharp ballistic speed. Often taught as a breakout from a double wrist grab, there are of course many adaptations. The classic name of this posture is: Step forward to form seven stars of the big dipper.

Press posture - back oblique - top and bottom

Tai-Chi Theory in Action

Pugilism and Tai-Chi Principles

To fight and conquer in all your battles is not supreme excellence; supreme excellence consists in breaking the enemy's resistance without fighting.

Sun Tzu

Fighting

Interpersonal combat (a.k.a. fighting) is both dangerous and wildly unpredictable. This form of encounter is best avoided at all costs, which is why martial arts have always emphasized: "for self-defense only", or "only in matters of life or death". But since this is a book about Tai-Chi and Tai-Chi is a martial art, this subject is both germane and unavoidable.

Pew research statistics (around year 2020) indicate that the numbers around these types of interactions hold fairly steady throughout the U.S.A. Aggravated assaults: about 250 per 100,000. Rape (which is less reliable because of under reporting): but is estimated at around 40-50 per 100,000. Murder and non-negligent manslaughter: toll 5 victims per 100,000 individuals. Fistfights: only account for about 5% of all U.S. homicides annually.

Even if it is only by accident, it is possible for an untrained person to kill someone in a violent street encounter. For example; an opponent may have an obscure brain condition, unexpected or unexplained seizures, or an undiagnosed terminal blood clot, thrombosis, or embolism. One could list well known fighters who's death resulted from such a camouflaged disorder.

Along that same vein, a well-placed shot to the sternum may stop a heart. And, a direct hit from a football helmet, or a line drive from a baseball can also result in the same effect. Given similar circumstances, a couple dozen young athletes a year succumb accidentally to such "unusual" incidents.

Ironically, more people are seriously maimed in street fights by tripping or falling down than by the impact energy from fists or feet. The most problematic? A vulnerable cranium impacting the pavement. The simple fact is: the law will not indite the concrete, only the hand that sent it there. Fortunately, the average individual isn't capable of striking hard enough to cause the same kind of traumatic head injury: which accounts for the statistics being what they are. But, if a specific medicine killed only 5% of the patients taking it, we would consider it to be too risky and questionable for therapeutic use.

In all reality, most fights begin over some minor offense and could easily be avoided or slimed out of. In these types of encounters; If you lose, you lose - and if you win you lose. You could end up being defeated; or you may be the one standing victorious over a motionless body. And then, you can tell everyone in prison how you successfully conquered your opponent. Either way: if you play idiotic games, you win idiotic prizes.

According to the Bureau of Justice's statistics (around the year 2020), the cost to the U.S. government to fund the criminal justice system averages $295.6 billion annually. This number includes managing more than 2.2 million people incarcerated, at roughly $134,000 per person. Half this amount, $142.5 billion, pays for police protection. The cost of maintaining and operating America's jails, prisons, and supervision (parole and probation), totals $88.5 billion. The judicial and legal system ring in the remainder at $64.7 billion. Fun fact: these are not fun facts.

It would be difficult to calculate the societal costs or the burden on families, due to lost income and strain on the social safety net, but one calculus allows us to create an illustration and commensurate one example. The court costs for each person arrested averages around $14,000. Multiply this times the 2.2 million people incarcerated and you can see this directly impacts family's another $30 billion nationally.

Private security in America is a $350 billion industry. Bureau of Justice statistics breaks it down to $282 billion in the private sector, and another $69 billion paid by the federal government. The annual nonfatal injury rate for security officers is 14 per 1,000 full-time employees (2017). Armored car services is 36 per 1,000 employees. The rate of cases that required days away from work or work restrictions was 9 for every 1,000 security workers; 28 per 1,000 armored car employees.

Municipalities require armed champions on patrol 24/7. Retail establishments pay private security to make sure no one shoves anything in their pockets. All of this pain and expense, because people simply will not do the right thing. And, all of this is to protect us from... us.

Outside of our borders exist menacing antagonists with differing ideologies as to the best way to manage a citizenry. Other envious regimes would invade and conquer if they could. The military of the United States maintains a fighting force of 1,417,370 active duty personal, and 857,261 reserves with a price tag of $778 billion annually. The U.S. military budget constitutes 39% of the worldwide total...which is $1.98 trillion. Adding the cost of clandestine intelligence agencies, which are reported to pull $62.3 billion for the national intelligence program, and $23.3 billion for military intelligence. These numbers are always notoriously under reported, as after all, they are spy agencies; and survival demands an imperative awareness of foreign threats.

The cost of war itself carries a hefty price tag in dollars and suffering. Discounting operations like Iraq, the war of 1812, and the American Revolution; a few of our major adventures have depleted us by:

Civil war...$68.17 billion / 750,000 deaths

WW I... $381 billion / 116,516 deaths

WW II...$4.69 trillion / 405,399 deaths

V/N... $843.63 billion / 58,220 deaths

Afghanistan...$910.47 billion / 2,285 deaths

People immersed in the fantasy of street fighting and combat video games may wonder why martial arts like Tai-Chi place so much emphasis on philosophy and spiritual understanding. For the same reason governments maintain a military, yet direct tremendous resources towards the diplomatic service.

Governments, like enlightened individuals, hope to dissolve and diffuse potential conflict before resorting to martial solutions. The prayer and introspection dismissed by superficialists, but emphasized so heavily in internal arts, differs little from the machinations of statecraft with peacekeeping programs and foreign aid.

The world will always be full of shallow, frivolous people who think there is nothing more glorious than to push someone's face in, and seek out professional training to do so more effectively. Whatever naive impulse that might have initiated one's odyssey, typically wind up producing the opposite kind of emanation. Those truly possessed of destructive power; like high level martial artists and military professionals, are very reluctant to execute, and are focused on trying not to ply their craft.

A peripheral assessment of such a metamorphosis in the base expression of an individual may suggest a diagnosis of schizophrenia. This, however, is decidedly not the case; but is the natural consequence of an immersion countermeasure which once again produces the opposite result of the one initially imagined. It is important to point out that this is not the same type of revelation as someone who has spent a career as a musician or golf pro and definitively declares: "it's not what you think it is".

Properly experienced and internalized, martial arts training should prove cathartic, eliciting a transformation that ultimately is an elixir; one far different from the ideal so fervidly coveted originally.

Simply put, the application of Yin/Yang in this personal arc, expresses itself in the most basic of divisions. Combat / non-aggression. Violence / peace. Pride / humility. Impulsive / judicious. Victory / long term thinking. And, ultimately - good / evil polarity.

Thaumaturgy

The speed of light is not constant. It slows anytime it passes through a transparent medium; air, water, glass. Light speed is only constant in a vacuum. Currently estimated to be 299,792,458 m/s. This means that the C (the speed of light constant) in Einstein's famous equation is subjective, rendering the whole idea relative. I state this humorously, because C changed over time as measurements became more exact, as did the length of a meter. This number is now very well established. We can now time laser light pulses using an atomic clock.

The shortest distance between two points is a straight line. This is an obvious fact, would seem to be a useful fighting tactic, and indeed many martial arts systems are founded on this principal. But as has been revealed throughout this book, rules are malleable, and laws are not immutable.

If you were on the shore looking out to sea, and fifty feet to your left, you observe a swimmer in distress. Given the emergency of the situation, you would probably not try to reach them by jumping directly into the water and swimming in a straight line to the person. You would conclude that the most expedient action would be to run down the beach until you were directly in front of the victim, then jump in and swim in a straight line to effect rescue. This is because you can travel faster on land than you can in the water. This means to be the most effective, it is not always the shortest distance, but the shortest time.

Fa-Jin and other types of rapid energy release techniques, shorten the time between launch and contact, minimizing the number of possibilities for change in the situation. Some tactics may employ time versus distance as illustrated in the example above, but that is not the only calculation.

It would be great if you possessed the complete package. Natural athletic movement, bull like strength, fearlessness. But few are endowed with all of these perfect gifts, collectively. So, if I had to choose one, or as in my case, having all said attributes reduced by age, and only being left with one; then let it be the most valuable one...speed.

This is not a contradiction of aforementioned attributes like timing which is also paramount. Or, tactics which are products of training the mind, determination, or size and strength. However, of all the physical qualities; speed, specifically hand speed, is far and away number one.

Because an organism must identify, process and initiate a response, action will always beat reaction. This is because it is difficult to intercept something which is already in motion. It is amazing how the "double shoot" technique, which requires setting the entire body in motion, can get to one before they can punch.

What would an encounter be like if the other person were moving in slow motion and you had all the time in the world to slip, counter or chose the best technique? A pill, incantation, or formula which could alter time perception, changing the relationship of bodies in motion, would indeed be super Kung-Fu magic. Increasing speed provides this elixir.

Those who hold the opinion that power is the dominate attribute, an exposition on the relationship between speed and power could prove elucidating. For example, in the game of billiards, the player imposes kinetic energy on the cue ball by striking it with the cue stick. If the cue ball collides with another ball, it slows down dramatically, and the ball it hit accelerates its speed as the kinetic energy is passed on to it. In short, kinetic energy can be passed from one object to another.

In billiards the collisions would be classified as elastic collisions. Ones in which the kinetic energy is preserved throughout the process. But, in inelastic collisions, kinetic energy is dissipated into other various forms of energy, such as: heat, sound, or binding energy (breaking bound structures).

Flywheels are an effective method of kinetic energy storage. Flywheels demonstrate that kinetic energy can also be stored via rotational motion. If one achieves sufficient spinning velocity devastating striking ability is an inherent result. Also, to avoid a take down, rotational forces are often a preferable option to solely linear power. This method of escape is extensively demonstrated by running backs in the NFL.

There exist several mathematical descriptions of kinetic energy. Yet, it is also helpful to consider real world examples and illustrations that demonstrate it in the appropriate empirical to scientific comparison.

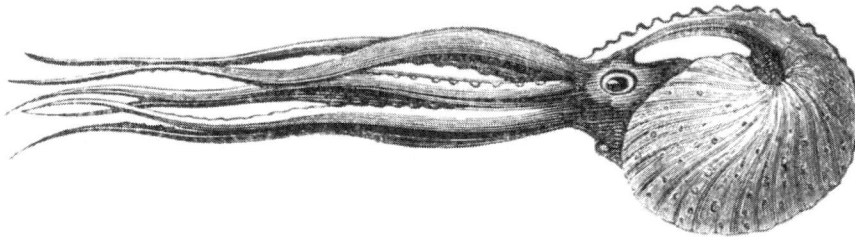

Kinetic energy increases with the square of the speed. An object doubling its speed has four times as much kinetic energy.

The kinetic energy of an object is related to its momentum by the equation:

$$ke = 1/2mv^2$$

where:

ke = kinetic energy

m = mass

v = velocity (notice its squared - i.e., my point)

Willem Gravesande dropped weights from different heights into a block of clay. This experiment proved the penetration depth was proportional to the square of the impact speed. Newton too approximated the impact depth of projectiles at high velocities; but based his notion only on momentum. He made no mention of what happened to the kinetic energy after the projectile has stopped.

For our purposes there is the obvious empirical data of energy transfer resulting in nerve impact, organ damage, and sheer force trauma to osteous formations. With a sufficient velocity, deep penetration and diffusion into the target is ensured, and the penetrating energy wave of power is transferred into the target; not allowing it to radiate back to its source.

Because the maneuver is thrown from a relaxed state, there is no noticeable fatigue with the doubling of the speed. This bears repeating: doubling the speed produces quadrupling the power with no perceptible drain on body systems or interference with structure or timing.

Leibniz and Bernoulli described kinetic energy as the living force. If European scientists are able use such blatant and descriptive language, then it's not much of a stretch to bind their sentiments to that of Eastern thought. This small step brings our perceptions one step closer to equating scientific principal with Tai-Chi theory; and ultimately melds the Yin/Yang relationship of the science world with that of the natural world.

Uweza

Suppose I walk into an insurance office and witness a conflict. One of the girls' boyfriends bursts in with a gun to confront her because "she done him wrong". Now, if this were a robbery at a convenience store, you would most likely not interfere. Because, statistically, the robber will probably just empty the drawer and leave. But in this case, the boyfriend has announced his intention to shoot. Keep in mind that you've just walked in and you're behind him. Also, you notice there is a can of soda on the desk within easy reach. You could simply pick it up and bean him with it.

Now, let's say that you're not a very good thrower, and can only throw at about 20-25 mph. This tactic might serve as a good distraction, but afterword you would have to jump him and wrestle the gun away; too many variables. Instead, suppose you just happen to be a major league pitcher and can throw at 100 mph. That's the end. It's finished right there. Because of your skill and training, you are able to deliver world class power when the projectile connects.

As martial artists we don't always rely exclusively on sheer power. The Yin/Yang aspects of conflict may call for vital area strikes, delivered with moderate power. But in the case of our baseball pitcher scenario, the prescription is power. So, let's take a look at why we are able to deliver an event ending (game changing) strike.

KINETIC ENERGY

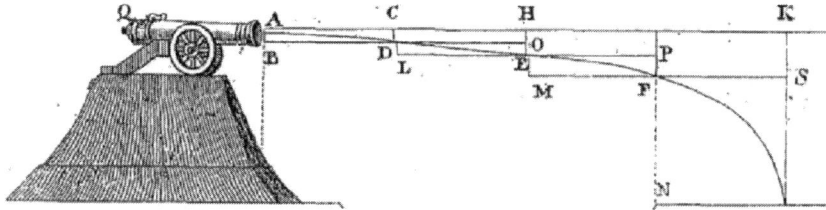

Kinetic energy is the power of motion. Anything with mass that is in motion has kinetic energy. Upon impact it has connectic energy. A stationary mass has no kinetic energy. An elevated mass has potential energy. Connectic energy is something I just made up because I am funny.

$$KE = 1/2 MV$$

KE – kinetic energy

M – mass

V – velocity

If you double the mass of an object in motion, it doubles its kinetic energy.

$$KE = 1/2 \, MV2$$

$$(2) \, (1)2 = 2$$

If you double the speed of an object, you quadruple its kinetic energy.

$$KE = 1/2 \, MV2$$

$$(1) \, (2) \, 2 = 4$$

This is the equation we are most concerned with...Speed equals power.

Back-up mass and gravity drop are contributing elements to power. However, it is speed that is the most reliable attribute. This is because one may not always be able to get their mass in motion. For instance, if one were locked or pinned to a wall. Speed also allows one to "beat him to the punch" - And, sometimes even if he is already in motion.

But, just to finish the physics; if we could somehow increase our mass by 3 and our speed by 4, it would look something like this.

$$M^x3$$

$$V^x4$$

$$= (3) \, (4)2$$

$$= (3) \, (16) = 48$$

The first bit of math is a standard equation used in physics to illustrate doubling the velocity quadruples the power. You're a martial artist. Good to know. But why the second equation? What is that an example of? Well, proper Tai-Chi application to be exact. And as always, the answer is Yin/Yang.

The above information is of use to any martial artist to more fully understand power enhancement. And it will allow for improvement in Tai-Chi fighting. But that is not real Tai-Chi, or more precisely not the highest-level Tai-Chi. Increasing speed, targeting acupoints, and having good push hands skills will allow one to, maybe, become viable in a real exchange. But what about Tai-Chi magic?

When one sees a demo by a real master performing incredible feats and barely moving, one is witnessing proper Tai-Chi executed employing the highest principals of the art. So the Yin/Yang is; one can develop their Tai-Chi like any other martial art, increasing speed and power, and fudging technique to make it work; but that is not real Tai-Chi.

Realistically, the master uses the same basic physics, because there is nothing else. But, he also includes a mind element; without which there is no high-level execution. Here is where the Yin/Yang marriage of mental and physical approaches the realm of the magical.

Again, what of the second equation? Is it possible? We've seen that one can quadruple power by doubling velocity, but can one triple their mass? No and yes. By employing proper Tai-Chi execution and principal one can affect the results of the math illustrated by the second equation. To be fair, it is visibly subtle and dynamic, but its results are devastating and effective. The highest level of attainment. The stuff of legend. Tai-Chi performing as advertised. This is real "super karate" power.

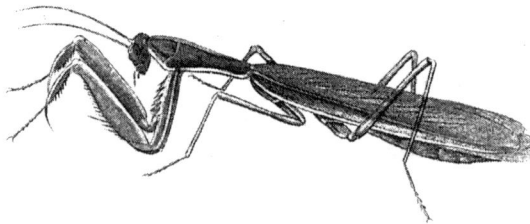

Well, it was a lot of fun describing those mathematics. Keep in mind that this is a real equation and important to know. But it is only really stated to begin a dialog. It would be truly useful if one could actually increase their mass. But is it possible? Actually, no. It is however possible to create a facsimile of increased mass that will function like the real thing.

While it is not possible to manifest increased weight, we can however redistribute the mass that we do have, to create a functional augmentation. The principal of hwa, or transformation, allows the practitioner to relocate the center of gravity to a lower position. This is achieved by affecting a Sung state and mentally allowing weight redistribution. Essentially, by removing tension and achieving a natural settling; no longer holding mass in a top-heavy position.

After all, you are just a bag of water. If one employs their muscles to support a majority proportion of their mass (mostly water) in the upper third of their structure, the organism is ripe for instability, and may be easily toppled. However, if the practitioner sufficiently relaxes, this allows gravity to pull the mass lower in the structure, resulting in the desired effect.

Yes, it is true that the mass has not been increased, but by enacting Sung and Hua, this allows for a realigning / transfer of a portion of the mass from the top toward the bottom. Effectively, the mass of the lower portion of the body increases, as the upper part of the structure no longer supports the same amount of mass it did before. The lower half has borrowed mass from the top half, creating a more stable structure.

If for some crazy reason, I was transporting 300 pounds of gravel in the front seat of my car, and became mired in mud; by transferring some of the gravel to the trunk, and thus over the rear wheels, I will more effectively achieve traction on the back wheels. This is because I have increased weight over the rear wheels, and that amplifies the downward pressure on that portion of the vehicle; thus increasing the total friction of the rear tires. Admittedly, this is a clumsy example, but it serves as an illustration that the total mass of the car has not increased, but by redistributing the load, the desired result was affected.

I have used the proportions of fifty-fifty distribution only as an illustration. But, for proper hwa transformation, it is best to regard the body more in thirds. The top third is: head to the navel (bai wai to lower ton tien). The middle third is: navel to knees. The bottom third is: knees to penetration into the earth. By effecting a Sung state and mentally allowing the mass to redistribute in a wave through the afore mentioned three zones, proper weight distribution is affected. This practice is commonly referred to as rooting. While I have described rooting to a stationary state for simplicity, it may also be employed while in motion.

Also, rooting is being attributed to a vertical plane, but during application (i.e. motion), it is employed on a majority horizontal plane. When rooting is applied in this matter it creates a wave that travels in a downward spiral of energy, elongating, (push or pull) and effectively driving the offender into the earth. To be more precise, one rides higher while moving and then transfers their weight lower in an effort to assist in maximizing power. In summary, this is all achieved by rooting at the correct time.

The mind element is critical here. By commanding one's bodily systems to allow the redistribution of fluids by employing the quality of mind intent alters physiology, maximizing technique. While it may have initially seemed needless to explore the physics at the beginning of this chapter, it was imperative that the reader understand that increasing mass contributes to power generation. And further, that hwa, as a facsimile of increased mass, can be used as if it were an actual mass increase.

The most common way a typical fighter increases power is by utilizing waist rotation and back-up mass. This is attained by using proper alignments and torque in an effort to contribute to the enacted body components; thus producing a type of energy gestalt. While this technique is common knowledge and is employed by martial artists of every stripe, the unique elements offered by Tai-Chi are presented here as an addendum to these more conservative principals of physics. Maximizing power is not always intuitive and commonplace; Tai-Chi demonstrates that the optimal results may be achieved with the non-intuitive.

Uweza - a Swahili word meaning: opportunity, ability, and ... power.

The Other Kind

The King Cobra is an elapid native to India and southeast Asia. It is the only member of the genus Ophiophagus.   The highly toxic venom consists of neurotoxins, cytotoxins, and alpha-neurotoxins that have cardiotoxic effects. Its diet consists mostly of lizards and rodents, which understandably develops encounters with the endemic mongoose.

There are twenty-nine species of mongoose and they do indeed attack and kill cobras. People have been fascinated with the mongoose/cobra match up ever since Rudyard Kipling wrote about it in Rikki-Tikki-Tavi in 1894. The mongoose is a carnivore of the suborder Feliformia, and has been venerated in many cultures including the Greeks, Egyptians and Okinawans. Fun fact, the beloved meerkat is a type of mongoose.

While mongoose feed primarily on worms, insects, small lizards, and rodents, they can and will kill and eat snakes; including the venomous King Cobra. They are quick, agile, and can dodge the snake's fast strikes; which makes for delightful spectator enjoyment.

But, when a mongoose does encounter the cobra's mortiferous fangs, they are able to survive its deadly venom due to a mutation in the nicotonic acetylcholine receptor that prevents the a-neurotoxin from binding, due to glycosylation; which is also a parameter in the optimization of drugs like monoclonal antibodies.

Cobra/mongoose fights used to be features of the undeveloped world; who also enjoy entertainments such as dog and cock fights. Things that enlightened societies find abhorrent. On the other hand, in the civilized world, we would never condone such cruel practices, and instead, pay humans to beat the shit out of each other.

Most pugilistic sports are highly regulated and combatants must perform within the confines of a predetermined set of rules, which make it understandable for observers; and thus qualifies it as a sport. For instance, in tennis you can't pick up the ball and throw it over the net or engage in other "anything to win" behavior; as this would be confusing, and lead to injuries that might eradicate all our favorite players.

Boxing is punching only, yet punching is prohibited in wrestling. Likewise, Judo and Muay Tai have their own regulations, which if violated result in disqualification. These certainly are methods of fighting and any one of them can be employed effectively in a street situation.

People have always wondered which style is best, and there have always been "anything goes" clandestine warehouse fights. During the early days of television, I remember watching some crossover events; and can attest to the fact that wrestlers have been beating boxers, by my recollection, at least since the fifties.

The Kung-Fu craze of the seventies and the proliferation of martial arts movies, featuring high kicking action stars; fostered the illusion that flamboyant, superfluous styles were viable; and created a generation of sport fighters that believed cinema graphic artifice translated into effective street technique.

Then the Gracies came along and changed everything. They promoted modified "no holds barred" events that pitted differing styles against each other. Any practitioner of any stripe could test one another in single elimination to determine which fighting system was best. In a formula that echoed with the scientific method, in every match up, the Gracie man won.

In a "that was then, this is then too" scenario that echoed the Kung-Fu mania; mixed martial arts schools and events were popping everywhere. At first blush, this seemed a rational response. After all, the grapplers were beating everybody. Here, however, is where this text must depart from the popular sentiment and outward appearances of the time. To build a case that things aren't always what they appear.

Back when MMA was still trying to invent itself, I recall taking my Pai-Lum instructor to a shoot fighting event. On our drive home, I asked for his opinion. After a few observations and carefully considered comments, he concluded with: "The reason the classic styles are the classic styles is because they work."

This response may seem counter-intuitive and even implausible, because after all, weren't mixed martial artists beating everybody? in a Yin/Yang, apples to oranges comparison, maybe. Only in this alternate universe in which most present day (at the time of this writing) martial artists live. Defenders of this myopic faith, declare that the proof is in the ring. They say, "anyone can try to disprove it", and they all lose. This may be true, as long as the contest tales place within the octagon, or if two people step outside to see who is the better man.

Recently, a friend was waxing monotonously about the supremacy of MMA. A conversation I have had to endure far too many times. He bemoaned that someone had offered a million dollars to anyone who could win a one-on-one against him, regardless of style. I told my friend, that I would take that bet.

Upon taking the challenge, the first thing I would do would be to work up a complete dossier and surveil the opponent for a month. Then, at an opportune time, snipe him from concealed cover. Why? Because this is my style. It's just the way I fight. For those who think that fighting only means stepping in to a parking lot are just as delusional as someone who thinks that the take-down is easily defeated.

Admittedly, one-on-one fighting is sometimes unavoidable. Perhaps someone may follow you into the men's room or catch you in a hallway with no avenue for escape. If I were jumped before I could produce my blade, I would rely upon my training, which may just surprise our MMA fighter. He would find that, I too, am not without my own set of tricks.

Confrontations that take place in night clubs and grocery stores rarely occur without some kind of buildup. You may have bumped into someone, or maybe they just want to fight over a chair or a can of beans. In these instances, a first strike may just be the antidote to the problem. If one can deliver any kind of power, at all, and are a mid-to-high level practitioner, a preemptive strike will result in a high likelihood of success. One important difference between a trained and untrained defender is their ability to capitalize on the entry. In essence, that is what all this multi-component technique training is about. Finally, anyone can deliver an initial punch, but to follow-up effectively requires master level or commando training.

From a defensive perspective, unorthodox maneuvers can be employed in many urban situations. Well established, yet oft overlooked methods, like: dive rolling over cars, utilizing unexpected angles, and improvised weapons can serve one well. For instance, if one is accosted in the parking lot or any relatively non-confined space, if one were to employ some of the more evasive tactics, the attacker would need to chase them to effectively engage them. Also, someone with the advantage of size and strength and ring experience may not expect such an unconventional type of strategy. In summation, the hubris of thinking that there is only one manner of fighting can dramatically tilt these situations in favor of a self-defense-oriented fighter; even if one is grossly out matched.

Pumped up wrestlers who mistakenly believe they can easily disarm a knife wielding opponent, are delusional to the point of severe damage or even death. And, have probably never encountered a teenage Filipino balisong aficionado on the street. Or, better yet, anyone with a knife. A perfect illustration of this point is my friend who was stabbed in just this kind of situation. He almost died, because he believed that he was just brawling; while the other man thought he was fighting for his life.

Fighting is very serious business. I must admit that I'm not really built for it, and could really get hurt. But, ring fighting strategies and submission type training, by others, provides an advantage for someone like me. Someone who feels that every fight is a knife fight.

There are many mental elements that separate sport fighting from self-defense. Some subtle, some so simple they confound the arrogant and overly confident. One who does not take into account my specific fighting style. A style which involves locating and enacting the tactics described in the earlier paragraphs. Or, one who foolishly thinks that the encounter is over when they walk away from a crumpled body.

My bag of tricks may just even the odds. Improvised weapons, mace, and throwing for distraction; are not generally encountered while working a submission; and are generally second or third tier priority factors with such individuals. Unlike sport, self-defense is a distinct style in its own right; containing many elements not encountered in octagon training. The "sport" strategy works best when two people are both just trying to get after each other. But, are not always viable when only one is trying to "fight".

As one small example, even during a clean, fast take down, there is a strong likelihood that I would be able to jam my spike, keys, or tactical pen into the neck or behind the ear. This is because I've been taken down before and I can maintain composure during the fall, allowing more than enough time to effect penetration. This tactic has a high probability of success due its surprise nature in relation to a take down expert's expectations and the fact that they are "fighting" and I am not.

MMA fighting is to be respected and has its place. To be certain, MMA fighters are well trained, admirable, and incredibly tough individuals. And, this is not a defense of classic arts nor a formula to beat the "new breed" of fighters. The successful application of fight science to street survival involves reversing the attacker's expectations and efficiently flipping any given scenario. The belief that there are only grapplers, punchers, and kickers gives the advantage to someone with commando style training. To repeat myself, MMA is to be feared and respected. But the milk-toast also has his trove of resources; like the blade you will never see until it's too late. In short, it's just a better way to fight.

The Other Kind

Batesian Mimicry

When I was a kid, it was easy to tell who the tough guys were. In the factory town where I grew up grizzled working men with calloused hands were readily identifiable as tenacious and resilient. And point in fact, this was usually true. Their hardened stalwart comportment was in stark contrast to the flocculent office worker; who only challenged their physiology no more than driving cars or pushing pencils. This is, of course, an over exaggeration just to reinforce a point; as many office personnel mowed their lawns; played golf, tennis, or some other sport; and so forth. But still, someone carrying lengths of pipe, swinging a hammer, twisting wrenches, or unloading trucks all day was obviously physically capable; and no soft, office denizen would dare consider any type of confrontation with a working man.

In the post-WWII years, as prosperity and leisure time grew domestically around the United States, national trends eventually cascaded into the Midwest. The desire for a fuller life and the free time to pursue it began to awaken in people; resulting in the previously unthinkable idea that you could change who you are. Media portrayed heroes as more physically capable, and average people began to develop a sense that had not existed before on a mass scale: body awareness. Fitness gurus, like Jack La lane, moved into prominence. This was accompanied by the embryonic science of body building and was championed by early pioneers such as, Dave Draper and Franco Colombo. Steve Reeves, as Hercules, prompted many individuals to emulate his stunning physical appearance.

In my youth, there were no gyms or health clubs - at least not in my end of town. And while I had a barbell set at home, I was one of the few people, during the sixties, in my area who was in any kind of shape. Anyone interested in physical culture typically had to go it alone; and martial arts schools were nonexistent. Ed Parker opened the first commercially owned Karate school in 1956, but that was in California. For those determined to improve physicality anywhere else around the nation, there was typically only the Y.M.C.A. or Golden Gloves.

Now with the new proliferation of gyms and martial arts academies, anyone could morph into a tough guy; or at least appear to be one. However, a roofer or stevedore were still recognizable as an actual tough guy, as opposed to a fraudulent impostor; because there will always be a discernible difference between a gym body and someone who throws car engines around all day. Regardless, still many believe that, "if it quacks like a duck..."

Batesian (fun fact: pronounced like Artesian) mimicry occurs in nature when a harmless species evolves to take on aspects of a harmful species. Just like the gym posers previously mentioned, the imitators develop the same warning signals of the actual dangerous entity, as a defense against predators. The phenomena are named for Henry Bates, a naturalist from England. While Bates received fame through his work with butterflies, for our purposes, an example such as the Scarlet King snake is more appropriate, as it developed a similar appearance to the venomous Coral snake.

As in nature, a human parasitizing the "honest warning signal" of the "model" gains an undeserved advantage at avoiding predation. After all, he has not expended the evolutionary effort to actually develop defenses; it just seems that way. In the natural world, the abundance of the "model" species is directly related to the success of the "mimic", due to frequency dependent selection. Predators avoid potentially lethal organisms only when the real threat is teeming in the locale. When the environment is filled with fakes, the tactic becomes worthless.

While it has been a lot of personal fun elucidating this phenomenon in nature; let us see if there is not some erudition that can be provided, giving us a practical application to augment our skills and tactics (i.e. we don't want to be posers). Because a primary theme of this book is to propagate the concept of Yin/Yang, rationality demands that... there of course must be an opposite or reverse.

If the hallmark of Batesian mimicry is the faux display of potential lethality, then the opposite would of course have to be the subtle art of concealment and stealth. In the natural sciences, this is known as crypsis. Cryptic behavior is not the sole domain of the animal world. In human terms, this leads to a very crucial survival skill; and that is the opaque world of the gray man.

In the natural world, prey animals employ a variety of measures to avoid demise. Camouflage is the first mechanism. Obscured, inconspicuous, invisible; by taking on the appearance of something other than themselves. At first blush, this tactic may seem like mimicry, but there is a distinct difference. The previously stated technique is to resemble a dangerous adversary. But in this tactic, concealment is deception. And in the world of the gray man, this is known as blending. This is because one becomes unnoticeable by virtue of the fact that there is nothing distinguishable between the practitioner and the environment. One literally blends into one's environment.

This can mean wearing a shirt the same color as the wallpaper, although in human terms, this is a really poor example. A better way to think about it is, one taking on similar characteristics as everyone in the immediate environment. In other words, becoming totally indistinguishable from the crowd.

For clandestine operatives, this may require learning a specific dialect, or even a new language. But for anyone else to survive among fellow creatures hostile to any outside presence, requires morphing a presentation and persona to avoid conflict. For example, in a school setting, anyone who dares to dress differently, or is naturally awkward or "weird" will become the recipient of taunts, insults, thumps, and wedgies. Later in life, these same individuals learn that in order to get along, you've got to go along.

Even among adults, bar patrons will become incensed because of non-regional mannerisms or the wrong sports logo. Although, highly developed social skills may help to diffuse confrontational situations. There are those who can walk into a biker bar in a business suit and wind up having everyone buy them drinks. But, the improper costuming only creates another hazard to be overcome. Better to blend in in all aspects. Appearance, behavior, and tactical language skills, all contribute to this tactic. While the current matinee idol may make millions for his performance, your's may save your hide.

Assuming an undercover persona is really an acting job. Surviving in a hostile, foreign environment is essentially no different. Most people have a manufactured personality anyway, so having prepared social techniques is just a form of preemptive defense. Most people naturally employ the Batesian and cryptic tactics, and this personality quirk is just the way in which they navigate their daily world. They just don't let anyone else know this fact. And, most times this performance becomes so innate that they fall prey to the belief that it is their "real" personality.

To deny that to one degree or another we all interact this way is to perpetuate the illusion of the spontaneous human being. Many of our reactions and responses are "pre-recorded" and selected from an inventory of responses proven to work throughout the day. Even though I am highly aware of this social mannerism, I am not immune. I consider myself to be fairly eccentric and, like everyone else, have learned to feign the mannerisms of "normal" people; often repeating phrases observed to produce proven results by others.

Even in the world of the gray man, sometimes reversing the process proves advantageous. Other techniques worthy of consideration, borrowed from the animal kingdom would be. For example, "Motion dazzle" is known to degrade a predator's ability to estimate speed and direction of a selected target. Often used effectively by fighters, motion dazzle can distort speed perception when properly implemented.

There are other animal adaptations worth mentioning, also. Visual illusions, such as the wagon wheel effect, which inverts perceived motion and confounds the opponent's perception. The barber pole illusion, where motion seems to be moving in the wrong direction. Each of these methods is used effectively by prey species to avoid capture.

Fun fact: Most karate tournament competitors use red gloves. But, it is tactically advantageous to wear standard white hand gear; as it blends in with the traditional white uniform making it difficult to see coming.

Emulation and proficiency of animal styles means more than just moving and fighting like a particular animal. If we are truly and completely to benefit from our observation of our fellow creatures, the utilization of mimicry, blending, deception, stealth, camouflage, etc. prove to be countervailing survival tactics worth incorporating. After all, it has successfully served our animal "models" and the primary reason we take on their specialized characteristics. The truly aware practitioner learns more than just how to fight like a tiger, he should consider the purpose of his mindset... and his stripes.

War Horse

I have never owned a horse. I've been around horses. And I do ride, though scantly more than a memorable number of times. I like horses and consider myself a friend to all animals. My animal friends have included; birds, both wild and domestic, squirrels, cats, iguanas, hamsters, gerbils, frogs, turtles, and rabbits. My brother and I kept a pet mantis once for an entire summer.

Dogs, on the other hand, I know well. I have had dogs all my life. And feel incomplete without one. The best dog I ever had was a coyote/wolf mix. Our shared adventures could be a book in itself. Having a big dog as a partner, evolves into one amorphous gestalt. Because the animal possesses qualities I do not, the alliance makes me more capable than I am. The dog too is benefited by the human's ability to navigate the perils of a complex society. Properly amalgamated, this union is the kind of symbiosis that a Sheppard has with his canine partner; a synergistic, confluence, adapted for modern times.

This is the way I imagine it to be with horses. While, I must admit that I surmise this, based upon my limited experience with them. I am not as familiar with horses as I am with dogs. Although, I do know something about many of my other animal friends. And, I must begrudgingly admit that I know more than I want to about people. I relay all this because I would like to use this diatribe to illustrate equivalencies from different perspectives - in order to make a point. No horse sense required.

There are areas of expertise, and there is skill combined with experience (kung-fu roughly translated). Within musical settings, a conservatory trained musician could run circles around a street performer in a comparative skills judgment breakdown. Competing for the approval of a critical evaluator has its place, but only provides one type of external pressure, similar to one needing to qualify at the rifle range.

I watch singing competitions on television and am happy for anyone who can step from their bedroom onto a national stage. I, like many others, possess only a moderate skill-set, but a deep experience. As a touring musician who has played many thousands of nights in every kind of environment; my background includes serious productions on radio and television, along with studio work - which requires the ability to excel in a variety of genres. Any seasoned professional, proven to produce in a zero-tolerance environment, constitutes immersion evaluation at the highest professional level. I note this only to emphasize the impeccable expertise required in this context. There is a difference between a musician like this, and someone who wins a singing competition.

Most martial arts studios teach self-defense responses to static grabs and single punches. This is fine, as it does ingrain a pre-programed responses to some common situations. Advanced students who train in these approaches know that these techniques are examples, like math problems presented to illustrate a method based on specific principals. Most of these studios supplement these rehearsed examples with tournament style sparing, to incorporate the random, unexpected aspect; while emphasizing the ability to express oneself extemporaneously. This relatively adhoc training methodology provides a baseline that the individual student is expected to fill-in with street sense. Most proponents of this specific approach are fairly realistic regarding its limitations.

On the flip side of the coin, are schools that offer a composite of grappling and kickboxing with a 100% conviction that whatever works in the ring is suitable for any and all encounters. These schools almost never train club or knife defenses, or multiple attacker scenarios.

When questioned regarding this mélange, the response is almost always, "let's put on the gloves" or "you and I should step outside". Confidence is high because my buddy could not possibly be furtively waiting with a ball bat. While adjourning to the parking lot, to see who's the better man may be customary; it may not be wise. Because it is possible that I am surreptitiously producing an equalizer from my belt.

When an individual has won most of his ring fights and indeed did knock out some drunk two years ago, it would be easy to develop the attitude that all fighters who fly under his banner are invincible. When discussing mental toughness and the machismo attitude of raw marines, an insightful Major once told me: "Any time you convince someone that he is worth ten of the other guys, you've got a problem". This, said by an indisputable war horse with deep combat credentials.

It is true that this current amalgam of fighting styles is proven effective in one-on-one, ready-set-go situations. Many have indeed mopped up the bar with all comers. Real world scenarios against sneaky, desperate individuals can, however, prove problematic. One could even have deep expertise in specific areas. Ring champion, bouncer, and still be shanked by an inferior pugilist. This is only a caution to address the hubris projected by many trained in M.M.A.

I am not a tough guy - far from it. I've boxed a little. I've been in so many fights, I can't remember them all. Lost most, but I've always survived. I've competed in so many karate tournaments that they all jumble together. I've been around a lot of violence; witnessed the success of erratic, unexpected surprises; and seen a lot of things go wrong. I have been around a long time and am entitled to an opinion.

Commercial schools and classic martial arts styles are not worthless. Without question, there is merit in the time proven, accurately disseminated principals artfully preserved in founding styles. And, selectively mixing them together into a hybrid brawling style is not the panacea their enthusiasts are overwhelmingly convinced it is. To be sure, these statements, of course, will convince no one. This, owing to man's predilection to reach conclusions - based on a limited data set. Which is why most guys are convinced that they are a sex god and a bad ass.

You've bought my book, now at least hear my advice: Fighting is a highly unpredictable enterprise. Even the toughest champion can be hit over the head or stabbed from behind. A humiliated, injured wimp, may lie in wait another day.

Weapons, confederates, uneven terrain, all provide elements of unpredictability. Every component of the equation contributes to, or diminishes your chance of survival. Besting someone in any type of competition is an important factor, but far from the full equation. Mike Tyson is one of the toughest guys ever. But he still has bodyguards. Who do you think you are?

A plow horse can offer impressive, displays of grit, power, and determination. A quarter horse, in competition, seems the epitome of equine development, speed, and impressive musculature. When watching this organized competition, one can be expected to be seduced by the intoxication of victory and the accolades of the crowd. Although, In another era, and during lethal hostilities, either animal could perform unpredictably.

Participating in a limited number of engagements, or even just being in or near a war zone technically qualifies one as a combat veteran. However, only regular, sustained, heavy combat makes a warhorse.

Thanatophobia

There is a gorilla in the dojo, and it has nothing to do with ape movement. This martial twist on the "elephant in the room" refers to any obvious disturbing subject that would prove detrimental or uncomfortable if discussed.

There is much swagger and hubris among martial arts technicians who feel that because of the superior science and systematic method employed by their art and their training that they are ready for anything. One falls prey to the rationale that a well-rehearsed defense against a single-leg take down or a left-right combination, works flawlessly in practice; and therefore, they can easily and seamlessly transfer their acquired ability into surviving a life-or-death setting. I have personally seen this fallacious scenario many times. That having a practiced, logical, and lethal response immediately allows one to use their rehearsed, retaliation under high stress conditions; and that any-and-all situations will allow this pre-programmed answer to work effectively, automatically, and as practiced.

A practitioner may have the greatest technique in the world, the utmost skill, and the bravado of a bull, but none of it will do them any good if paralyzed with fear. This is such a problem in the real world that many drills and simulations have been created in various enterprises to simulate the very real probability that one may fall prey to a psychologically induced, chemical dump immobilizing muscles and glaciating brain function.

A commonly known example of this is the harassment and stress of military recruit training. This type of harsh indoctrination is designed to identify individuals who may crack under pressure, compromising mission success or jeopardizing their other team members. A pale imitation of this strategy is replicated in some martial arts schools. Where instructors bark commands in the manor of a drill sergeant. This inferior approach is easily identifiable as theatrics; as it lacks the violent consequences of military training.

I identified this conundrum early on in my career and, in contrast, have always strove to maintain a jovial easy-going atmosphere in my dojos. Any potential student is quickly made aware that I am not a drill instructor nor a fitness trainer. They are informed that they may, and should, do pushups on their own time; and should quantify their toughness through personal challenges outside of my studio. My belief is that class time is much too valuable to waste on histrionics. If one trains with me, they train to be a technician - I show them how it works and how to properly execute it. Adjunct attributes, vital though they may be, must be drawn from other sources.

That said, fear is still the primary eviscerating constituent of nonperformance. Without question, controlling this debilitating condition is paramount to survival. This is far more vital to one's potential collapse and ruin than ability, strategy, tactics, or good technique.

Psychasthenia, as a chronic condition, is generally not germane to this conversation. That aside, in a crisis situation fear and immobilizing terror are some of the most influential demons that can interfere with one's ability to execute. In contrast, one who may appear timid; in a pinch, brawls like a tiger. Or, even one who appears to suffer from neurasthenia may surprise any and all involved by fighting like a barbarian. Fun fact: neurasthenia is nervous exhaustion in absence of objective causes.

Fear of death and injury is a natural survival mechanism inherent in the human psyche. Without it, human propagation may not be able to keep up with population decimation. What sensible people describe as stupid decisions, such as: "I can make that jump", "I should be able to stick my hand in there", and a thousand other options; offer examples that a healthy amount of caution prevents us from engaging in.

This, however, is not what needs to be addressed here. This conversation is to focus attention on a neglected aspect of martial arts training, and that is: controlling, challenging, or eliminating fear. Some people are naturally fearless, and others barbarous and brutal by nature. For the rest of us, fear can be a debilitating mechanism, when faced with a situation that demands action. Everyone has their sublimations, and others may spend a lifetime under the delusion that fear will never be an element; only to regrettably become paralyzed by an unexpected terror. In such a case, one's survival may demand this obstacle be addressed.

As one solution, some have developed aggression as a part of their personal arsenal. Within this vein, and very similar to a Ki-Ya shout, one may use psychological intimidation as their go-to solution. This solution can be characterized by engaging both mentally and emotionally, before any physical contact is made. This interaction is executed not as a diversion, but as an actual bludgeoning, psychological hit; one that impacts and engages the opponent prior to, and maybe in place of, physical contact.

There have been countless times that I have personally been able to prevent engaging, by simply becoming artificially hostile and/or belligerent. Bullies seem to regard one differently, when they come to the realization that they misjudged their target. This is especially true when they were only half serious about engaging. The caveat is, of course, that one must be prepared to fight; as this technique does not always work or may elicit the opposite reaction to the one intended.

As an example from nature, I have seen cats back down much larger, aggressive dogs only by standing their ground. In an object lesson, proven by an opposite example, my ex in-laws had a white German Shepard that was a cat killer. Often, I witnessed confident felines attempt to employ this tactic; only to learn, post mortem, that an animal with equal commitment and twenty times the body mass will most assuredly prevail.

The ultimate lesson one should take away from all this is: that psych, bravado, and intimidation is definitively reversible by physical momentum, inertia, and commitment to engage. Because of this, and keeping with the principal of Yin and Yang, a defender who attempts to employ this type of preemptive technique, and fails, must be able to immediately revert to their fighting skills.

This strategy should not be conflated with employing psychology as an attempt to avoid engagement. In almost all scenarios, the best first option is to attempt to diffuse or deflect; in an effort to avoid a physical encounter. Unfortunately, many times a confrontation quickly erupts to the hostile state, requiring immediate physical push-back. In contrast, situations that begin due to disagreement or minor offense, can frequently be interrupted in the developmental stage. A savvy defender will know when each option is viable.

At this juncture it might prove helpful to provide a look into the chemistry and influence that fear effects on the human body. But, all the salient details of this have been referenced in other chapters. While having an academic appreciation of the perilous effects of endogenous chemistry, it enhances one's understanding and achieves our overall objectives for one to acquire the ability to manage this caustic emotion. An emotion that has the high potential of negating any advantages that may have been gained by acquired fighting technique.

Here again, it's useful to appreciate both a macro and a micro understanding of this third opponent in an encounter. If one were starting to wade into a fray, and they had someone gripping onto one of their arms, we would all agree that this would probably place them at a distinct disadvantage. Likewise, the grip of fear can prove to be far more debilitating. Even having more of an impact than wearing a coat of thick chains. Like following a career path, or pursuing a love interest, sometimes one of the greatest liabilities is your own mind. But, what can abate this pernicious enemy?

In the large sense, conviction and a strong overriding philosophy can help assuage disabling panic from slowing movement and incapacitating decision making. For example, zealots in religious wars and fully committed warriors like berserkers, will walk through a field of fire with complete conviction of invincibility. In our own culture, war fighters with strong religious faith, often credit the almighty with providing an extra reliance; enabling adherents to push through during hazardous duty.

Even a nihilistic philosophy; believing that nothing matters, or "we're all going to die anyway", can set the mental stage for the calm discharge of focused purpose. A seemingly inimical sentiment like resignation, can still eliminate fear through abdication. Many faced with chronic hostility, who feel they may not be going home anyway, resolve to go ahead and do the job as best they can.

In contrast, panic begets chaos: like wild horses unresponsive to their driver's commands. A Multitude of frenzied emotions produces an uncontrollable synergy, often inducing paralytic behavior or even cowardice. Much like a threatening opponent, one's fear may need to be preemptively struck down before they become overpowered. Panic, rapidly welling up within an individual, necessitates even more powerful mental control. If one's hope is to utilize their innate power, or mind control techniques, outcomes are often mixed. Regardless, this paralyzing fear must be squelched and brought under control.

A lifetime of training and societal limitations holds in check most people's natural killer instincts. For some, to overcome this conditioning, often it is as easy as granting permission to indulge in these extreme behaviors. Yet for most people, some type of mental conditioning is required, such as: dehumanizing of enemy combatants; which is used to varying degrees in modern armies. Typically, most successful methods employ both subtle and extreme mind conditioning, with the goal of encouraging fearlessness and bolstering perceived superhuman invincibility. Usually, a highly suggestive person is responsive to methods of this type. Whereas, a rational person may simply be able to affirm that their courage is stronger than their fear.

When looking for spiritual development or meditation techniques, one may understandably look to the East; but the opposite tutelage may require guidance from the side of the planet closer to our home. The prescription needed here is not serene contemplation, but frenzy and psychotic rage. The most extreme example of this in the history of our conspicuously violent race, may just be the Northmen, the champions of berserker gang.

The Northern Warrior tradition, began as hunting magic and similar to the way that kung-fu styles focused on the development of physical movement. Vikings embodied this psychotic temperament; creating a strike force with a methodology to induce trance, fury, and violent, out of control incursions. Focusing on a high degree of frenzy, they would hack through any resistance, demonstrate that they are tasters of blood, and destroy with ferocity. Terror proceeded them because neither fire nor iron tolled upon them. They met little resistance due to displays like shield biting, fire eating, and rumored immunity to swords.

Constantine VII, in the book of De Cerimoniis describes Berserker rage as, "...shivering, and shaking, as if chilled, with chattering teeth, face swelled and turned red, literally hot headed". Once enraged, these men killed indiscriminately; enemies and comrades alike. Even their own compatriots maintained a safe distance, when exposed to this self-induced hysteria and howling rage.

This timeless and effective method of fear management is not exclusive to Byzantine Viking mercenaries. It is common to the chaos of war, regardless of era. For those of us unaccustomed to the eccentricity of berserker rage, this phenomenon has been alluded to in modern cinematic offerings. Some directors, under the tutelage of combat veteran advisors, hint at episodes when our own war fighters, immersed in the extreme sensory overload of exploding ordinance, death and confusion, throw the switch, becoming deliberately psychotic; screaming, firing wildly, charging enemy positions in a fearless killing frenzy.

Berserkers were outlawed in 1015 by Jarl Erikr Hakonarson of Norway. By the end of the twelfth century, they had all but disappeared. If we can learn meditation from the Hindis, and logic from the Greeks, then the Yin/Yang implication of survival mode may be to swell to full Yang; to out frenzy an attacker who is unresponsive to either redirection or science.

Personally, I have relied upon this very method; walking away on more than one occasion. Other times I have been able to defend with a calculated scientific efficiency. Sometimes a sledge hammer is needed; other times a soft bristle brush is the best tool for the job. Defending against a knife in an alley in San Antonio, is just as serious as the battle of Hafrsfjord, or an ambush in the jungles of Cambodia. Dead is dead; and all violent encounters court the same consequences.

One emphasis of this discourse has been to suggest a default action with a quirky type of mind science; when the reasonable course of action is typically to dominate a violent encounter in a calculated manor. This chapter, while focused on addressing and overcoming fear, is also presenting an alternate attribute. While admittedly this is an abnormality. One which has a long history of success in real world applications.

Think back at a time when you have been witness to a maniacal rage; and how frightening it was. Not only the physiological factor, but also the sensory receptors were overwhelmed with the perception that this person simply could not be hurt; that any onslaught would simply bounce off - as if they were shielded by some kind of physic armor. You, and everyone else, stands clear.

In all reality, some individuals are simply not suited for the above formulated type of response. Admittedly, this is an aberration and not generally included in the catalog of aegis in organized, structured martial arts. But, if training best practices, belie a "one size fits all approach" to technique and strategy; certainly, psychological factors are quadrupled in importance. Only when overwhelmed by panic or circumstances is the above ethos offered as an option in a desperate crisis. Instead, the cool, level headed response, allowing access to apex mental faculties, and allowing a clear decision-making process is always the preferred course of action.

Fear is not always the sole reason for hesitation. A secondary consideration may be an unwillingness to cause harm to fellow creatures. In this case, there exists a deep-seated conviction; one that governs even during challenging times of duress. For these "normal" individuals, standard training is probably applicable; with a reliance on technique, conditioning, and composure.

Yogic breathing can offer amelioration, if time allows. But since most attacks take place immediately or build over a score of seconds; there usually isn't time to stretch, recite affirmations, and do some deep breathing. This again, is why preparedness; as an ingrained, elemental attribute; and toughness as a quality, are the hammer that is always cocked.

Combat preparedness must include mindset as an intrinsic condition. Either, always cool and composed; or possessed of an innate, mental toughness; and in some cases, possessed of the nuclear launch sequence. The ability to toggle back and forth between these states is the Yin/Yang of survival. The body can be trained to respond, but to truly be prepared, time must be invested in an honest assessment of one's ability to function in a crisis situation. Even the greatest technician, if untested, may prove to be a hazard to himself and those he needs to defend.

LUM

I knew a girl who grew up in Boston. And once when speaking about regional accents, I asked her: "Do you mean to tell me that in the Boston school system the teacher will write on the blackboard, *mark parked the cart*, yet say: *Mack packed the cat*". Her answer was: "that's exactly what I'm telling you".

In America, professional speakers employ a dialect referred to as Broadcast English. Because news commentators and television personalities appear more authoritative when speaking with a clear, flat annunciation, devoid of any regional dialect. It is always surprising to read a bio and learn that a given personage spent their formative years in a New York borough, or hailed from the deep south. The word "fire" is pronounced differently in new England and Tennessee. Cockney and proper English, Castilian, and Street Spanish, Classic and Kitchen Greek, are all examples of the Yin/Yang of a given lexicon.

I often reference the Boston story when people correct my pronunciation of Chinese words. Many Americans involved with Chinese history, philosophy, or martial art, feel that Pinyin is the only correct way to write and pronounce Chinese words. Being of an earlier generation, I am most comfortable communicating within a system with which I am more familiar. Throughout this book I use a well-established historical method of translation.

Thomas Wade was a British ambassador and Cambridge professor who published the first translation of Mandarin to English in 1867. The system was modified by Herbert Giles in1892 and remained the standard during the time I was discovering the Chinese arts. Several romanizations were developed over the years. In 1928, 1986, and Tongyong Pinyin in 2000. These systems are best suited for authorities of more recent citation. Not only is the delineation of information more accurate for me as a teacher, but I purposefully continue to use the Wade/Giles system because it establishes me as someone who received their training in the 60's and 70's. I am under a firm believe this facilitates a better understanding of my perspective.

Up to this point concepts have been presented with language familiar to our time and place. As abstractions with no real translation ensue; use of more traditional terms will be required. To set the template for communication, familiar terms used will be Chi not Qi, Yang not Yong, and Lum for dragon instead of Loong. The focus of this essay is Si shou dai. Due to the importance of the subject at hand, American English terminology will be used here for visceral impact, and image retention.

SUNG * CHI * FA-JIN

SI SHOU DAI

Super karate power is real. It seems like magic, but it's just physics. Energy transfer seems like a mystical process, but it is really just the science of getting out of your own way. It centers around the first principal taught early in the study of the art, and that regards the Sung state. This is not to dismiss thought transference, or psychic energy projection, but they are a separate study and phenomenon.

Energy transfer in this discussion is the art of "dead-hand" striking, and this type of energy transfer can only be properly executed from a properly effected Sung state. Much of the "dead-hand" type movement in Tai-Chi is similar to long fist whipping type motion. This motion connects with "dead-hand" penetration, but is initiated from rotation of the core. In short hand application, "dead-hand" striking is often initiated by a Fa-Jin energy release, and concluded with "dead-hand" energy. Although also initiated from a Sung state, Fa-Jin is not "dead-hand" striking, but the impetus; just as the projectile that delivers the energy is not the rifle cartridge that propels it.

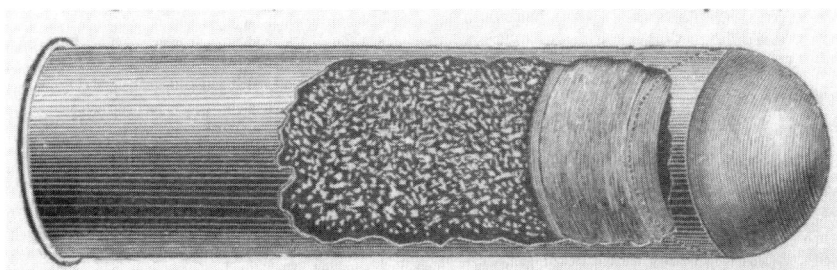

In Tai-Chi generalist theory, it is often said that what is proper health technique is also good for fighting. This seemingly murky and occult statement, is actually spot on. The same Sung state that allows for proper fluid and energy circulation is the same body energy state that allows for deadly Tai-Chi striking, which is the unimpeded transference of kinetic energy.

Sung, the state of profound relaxation is important to the health nurturing aspects of Tai-Chi. This body energy state allows a natural fluid or nerve impulse to circulate unfettered by the constriction of muscles on vascular structures and nerve pathways. Constriction is restriction for both biological thoroughfares and kinetic energy.

One of the precepts of Tai-Chi, states that muscular tension retards the flow of Chi. In health nurturing protocols this is critical for allowing biological processes to function without engaging baroreceptors and other regulating systems. Unrestricted, unencumbered free flow of kinetic energy is essential for fighting application. The relaxed body state allows for the maximum transfer of kinetic energy from the delivery mass into the receiving mass.

If a subject were prone on the ground and three, 50-pound barbell plates were dropped onto their torso, the most probable results would be broken ribs, a cracked sternum, and internal organ damage. This would even be the case if that amount of weight was released from only an elevation of a few inches.

Now shift you image to the same 150 pounds, but as a human who is able to effectively use their entire mass. Theoretically, that would be great. But this is only a theoretical example, so for now we will disregard angles, vectors, torque, rotation, and any other miscellaneous factors.

Now, if a 150 pound ball of dense material (for example, depleted uranium) were substituted for the iron plates; the penetration would no doubt exact fatal injuries. This is because the same energy is concentrated into a finer point of contact. Very convincing results of this important concept can be graphically demonstrated when performed on ballistic gel.

In contrast to the penetration of ballistic energy, cars rolling on adepts tensed midsections introduce the weight incrementally. Despite the impressiveness of this demonstration the energy and weight is specifically transferred without the jolt of energy transfer and on a large as possible surface area.

A vertical mass moving horizontally is simply unable to transfer its potential for a host of obvious reasons. One's effective power may be augmented by forward momentum accentuated with weight drop, but to achieve the results in the above example require the synergistic usage of the adjunct power resources provided by torque and rotation. A golfer who is 90 pounds and 90 years old, is capable of impressive tee shots, because he is basically striking the ball with "dead-hand" technique.

In golf, they call this technique "head speed". But their technique also references the importance of a smooth continuous delivery and follow through, resulting is a more effective transferring of kinetic energy. This can be almost directly translated into a similar transfer of energy in a martial arts sense.

Limply gripping the shaft allows for dissipation of power radiating in all directions. Conversely, (Yin/Yang) tensed muscles restricts the generation of energy created by weight transfer and waist rotation and the transfer of that energy into the ball. All golfers know trying to kill the ball is anathema to any hope for a powerful drive. A panicked or angry fighter, completely tensed, is equally ineffective.

"Dead-hand" striking can only be learned with the help of a living, intelligent deputy who is able to provide feedback as you coordinate the various components of this technique. Subordinate factors may increase power by degrees, but the primary effectiveness is achieved by the ability to withdraw intent, keep the muscles relaxed, and allow the strike to naturally penetrate without any restriction from the deliverer's muscular system. In a crazy "less is more" paradigm, the Yin/Yang aspect of this method of striking delivers an almost magical intensity of power no amount of muscle-based slugging can ever hope achieve.

One reason Tat-Chi is practiced slowly and relaxed, is because on those infrequent occasions when the adept does practice properly executed "dead-hand" strikes, the toll taken on the practitioner's body is devastating. The full speed loose velocity without any fixed stopping point, can tear relaxed muscles. These strikes whip at speeds and intensities unattainable with tensed, boxing style delivery. With no objective to absorb and diffuse the energy, this extreme velocity is hazardous to the practitioner without any potential target to protect one's musculature. Just executing one or two properly dispatched strikes into thin air, can create significant damage, thus requiring long periods of recovery and limiting training time.

Since "dead-hand" blocking and striking are the only kind of blocking and striking used in Tai-Chi, for the most part, practicing all movement in a relaxed, Sung state ingrains this type of execution. This is specifically done to reenforce this methodology as the only type of energy transfer being utilized. Disparity in size and strength would seem insurmountable, but this is most definitely a technique that may be used to equalize, and potentially gain advantage. This is a superior method which buries its kinetic power deep into tissues which may be inaccessible by standard surfaced focused strikes. As always, the answer is in opposites. The secret is: to project energy, one must purposely eliminate all impediments. To maximize force, one must purposely minimize intent.

As far as effective enhancements to fighting technique, these three paragraphs may be the most significant in the entire book. Of all the possibilities of options that may provide a telling difference, executing blocks and strikes with Sung energy is one of the single most effective things that can be done. When you project and transfer so much energy that you can't even practice it with full intensity, there is only one way to review and ingrain that type of movement; slow and relaxed. Critics of Tai -Chi are like children who pretend to have shootouts, but have had no exposure to actual gunshot victims.

In American English, dragon can either be pronounced as Lum or Loong. Some dialects may even sound like Leung. Some assign accent marks to various positions. The dragon possesses a mystical power, a penetrating destructive type of vibrating, penetrating energy that destroys bones and explodes organs. The reason this type of penetrating energy seems so elusive, is the essence of Yin and Yang. To fully emanate this type of devastating power, one must do the one thing that seems impossible, strike with no effort.

Lum is dragon.

Super Karate Power
(An Introduction to One of the Mysteries of the Arts)

One of the unspoken secrets of why someone might start training in the martial arts is the idea of obtaining super karate power. Super karate power can be summarized as the ability to generate bone breaking, organ exploding power. But is this a real thing?

But before we answer this question is might prove helpful to quickly address some of other reasons why someone might be attracted to the martial arts. Probably the most common reason outside of the obvious, exercise or increased confidence, that must be stated is that technique alone will allow an uncertain defender to triumph over a bigger, stronger opponent. The second reason is more closely related to the subject of this writing; that through proper training and divulging of some occult secrets, a practitioner is able to acquire skills, ability, and knowledge that they can use throughout their life.

Among adepts and novices alike, the ability to manifest these paradigms are well known. These techniques include: penetration, energy transfer, and detached shock waves in more than one direction. Expression of these phenomena have been extensively explored at many institutions including, Cal/Tech and Jet Propulsion Laboratories. Undoubtedly, applications such as these do work; although a thorough understanding of the underlying sciences is not a requisite for materialization, as a they work whether one knows what they are doing or not.

That being said, a brief review of energy, as it specifically relates to our efforts, is probably in order. One technical definition of these principles does include, the potential energy stored by an object's position in a force field; such as gravitational, magnetic, or electric. But for our purposes, and to be more specific, we should focus our attention to either the elastic energy stored by stretching solid objects, or the kinetic energy of an object in motion.

Within this context, elastic energy is created through muscular activity; and kinetic energy is delivered by a martial art strike. Applying this as an application, adroit combatants are able to direct power via the fluids in the target body. Although the energy is isotropic, equal magnitude in all directions, it may be effectively directed. And, due to the law of enthalpy, the changes in kinetic energy (work, heat) may be canceling; but the enthalpy remains unchanged. This is because energy is a quantitative property.

The work performed by the energy transfer is governed by the law of conservation of energy. Energy can be converted in form, but can neither be created nor destroyed. Because of this principle, the martial artist is able to direct the power of penetrating strikes through viscous humors, skillfully directing it to the structures of interest (frequently vulnerable areas of the opponent).

In Tai-Chi and other martial arts, this type of directed force is commonly achieved through what is known as "dead hand" application. In punch / push power delivery of "dead hand", a radiating energy is transferred through protective layers of bone and muscle to disrupt function at a selected location. But to be more specific, it is both the combination of Fa-Jin energy release in conjunction with directed "dead hand" application that allows this seemingly paradoxical ability to successfully manifest.

This book makes several attempts to provide further exemplars of this phenomenon; which with this modest (and maybe even a more complex) explanation may seem to be a physically impossible peculiarity; but, in truth, is a nonpareil actuality.

As stated at the start of this writing, this is undoubtedly the number one question neophytes have regarding the "secrets" of the martial arts. Yet, in public, this mis-understood and mis-represented ability is only vaguely implied to be a factual reality trough through historical accounts and modern-day cinema. Therefore, I deemed it worthy of an expanded explanation.

Ho'o.loli

Suppose there were a real-world situation where an automobile manufacturer wanted to replace an automobile's existing drive train transmissions with a belt drive. This is a practical example with functional results and consequences. The salient point to this scenario is that the engineers, while addressing this issue, would need to communicate in a specialized language, using coterie terms (a.k.a. trade jargon), and words that only apply to a specific technical cabal, in an effort to complete their goal.

Likewise, there exists a nomenclature specific to Tai-Chi and its implementation. This is because there are no English words or directly translatable concepts for many of the ideas present in the world of Tai-Chi. These are words not only of Chinese lexicon, but also a specialized language that only applies in the arcane world of the internal martial arts.

For instance, there has been great emphasis throughout this book to explicate the idea of transformation, or change, as a foundational concept; quite often through the expression of Yin and Yang. The philosophical and practical implications of this endeavor serves as an aid to understanding the benefits in health and other affairs, both cosmic and mundane.

Many examples have been given of opposites and reverses, along with comparisons and metaphors to annotate the universality of this most basic law of reality. As an example, the chapter on five element theory, underscored the importance of the fact that the transformation takes place on the edges: That all important place on the Tai-Chi diagram where Yin diminishes into nothingness. That indescribably small region that dwells only within a nonexistent border. That area just before the first micron of Yang emerges and the change happens.

Also throughout this book, It is frequently emphasized that Tai-Chi is a Yin/Yang art. And, that internalizing this precept is tantamount to effectively employing Tai-Chi as a martial art. This, however, is but one recondite aspect of Tai-Chi. In fact, Tai-Chi shares many concepts and principals with a host of other Chinese fighting styles. This, along with a vast number of principals of physics from fighting systems of more prosaic origin.

金

Let us start to explore some of the Tai-Chi lexicon with the word Jin. Jin is one of the five hundred most common Chinese characters. Some examples of words containing Jin are: Jin-Bu (progress); Jin-Gong (attack); Jin-Kou (import); Jin-Lai (enter); Jin-Xing (proceed); Qian-Jin (advance). Jin is also a Chinese language spoken by sixty million northern Chinese and Mongolians. Depending on the dialect, it could have scores of meanings from saliva/sweat to gold; or it may be a family or place name. A good English comparison to Jin is the word bore/boar. This word can mean a mood, an animal, the interior of a tube, or the process of making a hole.

Today, Jing is more accurately transcribed as essence; although in the day of the Wade/Giles translation it was used interchangeably with Jin. Because pinyin has become the parlance of these times, regional dialects notwithstanding, and writing for a pedantic audience accustomed to pinyin, this essay will use the contemporary term - Jin. And, for our purposes, we are only concerned with Jin, defined as: strength/enthusiasm/spirit/expression and energy.

In this vein, Fa-Jin, in martial arts parlance, is usually understood as a specific technique for the discharge of explosive power, and is a traditional method used throughout Chinese martial arts to launch movements energetically. Jin, in this context, is not a type of energy. Instead, it is the expression of a method used to release energy. In contrast, and from a martial art energy viewpoint, there are thirty or forty types of Jin.

换

The Chinese word Hua essentially means transformation or change. Hua-Jin is translated to transformation of energy; or more simply put, change of energy. Every movement within Tai-Chi contains a degree of Hua-Jin. In some Tai-Chi applications, Hua is a neutralizing energy, where neutralizing is the change. Hua, in this context, refers to what happens to the energy (or force) of the opponent - the moving, reducing, and/or eliminating of it.

As mentioned elsewhere throughout this book, Sung is a primary body state of Tai-Chi. Without Sung, there is no Hua. Sung is the conduit for the efficient reducing or moving of the opponents force. Effective Hua is made possible because of the Sung body state - one of profound relaxation. In contrast, a tense or rigid person can be unbalanced or toppled with much greater ease.

To illustrate this point and as a mind experiment, imagine that an angry person enters a room and violently kicks a wooden stool. This energy is directly transmitted to the stool without any dissipation, therefore the stool flies across the room. Now let's take the same scenario, with a slight twist. The difference? Someone strongly kicks a beanbag chair. In this scenario, the power is dissipated in all directions due to the beanbag's lack of rigidity.

The Sung body energy state is more akin to the beanbag than the stool. In the Sung scenario: the opponent pushes, the center absorbs and dissipates, the inside is empty, the power connects with nothingness, Nei-Gong.

One key point about Hua is that Hua is passive. This Jin has a quality that creates connection because it is passive. As power transforms, this is Hua. Energy dissipates using Sung, but it is Hua that is the ingredient which makes it possible.

A human being is not a beanbag chair. Because of this, a human being can do things the beanbag cannot. For instance, the defender has tendons and ligaments, bones and muscles; and can use these bodily elements to manipulate a kinetic energy wave; even to the point of redirecting it back to its source. Yet still, this is entirely a passive action. Yin creates Yang, passive creates active.

In a real world sense, force is simply a vector; one of magnitude and direction. Hua is both a quality and an essence. Hua is the transformation of the force. Hua is the change of the magnitude and/or the direction.

One final thought, Hua uses the tendons and ligaments of the body as its primary vector for manifestation.

朋

As a technique, these qualities do not manifest without proper Peng. For example, nailing a board together requires more than a well-executed hammer stroke. The nail must be held by the opposite hand and properly positioned, left working in concert with right. One must tilt the nail at the right angle and time the stroke. Strong hammering is but one small aspect to masterful carpentry.

The Sung body state is open and relaxed; Jin is energy; jie-jin is receiving and connecting energy. Once energy (power) is received, it is connected to and managed with the goal of Peng-Jin. But it cannot become Peng-Jin without other elements (Jin) being present. Critical to enacting proper Hua are structural elements such as alignment and structure.

Often, Peng manifestation is described as a springy kind of returning energy. Very similar to an inflated inner tube: if the inner tube had the ability to send back the power to its tactical advantage. The song of Peng says, to apply Peng, one must do two things: hang the head, and sink the Chi.

On the other hand, nei-jin is the quality of your power from inside. Where Peng is the skill in which that power is manifested or expressed. Peng, expressed in this way, is an uprooting expansive type of energy that interrupts the attacker's connection to the earth, breaking his root.

There also exists many other physical techniques. For instance, a circular redirection of the opponent's power, where their energy is ultimately sent back to them. In yet another example of Yin and Yang, once connection is made, and energy is received, the kinetic energy is circled down and sent back, arching up towards its source. But, this is a technical skill, when Peng is utilized as a quality. It is still Peng, but in the subtlety of expression, it has become something else.

Now, it is possible to train Peng return energy as a physical technique and refine it to the point where it performs as advertised, but still not manifest Peng - just being a mimic of Peng.

Finally, Peng is an internal quality. But this is only in a large sense. So, Peng is both a quality and a technique. But Peng, like the essences we discussed earlier (Sung, Hua, and Jin) is also an internal quality.

Peng, coordinated with internal Hua expression, are the methods of execution of Tai-Chi. Like magnitude and direction, quality and technique are a vector of Peng expression. As another example: both Orlando and New York are north of Miami. New York is a further distance. North is a direction. Both cities share this quality, one has no more "northness" than the other; this is just a matter of degree. So, both the technique and the quality of Peng are Peng. One is external, and the other is internal.

结构

Structure must be present in order for Peng to manifest. Hang the head and sink the Chi. Ding-Jin, which is a mental state; is the empty force at bai wei. In this posture, the mind creates an uplifting sensation, a pulling up from the fontanel. This is hanging the head. Concentration is directed to Ton-Tien (sink the Chi); align Zong-Ding and Peng will happen.

For those unfamiliar with internal arts, or Chinese terminology, the previous description may all sound rather obtuse. Where others, those trained in this type of understanding, will recognize this as the formula for gunpowder.

朋 刘 几 安

The four fundamental forces used within Tai-Chi are Peng, Liu, Ji. and an. Unfortunately, it would require a volume at least the length of this book to even begin to transmit a basic understanding of each of these. And even with all that, it would still also require hands on instruction from a competent master to develop the skill to use them. But, in a simple, yet incomplete, attempt to broker an introductory understanding of Tai-Chi power for the uninitiated, I have tried to outline the methodologies and essences used for the comprehension of one, small concept - Hua.

I had originally planned for this section to be simple, after all, it is a beginner's guide. But once commenced, even a basic explanation becomes a runaway train. And, like the example of re-engineering the transmission, it is impossible to relate Chi-Kung without Chi and Jin.

Any discussion of Kung-Fu requires a cohort of accompanying concepts and terminology. I love metaphor, I believe it provides different angles for understanding. But at some point, actual language peculiar to a specific enterprise must be used. A genuine effort was made to keep this discussion simple, and to maintain a logical thread. I am hoping to have communicated opaque interpretations in a somewhat understandable way.

Ho'o.loli

Ho'o.loli is the Hawaiian word for change or transformation. And while the concepts outlined above are not a component of any indigenous Hawaiian martial art, yet the Hawaiian culture understands the essence of the meaning; although not originally applied in the same context. With the influence of Chinese immigrants to the islands, many Kung-Fu enigmas from the mainland seeped into native arts like Lua. None the less, I have chosen to title this discourse as an homage to a martial art of Hawaiian origin with which I am most familiar.

Kenpo is a hard-hitting fighting style with its modern foundations in the islands. This art features, among its many revolutionary concepts, explosive devastating power. The speed / power methods of execution in Kenpo are not Fa-Jin; rather a type of energy release that belongs within this classification. It is different than Fa-Jin, but it is as equally effective as any Chinese internal art. And, although a modern creation, if de-evolved back far enough, surely must share a common origin. The point is this: it doesn't matter what you call it, or its source, or how convinced you are of the exclusivity of tribal secrets; a rose by any other name...

Lastly, this book is not so much an instruction manual as it is a commentary with a high potential for instruction. All-in-all, this book is highly tilted toward explanation over how to. Specifically, the above discussion is fundamentally designed to answer some simple, basic questions, as well as hopefully point one in the right direction for further inquiry and more in-depth analysis and study. And, I take comfort in the fact that even if I did not explain every concept in the greatest of detail, my discussions will provide a springboard to spur any motivated reader further; using this book as a foundational guide as to where and what to look for.

Iron Men

The largest percentage of people attracted to Tai-Chi do so for its purported health benefits. A fraction believe internal styles may offer some advantage in fighting. But, many practitioners, and most instructors, are just retread karate people; slowing down, recovering from injuries sustained in other martial arts, or commercial instructors wishing to expand their student base.

I have trained several prospective and pro-fighters who hope there might be some advantage to going around the other way and incorporating soft style techniques into their arsenal. Almost universal among American fighters, who recognize the viability of applications in Tai-Chi, is the idea that soft style techniques can be enhanced by the addition of muscular conditioning and strength training.

If a young person was being advised on which profession provides the best living, they may vacillate between doctor and lawyer, but one doesn't choose both. You don't need both. Either one will provide an adequate lifestyle, societal position, and self-respect. Trying to be both is counterproductive and unnecessary.

Individual martial art styles evolved to be complete in themselves, the same way an animal species evolves unique mechanisms for defense and offense. What makes the cobra / mongoose fights so intriguing is the difference in fighting capabilities and specialties. Some "medical vandal" doesn't need to come along and surgically graft together a cobra and mongoose; just because he has the ability to do so.

A foundational concept of Tai-Chi is the idea of having a strong, substantial lower body and a soft, pliant upper one. The health aspects require loose, unrestricted, flowing movements; enhanced by breathing techniques and internal organ massage. Whereas, the fighting techniques depend upon loose, whip-like movements, and the ability to meld and blend with the opponents movements. All of which are restricted by extreme muscular tension.

If someone were to inform me that they were a genius and had developed a Nautilus machine for tigers, I might be surprised to learn that tigers require functional enhancement. The developer could go on to explain that he had researched engineering and medical data on tigers, and was now the world's foremost authority on tiger anatomy; and could make tigers better and stronger than they were before. After in-depth exposition on cam ratios and graphs on feline response to resistance training, he would build a case for the proposition that these animals need to be supercharged; because they are just somehow inadequate in the natural state.

This could be done, if the goal was to produce a genus of felines with half the population non-functional, like teams in the NFL, where a large percentage of the roster is out on injured reserve. Exceeding design parameters invites residual ramifications and consequences. Once past the zenith of peak conditioning, over-training enacts the law of diminishing returns.

The type of movement and exercise a tiger encounters in its natural environment is exactly the right type to keep it at the top of the food chain. The challenges that evolved as a part of tiger natural selection, adapted this organism to meet the demands; and produced this apex predator.

Violating Yin/Yang theory invites impaired performance, at least, and disaster, at worst. If a particular type of development is required for some special application, Sumo wrestler for example, then by all means pack on the pounds. This decision needs to be weighed against the physical limitations, compromised daily activities, health ramifications, and social difficulties induced by this type of training. An athlete may have an enviable career as an offensive lineman, where massive weight and increased strength produces a lifetime of respect and monetary gain. If he somehow found himself aside a jungle explorer with the need to jump a ravine to escape a tribe of incensed locals, the specificity of his conditioning, in this instance, would prove a detriment; where a normally proportioned man, in good shape, could make the jump.

Recently, there was a year of televised riots, replayed endlessly on all the news channels. Aside from the obvious negative aspects, there was repeatedly illustrated examples of this very point. In the confusion of assault from every direction, the top-heavy, overdeveloped participants fell down an inordinate number of times; because their inadequate base simply could not accommodate the power and forward momentum generated by enhanced upper-body strength. Aided by the enthusiasm of frenzy, and they tripped over themselves like weevils.

In contrast, the naturally proportioned rioters fared much better. Slipping in and out of confrontations; blending and falling (to the exposed position of being trampled) to the pavement far less frequently; able to scale fences and mount edifices their bulky counterparts were incapable of breaching. To be sure, when directly opposing a larger irresistible mass, they would be moved, but survivability and mission success invariably went to the normal man.

I'm sure that back at home, in the gym, these androids are a force of nature. When squared off on a flat surface, facing one opponent, they probably are formidable. The blatant, undeniable example of performance in the riots confirms an observation well known to astute observers. Know what you're training for. If intimidation and ring fighting are the primary goals, by all means bulk up. But, surviving any type of erratic fracas requires agility and dexterous movement.

Without doubt, health objectives are reduced when demand exceeds nature's designs.

An already unhealthful situation is exacerbated by the addition of questionable nutritional supplements, of unknowable origin, and indiscriminate use of anabolic, androgenic steroids; the deleterious effects of which are well documented. If the need or imagined results justify the unbalancing of the delicate human biology, just to trip over yourself in an unpredictable melee; perhaps having a state-of-the-art, over-conditioned tiger would help.

Zoomorphism

Each martial art has its own origin story. Some are fantastical, some mundane, others, entertaining. For some, inspiration occurred by watching a snake and bird fight, or by observing the adaptive coiling movements of a monkey. There is no animal endemic to China, real or imaginary that doesn't have a king-fu style imitative of its peculiar movements.

Much effective technique and energy release methodologies have been gleaned by watching animals, to acquire an advantageous approach to fighting. While much precedence has been gained by this method, in one of life's great irony's, turns out that Human being style, (boxing and wrestling) prove comparatively effective, compared to movement designed by nature for, and often, best suited to another animal.

This does not mean that they are not effective methods, or that they have not enhanced proficiency of martial technique; just that certain mechanics and movement are best suited for creatures who inherently possess certain physical characteristics.

This is not meant to be dismissive of animal movement, but to emphasize that animal technique never has been an exact replication of the animal model, rather an adaptation of mechanics and procedure learned by observing fellow creatures. A combination of human and animal; a chimera of technique, and yet another illustration of Yin and Yang.

People who have been sheltered or raised in isolation and have never observed either pugilism nor animals in the wild, when forced to fight, usually tense up completely and swing wildly. While others slap punch protectively in an impotent parody of boxing. And still others swing for all their worth - inherently utilizing hip and waist rotation with all their weight behind it, being so committed that they throw themselves off balance. These are naturally occurring movements endemic to the human organism. Most individuals' minds instinctively prod them to put everything they have behind it; to step in and use shoulder power, the same way a bird naturally pecks.

Europe and most of the west developed systems of everything under the influence of the scientific method and Newtonian physics. Wrestling and fist-fighting styles were also refined in an attempt to maximize power and leverage through experimentation and analysis of the human anatomy. Occasionally, there were animalistic references made, such as: implying that someone butts like a ram, or kicks like a mule; yet to my knowledge no serious, organized attempt was made to pattern a fighting style explicitly after the movements of any particular animal, anywhere in the West.

On the other side of the world, where things were looked at a little differently: philosophy, religion, and medicine took on a sweeping, inclusive comprehension. There was a cultural inclination to inculcate everything with examples from the natural world.

When attempting to define the nature of the almighty, people of the West, Near, and Middle East logically concluded that, "of course, god must be like a mighty king" (Yang). In the Far East, where all things were perceived as intertwined in a vast universal matrix (Yin), this opposing cultural mindset sprang forth with a completely different evolution of everything arising from the same conundrum. Their observations of cosmic bodies and animal behaviors, set a precedence for ascertainment of patterns found in the natural world.

Tai-Chi is an understandable outgrowth of this type of thinking; a mentality that perceives all things as interconnected. Any analyst who begins with the Eastern thought perspective as their starting premise, inevitably will deduce that two antagonists at some point join as one, in order to coincide with the order of the universe as understood by Tao.

In contrast, a society (Western) with conflict as a fundamental doctrine; one that perceives all things as billiard balls banging into each other, and one in which the harder and/or stronger billiard ball always wins; can reach only one conclusion on victory and dominance... bigger, faster, more powerful.

In a cultural Yin and Yang, most of the other side of the planet surmised a completely different approach. What if we went around the other way and became one momentarily joined with the power, as well as the anger and intent; riding that until both momentum and intent are exhausted, causing the inevitable change to occur. Then in a second Yin/Yang reversal, switched from soft to hard, from harmoniously combined, to powerful and penetrating.

It was this culture and ideology that produced Tai-Chi; an approach that simply could not have happened in the west. Despite all the intelligence of individual minds; collectively, the societies of the Western world were simply incapable of producing this type of paradigm.

Among some of the Western elites, there was an elevated pugilism. But for the common man, fighting was considered a natural function, like breathing; which required no enhancement nor amelioration. The concept of enhancing this natural process was not collectively entertained.

Can movement or breathing be therapeutic? Not even considered in the West. These same people, I'm sure, could not help but be impressed by the power and agility of animals in conflict, but in a kind of universal delusion; combatants, for the most part, relied on a disorganized wild slugging and grappling form of pugilism.

At this point, it is worth considering the Eastern concept of man's place I the universe, because it informs our understanding of the Eastern fighting arts. People in Europe and the East both observed animals fighting, but owing to a complete disparity in the cultural mindset, the Chinese saw tutelage and the impetus of an idea; in the same way they looked at the heavens and saw systematic harmony.

If you were to watch a video presentation about nature, most of the program would be visages of predation. Whether insect societies, or the African savanna, something is attacking and tearing apart a vulnerable victim. Even in our sanitized society, where I pay someone to slaughter my chickens, there is predation everywhere. Corporations and individuals prey on vulnerable marks for property or financial gain. In schools and on street corners, bullies assail the defenseless as surly as any predator stalks and besets its quarry.

Different continents may harbor distinct, indigenous species, but the people seem to be the same everywhere. It should be noted, that this does not contradict the difference between cultural mindsets, but individual human tendencies when left undominated by the society at large.

China is a vast country, and Yin/Yang dictates that even though Tai-Chi style fighting was a product of Taoist thought, there would be pugilists who understandably concluded that speed, power, and slick tricks were obviously a better approach. But still, the cultural influences were so powerful, that even these practical thinkers considered the environment for insight and inspiration. Directly influenced by all of the above factors, a large number of these results evolved from animals. Here is just a few of the styles emanating from these observations.

TIGER

The body of a tiger is very powerful. But it is best understood as a weapons platform positioned by stalking and leaping skills. The most instructive element conferred is that Tiger is always cocked and ready to spring from any position. As the animal creeps, using stealth to acquire range, he remains crouched. Even as he lifts a foreleg, there is no point at which he needs to reposition. Even as he takes a step, each increment and weight transfer is poised for action at any time. Never out of position. So too, in Tai-Chi, as we smoothly adjust to the changing situation, we continually adjust alignment; poised to deliver power at the opportune junction. Flowing in a constant state of readjustment; morphing to the changing situation; waiting to transfer coiled energy when a balance vulnerability is sensed.

BIRD

The bird is a delicate animal. Self-preservation demands that the bird not directly engage when confronted with a formidable aggressor. Flair feathers to appear larger, blind with a wing, master of evasion, pecking vulnerable areas. Bird can't trade power shots. But rather, concentrates their slight power into the point of the beak. Bird does not possess a lot of mass, but has animal commitment; is capable of killing small mammals, and dive bombing two legged intrusive ones. These defensive methodologies, as used by a weaker and lighter animal, can provide excellent examples and prove instructive. The natural evasive techniques of Bird, is exemplified by the Crane and Eagle styles, along with influencing Tai-Chi in fundamental ways.

APE

Ape and monkey are two different animals, as everyone who has ever been to the zoo knows. An ape is confrontational and direct. A monkey would rather run up a tree and throw a coconut. Since simians are much like us, anatomically and genetically (chimpanzees share 99% of our D.N.A); for the sake of expediency, let's lump us all together. One major difference does exist though. It would be tempting to assume that all primates possess a natural wrestling style. This, however, is not the case. Wrestling is a uniquely human science, relying on leverage and technique.

Ape relies on massive strength and grip with a natural inclination to rip and tear. Like most mammals gifted with powerful jaws and massive canines, biting extremities, and finishing by tearing out the throat; while also being pinned with inescapable, iron-like hands and feet. Stepping through and dropping an overhead hammer-fist, is an adaptation humans have garnered from this formidable creature. One kung-fu ape style features prominently a maneuver called monkey bite, a hallmark tearing technique.

Monkey, on the other hand, possess a different physiology and psychology. Monkey uses flowing, deceptive entries with the ability to adhere to the opponent. Monkey is purposefully non-graceful and chaotic, yet also very relaxed. Monkey flows around, gets in, confuses and dominates with jumping, dropping, rolling and other evasive and entry maneuvers. Monkey is a deceptively effective style. Monkey's seemingly erratic movement produces results that are undeniable. Monkey is specifically confounding to most humans. I personally love monkey style.

SERPENT

Serpent covers a number of reptiles. But, it is best for this summary to limit this category to one representative: Which of course is Snake.

Coiling, wrapping, constricting movements are emblematic of Snake. Snake also places much emphasis on specialized striking. These strikes emanate from the wrist, usually utilizing only one or two fingers. Contrary to the precepts found in many of the other fighting styles, there is often no power borrowed from rotation or weight drop. The formidable eagle claw, although technically Bird, can often be indistinguishable from Snake. Constricting maneuvers, which would seem like Snake, are more the province of Chin-Na. There also exist various blending, morphing and admixtures within schools and from individual sects of Snake. As a corollary, special ops forces have distinct yet similar missions, but are distinguished by branch of service. A rose is a rose, but a snake can be a deadly viper.

MANTIS

The king of insect predators and the most adaptable to human movement, would be the praying mantis. From the order Mantodea, there are over 2,400 species in over 460 genera.

Mantis are admired for their fearlessness and ambush predation tactics. They have the ability to conquer and intimidate opponents many times their size, without fear. This relatively small and weak insect can often escape from or even best a more capable predator. Their raptorial forelegs serve as the inspiration for Mantis style kung-fu. Where other stylists adopt their other offensive characteristics. Observing the defensive and predation habits of insects might seem like a stretch, but there are, however, many surprises and upsets within the insect world. An astute observer can learn many things from witnessing such exaggerated mismatches and unexpected outcomes.

Fun fact: Females are known to engage in cannibalism of their mates. A Mantis behavior I have experienced personally during divorce proceedings. Finally, my brother and I kept one as a pet for an entire summer. Fascinating creatures.

Before television and the internet, people hoping to improve output and systems observed nature or stared into the fire for inspiration. Other than existing primitive contrivances, animals offered an example of successfully evolved mechanics and group organization. Other than ideas gleaned from dreamwork, there simply was nowhere else to look.

Many of the tactics lauded in Sun Tzsu's military classic, *"the art of war"* was developed by lessons culled from kung-fu animal styles. By thoroughly understanding Yin/Yang inference and not attempting an exact reproduction of animal mentality, but allowing to serve as inspiration and suggestion. Tactical lessons sparked concepts that pared animal patterns of behavior mixed with the capabilities and advantages of the human mind.

Our culture too considers environment, and is not devoid of learning from, or utilizing animal examples, as Charlemagne did. Witnessing enough animal behavior offers a type of immersion therapy for those astute enough to learn. Newton was proverbially jolted into revelation by an occurrence from the natural world. And, Orville and Wilbur finally deduced the concept of lift, not by increasing degrees of bird power, but by replicating the shape of the wing.

There are five major animal styles in the pantheon of Chinese martial arts. Owing however, to China's vast land mass and population, every creature imaginable is represented in a fighting style. For instance, dog boxing is a type of ground fighting; cats, both large and small; Insects of every type, there are even styles based on the footwork of a rat. Animal influence is not exclusive, there are also systems based on purely human morphology and movements. There are stand up styles similar to Western boxing and Chin-Na is a joint locking curriculum peculiar to the human anatomy.

Before the appearance of mixed styles, scientific training methods, and anabolic enhancements, Eastern martial arts offered the only advantage in tactics and physics. Vital area striking is still a thankfully misunderstood adjunct study, and while generally dismissed, animal systems still offer an unexpected advantage on survival.

Competition fighting disallows many of the techniques and weaponry that produce telling, injurious results. The octagon styles are formidable despite rules that disallow even obvious prohibited targets, such as: throat, groin, and eyes; along with the requirement of padded gloves, which purposely prevent access to most vital areas. Still, just as judo remains plenty rough, even after the removal of dangerous techniques, so are these other pugilistic styles.

Classic arts have fallen into disfavor in recent years, as their sport counterparts gain in popularity. Despite the lack of respect given by the new generation of practitioners, and young fans, there is still much to be learned from the ancient wisdom. Kung-fu secrets still exist, and even though modern fighters think they know everything, there are still power secrets and the cunning, unexpected tactics that can only exist in classical fighting styles.

Modern ardents of Eastern fighting arts may have to devote more intense training in order to vie with chemically enhanced, near pro fighters. But then again, martial art has never been about competition. Most styles were developed as their name implies - martial arts. These systems were spawned and developed for survival, not competitor domination or prizes. But after all is said and done, this new breed of martial artist is predominately dependent on a Western, Newtonian thought model, not an interdependent matrix arising from the natural world.

You don't know what you don't know. If history is to serve as any example, then it would be incautious to dismiss the unexpected or the ability of an opponent to fight like an animal.

Strategy and Tactics

No concept of human conflict is more nebulous than strategy and tactics. Often thought of as interchangeable, the difference though linguistically subtle, can be dramatic for survivability. In brief, strategy can be thought of as the general plan, and tactics as the methods and actions used to execute that plan.

A boxer's strategy may be to let his opponent wear himself out, then go in for the finish. His tactics would be the rope-a-dope, slipping and rolling (to dissipate incoming power), conserving energy, then at an opportune time, exploiting whatever weakness were picked-up from the opponent during the execution of the plan.

Guerrilla groups, often outnumbered and out supplied, use the tactic of hit and run with the overall strategy being one of attrition. Sniping and propaganda campaigns are tactics. To cripple, exhaust and eviscerate the enemy's will to fight, is the strategy.

To meet women, one strategy is to pretend to be something you're not. The tactics are charm, confidence, grooming, wardrobe, and lies. The secret to making this tactic successful is sincerity: once you learn how to fake that, you've got it made.

I don't think I ever won a fight where I squared off. Maybe one or two, but that would be it. In my particular case, experience has taught me If I am to survive, I must rely on stealth, subterfuge, and surprise. Mostly that means to strike first and unexpectedly.

As a martial artist, I absorbed and now possess thousands of fine points, hundreds of techniques, and some impressive skills and abilities attained throughout my career. Also, I can provide great physical demonstrations and can lecture for hours. But, of all the prowess I may be able to employ (or in rare instances, mimic or even fake), probably the single greatest ability I have acquired from the martial arts is that it has made me better at my preferred strategy and tactics.

Fun fact: The vast majority of violent attacks are initiated by people known to the victim.

Regardless, even a robbery or misunderstanding in a club usually has a buildup of some kind. This is where my strategy is best suited. While it may be the credo of most styles that karate is for defense only; I, on the other hand, have developed a catalog of pre-emptive techniques. Life has taught me that if I am to survive, I must move into action first. That usually means hitting them while they are talking, otherwise engaged, or purposely distracted, and then relying upon the skills I've gleaned from my martial arts training.

Some may consider this not self-defense, but I believe it is. I only employ this tactic when my substantial experience tells me that a physical dispute is imminent. As the saying goes, "Better to be trialed by 12 than carried by 6". I understand that this may be a controversial statement, but I firmly believe that you can move into action first and morally still be the defending man.

A good place to start mentally accepting this strategy is to think about anytime you've had your head handed to you. Consider how the conflict might have ended differently if you had the confidence, composure, and power to strike first. But, if you allow fear or intimidation to impair or otherwise stall your abilities, encounters such as these may end badly. As American Kenpo Grand Master Ed Parker said, "He who hesitates, meditates in horizontal position".

One key point about this strategy is: if you feel that you have to cock, telegraph, or set to deliver your strike(s) effectively you have missed in your training.

Further, one of the most difficult skills to acquire in fighting is to create an opening to capitalize on. In contrast, if you strike first and at the time of your choosing, the opening will already be there.

Another consideration is that most outcomes are already decided in the critical pre-engagement seconds. Therefore, one must move into action first if they hope to survive. This is where misdirection, acting, and throwing for distraction are fundamental self-defense moves.

While it is all well and good to have well practiced fighting strategies and self-defense techniques; making the mistake that assuming the fight doesn't start until the opponent grabs or punches, robs one of the critical first strike advantage and preemptive opportunities.

I teach authentic animal movement and traditional martial art. This is to build confidence, skill, and many strategies. But as a more street savvy lesson, I also provide realistic, defense scenarios where some students play a drunk, a robber, or ruffian. I find that this form of training is imperative, because this is where one can learn to "stack the deck" and ensure that an encounter such as this is resolved in their favor.

In summary, my preferred self-defense strategy is to be prepared and give myself every advantage. That means cheating, improvised weapons, or having practiced scenarios. Scenarios where acting and psychology are used to distract, misdirect, and/or buy crucial seconds to execute a preemptive strike. These are the tactics used to employ this strategy. To end with another famous quote: "the best defense is a good offense".

Fighting Styles

Of all experiences within a human life, fighting has the most diverse opinions of definitions. I can't think of any other single event or expression in the human experience that has less agreement on what it even is. Even abstract concepts like love or God have a more universal understanding than this well-known common occurrence.

In my humble opinion, all styles have something to offer. Yet, success depends more on the man behind the style than any structural advantage inherent in the system itself. I admit that some ideas are better than others. For instance, not cocking, but rather throwing from where it originates is a prime example of a good idea. Other good ideas include: utilizing physics to maximize power and leverage, strong basics, and especially good tactics. Regardless of style, almost all recognized systems employ these essential concepts and physical practices to one degree or another.

Most normal people have very little experience with fighting. Aside from schoolyard conflicts and some confrontations and tussles, here and there, most people at least in this country, get their opinions on fighting from movies or from watching combat sports on TV. This produces an unrealistic idea of what a real exchange is like. It fosters exaggerated ideas of how much punishment a human body can take as well as effectiveness of dubious techniques.

One positive attribute of movie fight scenes is that determination can often be the telling difference. And, often on the screen protagonists will muster deep inner fortitude and persevere. This is good propaganda, because the fight always goes to the toughest man. Although this may not be true reality, in many cases; I personally have seen guys, in real encounters, just keep coming with their nose smashed all over their face.

This book is written with the neophyte, unfamiliar with martial arts, in mind. The following is a panoply of some of the more well-known fighting styles. This list is purposely far from complete and is only written as a general summary of some of my personal observations of their strengths and weaknesses. I am sure that another seasoned martial artist may have produced different conclusions and/or observations. But please keep in mind, that this section is provided for the less experienced or more myopically focused practitioner.

BOXING

Boxing movement is probably the most effective type of movement for stand-up self-defense. Angles, slipping, and basic principles like footwork and waist rotation are essential in hand range.

HOWEVER...boxing relies on one attribute - power punching. Limiting one's repertoire to punching, only excludes proven fight ending tricks, such as: eye gouging and groin kicks. Also, eliminating soft targets restricts one's options. This, along with a lack of experience with ranges other than just arm range and multiple attackers can be a deadly inadequacy in a real encounter. Even if one doesn't believe in Dim-Mak, vital area strikes, ear slaps, shin kicks, and throat punching could prove helpful when outnumbered or out classed.

The reason boxers wrap their hands is because they are surprisingly easy to break. The small metacarpals are no match for the frontal bone of the cranium. While it's all well and good to develop punching power on the heavy bag, but fracture your wrist or hand bones and now you can't use that hand.

In short, boxing movement is a foundational and proven fighting skill. But recognize its limits. I know there are mechanics who can fix anything with a pair of channel locks and a roll of duct tape, but don't throw specialized tools out of your tool box. That clutch head nut driver may be just what you need someday.

AMERICAN SPORT KARATE

I have included this "style" because there is a hidden jewel within. We, martial artists, all love to trash talk tournament fighting as an unrealistic game of tag. But hidden in plain sight is an essential tool overlooked in the minutia of complex martial arts systems.

A parable among many experienced fighters is: "Whoever gets in the first lick usually wins". This truth has been born out across cultures and generations. Regardless of knowledge or skill, getting dazed creates an opening for a slick fighter to capitalize on. If that initial, first contact takes the starch out of you, your opponent has full resources to finish you off.

Sport karate is all about developing and demonstrating that one skill. He gets in with that first strike and "point". Often times there is a longer exchange series until the judges observe a clean unopposed score; one that would create the opportunity to set up a finish.

Whatever style one practices, it is presumed that there are a number of potential lethal follow-ups; ones that would prove too dangerous for weekend hobby competition. Since there are many styles with trips, throws, and neck breaks; it's enough just to show that one can get in first with a telling shot. It is assumed one will follow up with bone breaking, organ disrupting techniques.

BRAZILIAN JUJITSU

In my day, I only knew of one Ju-Jitsu from Brazil: that was Gracie Ju-Jitsu. In the sixties, circulating around karate dojos were 8mm films later known as the Gracie tapes. These were videos of the Gracie family and their students taking on all comers with one inevitable outcome: in every contest, the Gracie man wins. At that time, the Gracie style was a complete system with knife and club defenses, multiple attacker scenarios, and self-defense techniques that looked a lot like Japanese Ju-Jitsu.

Then they "brought it to America". With the success of the U.F.C. there emerged an explosion of Brazilian grappling styles focused on tournament competition and seeking the "tap-out". The same thing happened with Kung-Fu in the seventies. Kung-Fu became diluted and phony and produced a plethora of charlatans. This has not happened as much with B.J.J. They have kept tighter control and have managed to maintain a high standard. Having said that, most schools that I know of teach only for one-on-one, tap-out competition. Gone are knife and gun disarms and their original Judo style club defenses. They have transformed into being one-on-one specialists. And yes, it is effective one-on-one. But, three guys with ball bats in the alley?

JAPANESE JUJITSU

If you can find a traditional Japanese Jujitsu dojo, it's probably right next door to the John L. Sullivan school of boxing. Original Jujitsu was a war art. Incapacitation, maiming, and killing were the only techniques. Arm bars were delivered with ballistic power and always resulted in a break. Kyuoshu vital area strikes were a refinement that made it only more lethal.

In the late 1800's Dr. Jigro Kano developed a new sport called Judo by removing the deadlier aspects of the parent art and focusing on the throwing and unbalancing aspects. Don't misunderstand me, Judo is still plenty lethal. Throwing someone is one of the most dangerous things one can do to a person. I love Judo.

Fun fact: My first published article was in the Kodokan magazine.

KARATE

Many of the observations relayed about Jujitsu can also be said about karate. If Jujitsu is summarized as death by grappling, Karate is death by striking. It is characterized by its strong linear power kicks and punches delivered with full commitment. Four-foot nine, rock solid, come and get me is its most distinguishable persona.

When US occupational forces sought instruction after the war, they were mostly taught a basic curriculum with the more lethal aspects hidden, due to national pride. Things didn't fare much better when the art came to America. Most of the first karate instructors in the USA were lettered men. Teaching academically at universities and having Karate clubs on the side. Commercial studios really didn't come online until the sixties, with second and third generation students trying to carry the mantle. A few outstanding practitioners became well established, but the American Karate business overwhelmingly belonged to the Koreans at that time.

TAE KWAN DO

The Korean arts in America are more a tale of business success than occult pugilism. As advertised, the hand and foot art teach basic self-defense, discipline for kids, and exercise for all. That's not to say there are not high performing practitioners produced by this art. I have seen some impressive demonstrations of Tae-Kwon-Do. But the admiration is always more for their athleticism than content. Anyone who can punch and kick or knock away a grabbing hand is better off than they were before. I'm sure the high-level Koreans have as many "secrets" as anyone else, but do they trickle down to the white devils? Doesn't matter, they are here to peruse the American dream.

I never liked that they made American students bow to the Korean flag. Undoubtedly, one of the most prolific styles in America: they know how to open schools. We used to call newly arrived instructors, T.W.A. black belts. This is because when they got on the plane in Soul, they were a third-degree brown belt, and when they got off the plane in Milwaukee to open their school, they were a ninth-degree black belt. Oh yeah, and every one of them was the president's bodyguard. Still, one must admire the business acumen and political influence. Of all the martial arts, Tae-Kwon-Do is the only Olympic sport. This is due to the rather new custom that the hosting country could add an event of their choosing. Guess which one Korea added in 1988?

Fun fact: My first studio's t-shirt sported the moto: "Don't bow to a foreign flag!"

M.M.A.

Every criticism of M.M.A. always ends with a challenge to step outside. Of course, world class practitioners in peak condition are dangerous. So is a linebacker for the Steelers. I admire M.M.A. the same way I admire The N.B.A. or any other top athlete.

For me, classic styles are self-defense styles. And, the enjoyment of perfecting a skill, belonging to a club, and absorbing the culture and history; for many, was part of the attraction. I don't understand why it can't be regarded as an avocation, like dance or tennis - participating for the sheer joy of it.

M.M.A. practitioners love to point out that they usually destroy any of the classic arts. And that's usually true within the octagon. Amateur fighters and over confident B.J.J. enthusiasts should be as careful as anyone else. Someone 4'9" and unassuming can still be a lighting fast killer.

For example, the true expert is counting on the M.M.A. fighter to be so confident in his double shoot that he can slice their jugular with their blade that was never seen. There is an old Chinese story that says the rabbit usually beats the fox because the fox is only running for his dinner and the rabbit is running for his life.

For another reference, see the anecdotal story "friends" in the last chapter.

MUAY THAI / SILAT / LUA

Many fighters cross train in Muay Thai, because it is more martial art than boxing. But, here again - gloves and hand wraps. That is why self-defense arts use the palm and hand-sword (shuto): to be able to keep fighting with that hand for an extended period of time and contact.

Personally, I love the Filipino arts. Primarily because of the science, but also because of their impressive, down-to-earth skills. For instance, you really don't want to have a go with some street kid from Manila holding a ballysong, or even just a rattan stick.

If they were available at the beginning of my training, I would have definitely pursued the Indonesian arts. But they weren't. Yet another series of arts that are fascinating and compelling. From a purely martial art perspective, the Indonesian art are like Kung-Fu and Kenpo mixed.

SUMMARY

I could go on to list many more arts, but I think you get the idea. In short, all styles have good and bad and it really depends on what you like and what is best suited to your personality and body type.

It is a total waste of time to point out perceived flaws in every art. That was not the purpose of this chapter. The chapter is about fighting and every art has its strengths and weakness.

Fighting has always been with us. Still, the vast majority of the time, it is a stupid, wasteful endeavor. A highly unpredictable fool's errand. Life is a gift and having a whole, unbroken body with which to enjoy it is a real blessing. Yet, many people willingly take a chance with their health and exacerbate small matters - Insults (real or perceived) and small mistakes or accidents. I'm not going to fight over a chair or a word, but those who would are legion.

One must always keep in back of their mind that physical conflict has consequences, such as: injury or death, prison, and/or revenge. Instead of a blustering intimidator, a smart person develops his grey man skills. They slip in and out of situations. They always try to blend in and typically go unnoticed.

I have never been happy when people use the word reality when talking about fighting, because the reality is different every time. The types of situations I've encountered here in the good old U.S.A. are very different from some kid who grew up on the streets of Manila, Panama City, or Beirut.

The good news is; one can prepare for two types of encounters. Someone who comes at you crazed, swinging for all their worth. Or, someone who tries to box you. If they're sparing around, don't engage, just leave. If they are coming for all their worth, the self-defense stuff has a high probability of working. This is due to their over commitment. Of course, today one must be prepared for the wrestling take-down.

That said, almost all fights can be avoided; unless the impetus for the encounter is robbery, or you gave an antagonist some good reason to go after you. Just about every other potential conflict can be mitigated. Yet admittedly, some conflicts may still be initiated by someone with a bully mentality.

While there are many truly tough dangerous hooligans, most people aren't as tough as they think they are. Most of these antagonizers are not really fighters, rather intimidators. They revel in the cat and mouse. This provides the aware defender a window through which to employ a first strike advantage. Run when you can, but you can always end it quickly by moving into action first. The facts on the ground haven't changed since your grandfather's time: bullies are cowards.

I am happy to announce that there is now an official organization for individuals possessed of this mentality. It turns out that the pre-professional M.M.A. association has joined forces with the American body builder's doping guild and the one world Tae-Kwan-Do cooperative to form a new, world changing collective: American Society of Super Warriors in Pursuit of Excellence. Although, they are better known to the general public by the acronym, A.S.S.W.I.P.E.

The world I sought to escape was one of unrelenting; "What are you looking at?" and "You got something to say to me?" thugs jumping out of cars and chasing you down - fighting, fighting, fighting. Fortunately, I don't get a lot of that now. First, I'm older; but secondly, and more importantly, I'm far less confrontational. Maybe it's just me, but I also think the world has evolved. I now see more tolerance and cooperation. Less fighting. I am hopeful that this is so. Who knows?

Weapons

FIREARMS

Guns are an effective means of administering deadly force. But there are many problems with owning, carrying, and defending the use of firearms. Also, its only useful if it's loaded, cocked, and in your hand. Otherwise, you need time to reach into your bag or pocket, unholster, draw, and fire. Equally relevant, You probably could have figured some other way to dissolve the crisis. Finally, practicing at the range is only one set of skills. One needs to master many others, such as: drawing from awkward positions; firing from their back, kneeling or crouching; or dive rolling over cars and awareness of other environmental factors.

I was sitting at the bar with a friend of mine and he was getting into a heated argument with another patron of the bar, sitting on the other side of him. The gentleman exclaimed, "I've got a gun!" Tom asked, "where is it?" "In my car" Tom retorts, "go get it...I'll wait". Instead, Tom beaned him with a pool ball.

KNIVES

"Charge the gun, and run from the knife". I have personally carried a knife every day for over sixty years. And I was glad to have one on more than one occasion. Most folders that people carry are not kept sharp, either due to use or other factors. I keep mine sharp, very sharp. A sharp blade is deadly if you really know what you are doing. If you carry a knife for self-defense and it is anything other than razor sharp, you have decreased its effectiveness dramatically. Likewise, if your defensive tool is only capable of poking, you might as well have a screwdriver, it's easier to defend in court.

If you are anything less than well skilled in knife fighting, it is best to think of a knife purely in defensive terms. One should always keep in mind that If you extend to reach the opponent, you run the risk of being disarmed. Also, they now have the legal standing and emotional state to turn it against you.

Personally, I favor a reverse grip, held close to my body and will cut anything coming in; using an execution similar to regular blocking motion. Always be cognizant that a blade cuts by drawing. Using this knowledge, roll around or rake the incoming projection. But, if you do need to thrust, do so with the knife blade in an upward facing position, raking back with an upward draw. This motion is almost like you intend for him to block your knife hand, so you can take advantage of the situation by cutting on the pull back. Finally, never use your knife as a threat or an attempt to intimidate. It is an option of last resort. Never let it be seen until after it is felt.

HOOK CANE

This is my absolute favorite weapon in the world. One can carry them anywhere, and they are always in your hand. Totally adjustable in length, obliquity, and application. It can be used as a bludgeon, whip, or lever - just to name a few of the more common applications.

When I see the techniques promoted by many cane experts, I am reminded of the Angelo Dundee quote about the uppercut: "The punch nobody knows how to throw". This most certainly applies to the hook cane. "The weapon nobody knows how to use". I have been fortunate enough to be exposed to some of the "magic" of a traditional cane system. These legitimate experts are capable of producing supersonic whip and bone crushing power, but that is only the more visual application. These battle hardened systems are nothing like the self-proclaimed cane masters of the modern era.

STICK

The straight stick, like the hook cane, is adjustable in performance. Also, some of the same principles that make hook cane devastating may applied to the stick; to a certain degree. One advantage of the stick is that there are cultures that have refined this type of fighting to a fine science. Used properly, the stick, again like the hook cane, is capable of producing crushing injuries that can leave one with a permanent disability: unlike a cut, which may heal sufficiently to restore to full function. Also, the stick doesn't need to be straight. It may actuality contain bends and other adaptations.

One final thought, the thing about training with martial arts weapons is that once you know how to spin things, everything becomes a weapon.

BAT

It's not sexy or exotic, but even in the hands of the untrained, a bat is to be respected. A determined adversary swinging a bat can be very difficult to overpower; and is potentially very dangerous.

In this same category is the golf club. It is like a steel whip with a deadly blade, or bludgeon, at the end.

Swing either of these weapons with conviction and authority; low, or low to high.

Also, one should pivot 90 degrees after each swing to expand their peripheral view. As with each of the weapons described in this section, one should avoid tunnel vision on a single opponent. Always remember to watch your back.

SWORD

I consider myself a swordsman. I have a sword collection, but would never run outside with a sword. Using a sword for self-defense just makes you look like a nut job. Each one should come with a sticker that says, "arrest me". One may be able to mount a reasonable defense if they use a bat or a golf club. But, even the ball bat has a sinister reputation, so choose the golf club if given an option. In my humble opinion, swords are useless for self-defense.

PEN

The pen is one of the best innocuous, short range self-defense weapons one can choose. Any pen can be used for limited defensive purposes, but for adequate results, it must have a steel case with a blunt top and a twist open; not a push button.

Probably, the standard plastic pen is your worse choice. Many of them will shatter or bend, becoming as much a problem to you as a weapon to them. A better choice would be a standard wooden pencil.

There are multiple ways to hold the pen, but my favorite is to place the broad top in the middle of your palm and extend the point between the fingers, your choice. I call this the punch grip.

In use, one should punch for speed and primarily target the throat or other acupoints and using a snapping (over thrusting) motion.

Another one of my favorite grips is to hold the pen in a fist, tip down. I call this the hammer-fist grip. Use this grip to hammer-fist the groin or other delicate areas. Although, one may certainly attack the groin with the punch grip, it is bettered suited for the hammer-fist grip.

Tactical pens are currently available for purchase. The major downside? They look like a weapon. Once again, court.

GRAVEL / COINS / LIQUID

Throwing for distraction is an excellent way to gain a half-beat so one can get the upper hand. So, unless you're jumped from out of nowhere, you can probably see it building. This will potentially give you time to "arm" yourself. One easy tactic is to throw dirt, coins or liquid at the face, then attack low. Or, pick up something solid and start swinging.

MACE

Pepper spray is very effective and efficient. I like it. When in doubt, hose 'em down.

One must be very judicious before defending with a firearm. Am I sure? Is this warranted? Justified?

But with mace, an overreaction means controversy not prison. However, one must follow up immediately. Kick them low, then throw combinations. Or just run.

BOTTLES

The best way to employ a bottle is as a club. The opponent's head will absorb the impact, similar to the stick. There is a low likelihood of shattering your weapon, but If it does break, start grinding. You may cut your hand but it's his queen, your knight.

Breaking a bottle to produce an edged weapon is risky business. The idea that a bottle will break off perfectly leaving you with a nice handle and workable cutting edge is a bad gamble. More often than not, the bottle will break in your hand, leaving you with a bleeding wound. Now you can't use that hand and are worse off than before.

CANS ETC.

Most objects found around the house are best used as a projectile weapon over a mere distraction. Hurling cans, books, statuary, or other loose objects is just to create an opening to apply martial arts. Or, in some instances can be used the same as gravel / coins / liquid.

Throwing a can is likened to throwing a rock. But when used as a hammer, it also has a formidable edge that can produce a fight ending impact when delivered to the face or head.

EVERYTHING ELSE

All objects in one's environment are potential allies in an altercation. If it has a point, thrust it. If it has mass, slam it. If it has a natural, jagged edge, rake it. But, one's greatest assets are their agile mind and good street sense.

Just like one's natural weapons, improvised weapons must be delivered with conviction; and in most instances are better because they can't be hurt, unlike a natural weapon.

For instance, a novice or untested black belt with a stapler in one hand and a pair of pliers in the other, is just that much more dangerous. Also, a high-level martial artist can have his rhythm, flow, and energy impaired by inserting objects into the equation.

Finally, use whatever provides an advantage and be more determined than your assailant.

Tai-Chi Fighting

Tai-Chi-Chuan, i.e. grand ultimate fist. Not only a healing health practice, but also a devastating martial art. This line invariably appears somewhere in every book on Tai-Chi.

Indeed, there are some very impressive demonstrations to bolster this claim. But, when you see Tai-Chi techniques or fighting application, the word devastation does not immediately come to mind. Seeing someone pushed up and off their feet to have them stumble another twenty feet may be worthy of respect, but where is the deadly incapacitation implied by proponents? To compensate for this type of critique, many instructors show some redirection of power and a dramatic uproot ending with an impressive discharge. And then they will hint darkly that there are other, more lethal techniques known only to the occult inner circle.

In reality, this hint turns out to be mostly true. Yes, there is deadly Tai-Chi power. And yes, there is the more benign, humane application that most people think of when Tai-Chi application is sited. Disrupting or redirecting an energy vector is indeed the grand ultimate as it maintains harmony by initially offering a less lethal option. That is the reason why it is the most commonly articulated expression of Tai-Chi.

Crushing a larynx or eye orbit is unnecessary if the attacker can simply be repelled. Internal organs can indeed be damaged by violent, concentrated power; directed for that purpose. These Ying/Yang approaches seem to be the two main options of the external power expression. Some Tai-Chi styles feature an arsenal of trips and throws, and there is even a posture that occurs in all forms called parry/punch. One could legitimately wonder if it's Okay to punch extemporaneously in a self-defense situation, and would one still be doing Tai-Chi?

Of the three Neigong sister arts, Tai-Chi is the most internal. Properly applied, internal aspects such as Hua and Peng can be effectively employed to transfer energy; usually resulting in a dramatic uprooting discharge. Receiving and transforming an incoming force and redirecting it back to its source, is the hallmark of the style.

With the proper investment of time and effort, the principal qualities espoused throughout Tai-Chi practice will indeed perform as assured. This is a goal well worth attaining, and even worthy of the moniker, "grand ultimate". To personally experience the total physical control and operational shutdown of one's entire organism is quite eviscerating, and would make anyone respectful of the internal arts.

It comes with a caveat, however. Anything shy of true master level execution could prove problematic within a life-or-death scenario. At the point when one's highly developed internal power becomes a quality, it becomes available at all times. Like toughness, when this quality is fully realized, it transmutes into what that the person "just is". As an analogy, if we were think of this quality as any type of force, such as photons (a.k.a. light), it would be radiating at all times. As such, even if an unexpected, fast punch or take down where attempted, once within the "field of Chi", this threat would be intercepted and dealt with in harmony with Tai-Chi protocols; without hesitation or thought.

Empirical understanding of soft style fighting dictates that anything less than an extremely high-level ability can be overpowered by superior strength, and determination. A little self-defense knowledge would prove helpful against an untrained attacker, but a little Tai-Chi, could almost be a detriment. A victim may be better off slugging-it-out in a natural fashion, rather than relying on internal power that is anything less than fully developed. Applications that execute flawlessly for a master may prove unreliable for anyone else.

If Tai-Chi is promoted as a Yin/Yang art, then there is no concealment or subterfuge as to the nature of this frank reality. There must be a second side. For instance, the common exercise of "push hands" emphasizes only the dissolving and redirecting aspects of the art. The ballistic power striking inherent in Tai-Chi movement, the other half of Tai-Chi capabilities, is purposely omitted.

From a more practical perspective, the Hua and Peng aspects of the art are its primary feature. Where energy is received and redirected back to the aggressor. You provide no point of arrival for the opponent's attack. There simply is no destination. You lead them into emptiness.

In contrast, is explosive ballistic striking. And in concert with that goal, push-hands may serve as an entry to set up Fa-Jin strikes; just as Chi-Sau sticky hands may set up the Chin-Na. But, once engaged, belligerents are positioned for the customary Tai-Chi dissolving and blending actions. There exists however, the option for the practitioner to apply the power slap, palm techniques and "dead-hand" strikes.

As traditionally practiced, Tai-Chi does not require any Li (a.k.a. hard style) techniques; it is a complete art. Most adepts, however, have deep histories in other martial arts. They can, and will, resort to Li (external power) when necessary. Neijing (internal) arts are considered by most to be difficult to internalize. And as such, can be problematic to apply until mastered. In such scenarios, it may prove advantageous for one to be able to move in and out of styles. This is especially true for the journeyman practitioner.

Defaulting to external technique is not an inadequacy or a failure of Tai-Chi, just an acknowledgment of a practical reality from an individual standpoint. In all reality, default protocols (i.e. untrained combat) are not exotic, nor are they arduously integrated as viable options. But the simple truth is, these protocols are Shaolin movement; and are just an expression of Kung-Fu hard style technique.

Also, if one's energy is disrupted, or their concentration is broken by an unexpected punch or kick; one that causes pain and breaks the Chi, the defensive energy stream can instantly become useless. Therefore, one had better have a default system in place to address this type of deficiency. A default option is for one to rely upon toughness, will, and powerful technique. Also known as martial art.

A GLOSSARY OF TERMS

FA-JIN
Power generated by initiating movement from a relaxed energy state. Coordinating whip, waist rotation and backup mass in a chain reaction as required.

CHIN-NA
Joint locking...
Often executed with a striking motion.
Not an incremental applied pressure as used by bouncers or in police come-alongs.
A ballistic explosive pressure that turns an arm bar into a break or a headlock into a fractured jaw.

NERVE LAUNCH
A strike or other movement initiated by the business end of the weapon. Bringing the larger muscles into play in an explosive chain. Yes...it's different from Fa-Jin

DEAD-HAND
A strike delivered in a totally relaxed state.
Tense muscles mute the transfer of kinetic energy generated by waist rotation and weight drop

DIM-MAK
This is a specific term that over time has become generalized.
Kind of like cool, where it's perfectly acceptable to describe a bar-b- q that has come up to temperature or a hot sandwich as cool.
Originally words that meant artery press, seal the breath and seal the vein, in the western world at least, all now generically fall under the term Dim-Mak.
Techniques that target the nervous system for ease of communication also use this term.

SUNG (SOONG)
A profound state of relaxation. From which movement is launched.
Muscle constriction retards speed.
Angry, flexed, swinging from Missouri is the polar opposite of blending, riding and burying strikes that concentrate power and velocity.

ZHAN Adhere
A sticking energy. Once in contact with the opponent, you become attached to him, crowding, riding, waiting for a mistake or a change.

Dong Jing
Understanding energy. Confidently interpreting what you feel. All sensory input follows a familiar path. Experience allows you to interpret and predict what will most likely happen next.

CONCEPTS TO STUDY

TING	listening
DONG	understanding
HUA	neutralizing
FA	issuing
LIAN	connected
SUI	follow
NIAN	stick
ZHAN	adhere
CAI	pluck
LIEH	split
JO	elbow
KOW	shoulder
PENG	ward off
LIU	rollback
JI	press forward
AN	press downward

These are all definitions and terms to be understood and utilized in Tai-Chi application. They are however concepts beyond the scope of this book. My purpose here is to develop an awareness and type of thinking that will help you become a more intuitive and interpretive practitioner. More able to process viscerally and express extemporaneously.

These lists, of course, are far from complete and there are many principals that Tai-Chi shares with other martial arts. Universal concepts, such as: waist rotation, gravitational marriage (smartly using gravity to one's advantage), and back-up mass. Although executed subtly, in Tai-Chi, these principals can still be expanded upon and transformed from a Yin type of execution to a Yang approach through the use of angles, bracing, and muscular force. The Tai-Chi diagram clearly illustrates this ability as a practical, universal criterion. In fighting, as in life, there sometimes exists the need to adapt and go around the other way to reach the mountain top.

In an effort to avoid allowing the intent of this volume to be confused by trying to list and categorize every possible concept in Tai-Chi; technical overload will be avoided by applying a notion used by investigators when an issue seems insurmountable; break the task into solvable portions. In this instance the idea is to prepare the reader for the occasions when it is necessary to morph from Yin to Yang.

For example, if ballistic striking is not readily visible within your Ta-Chi form, one should consider possible options at a given juncture; especially if a disruption occurs. By scrutiny and expansive probing, one becomes adapted to a fuller understanding of the inevitability of Yin/Yang change; also known as, things not always going according to plan.

And, of course, the opposite is also true. If one has the proclivity to be a slugger; one could switch it up with Hua and Peng; adding to their ever expanding toolbox. Always remember, this is an art. This means open to personal interpretation and expression - not an automaton who is an exact replica of everyone else.

In music, a symphony player is more akin to a robot that reads exactly what's on the page. You, as an individual, should strive to be more like a jazz musician; one who can express himself extemporaneously and adjust to the unpredictability of the other musicians. That is the true measure of an artist.

If your martial system is a rigid, one size fits all approach, it is not being taught as an art. A martial science is fine, but different from an art. A dogmatic: "he does this; you do that approach" will never allow you to develop to your full potential. Wisdom demands that one adjudge the dilemma of being benefited by sound principal, and being stilted by dogma and bureaucracy.

An old adage says: "no military plan survives contact with the enemy"; which is why a marine corps slogan is: "adapt and overcome". Lao Tzsu wrote the manual on this fact...The Book of Changes.

Options

Tai-Chi is a pushing art. The classic response is to dissolve the incoming energy, and effect discharge by driving the attacker's entire body off to an awkward angle with a powerful shove. The sister arts of Bagua and Xing Yi could be thought of in a very broad sense, as Tai-Chi with strikes; while also employing disparate strategy and tactics.

Chen style was the original Tai-Chi, and was thoroughly a martial art. Subsequent generations of teachers modified evolving versions with personal preferences, to become the main styles that we know today. Sun, Wu, Yi and others were widely practiced for both health and martial art. Yang style became renowned for Chi-Kung health nurturing aspects, and evolved a reputation as a healing modality.

Subsequent practitioners alloyed aspects of other martial arts to assuage perceived inadequacies of fighting operations. Many hybrid styles emerged, especially in the modern era. Some are even being promoted as "combat Tai-Chi". An experienced master can move in and out of styles and apply a technique that may be more appropriate or comfortable for a given situation. Be it personal conflict or species survival, adaptability is always the key to triumph. And, the optional movements presented here have been acquired from curricula that are not, strictly speaking, Tai-Chi.

A skilled culinarian may concoct a jalapeno desert cake or make a pineapple pizza. Though ostensibly incompatible and confounding to a regimented type of thinking, a master of his craft can interpolate unconcordant components and make it work. Though our programmed thinking and conditioning excludes options because they seemingly originate from disparate traditions. Originality defines art.

Options for biting, choking, or roundhouse punching may not amalgamate once engaged and set for a Tai-Chi discharge. There are however appropriate inserts that are accommodated by Ta-Chi movement, and strikes from related curricula that may be prescriptive at an opportune juncture.

Since this is a book not only about one specific art, but also fighting in general, it may prove thought provoking for the curious to be made aware of options to insinuate into application. Offered here is a limited assortment of animal repertoire inserts from the Chinese Boxing curriculum.

Monkey

Key Elements

- Weapon: varieties of monkey fist

- Target: supratrochlear, infraorbital, temporal branches

- Location: vital areas of head and other pressure points on body (as demonstrated in illustrations)

- Attack: single or double incoming attacks

- Execution: (knuckle / bone) strikes and (usually) grinding

Monkey is not an ape. It is a more delicate creature with a different temperament. Where an ape will engage aggressively, a monkey will run up a tree and throw a coconut. Monkey martial art is evasive and blending, generally coiling around an attack rather than engaging directly. Once incoming energy has been dispersed by circling or spiraling, direct linear strikes are often launched. Various types of slapping is also employed. Monkey is the Yin to tiger, being cagey, evasive, and entwining when in close. Also, very loose (almost wobbly) and deceptively unbalanced (visually), while simultaneously entertaining and enchanting (to the point of distraction).

Monkey Options - single punch / two angles, thumb strike, double punch

Mantis

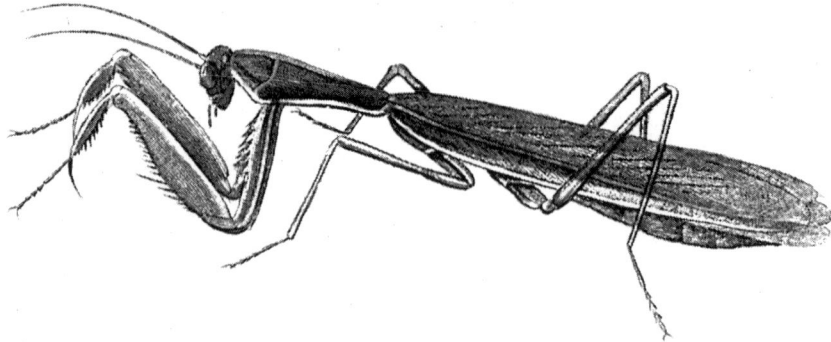

Key Elements

- Weapon: mantis hook / strike

- Target: vital areas of face and head, along with various other pressure points

- Location: pressure points on body (as demonstrated in illustrations)

- Attack: single hand straight punches / two hand push

- Execution: snapping launch of Te-sao

Mantis employs strong hooking / pinning action with forearms. The mantis hook provides a tighter grip compared with crane's beak. Strikes are delivered with cai energy, which is the snapping release often compared to the action of plucking fruit, as referenced in the Tai-Chi classics. Mantis, while relatively aggressive, is still more evasive and deceptive than tiger; relying heavily upon hooking, trapping, and unorthodox weapon choices executed primarily in a whip-like manner.

Mantis Options - punch divert, punch strike, push divert, punch counter

Snake

Key Elements

- Weapon: tips of fingers (one or more)

- Target: stomach 4 & 5, eyes, radial / ulnar nerve

- Location: head, neck, arms, other soft targets

- Attack: two hand grasp of upper arm / one hand grab to extremity

- Execution: strike (dotting) / pressing and/or grinding

Snake is an adjunct style for most kung-fu practitioners. It would be rare to find someone who practices snake exclusively. When tight, trying to clear space, or garner release, interspersing snake technique between other hits can sometimes prove prescriptive. Usually a retaliatory shot with a dotting action, pressing or grinding is also employed. Snake is direct, like tiger, but not as directly aggressive; employing quick, well-timed offensive maneuvers, executed almost entirely with the finger tips.

Snake Options - break grab, eye spear, double poke, poke with whip

Crane

the greater indian Crane

Key Elements

- Weapon: crane beak, crane wing

- Target: soft, vital areas, suboccipitals

- Location: primarily neck, torso, and eye sockets

- Attack: kick, grab, push, tackle

- Execution: pecking, hooking, evasion, crane wing penetration, kicking, and single legged stances

Crane is a delicate animal, with slight muscle mass and hollow bones. Legendarily developed in Fukian province. There are many versions of this well-known system, such as: white crane, black crane, and imperial crane. Utilizing evasion, hooking, pecking, blinding, and crane wing penetration. Cat stances and a variety of kicks are hallmarks of these styles. Crane is the Yin to tiger, being elusive, indirect, and delicate; relying heavily upon edges of mostly flattened weapons, with many blinding maneuvers followed up with offensive strikes.

Crane Options - kick, grap (or punch) , double thumb strike, double hand strike

Tiger

Key Elements

- Weapon: tiger claw, large tiger mouth, small tiger mouth, biting

- Target: face, bones, vital areas, dermis

- Location: flesh, organs, harder targets

- Attack: high tackle, punch

- Execution: rooted, strong stances, powerful kicks, aggressive, ripping and tearing

Known as Hun-Gar in the Sino speaking world. Tiger is an effective well-known, powerful Kung- Fu style. In five animal styles, tiger is taught first because it is simple, strong, and it works. Tiger is widely taught in China. In Tai-Chi, the posture "push" is a type of tiger movement. Tiger is the Yang to monkey and crane, being aggressive, directly devastating, and focused; relying heavily upon semi-open hand strikes for penetration, ripping, gouging, and crushing..

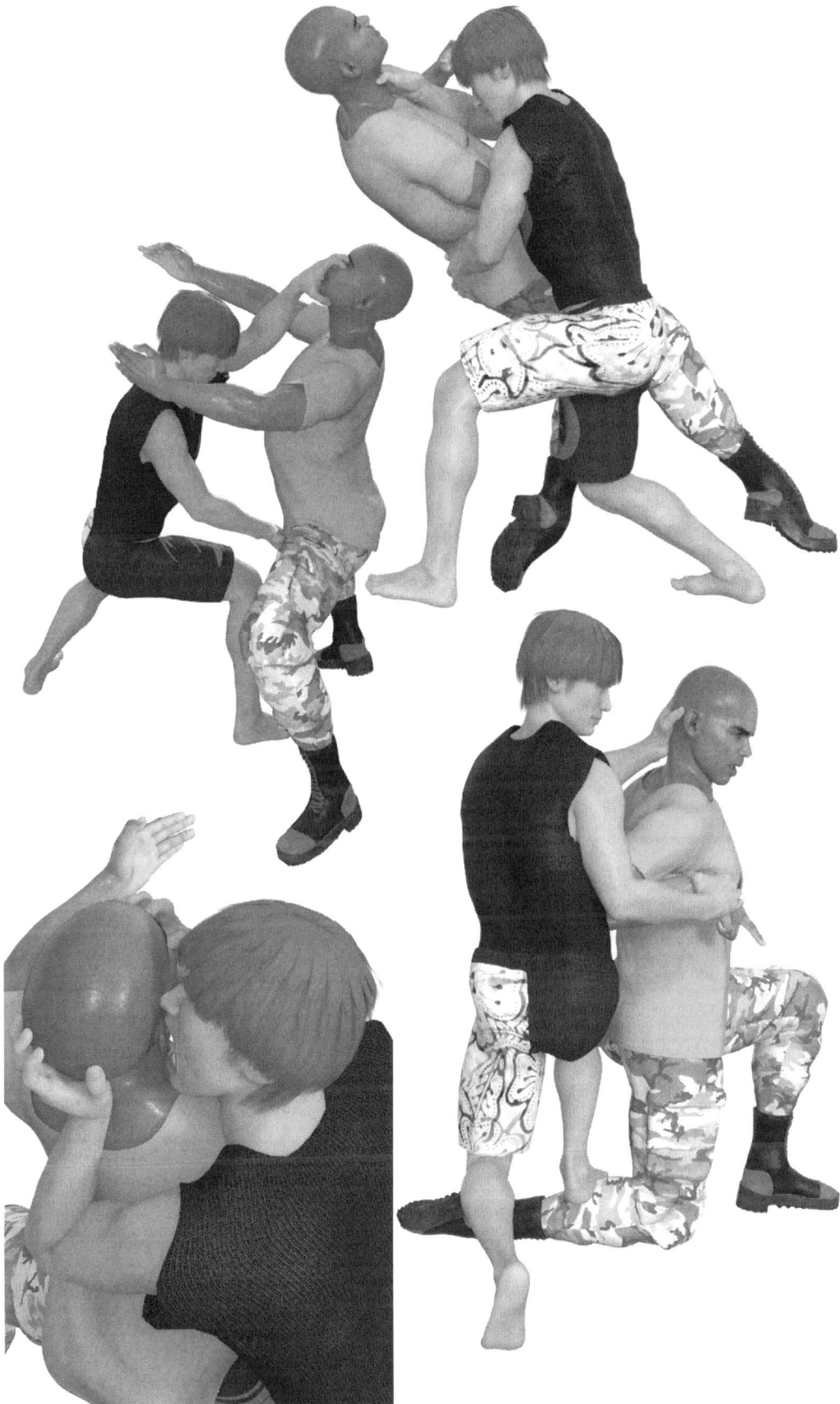

Tiger Options - double claw, unbalancing, biting, stomping

Nautiloidea

Cephalopods: this mysterious creature has bewildered and confounded mankind for centuries. From their copper based blueish blood and bioluminescence, to color morphing camouflaging techniques. People have always been fascinated with this unique creature. The study of Cephalopods is a branch of malacology called teuthology. As of late, these beings have begun to receive some well-deserved attention. And, these observations have spawned research that has revealed mechanisms responsible for their amazing characteristics.

Cephalopods are a phenomenon of nature, possessing a large number of amazing abilities.

Through chromophism, cephalopods are able to affect a camouflage in milliseconds. They can expand or contract, chromatophores, as well as other components within their dermis, such as: iridophores, lecuophores and photophores. These ocean dwelling creatures can also live in deep marine crevices - those crack-o-phores. Animals posed of these abilities, can perform astounding adaptations, and are able to command chromatophores like a muscle on demand; producing a coloration change in less than a second.

Likewise, cephalopods are also capable of bioluminescence; which is produced by bacterial symbionts. And, the Yin to the chromatophore and bioluminescence Yang is that they also possess a highly enhanced chromatic visual spectrum, greatly improving their visual acuity.

Another behavior worthy of note is jetting, the ability to fly through the air for distances of over fifty yards on a spray of water in a form of jet propulsion. These animals are not structurally aerodynamic, yet are able to eject a powerful jet of water from the funnel as they consciously spread fins to form a type of wing and create lift. An alternate type of flight.

And although these peculiar characteristics may seem disconnected from our Tai-Chi discussion, these aspects, both baffling and enigmatical, will be of great benefit.

While there is much cephalopod biologically one may explore, for the purposes of this inquiry, we will limit our examination to some of their more applicable aspects. Further understanding of these amazing characteristics will hopefully provide another perspective from the standard analysis; and utilizing the scientific method, help us comprehend the idea of energy transfer. To accomplish this, it may prove helpful to acknowledge a very real phenomenon employed by animals in this class and that is nothing less than alchemistic.

Most experimenters, in the pursuit of human powered flight, tried to replicate the mechanical action of a bird's beating wings as the primary R&D. It wasn't until two intrepid bicycle shop owners blundered onto the revelation that lift was created by the shape of the wing; With that revelation, aerodynamics was born. Prior to this, it was a hidden mystery that birds were able to command this "force" by morphing their body, capitalizing and controlling lift.

Just as the octopus wills the molecular structure to cause a color change and the dove shapes her wing to control and direct the conspicuous, omnipresent gasses on which she rides; the Tai-Chi master receives incoming power, morphing the body to manipulate and redirect the wave of kinetic energy to their will.

But even though it looks like kung-fu magic, do we attribute it to voodooism when a bird commands natural forces to become airborne, escaping a predator? Or is it a conjuring when an octopuses directs their bodily processes to alter their appearance, confounding the observer? No, these animal are displaying their natural abilities to manipulate their physical biology. The point is that Tai-Chi energy manipulation, as controlled by processes like Hua and Peng, may seem equally unbelievable as disappearing, instantly blending into the environment, or lifting off the ground and soaring atop a tree.

Birds don't amaze you because you see them all the time. But, cephalopods are a little more mysterious, due to their relative rarity in the experience of most people. Tai-Chi internal power, which has been deliberately kept hidden until the deleterious information age, is just another phenomenon of the natural world.

As young masters seek ego gratification and recognition on the internet, there will be more demonstrations and explanations until this once secret aspect becomes routine. For instance, there was once a time when kicking skills really did provide an advantage; until it became common practice. Also, take downs were the next enigma exploited; until everybody started doing them, and learned to build defenses to defeat them. Finally, internal power secrets, which seem so impossible to the uninitiated, will one day be a part of everyone's arsenal. The occult wizardry of the internal arts is becoming as endangered as rare Cephalopods. Tai-Chi power secrets, now palpably displayed as a peacock or bird of paradise, where once concealed: they blended into the ocean floor.

Shuangzizuo

I have a friend who is of Polish decent and loves to regale listeners with reminders of contributions given to the world by the Polish people. It is an impressive list, and includes a litany of famous names, and invariably includes Copernicus. Those of Arabic heritage would also be justified in presenting a collection of benefactions given to the world. This would also be equally true for Greeks, Italians, and everyone who thought and/or wondered.

Likewise, the culture of China is responsible for bestowing many enrichments; mechanical, cultural, and philosophical. These dispensations are arguably more influential than those of many other civilizations. The cumulative effect on human life is impossible to calculate. Historians officially credit China with four notable inventions: the compass, gunpowder, paper making, and printing. All innovators are anonymous except for Cai Lun, the inventor of paper: A first century eunuch who served both emperors Ming and Zhang.

Other notable contributions to history and culture are diverse, such as: metallurgy, hydraulics, horology, and pasta. Although these benefactions are well known; people from other parts of the world, when ranking Chinese contributions, always near the top of the list will be Kung-Fu. The term's literal translation is: "time and effort". And, the more precise translation (Wade/Giles) does not necessarily connote martial arts skill at all; instead it simply refers to any practiced conduct that produces expertise.

In China, if one were to verbalize the term "Kung-Fu" to an adjunct Chinese speaker, they would wonder who you were referring to. A baker? A wheelwright? Actually, anyone who has invested toil and energy in cultivating a high-level skill.

Tai-Chi is a kung-fu style, and it certainly requires time and effort to perfect execution and understanding of this arcane art. But like any journey to a remote location, one learns much along the way. Consider one's relocation from Miami Beach, Florida to Los Angles, California. Traveling this journey by air, would not be the same as driving or hitchhiking. By ground, one would meet many people and encounter numerous situations as their odyssey unfolds. This would be a far shorter and less rich experience by air. Like nutrients in an elixir, one drinks in the passing culture, atmosphere, and essence of each region, person, and moment as they experience and interact with them.

As an example from a personal perspective, show business took me to places I never would have deliberately chosen in a more mundane, pedestrian endeavor. While I can fondly recall specific people and events, it was the music, the art, that provided the impetus and served as the underlying catalyst. In short, a significant, intimate motivation changes everything.

As in other internal styles of martial art, Tai-Chi is difficult to learn; oft times people begin to feel the goal does not justify the arduous journey. But the analysis and internal fortitude that is required to attain erudite levels of the art, can be nothing short of transformative. The internal alchemy is commonly understood to supervene on the physiological and physiological plane of the human organism. But if signposts and realizations encountered along the way are properly considered, compensations are titanic. The reverse is dire. To paraphrase Socrates, an unexamined art is not worth doing.

From another perspective, it requires much time and effort for someone to become a competent musician. But, once some skill is obtained, simply "working" or just creating sounds, without enjoyment or desire would be a dry, empty pursuit. Ultimately, competence is not the totality of one's struggle to obtain such proficiency. Ideally, one does this not only for mastery of the skill, but for their own personal development, enhancement and in many cases enlightenment.

Moreover, and holistically speaking, once a level of proficiency is achieved, the practitioner should sense an ethereal elevation. An "out of body" awareness of their higher mind observing and serving as witness as the body performs on automatic. To at once feel as the doer, but also observe, in an altered state as a disconnected beholder.

The creation of music can be its own kind of joy. But on another level, not dissimilar from the sensation experienced by a leaping dancer, a jumping wide receiver, or golfer whose soul momentarily sails aloft with the ball on a satisfying drive. An experience that reaches an exalted state; finally realizing the reward of instruction and practice.

With any of the above referenced endeavors, if a neophyte steels his resolve, and dedicates sufficient "time and effort" to attain Kung-Fu, the reward is the Zen experience; a gateway to an ethereal realm where existence is transmuted. This altered state is the experience of an elite class of individuals who transubstantiate. Although it is an exclusive club, the good news is; anyone can join - it only requires Kung- Fu.

But, anyone can develop martial arts skill, and it is understandable that a brute would have no need nor interest in the philosophy. But as stated elsewhere, and repeated here: this book is not a "how to", but more of a how and why. Using different words: is one's mental acuity enhanced by immersion in the art? Yes. Healthful? Yes. Fighting moves also? Absolutely. But that is not the real point here.

What is the point? When an avocation, occupation, mania, or delusion is internalized, there is gestalt. When the resultant outcome becomes more than the sum of its parts; when it is more than just what it does; transformation can be realized.

In the great cultural mix that constitutes our world today, and the polyglot that continues to be a hallmark of the United States; ideas, once hoarded, spill over into the whole world. A trend toward liberalism of interaction allows outsiders to savor processes and traditions from many cultures. As barriers fall and exchange, previously prohibited, transpires; more people can benefit from exposure to ideas and methodologies once shunned, due to elitism and zen-o-phobia.

But, the Chinese are the ones who initially developed this particular path of experiential Kung-Fu. A method whose end result is not entirely unlike other evolved perceptions of the universe. Yet serving as a philosophical big bang. But, once this concept began to seep into the western thought as just a seed, a small breach; but one that opened many doors into new ways of thinking about what was previously "known". Something that once absorbed by the west, resulted in a huge difference of perception. Yet realistically speaking, the west was only exposed to a little tweak in thought, a slight divergence philosophically. But, one that allowed for the concept of Yin and Yang to permeate the consciousness of the west.

Other western cultures, including our own in the United States, observed only the binary nature of things and events. But the eastern mind, informed by the absence of Newtonian physics, developed on a separate, yet parallel course. One that, once manifested, could teach, conceptualize, cognizance, and inform; functioning in every facet of our experience. It is this approach and acumen that Tai-Chi reveals; a concentrated tutorial in altered (full) awareness.

Yes, the world requires mathematics, paper, and sophisticated navigational aids to advance. But the comprehension of what unfolds as a result of our introspection in these efforts is a subtle adumbration of the overall worldview of the culture that produced it.

Zen-O-Phobia

Owing to genetics, the basic nature of the ego, and the need of tribalism for survival, man possesses an innate predisposition against difference. This predisposition can manifest in many ways, including: protectionism and exclusion of concepts, customs, and people regarded as other. National borders have always provided a metric by which to claim both a personal and national identity. The inescapable doctrine of Yin and Yang dictates that despite well-defined disinclinations, there have always been interaction and cultural exchange between even disparate groups.

Fun fact: it is estimated that up to six percent of people with European ancestry may have neanderthal genetics.

Marco Polo was an Italian explorer and adventurer who spent fourteen years exploring in China. As everyone knows, it was Polo who introduced noodles to Europe. This delicacy is indigenous to the Chinese mainland and prior to Polo was only enjoyed in that locale. Although, this factoid is typically common knowledge, when anyone mentions pasta almost everyone's first thought is of Italy. Our association is that deeply ingrained. The same holds true for the subject of Zen. The mention thereof, automatically invokes images of Japan.

Zen thought and practice, however, is actually a product of China; which itself Imported core fundamentals from Sanskrit writings and practices of India. The precepts that would become Zen, began as doctrines of a Chinese practice called Chan; an offshoot of Mahayana Buddhism.

The most popular modern religion practiced throughout most of the Americas is one that grew around the teachings of an enigmatic prophet from the Middle East. And, this doctrinal nucleus is based around an even more ancient belief system that had grown out of the primitive traditions of Babylon and Mesopotamia. Modern descendants constitute a small but influential minority throughout the world, and have survived through tumultuous times; in a remarkable example of overcoming bigotry and adversity.

Since the majority of the North American population embraces a belief system that is itself an import, one would think that it would be more attune to openness and acceptance regarding spiritual postulations of alien organ. This, sadly, has not proven to be the case; as tribalism and distrust of "other" is deeply rooted in the human psyche.

Even if only as an academic study for purely historical reasons, the mere mention of eastern belief systems ordinarily alarms fundamentalists of every stripe. Further, some believe even scholarly pursuit is tantamount to swearing allegiance to a foreign divinity. It is possible, of course, to train in martial arts without any thought of spiritual affiliation. After all a punch is just a punch and a kick is just a kick.

The complication arises when genealogical defenders of a doctrine contrive a peccadillo in benign, ubiquitous principals like those found in Tai-Chi. Purely objective and phlegmatic principles where an acceptance and consideration of Taoist thought is integral to understanding of the physical function. While blending and joining momentum with an opponent's force can be learned solely as a physical technique, the mindset that drives that action is rooted in an understanding of cycles. Ones not only of physics and body mechanics, but also phases, degrees of emotions, and bio-function - as well the sky that looks over them.

Because Tai-Chi is more than just a "he does this, you do that" (i.e. action / reaction), one's performance and results are enhanced by an all-encompassing, synergistic amalgam of the entire organism, where the mind is connected to and working in concert with body. And yes, because an advantageous outcome is instated by union of forces, both seen and unseen, mind and body functions better as a unit: especially when all systems; including an involved, cultivated physiology; function harmoniously.

To be very clear: these elements are not beliefs, but understanding. Taoist interpretations are not a religion, but more of an amalgamate of science and empirical observation by generations of enlightened attestants. When one gains an acute comprehension, or even taps at the door of enlightenment, it is the result of introspection fostered by concepts like those found in Tai-Chi. A recipe of properly assembled components producing effectiveness because of working within principals. If one is to consider the results, the cost/benefit, and rewards vs. investment, even a skeptic might find merit.

Witnessing patterns such as planetary orbits or seasonal changes is not, not, not a religion, more exactly an organized observational account of natural phenomena. An application thereof for accentuated functioning between man his environment, and mitigation of situations that arise from entwinement therein.

Most prophets that have risen to prominence, never set out to or declared an intent to build a religion. Usually their teachings are meant only to disseminate understanding and initiate enlightenment. Taoist proselytizers have followed the same path seen in the evolution of many religions. Predictably, their followers, owing to reptilian brainwave patterns, insisted on categorizing, collating, and organizing the message. They collaborated, revised, and produced a final edit - approved by committee. A governing hierarchy was established, with a regimented chain of command; and of course, require graded levels for advancement. Yes, there are now Taoist "priests", services, and canon; but like the other paths to enlightenment that came before, the original revelations intended only to serve as guides for fellow seekers.

People die here and in "heathen" countries. We all experience life's phenomena in the same way. Religion should be about unity, not division. Fear of other, and hatred for all things foreign, is contrary to the central message of unity fostered by most paths. I once saw a televangelist proclaim that followers should not allow their children to train in karate. His rationale was that karate came from a Buddhist country, and contamination would take place just by learning the movements.

I have learned much from Arjuna's lessons in the chariot. The yoga I was led to is called "the science of God contact", and I would have to agree. No matter how legitimate the institution appears in the locale, those who promote tribalism just to appeal to man's base nature, foster a cult and have failed to walk the razors edge.

Like a bigot who would prefer to die rather than accept a transfusion from a vilified infidel, this is irrefutably self-mutilation. To be quite frank, this premise is completely inconsistent with not only Tao, but any naturally rational human impulse. It should be quite apparent to any thinking being to recognize if a message is healthy or not. As a well-known visionary from the middle east once said, "let us reason together".

If a friend offered you some helpful advice, and you later found it was a quote from the hated "other", would you ignore the wisdom? To draw a distinct line between faith and a path of wisdom, is a subjective division. One collectively agreed upon observation is that religion is simply faith organized into a corporate structure. Tao, like most wisdoms, did not start out with this complex of an organization, but similar to the teachings of the humble son of Nazareth, is most efficacious if kept in its simple, original form.

85 percent of the world's population follow some type of organized religion. Most belong to one of the mainstream faiths. Listed alphabetically: Baha'i, Buddhism, Christianity, Confucianism, Hinduism, Islam, Jainism, Judaism, Shinto, Sikhism, Taoism, Zoroastrianism. As unbelievable as it seems, there are 45,000 Christian denominations worldwide. How fortunate, to find right one.

Many altruists have dedicated entire lives to try and assist the expansion of the world's understanding of spirituality. It is at least worth consideration. Pax.

Brubaker's Law

1. The fight always goes to the toughest man.

2. If it lasts more than three seconds...you're in trouble.

3. If you're fighting...you've made a mistake.

4. A weapon is an incredible equalizer.
   Use it first, but make sure they never see it.

5. Whoever gets in the first lick...usually wins.

6. You can strike preemptively, and still be the defending man.

ADDENDUM TO BRUBAKER'S LAW

1. Just because you are confronted, doesn't mean you are going to fight.

2. Just because you are fighting doesn't mean you will be seriously hurt.

3. Just because you are hurt doesn't mean you stop fighting.

4. Just because he pulls a gun doesn't mean he gets off a shot.

5. Just because he shoots it doesn't mean he will hit you.

6. Just because you are hit doesn't mean you are seriously wounded

7. Just because you are wounded doesn't mean you will die.

8. Just because you die doesn't mean...O.K. I guess it is over.

The scenario does not end. Even if you are shot. You never give up. It is not over just because you have been hit, knocked down or shot....Keep fighting.

Yin/Yang in Tai-Chi Application

If Tai-Chi is a fighting style and a healing art, why the emphasis on philosophy? What does Yin/Yang theory contribute to either of these two aspects? In other chapters, it is stated that there was an emphasis and need for biometric balance. In contrast, this section is concerned with fighting application and how the principals found in Tai-Chi can contribute to more favorable outcomes for the practitioner.

In the ebb and flow of any conflict, there is always an exchange in dominance. There was much loss and many stalemates to arrive at Appamotox; In basketball, the lead changes constantly; in tennis, the volley continues until someone outwits, bamboozles or makes a mistake.

Superior strategy and tactics has altered the outcome of most world changing events, and interpersonal conflict is no different. Martial artists recognize the need for physical conditioning and mental toughness as important keys to victory. The strategies employed by some less sophisticated practitioners amount to working angles, capitalizing on an entry, or the reliance on slick tricks. But, even these individuals, however, learn to read subtle queues, and feel intent.

Imagine someone with zero game; no mind element at all. When attacked, they will typically either become paralyzed with fear, or engage in a "this isn't happening" fantasy - both resulting in disaster. The experienced fighter remains mentally cool: "his shoulder twitched, he's stepping, it's an overhand, dodge left" - using their mind as an elementary element of engagement. But why stop there? Perhaps the mind can be employed to function on a superior level; engaging a sense, a feeling - challenging their mind as they do their body.

To many beginners and the uninitiated, the concept of engendering an overriding philosophical idea and higher state of mental acuity can appear to be somehow impractical and unnecessary. Dissimilarly, in a "he does this; you do that" approach; one is always playing catch up, setting up a trap, or engaged in a volley.

If, however, your fighting style has an additional layer, pervading every thought and action before it is fully formed, you would be functioning in accordance with the Tao; and moving in harmony with opposing forces, as if receiving assurance and advanced information. This approach can seem unworkable and fanciful, but is utilized to varying degrees by pragmatists in many arenas. Confidence, attitude of victory, and visualizing outcomes are techniques of engaging the mind on another level to enhance physical actions. Wane Gretzky was not the fastest, toughest, nor biggest player; but undoubtedly was highly successful and a big scorer. He attributes much of his success to the fact that he could clearly see the puck going into the net. This statement exposes his underlying mindset and certitude of his actions.

The Tai-Chi mindset is one of harmonizing with all aspects of the engagement. Including, but not entirely limited to, aspects of mind and environment. Blending, instinctively employing Yin and Yang, accompanied with a serenity and in-depth understanding of the changing action, engages a mental aspect that transcends an "act and react" approach to surviving a violent encounter. This pervasive quality is a critical principal employed in Tai-Chi fighting.

There can be no fight without two. Like the electric current that can't flow without an end point, there is no injury from the punch, without a destination. I have purposely used this concept in practice several times. I avoided the attack by merely dancing around. Evasion, by using footwork, until they burnt out. I simply did not engage them. But, when two parties close, they enter into an agreement to see which Yang energy will dominate. Removing the point of physical contact changes this equation.

Of course, this approach is not unique nor exclusive. Aikido, Silat, and Systema share many aspects of this strategy, if not philosophy. The opponent is introduced to the sidewalk; they do it to themself. By blending and redirecting an opponent, a reverse of power and intent occurs. Similarly, an application of the pressure point curriculum provides a comparable example. Introducing a neurological stimulus causes the attacker to reverse their decision. The jolt of pain creates an opposite mindset without the need for serious debilitating injury. Opposite and reverse, Yin and Yang.

Recently, an entirely new class of the defensive arts has been crafted out of this concept. Total evasion. This class of art is coined after the word peace in a dead language. I respect the idea, and support its creation, if only as a counter-balance to all the violent and aggressive styles. There is a need for a completely passive approach to fighting as a safety valve and as a finger, pointing to a laudable idea. Also, this is a prime implementation of the concepts presented above. This approach, however, is inherently incomplete because it violates the apodictic principal of Yin and Yang. It is exclusively Yin. Not allowing any Yang. One would need to violate its principles to engage in Yang.

Without the ability to engage and reverse the attackers intent, one does not ride the wave of the event in a natural cycle, like the seasons. One relies solely upon the change of mind intent or the opponent's exhaustion. Simply put, this approach is completely one sided. Instead, one should have the personal decision to engage as needed with the opponent in the learning process, helping them change their mind, if required. Otherwise, there is no harmony and balance.

Total passivity is in counter-point to the position of tough guy fighters. They are exclusively Yang. Bigger, stronger, better conditioning. This too can be a casualty to its own excess. It is subaltern, because it is only one thing and lacks flexibility. In a storm, the oak is uprooted, the willow survives.

If you ball up and just lay there, you have just changed the situation to a different Yin/Yang equation. Attacker and victim. You have still provided a final point of arrival for the attack. A far better and effective strategy would be either evasive or equally tough. Either one of these approaches may work on any given day, but it is tactically superior to have the ability to adapt and choose, based upon the immediate situation. To implement the understanding of E-Ching theory; to flow with the storm and calm and not be restricted to either.

An explosive flurry by an enraged opponent will flare and burn itself out. By retreating to a Yin state and not engaging the attack, during its developmental stage, the Tai-Chi practitioner waits for the Yang to Yin transition. After the furry subsides and the Yang energy has diminished, one swells from Yin to Yang launching a powerful retaliation; capitalizing on the receding explosiveness - blending and pressing, reasserting dominance.

The nimble and wise military commander, familiar with teachings of Sun Tzsu, employs this concept on a macro scale. In Viet Nam, Westmorland was often criticized for his many strategic errors. And, while it is true, what's often said about him - he was still trying to fight world war II, his biggest failing was his unfamiliarity with eastern guerrilla tactics. This tactical failing proved his ineptness, and ultimately cost him his command.

The technologically inferior and under-resourced Viet Cong utilized ambush hit and run tactics; seldom directly engaging the superiorly equipped occidentals. They executed surprise assaults, then quickly and quietly melted back into the environment; in accordance with the principals of Yin and Yang. Frustrating and ultimately neutralizing the mighty American war machine.

While it's true the Americans won every major combat engagement of the war, in the end, after three million causalities and saturating the pristine country with dioxins; the powerful Yang energy of the foreign occupiers collapsed under the weight of domestic political intrigue. Overwhelmed by the Yin energy of the peace movement.

Massive geography changing events like the Mongol tide that conquered most of Asia, finally receded into a Yin state, after having carved a huge swath through most of their known world. Powerful civilizations ebb and flow in a predictable pattern. A flare of dominance and conquest, then diminishing and ultimately being absorbed into the annals of history. Rome, Greece, England. Power and privilege are great for individuals lucky enough to ride the wave of a given regime. Collectively, however, societies should be aware of history and the basic phenomenon of Yin and Yang.

The concept of Yin/Yang has been a governing principal of all aspects of existence in the East ever since the old philosopher delivered his treatise to the gatekeeper and disappeared. So called "soft style martial arts" rely heavily on this concept as a starting point; before tactics, strategy, or technique manifests. If we are to derive maximum advantage from martial arts training, especially if our approach is based upon fighting styles of the East, employing this fundamental precept should not be overlooked.

Tai-Chi Death Touch

Pressure point fighting, "push button" karate, and death touch have always been part of the attraction of the martial arts. Big, strong, tough guys dominate in every situation; unless someone possesses some secret ability to even things up. The movies usually present the protagonist as having superior skill. Faster hands, higher kicks, unorthodox, confounding techniques that leave an attacker exposed for the delivery of bone breaking power.

That scenario is the description of a tough, highly skilled, fighter whose years of training have given him a competitive advantage. This, however, is still just regular fighting. Somewhere inside everyone whoever walked into a dojo is the hope that knowledge of anatomical vital areas will allow you to neutralize anyone with a simple tap.

In yet another example of Yin and Yang, this is both true and untrue; with shades of gray. You may rest assured that there are most definitely vital area points that can kill or incapacitate an attacker. The bad news is they all don't always work on everyone and are not always easy to access. These areas and the techniques for taking advantage of them should be considered an adjunct skill, not a primary method of defense.

In certain instances, if the attackers' hands and attention are engaged, in a grab for example, a pressure point release can provide a dramatic discharge. However, in an actual fighting situation, one must possess the timing, skill and toughness to hang, in order to manufacture the proper circumstances to apply a pressure point technique.

The term pressure point has fallen into disfavor in recent years, reverting to traditional indigenous terms. Regardless of what you call them, there are areas of the body that are more sensitive than others. Nerve centers and unprotected internal organs can become damaged or produce incapacitation on which a competent fighter can capitalize.

The term Dim-Mak is most commonly translated as artery press, but also encompasses other deadly techniques, such as sealing the breath or vein. For example, if a wrestler snaps your neck or chokes you 'til you are dead, you have essentially become the recipient of a Dim-Mak technique.

This category of techniques include: interrupting the supply of blood or air, rupturing vital organs, damaging the brain, or producing subdural hematoma. These are all considered both dangerous and damaging. Various ruptures and/or other damaging methods may not create immediate or complete dysfunction, but may cause slow leaking damage; would be classified as a delayed death touch. The use of other autochthonous terms changes not the result. And, although sealing the breath, sealing the vein, and artery press are technically part of the Dim-Mak classification, they will not be addressed in this volume.

Like knife fighting, Dim-Mak killing techniques are mostly theoretical in nature. Mr. Parker said that Mr. Chow took him into the fields of the Parker ranch to snap the necks of cattle, because the vertebral structure is the same as on a human. I have to accept this story on his authority (although I would not be surprised to find out that he had), along with its accuracy; having never snapped anyone's neck myself.

Boxing and wrestling techniques are fully applied as taught, and not hypothetical in nature. One reason I have an affinity for Judo is because they use their methods fully, not theoretically, during randori. In contrast, untested, secret knowledge passed down and reinterpreted for generations can be easily corrupted. Empiricism is the bulwark of my teaching method. I can only genuinely pass along information that I can demonstrate and apply myself. For that reason, we will limit the discussion of vital area techniques to the less lethal and verifiable, usable applications.

Zygomatico Facial Nerve
(GB 1)

Supraorbital Nerve
(BL 2)

Infraorbital Nerve
(SI 18)

Facial Nerve
(TW 17)

Greater Occipital Nerve
(GB 20)

Great Aricular Nerve
(SI 17)

Transverse Cervical Nerve
(LI 18)

Brachial Plexus Nerves
(ST 12)

Mental Nerve
(CV 24)

Hypoglossal Nerve
(ST 5)

Cervical Nerve Roots
(ST 10-11)

Supraclavical Nerves
(KI 27)

Suprasternal Notch
(CV 22)

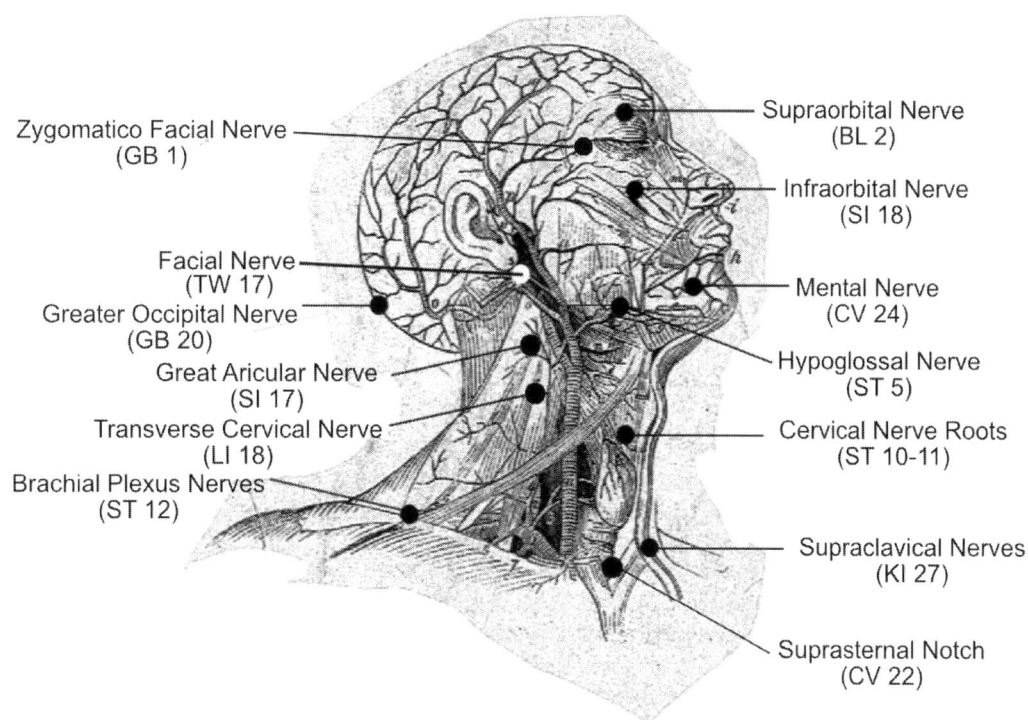

Nerve target / Acupoint approximation

The Chinese joint locking system Is called Chin-Na. Sankajo and kotegaeshi, although Japanese terms, are common joint manipulations one would find in Chin-Na. And likewise, Chin-Na implements many of the same general techniques of Dim-Mak, such as: artery press and sealing the breath or vein. In the West, one would recognize many of the other Chin-Na applications as: ankle-lock, arm-bar, or full nelson. In Chin-Na, one would find there also exists a fascinating study of aggravating the nervous system to elicit an immediate response. In reality, joint manipulation is just a specialized version of this same study. And it is within this study where we will concentrate our amended analysis of the human anatomy.

Almost all of the direct attacks to the nerves involve grinding, pressing, or stretching a nerve across a bone. There are anatomical locations where nerves are exposed, lying close to the surface, where they can be manipulated. Also, nerves may be found exiting a foramen, and can be pinched against the side of the hole. Likewise, there exist both press points and grind points. Some of these points only respond to one type of breach, others to both. Many of these points require a precision and manor of execution that can only be learned from a competent master. Others need only to be remembered.

The most common natural tool used to attack the nerves is the knuckles. This encompasses all knuckles, both individually and collectively, at all joints of the metacarpals and phalanges. Other common natural tools include, but is not limited to: the elbow, the ulnar stylus, the fingertips, or even the chin.

Finally, it must be stated that follow up strikes are essential. Vital area or not.

Because this is not a technical manual and because there is an unlimited array of information on the internet about this subject, I will avoid any detailed how to. This book will, however, generally reference a couple of my favorite applications, as the opportunity to access them occur frequently both in survival situations and the Tai-Chi form.

Since attacking internal structures is part of an internal art, we should first impart some simple, basic, and yet vital information. Exploding organs or stopping the heart are dangerous, unnecessary techniques. Interrupting intent and neutralizing aggression, with nerve attacks, is generally sufficient; if properly capitalized upon.

Being pinned down and pummeled in the face is a horrible experience, but one that can be survived. Broken nose, fractured jaw, blood, but if personal toughness is high and one is imbued with determination along with an indomitable will, one may be able to muster a counter. Employing Dim-Mak techniques that are immediate, attack baroreceptors, and/or directly interrupt the nervous system are typically sufficient to override any amount of obstinacy or tenacity.

Pressure point and vital area strikes can often be dismissed by many modern day fighters as superfluous or unnecessary. This is often done because these types of maneuvers are either disallowed or rendered relatively ineffective by mandatory gear.

One element common to all stand up styles is the very likely possibility that you can be lifted off the ground by a bigger, stronger man. This action immediately negates most leverage, back-up mass, or using the ground as a brace. Regardless of your technical approach, in this situation, concentrating retaliation to these targets may be one of the few viable options left. All techniques disallowed in modern sport fighting systems.

Alternatively, a release gained by a pressure point application could mean the difference between hospitalization and beers at the New Barge Inn.

This is in contrast to life or death encounters, extreme circumstances, or covert operatives; where knowledge and the skilled implementation of true Dim-Mak technique prove invaluable. Super karate power is real. If you don't possess it, then you are just training to be a fighter.

Applications

True Dim-Mak consists primarily of "sealing the breath" and vein techniques, as well as properly focused power strikes, capable of severely damaging internal structures. These applications necessitate instruction from a competent master, and therefore exceed the scope and intention of this book.

As stated in the title, this is a beginner's guide; and as such, this section will only offer a beginner's introduction into vital area incursions. Offered here are a variety of examples of pressure point release, and although technically not Dim-mak these illustrations are provided to acclimate the neophyte to the idea of neurological disruption. Also, to facilitate this elementary presentation, all examples are shown as responses to static grabs, as this situational context negates the high-level skill of intercepting an incoming projection.

To be sure, there are also strike points, combination methods, and power hits that can affect internal organs. But the techniques offered here are designed to only irritate afferent pathways near the surface by pressing, pinching, or grinding a nerve as it exits a foramen.

Finally, these techniques are purposely non-complex and need only be remembered for implementation. And, since these applications require no timing, body mechanics nor footwork, they serve as an excellent confidence builder and starting point to internalize and comprehend the equalizing power of martial art.

Rat's Claw

Key Elements

- Weapon: Rat's Claw

- Target: Suprasternal notch

- Location: Shelf of bone at top of sternum

- Attack: standing side headlock

- Execution: downward penetrating pressure

A properly executed side headlock is unbelievably painful, and instantly negates any type of counter. The term headlock is a misdirection as the real technique grinds the attacker's radius into the victim's jaw. Fortunately, most novices attempt to constrict the neck. Since the airway is in front, and there is another blood supply on the non-constricted side, valuable seconds may be procured to effect release.

While the attackers' hands are engaged, attempting to affect the lock, the defender reaches up with the right hand and locates the jugular notch at the top of the menubrium. Pressing down, impact fully, and continue with a constant pressure. This application ordinarily causes the attacker's knees to buckle. While temporally distracted with pain from the nerve attack, the defender pushes the attacker backward with a right heel palm to the sternum; while the left hand, which has remained at the small of the back, pushes forward. This application resolves into the customary Tai-Chi "carry the ball" posture. Proper weapon formation is extended index and middle fingers, with middle finger wrapping on top of the index finger, as reinforcement. Similar formation to two-finger sword but with fingers overlapping; thus more properly executed on a downward trajectory.

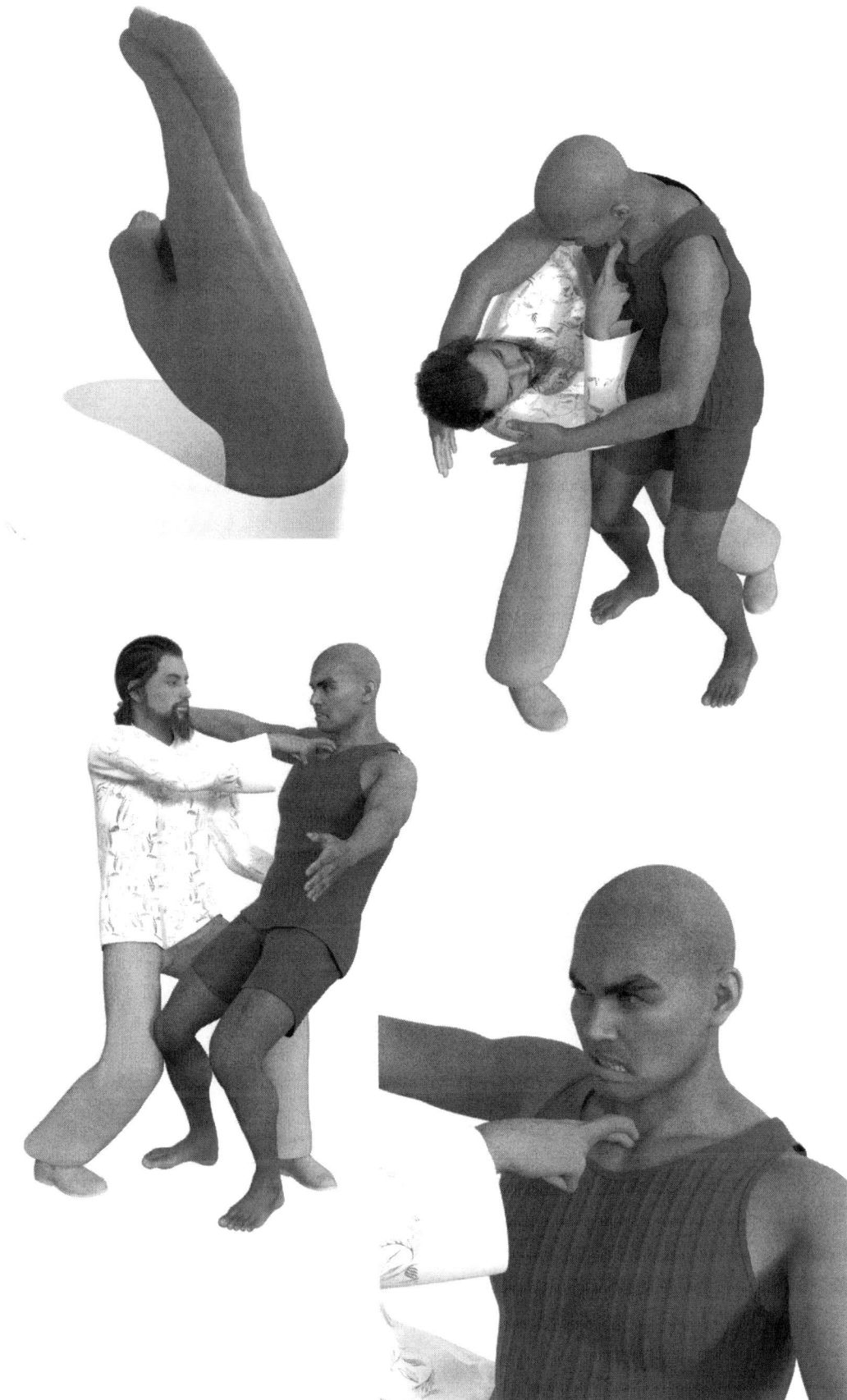

Eya of Phoenix - weapon, possible attack, response side view, response detail view

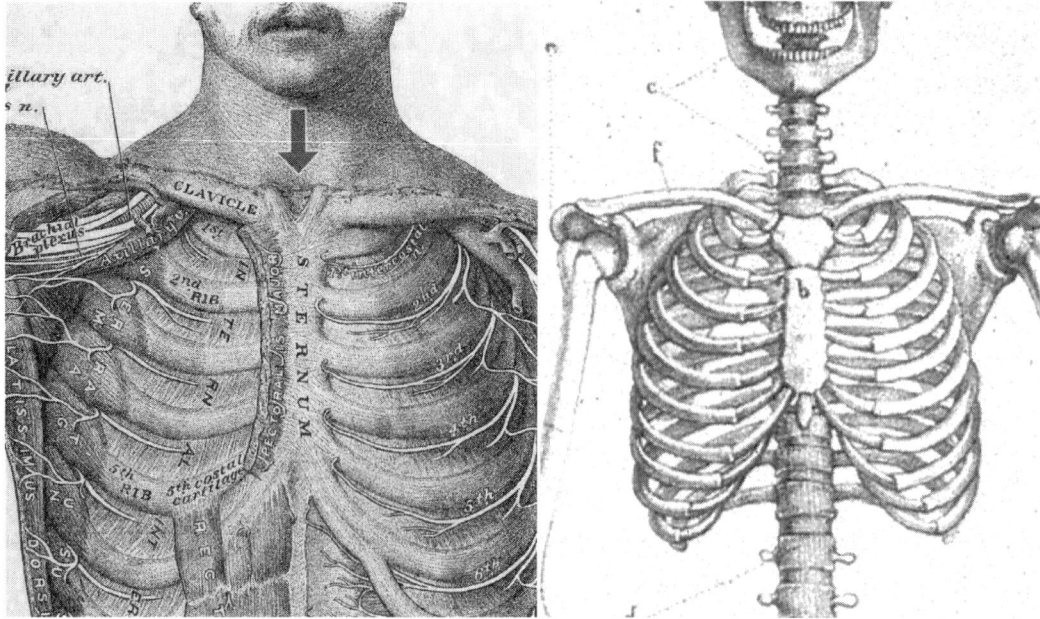

Rat's Claw - application point details

Eye of Pheonix

Key Elements

- Weapon: Eye of Phoenix

- Target: facial nerve

- Location: point of jaw under ear

- Attack: front bear hug - arms free

- Execution: grinding motion - towards center of attacker's neck

It is always preferable to interrupt an attack in its developmental stage. In this instance, before the contraction is fully executed. This technique, however, will provide release even if compression has already begun. The assailant will generally release and move back and to your left, allowing the defender to commence follow-up strikes at a 45 degree angle. This also provides the defender with a customary left fighting stance.

Most untrained attackers utilize a bear hug as a restraining hold, which allows for successful implementation of this technique. An experienced fighter will, however, execute an embrace with a ballistic explosiveness injuring the ribs and infusing a jolt of pain. This method is executed with the purpose of attempting to nullifying an effective counter. The defender should affect quickly prior to the full engagement of this crushing maneuver. Proper weapon formation is fist with index knuckle extended, reinforced by the thumb.

Eya of Phoenix - weapon, possible attack, response side view, response front view

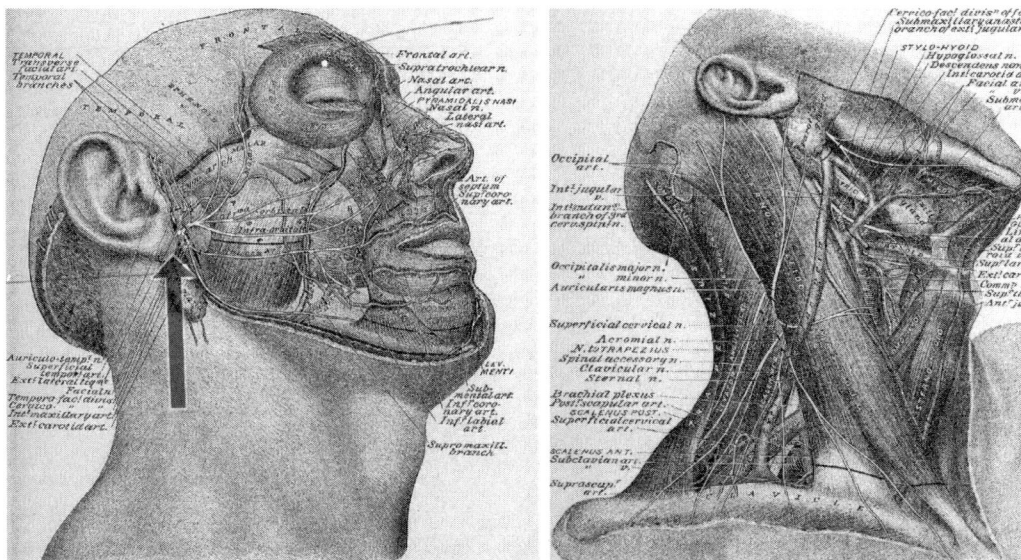

Eye of Phoenix - application point details

Two Finger Sword

AKA - Immortal Man Pointing the Way

Key Elements

- Weapon: Two Finger Sword

- Target: trachea

- Location: straight into throat

- Attack: front choke or two-hand lapel grab

- Execution: thrusting motion towards spine

As long as the attacker has not dug his thumbs into your trachea or other vulnerable structures; if you swiftly poke this hand formation directly into the trachea, a dramatic release is generally affected. When practicing with a partner, gently place fingers just above the jugular notch and press forward, slowly, and incrementally. During self-defense, a strong thrusting motion directly forward and toward the cervical vertebrae is recommended.

Ordinarily, all of the attackers' conscious controls are shut down and they will take one or two steps backward, allowing the defender to launch a flurry of strikes. In the illustration, the tough, determined attacker only reacts partially, prompting the close-range response of a knee, but most often this would resolve into a longer range kick. Proper weapon formation is extended index and middle fingers, each aiding the other in reinforcement of the whole. Similar formation to rat's claw but with fingers side-by-side; thus more properly executed on a forward trajectory.

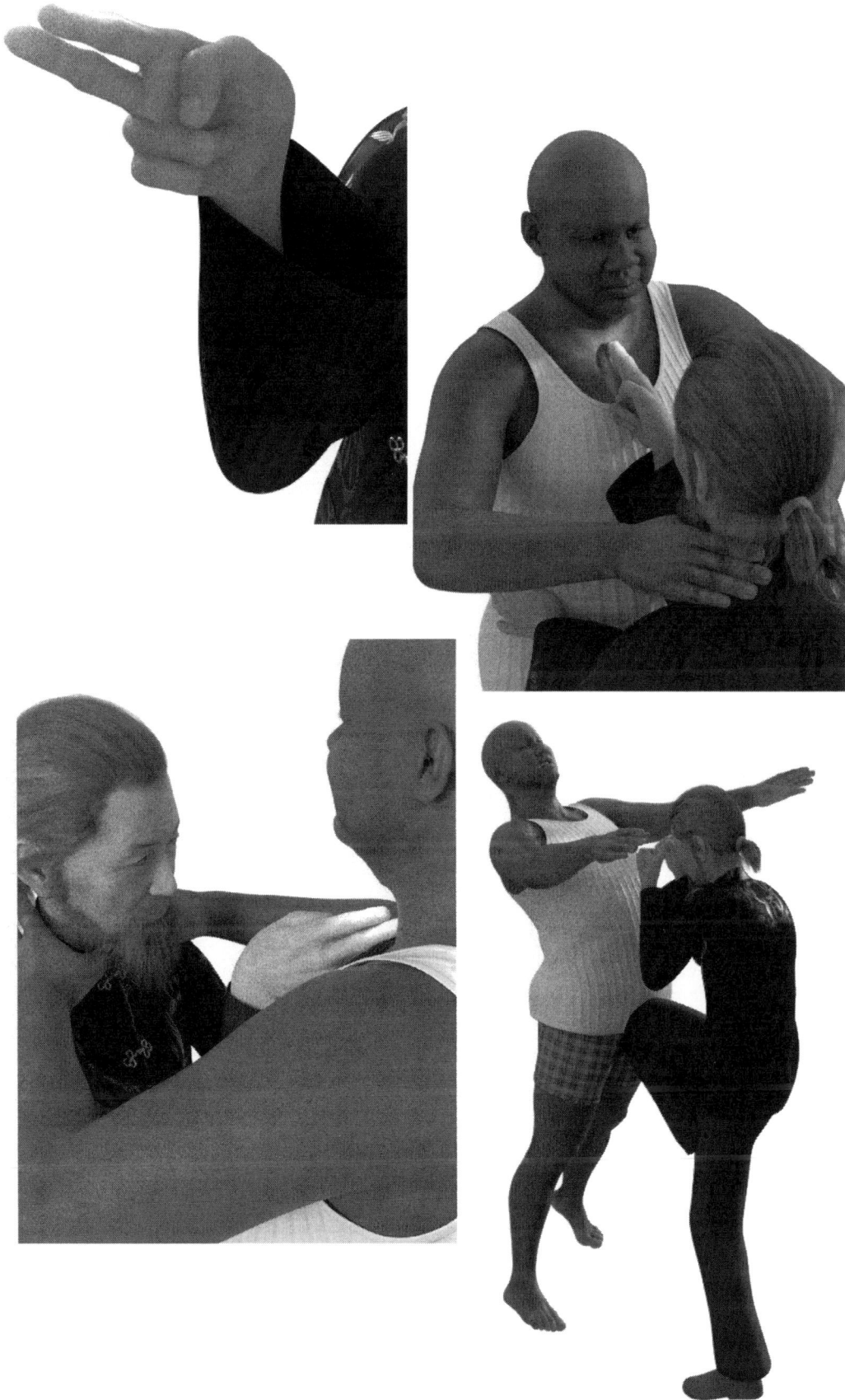

Eya of Phoenix - weapon, possible attack response, response side view, response wide view

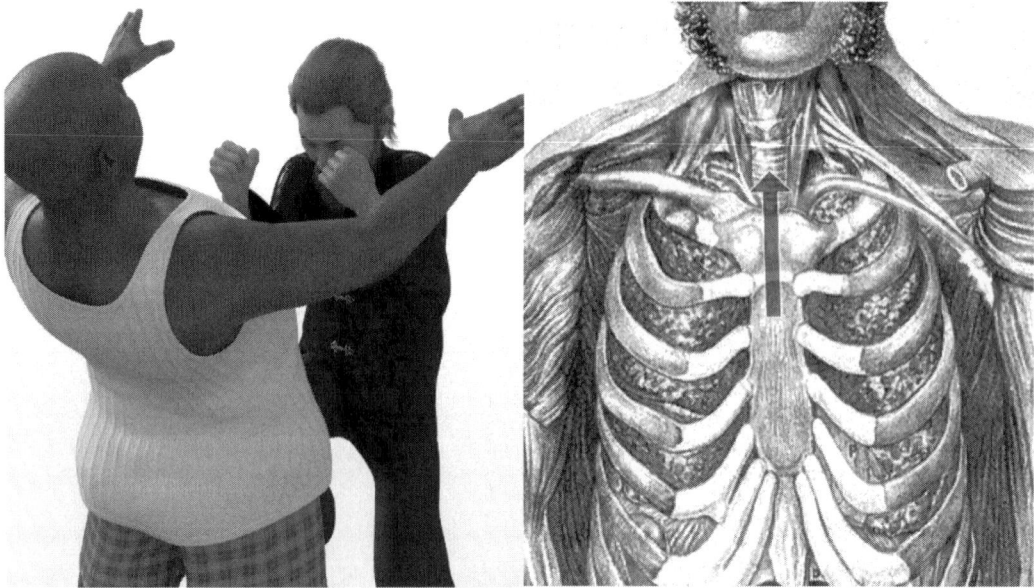

Two Finger Sword - response front view / application point detail

Tiger's Mouth

AKA - Suôgû

Key Elements

- WEAPON: Large tiger's Mouth

- TARGET: ST5 / hypoglossal nerve

- LOCATION: Mandible, mid-line between the chin and ear

- ATTACK: Standing embrace escaping guard, or varied

- EXECUTION: Thumbs dig in with authority, with an upward and outward pressure, while tips of thumbs impact the hypoglossal branch of the facial nerve, grinding against the jaw

As with all pressure point releases, follow up is crucial. Incapacitation is fleeting, Fingertips are poised for eye scoop. Controlling locks or finishing strikes are essential. There is also a small tiger's mouth which is not depicted in this example. Proper weapon formation is similar to trying to grab a basketball.

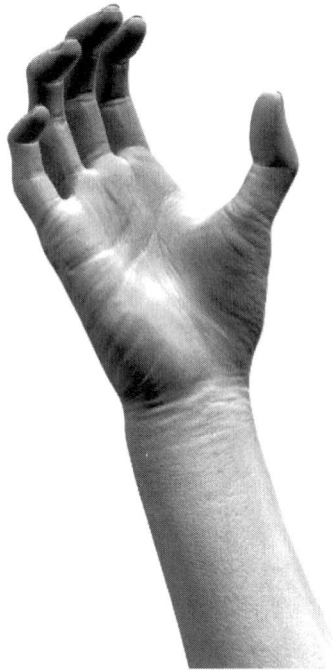

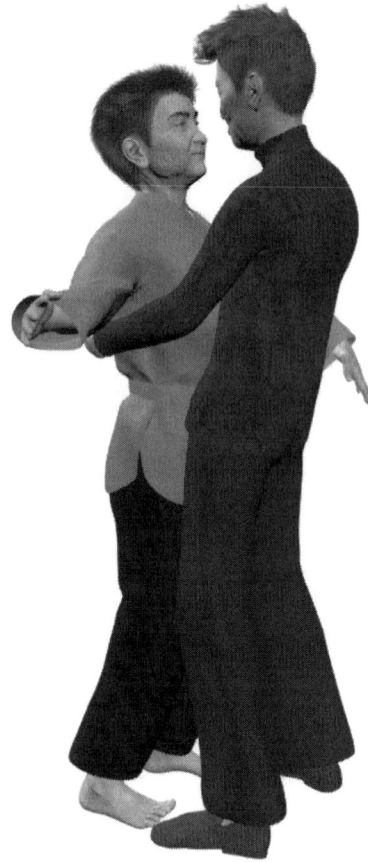

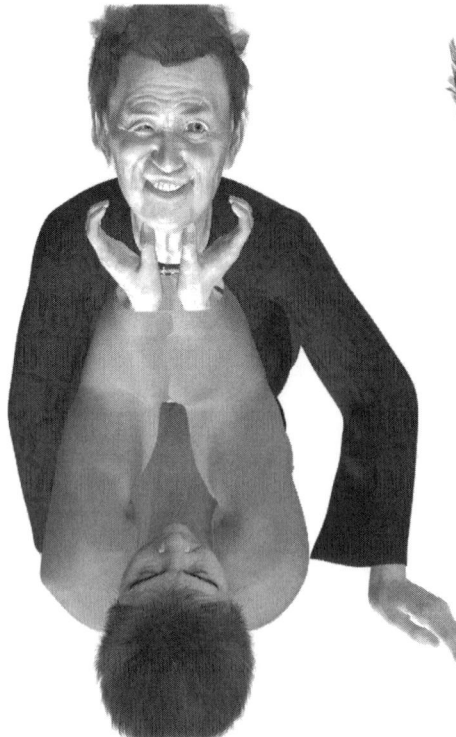

Tiger's mouth - weapon, possible attack, response top view, response side view

Tiger's Mouth - application point details

Dragon's Head

Key Elements

- Weapon: Dragon's Head

- TARGET: gb1- si18- tw17- st9/10

- LOCATION: as indicated in diagram

- ATTACK: double wrist grab, Front bear hug, punch

- EXECUTION: a precise, rigid instrument is employed to grind a nerve against a bone, usually as it exists a foramen

Relentless driving pressure, while twisting the weapon, produces the best results. Fa-Jin claw or palms are deliverable if launched immediately. Follow up strikes and throws are required. Proper weapon formation is fist with middle knuckle extended, reinforced by the thumb.

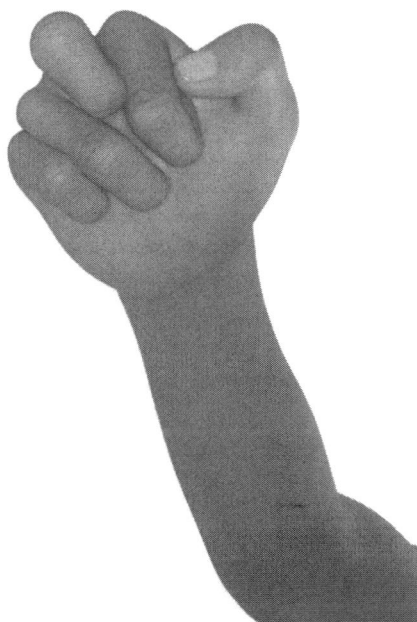

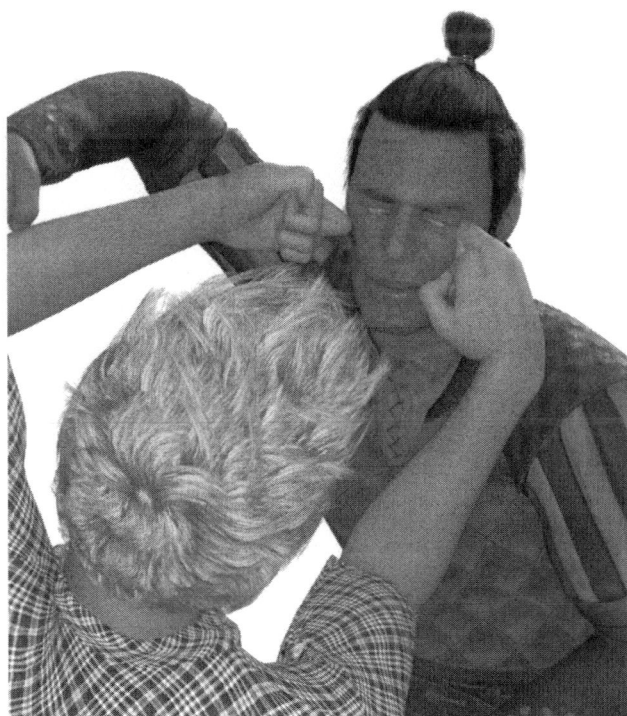

Dragon's Head - weapon, double response from rear, front, and inside pumch

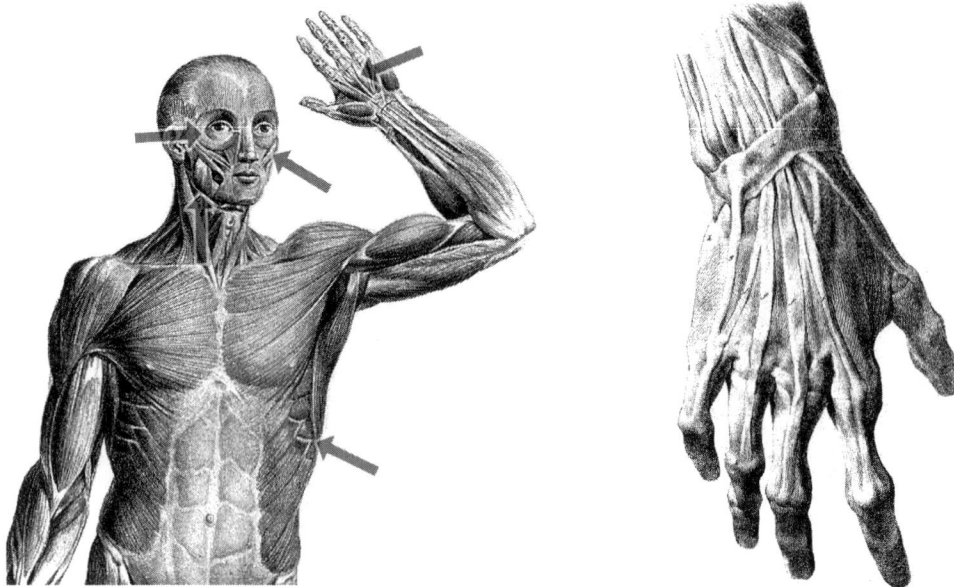

Dragon's Head - application point details

JOHN L. ZHANDOUJI

From our perspective in the modern world, it is tempting to deride many of the ideas of our forebears especially in the arenas of science and medicine. Since it is human nature to look askance at anything that is not fully understood, it is common practice to disparage the strategy and techniques of turn of the century European fisticuffs. But like many other misunderstood endeavors, the secret is revealed right there in the name. Bare knuckle boxing. Fighters of our era assume that these primitives simply hadn't figured out the mechanics or necessity of power punching. The turnabout is that, simplistically, they didn't need to.

As the name indicates, it was a style that principally featured vital area attacks with the points of the metacarpals. Many of these targets are the same pressure points outlined in the above illustrations (such as Si18 or Gb1). Empiricism had taught that these targets require no more than a moderate tap to produce a reaction. The fact that the weapon only needs to be retracted a few inches allows the fighter to continue to hide behind his hands. Throwing a massive overhand can leave one dangerously exposed, due to the waist rotation requirements of a torque punch. Many boxers capitalize on this defect, and time an exposed head, while his opponent is recovering their position. Padded gloves were developed to avoid injury to the hands. This made for a better spectator sport, but negated the finer points and consigned power as the only way to deliver injury. Because of this "innovation", knuckle strikes were lost forever.

To be sure, these early proponents of fight science would pummel their opponent with a barrage of power punches once entry was obtained. Modern boxers take to the extra padding of the gloves so well, because it is only natural for our species to slug with back-up mass and waist rotation. The classic bare knuckle guarding position however, so imperiously ridiculed by modern fighters was one component of a martial arts style that was very cognizant of vital area striking.

Tai-Chi Theory and Philosophy

Philosophical Implications of Tai-Chi Principles

The point of philosophy is to start with something so simple as not to seem worth stating, and to end with something so paradoxical that no one will believe it.

Bertrand Russell

Forward

Anyone who considers themself an authority on a subject has learned, sometimes quite painfully, that; "the more you know, the less you know." The more expertise one acquires, the more questions arise. Finally, one becomes patently aware of just how much they still have left to learn. I must admit, that like the innumerable aspirants before me, I have fallen prey to this paradox. And, despite acquiring this revelatory truth, I have persevered.

The original goal of this book was to answer basic questions for the beginner, to clear up some misconceptions held by even tenured practitioners, and finally to impart revelations from my own observations. In short, to eliminate confusion and provide elucidation. In years past, I pledged that if I were ever to write a Tai-Chi book, it would be an academic work; avoiding an abundance of pictures of techniques, and instead rely upon detailed instructions on execution and limited to pertinent information. I promised myself that I would purposely avoid the insolence of surreptitiously increasing page count that would result from illustrating a step-by-step execution of the form. I would consciously eliminate the repetition that one could easily find from other authors on this subject.

My initial hope was for this book to be voluminous. Like all authors, I wanted it to be the definitive work on the subject. But as I reached the later chapters, I began to suspect that I may have told my story; or the Tai-Chi portion anyway - in far fewer words than I had imagined. This topic is daunting; because it is vast. Still, I dreamed of sparking transformation. And, while there may be many minutiae, the subject can be formulated in a few simple truths. The difficulty about truth is, it too often is subjective. Although it would seem that in any definitive work, there would be only one truth; "truth" is subject to interpretation. For now, truth requires a more malleable definition.

We are deceived into believing that truth is the ultimate binary rubric - either on or off: true or false. Here again, the pliant, bulging visage of Yin and Yang is instructive for the comprehensive understanding of such a fiat. In fact, there are different types of truths. There is personal truth, and objective truth. Most convictions are personal truths. Someone may have a religious conviction that is believed with full confidence: but, this is still only a personal truth. Gravity is an objective truth: all objects fall at the same rate and is universal for everyone.

This entire effort is an expression of personal truth. As presented by me: even the science is subjective; filtered through the lens of one person's experience and understanding. This however (Yin/Yang) turns out to be a grand example of objective truth. One that can be comically and euphemistically compared to the Born rule: where probability density is basically amplitude squared. But, to many readers this theoretical equation may mean little to nothing. So, let's look at this theory from a more conversational and intelligible point of view. So, while there are trillions of energy points in multiple dimensions, there is still only one wave function; and that is the wave function of the entire universe.

I must make this final observation about truth. Personal truth and objective truth are not necessarily mutually exclusive.

For example: I can make an allusion to the dysfunction and/or incompetence present in bureaucratic or bloated organizations. This may arise because I was a personal witness to incompetence and a magnitude of dysfunction present in these departments and agencies. This fact provides me with a personal truth; in contrast to the general, objective truth. The fact that this is a personal truth is unaffected by the fact that this is also an objective truth.

L'INSTANT CRITIQUE

It is often said in the martial arts, that once you accept an instructor, full acquiescence must be rendered. One must accept the instructor's truth. The same could be hoped for by authors of manuals such as this. To a certain extent, the reader must trust in the author's integrity. Personally, I will absolutely avoid promoting or postulating methods unless verifiable and proven. And, conjecture, speculation, or opinion will be stated as such.

With this arises a difficulty. The problem is: while principals of physics can mostly be verified, in the laboratory of one's own processes, many of these mechanisms can only be realized by one empirically and experientially. In contrast, inquiry into realms arcane, and things enigmatic can get very perplexing. Many times information of this category cannot be verified in a traditional sense and must be authenticated on a more personal level.

Proper information begets realization. The product of this achievement is an individual's personal truth. Full awareness becomes a functional form of enlightenment. In other words, it has become the whole truth and nothing but.

One's personal illumination is a direct product of one's personal odyssey. I can only hope that the information presented in this manual can play a part on your personal journey to this enlightenment - even if it is only a small one. The ideas, formulas, and procedures contained within this book, although unique to one perspective, have the ability of generating universality. If that arises, then both you and I can grow together: Yin and Yang. Overcoming the, "I explain, and you accept" narrative.

As the author, one of my most difficult tasks during the writing of this book was to not pontificate. I whole-heatedly believe that this oft disingenuous and typically haughty writing methodology can be a major flaw in any endeavor of this nature.

The original intention of this book's format was to present the information in a straightforward manner. The stated purpose, after all, was to answer common questions that I knew most people want answered. The initial layout was to title each chapter after one of these areas of inquiry, where subjects in the titles were obvious. Titles, such as: Speed, Internal Power, Energy Projection, and Energy Transfer. Yet as the project progressed, a transforming understanding was revealed. As it turns out, this is not the best approach at all.

A long-standing conundrum about information transfer has always been (to not only me, but I'm sure most everyone), "Why did they disperse information, seemingly randomly, throughout the system? Why not present the foundational truths in an orderly fashion? Why the obtuse, occult, mysterious egg hunt?" As I worked with the material I developed, a new revelation surfaced. In yet another example of the genius of past masters, the relevance of opaque formulation began to appear to me from the mist.

It turns out, that this not only is the best way, it is the only way. The Yin/Yang of it is, "only those who deserve it should get it, and only those who work hard to get it deserve it." Many teachers have tried to openly reveal secrets, only to have it fly over the heads of addlepates. Also, many "secrets" are so simple, that once revealed, are commonly dismissed by pilgarlics incapable of recognizing gold when they see it. "Good seed must fall on fertile ground." I too have learned this very difficult lesson. Despite the very best of intentions, the surest method of disseminating information of this type is the time-honored way; obfuscation.

My chosen method for compelling study and contemplation is to utilize challenging vocabulary. This is done in hopes that the reader will slow down and digest content, thus causing reflection on germane topics. There is pertinent information contained in this volume, much of it useful, some of it even correct. But it is only intended for receptive vessels. And, as this is in itself a type of natural selection, only those who resonate will be willing to connect the dots.

Despite the titular inference, this work is far from complete. Instead, it is intended more as a guide. The chapters are calculatingly concise; and are meant to serve more as signposts to trigger further inquiry.

And, because the curriculum is so vast, a detailed examination of each topic would be multitudinous. The format is more akin to expanded bullet points. The chapters purposely provide the reader with just enough information to launch a deeper dive into other, more detailed resources. But, no one likes a dry read. So, there are gelastic aspects that punctuate the otherwise desiccated discourse.

The simple truths contained in Tai-Chi, Chi-Kung, and even complexities like quantum field theory, are not necessarily mysterious. Rather, if properly understood, they are part of the landscape of the world in which we live. Just the way things fit together: just the way things work.

Although these patterns were identified through stringent scientific inquiry, they were also revealed by aware adepts: albeit though different paths. Similar to other areas of human inquiry. Ones that elicit questions, like: Did we discover math, or did we invent it?

Lastly, I would be tactically remiss if I didn't preemptively anticipate personal attack. Some may take exception with my content and presentation. And, while prostitution may be the oldest profession; the oldest avocation is undoubtedly critic. In more civilized times, appraisal came from a position of esteem or some recognized authority in a field. Or, someone able to rise through the tortuous gauntlet of journalism. Now, anyone with a computer, a bag of Cheetos, and energized by a power beverage can level acerbic commentary to the world from their mother's basement.

In modern times, a new type of predatory animal has evolved. The advent of Facebook, podcasts, and self-publishing has fashioned a new breed of critic: a snarky, vitriolic class of trolls spawned by these new technologies. I anticipate stringent review from arrogant martial artists and followers of new age philosophy gurus. The latter are people who have invested years and thousands of dollars subscribing under the tutelage of self-styled sages. Individuals who post profound, high-sounding aphorisms on the internet. And yet, in their personal lives, remain highly opinionated and judgmental.

I surmise that this type of person will find nothing between these pages. Why would they, they already have all the answers. But, if they were sincerely fully knowledgeable, imperious contempt would hardly be a defining trait. I would only ask this simple question: "Do they really know it all?"

The French have a saying… "Tout comprendre, c'est pardonner" - "To know all, is to forgive all."

Love is the currency of enlightenment, and the most obvious attribute of the true seeker. I intrinsically suspect that one day love may be identified as a type of dark energy. The ubiquitous substance that is the fabric of the universe. Until then, we must try and learn from each other and trust that this ambrosia is our spiritual endowment. Herein, I have tried to disseminate the most germane motifs. If you find in this book only one item previously unknown, reading this may have proved worthwhile. As a hedge against this probability, included are some tall tales and iconoclastic burlesque. I offer this in profound humility to fellow travelers.

Monoceros

Ever since Democritus halved the apple, scientists have been disassembling nature, dividing things into smaller parts, and dissecting into the microscopic. In order to fuel the insatiable desire to know what everything is made of, man has developed equipment to examine the unseen world. When even advanced instruments failed to disclose life's ultimate reality. Mathematical equations were developed to postulate the content of subatomic structures.

This, of course, has served its original purpose; but while unintended and in a backhanded way, has also provided mystic sojourners with a degree of comfort and understanding regarding a nagging fundamental question. That of course would be, how did the universe come to be?

To unravel this question, it first becomes necessary to elaborate on the methods used for examining the minutia of the cosmos. And this brings about yet another fundamental understanding: gaining a grasp of just how small is small.

An electron is three billionths of a meter. It is also one thousand times smaller than a quark. A neutron is two femtometers wide. A femtometer is, brace for it... one millionth of a billionth of a meter. A quark is two thousand times smaller than a proton, which is, in case you're keeping score, four hundred and thirty million, billionths of a meter. Just to compare this to something we're all more familiar with, a quark is sixty thousand times smaller than a hydrogen atom. In case you haven't handled any hydrogen atoms lately, that is two trillion, four hundred billion times smaller than a grain of sand.

I mention all these facts to set the stage for advancing a proposition that asks: just how small can anything get? Is there a limit to definable miniaturization? Where does lawful limits draw the line between a tangible reality and an event, or a phenomenon? What is a thing, and what is an apparition?

This proposition brings about the following questions: how small must something be before it ceases to exist? Or, due to cosmic laws, ultimately converts into something else? Is there an alteration point where a thing ceases to be a thing? When does an article that possesses mass or energy lose so much of its defining essence, that it is reduced until it not virtually, but actually disappears.

This thing, once possessed of vitality, experiences less and less virtuality and reaches a cosmic tipping point in accordance with some as yet unrealized cosmic law. The property must then undergo ultimate transformation.

I propose that at that critical point, when whatever is an infinitesimal fraction of a yoctometer, the essentia must exit the tangible and enter the realm of pure thought or emotion.

In all of recorded history, all scientific experimentation, and empirical observation by sentient beings, has noted that everything in heaven and earth experiences an arbor of transformation; a breaking point. An apex where quiddity has reached maxim saturation and simply cannot sustain status quo, and at this point must assuredly return back to its ultimate source.

At this stage in my premise, any attempt at metaphor would prove to be grossly inadequate. Regardless, in an effort to provide further clarification, I will make an admittedly incomplete and fruitless attempt.

An acorn is not an oak tree. It is a seed with the fundamental essence of a tree. The seed germinates and becomes a sprout. Still not a tree. The sprout grows somewhat to transform into a sapling. The beginnings of a tree. Further in its life cycle it finally becomes the grand oak tree. But ultimately, the tree dies and begins to rot. At some time there is a literal tipping point, where the tree must ultimately fall, and completely decompose; returning to its source.

A zygote is not a human. It contains the essence to become a human. After fertilization an embryo forms. Only the beginnings of a human. The mother can only become so pregnant before a transformation must take place. An infant is born. An undeveloped human comes into existence. This human grows and matures to a point where it must transform again. It dies and returns back to its source. Often after starting the cycle again with another human.

Everything you see, create, and know will come to an end. Every work of art, literature, creation, animal, or environment has a beginning and at some point will cease to exist. Ultimately returning to its source. In five billion years the sun will supernova destroying everything in its sphere of influence. One billion degrees will most assuredly bring about transformation all the way down to the quantum scale.

Every element on the periodic table has a half-life. That is the amount of time any quantity of "stuff" is reduced by half. This does not mean that it stops transforming, just the amount of time for one half of it to transmute. Some elements, such as hydrogen-7 have very short half-lives, others, such as tellurium, have very long half-lives. Regardless, every element known to man has a half-life. Where do these elements go? Back to its source. And given enough time, will ultimately degrade until there is nothing less.

To emphasize the point, that as a thing becomes less and less, if it is to retain any of its "thingness" it must transform into a non-tangible realm. Now, with the precept of Yin and Yang, the opposite and reverse is not only an arguable possibility, it is a foregone conclusion that thought and emotion are the progenitors of matter. To bolster this hypothesis, even the Upanishads state that all creation is just a dream in the mind of God.

To state that the universe simply "always was" or was "the will of God" is steeped in ambiguity and is, to many, unsatisfying. To curious, circumspect creatures who deserve at least, some kind of formulaic solution; extended here is an idea of the steps in the process. A process that may or may not correct or "fill in the blanks". Never the less, it at least begins a dialog.

Many scientists may certainly argue that this idea of transformation from incorporeal thought to tangible reality is absurd and unproven. Yet many speculations, such as those framed at the beginning of the previous essay, display a time lag between conception of hypothesis and proof of reality. I believe the premise proposed in this essay falls prey to this unfortunate certainty.

When mainline spiritual traditions maintained that God willed the universe into existence, or spoke the word (vibration) and matter became manifest. This exposition is accepted as truth by many, yet the actual mechanics of the process is declared a mystery. And, since we advance theories about everything else under creation, it seems reasonable to present some idea of how that process might actually take place.

If we can, without question, accept smaller and smaller units until reality disappears, then just possibly (Yin/Yang) creation occurred the other way around; manifesting from a realm of thought and emotion into what we call reality. Qualities of spirit that became so strong they simply could no longer be contained and erupted forth in a transformation from a realm of mind to one of a tangible presence.

This paroxysm of transformation is well established in other sciences, it is only a mild expansion of thought to entertain the possibility of a cosmic level tipping point. Where religious postulation is ambiguously vague about actual process, logic calls us to look to science for answers, where we receive only silence and blank expressions.

The possibility, of course, exists that religion has been quite clear and specific all the while. That the process of creation and the explanation of spoken word, or the dream of God, is the full explanation.

To date, science has only been able to offer us a partial explanation. Where a theory like the big bang tells us how the universe began, it offers us no assumptions as to why. Or, what was the originating impetus? And, makes no speculation of what came before.

An oft overlooked fact about the big bang theory is that it was not the beginning of the universe. In fact, there was a period of time where bound up in the fabric of space itself, was all of the potential that would ultimately become the totality of the matter and other energies present today. Scientists call this time the cosmic inflation.

There is now much doubt regarding a critical part of this theory. That there existed a singularity or a hot dense state that was the nexus of all that we know. This has remained the biggest single misconception about the updated theory. Where the big bang did happen, it appears it did not happen the way we were originally led to believe. The idea now presented is that space, in its entirety, began expanding everywhere. In other words, there was no place that was not the big bang. This event, is more accurately thought of not as an explosion into space, but rather an explosion of space.

Now, there is an insistence that the phenomenon of cosmological red shift supposedly conclusively proves this latest theory. This is predicated upon the fact that an expanding universe stretches light. But, in the not so distant past from this updated observation, they were equally emphatic that all matter was once condensed into a gravitational singularity. And at one time, that the earth was the center of the solar system.

Fields of inquiry alter positions as knowledge base grows, and technologies progress as systems advance. To ask, how the universe began is really a question of both science and religion. Just as the two halves of the Tai-Chi symbol swirl together to produce one complete whole; this issue, more than any other, may require the Yin/Yang approach to reach any satisfactory conclusion.

Most physicists demure when a non-scientist equates any aspect of physics with spirit. Today it is typically considered naive, stupid, or just intellectually blasphemous to compare speculation with numbers, with speculation of the heart. However, it is fair to ask how valid are calculations made regarding measurements of things too small to ever be seen.

One final word on math equations advanced to simulate measurements: How small can something get before it disappears? As stated above, a femtometer is one millionth of a billionth of a meter. A yoctometer is one billionth of a femtometer. All this is dwarfed by a measurement known as a Planck length. The Plank length is equal to $1.616255(18) \times 10^{-35}$m. This suggests that space-time becomes quantum foam at the Planck scale. If a grain of sand were inflated to the size of the observable universe, a Planck length would be the size of an actual grain of sand.

In conclusion, the process of transformation is a critical aspect of five element theory. The chapter called Phases expands upon and highlights this fundamental principle in detail. The Tai-Chi symbol offers not only a visual representation, but also a road map to such transformation. Contained within the circle, undefined energies diminish, then reemerge. Cycling: a perpetual self-contained eternal system, returning upon itself to begin again.

Phases

It might seem curious, that in a book about a Chinese art, there is very little focus on Chinese tradition or ideas. This is by design. This is a complete book on Tai-Chi and is implemented for practitioners of all levels and accomplishments, but also makes copious accommodations for the Western neophyte. For the person uninitiated in Eastern philosophy and attitude, but saturated with the dogma of more modern cause and effect training.

The fighting strategies and healing modalities in Neidan, as developed in ancient China, are heavily influenced by a concept of nature, born in a culture immersed in five element theory. There will be a brief tutorial on the subject presented here. But, this is only for reference.

As in many of the convoluted, labyrinthine eastern notions; the superficial principals are not really the point. This is because mastery of the art is not based on specifics. A focus on hard and fast rules, or even things, is kind of a dodge. A useful understanding of nebulous ambiguity is more illuminating than adhering to rigid concepts and fixed points in place or time. The adept is more concerned with process.

When one studies a five element diagram, it is understandable to assume that one's focus is on the elements themselves; and give great consideration to the specific aspects of each designation. Ah...yes...Fire is hot. But right up front, the emphasis is on process. Fire consumes Wood. Earth creates Metal. The familiar zen adage; "Don't mistake the finger pointing at the moon, for the moon", is illustrative here.

The goal of understanding this is to realize that there is no definitive description or fixed point of anything. Everything is in flux. Everything is morphing between states, on its way to becoming something else. The ghost of the movement, the space between the notes.

The event is the process. The consequence of transformation. Not the Metal or the Wood, but the transfiguration as it shifts and metamorphosizes. A continuing process of renewal.

Internalizing this can leave one with the feeling of trying to cross a river by walking on balloons. Nothing is fixed, everything is wavy, transforming, a pulse in a field....As Lao Tzu rightly observed....Changing.

Things that seem definitive...I am married, I am a carpenter; are not static situations. A marriage is an ever evolving chess game of tactics and accommodation. Carpentry is the epitome of transformation. The whole craft transforms wood into objects. Someone is 31 years 4 months 15 days 9 hours 26 minutes and 53 seconds old. Not anymore. They are now 31 years 4 months 15 days 9 hours 26 minutes and 53 seconds, plus some. It is a convenience to say 31 years. But, age changes every moment. And, the day before one turns 32, they are more 32 than 31, yet they will refer to them-self as 31. Also, one may not always be a carpenter or forever be married.

FIVE ELEMENTS
CYCLES OF GENERATION AND CONTROL

Creation Cycle (Sheng)
Overacting Cycle (Cheng)
Destruction Cycle (Ke)
Insulting Cycle (Wu)

+SI +TH
FIRE
Exploding (Pao)
-HT -PC

+GB
WOOD
Crushing (Beng)
-LV

+ST
EARTH
Crossing (Heng)
-SP

+UB
WATER
Drilling (Zuan)
-KD

+LI
METAL
Splitting (Pi)
-LU

Create / Overacts / Destroys / Insults / Creates / Overacts

CYCLES OF IMBALANCE

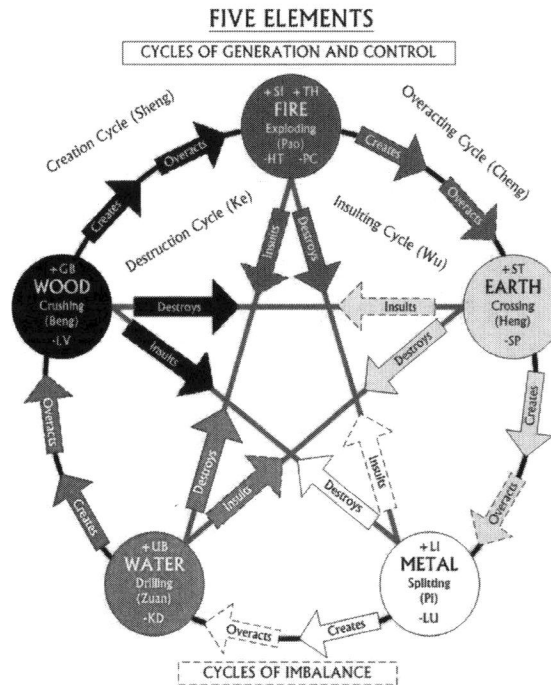

Tai-Chi as a fighting style concentrates the focus on riding the change, not directing a strike to a particular static point (although this does occur, frequently, as an illustration of the Yin/Yang of opposites and reverses); instead of commanding time and dominating space by enacting a plan (i.e. back-knuckle to the face, and when he lifts his hands to block, I will then execute my real attack; the reverse punch!).

This planned approach certainly works and is used all the time with varying results (because he's planning too). Tai-Chi tactics eliminate half the variables, by not imposing a outcome or prediction on an elastic situation. Riding like a surfer on a wave, will ultimately allow you lead the opponent into emptiness. There is a common saying in Tai-Chi fighting: "He does thus and so, and I wait for a change."

That is the proper application of Wuxing theory. We work the change. Many fighters know...hit him on the switch. When sucker punching, you don't say: "I'm going to put you in the hospital"; you say: "I'm going t...", then hit. Bruce Lee knew from his study of Wing-Chun that executing on the half-beat is advantageous to victory.

If our appreciation of all interactions in life displayed an awareness of this understanding, we would experience far less pain. If you lose your career, it's not the end of the world; you're transforming into something else. Attacking the boss or drinking yourself into ill health is focusing on a fixed point in time, which results in negative consequences. The master of Tao rides the change into the next phase.

This is why the Chinese glyph for crisis also signifies opportunity. The transitional phase is where opportunity exits. Making a deep study of five element theory is a bit of a ruse and a lesson in misdirection. The sailor relies upon a port or a lodestar, but continues his journey. The thing to be learned is not to be seduced by the deceptive importance of the Earth or Fire element. They are both constantly transforming. Give them their due, as you jump from one to another, but control your trajectory during the jump. Be savvy. It's all about process.

Time

Time and gravity are inexorably linked. Both are dynamic, mobile, curved, unified. As postulated in the concept of Tao, part of a network of causality. Causality is a fundamental aspect of time. Our experience of the flow of time is a derivative of brain function. Like proprioception, a way to keep us oriented in the world.

The definition of time is now more abstract than ever, and more malleable than is readily apparent. To declare that time doesn't exist, is of course an absurdity on its face. The practically minded will most certainly tell us that time exists. But before we try to build an alternate case, let's examine the time-gravity interaction, and build a possible platform for understanding uncertain realities and our equally uncertain perceptions. A position that seems contrary to both history and one's personal experience, has some pretty astute supporters. One of which said:

THE DISTINCTION BETWEEN PAST, PRESENT, AND FUTURE IS ONLY A STUBBORN PERSISTENT ILLUSION.
ALBERT EINSTEIN

Einstein, because of his understanding of relativity, believed time existed as a series of individual moments, like frames on a movie real. They exist permanently and all at once on the reel, but are perceived as passing because of the manner in which they are shown to us. Time is an illusion the mind creates to aid our sense of temporal presence. Neurons in the brain create a virtual perception of past and future.

Time slows down or speeds up because of the relativistic way mass warps space and time. An observer in strong gravity, such as Earth's, experiences time running normally, in relation to a weaker gravity where time runs more slowly. Mass warps the fabric of time - it's relative. In the famous twin's paradox, time passes differently for someone traveling at the speed of light relative to someone earthbound. Even two persons on this planet experience "now" at different times. Someone atop mount Everest experiences "now" fifteen billionths of a nanosecond before someone at sea level. This means that "now" is not homogeneous, it is warped by mass. Again, it's relative. Also, there is strong opinion to support the idea that time moves differently for different people, and may also be etched in the fabric of the universe.

Akasha is a Sanskrit word referring to a celestial storehouse of records. Adepts are able to access information from this cosmic library by yogic technique. An analogue of this concept would be a phonograph record. The music is encoded in the groves of the vinyl. It exists as a whole, but is experienced depending where one places the needle.

Look at differently, film on a movie reel is a record of a slice of time, each frame can be viewed independently, while temporally collectively held on the reel. Similarly, an image, say a ball, can seemingly move from left to right as one flips the pages of a book; but could also be made to progress backwards, perceiving the flow in a reverse direction; or stopped, allowing examination of each individual page.

This may seem banausic, but the idea of time being like a flip-book is not necessarily a far out or even new idea. The Sanskrit tradition conceives of a storehouse of information. A record of every thought, emotion, and event - of each individual person. Time, then, is a series of unfolding moments. A series of snapshots lined up to see every event as it has or will happen. But, no individual frame contains time.

Our brains perceive these individual frames as strung together and interpreted as the passing of time, like a novel. And, just like the other analogies, it contains the entire story, where one can move to any page, at any time; or read the pages sequentially. We just so happen to be wired to comprehend time as a flow. Our brains are time machines.

All moments exist simultaneously - past, present, and future; which is why religious traditions commonly assert that it is written. God knew your fate before you were born. Or, the creator chose you before time began. It is tractable to dismiss these statements as beyond our ken. But, for modern people who may wonder how this is possible; here is an answer. It seems mysterious to us because of the way our brains recon time. Time is not the same for everyone or every entity. This can be expressed simply through relativity or dysfunctions of perceptions, such as: dizziness, disoriented, lost, obscured sense of direction, and/or an occluded time sense.

Space and time are both fluid and affected by gravity and velocity. But from our perception, they are emergent properties. And, like the movie film, they are both real and illusory. General relativity works in the large-scale classical world, but quantum mechanics is needed to explain phenomenon on the quantum scale (Yin/Yang). And, each is governed by networks of relationships of causality. Within our range of certainty, space and time are not rigid, but rather react to the presence of matter. Furthermore, time does not degrade, and functions wholly outside the second law of thermodynamics, in the same way that it is believed that light exists outside of time.

The Copenhagen interpretation, for example, provides for a nondeterministic universe. In this postulation, time exists in an undefined state until observed, at which point wave function collapses into a defined state, but only as far as the Heisenberg uncertainty principal allows.

Physicists have many diverse ideas regarding this phenomenon, and are at no loss for ways that try to explain it. This includes the Von Nyoman interpretation, many worlds theory, and pilot wave theory; all of which imply a tangled network of sub-realities. These theories of a labyrinth web also bear a coincidental affinity with the Taoist concept of a systematic matrix, in which all things are interconnected. This is also in accordance with the idea that East and West are only using different cultural references to describe the same phenomenon. Indeed, both agree on a universal fabric of space-time, and that this network is malleable and changing - as Lao Tzu rightly observed.

A systematic review of diverse opinion would cause any investigator to conclude that a precise definition time is far from a settled question. Like many of the other unresolved inconsistencies of physics that have been amply noted in this book, we now have to objectively conclude that even the mighty western scientific machine is also lacking in this regard. Even modern and objective mathematicians are no more certain than the observations of the ancient philosophers. And, since practicality is the canon of this book, it is most expedient to eliminate semantics and dogma, and instead focus on a propitious weltanschauung.

To maintain proprioception, walk upright, and maneuver within the dominion of gravity, required the development of spatial awareness. Time sense, like kinesthesia, is a brain function that evolved, so that the organism could orient itself with its surroundings. Likewise, it was only precipitous and utilitarian to excogitate a sense that would prove serviceable for an emergent species. To count the days, to rotate crops and deliver goods in an orderly fashion, to organize sun and moon cycles, was only practicable for an advancing hominid.

Since perspective is imperative for motility within the dimension of space, let's apply the same intuition to our interaction with time.

时 间

Time travel never happened. This is a definitive statement, but because of a quirk of our language, I am obligated to say, "and never will". Because if it had, you wouldn't be here. Certainly, someone would have gone back and told their great grandfather to buy IBM shares. Someone would have killed Hitler. Someone would have saved Jesus. Benevolent forces would have delivered vaccines into prehistory. And, malevolent ones would have hijacked the Manhattan project for personnel power.

What we call time is merely a convention, a convenience, a way to keep appointments, plant crops, and regulate systems. Methods of keeping time are only markers of how often a system returns to the same, or a similar position; with each method of recording this transition being only semi-accurate. For example, due to laws of physics, even the moon or a pendulum lose position with each cycle. And, due to time dilatation, if the GPS system was not constantly being updated, positioning would be off by as much as seven miles in one day.

Never the less, time is merely a concept; one similar to love, hate, or ambition. We only see its effects through complex biochemical processes. One believes they feel something. But, time sense, like any other sensation in the human experience, is not a dependable metric. What we sense as time is very illusory. For example, time drags when bored or in pain, and passes quickly when happily employed. If one were marooned, one would have to guess, "seems like this should be Christmas".

In contrast, emptiness has no chronology. And furthermore, an empty void has no dimensions, not even time. In a total void nothing exists, not even time. An object must materialize in void to possess linear dimension. And without corporeal elements to experience process, there is nothing to have an awareness of change. Time only exists if there is someone to witness it. That means your brain is a time machine. Perception chronicles change.

Time can be measured, but does it flow? For science to present tangible empirical evidence, and not math, seems an impossibility. "The sun set 1461 times since the last election." Stonehenge has disintegrated in predictable periodicity; therefore, the degradation can be mapped. This only proves entropy, not necessarily time. Systems degrade, but this is merely the result of a process.

ت‌ق‌ل

As stated earlier, space and time are not rigid, but are influenced by the presence of matter. Immutable in its amaranthine nature: interminable is its abiding quality. And, our perception; only an involution. Similar to driving on a winding road through hilly terrain. Daniel Price observed: "Time is a landscape that stretches across all things, we are the ones who move across it." And, while we degrade, time does not. We are just flashes on the screen of time: Mere blips: Destined for dissolution - subjugated by entropy.

We experience process; our molecules disband, disunite, and succumb to the second law of thermodynamics. We too, transform, transition, and die. And like us, the mighty oak withers and disintegrates. Even majestic mountains succumb to the undeniable friction of change; eventually collapsing and crumbling. Lao Tsu rightly observed that all "things" change. But only in a dimension that is relative to its object.

Entropy is given - the destiny of all things. An amplitude of discord. A way to measure disorder. The only thing that distinguishes past from present. Time is a dimension; and like height or width, requires a reference point to be relevant. Without something governed by entropy there would be no gauge (i.e. a void), and therefore no time. And, if entropy is inevitable, why was the universe ordered in the past? And, who ordered it?

Ώρα

All of the above has been presented merely to delineate the point that time, like Einstein rightly observed, is an illusion. Yet it is within that illusion, and because of it, that we experience joy. Also, time is a gauge to facilitate communication and coordinate human intercourse. Another way to perceive this is that time is a landscape with entropy ruling all material objects. Okay, so there is no time, only process; tomato, tomatoe - what's the point? Perhaps only the biggest deal there is! - self-realization.

But there is another part of you. A part that that exists outside material reality and is timeless. Understanding this gives new perspective to pragmatists when confounded by the realities of the eternal. In all other human arenas, objects, emotions, missions, and creeds must have utility. Water, sunlight, gravity are all things utilized for benefit.

समय

What we call time is just a symbol that represents states and processes and doesn't really exist. Furthermore, our perspective of time is not only distorted, but also prejudiced. This can be related to a story, told in a previous chapter, of a father and son observing a horse race. The son, looking through the fence, could only see events unfolding in sequence, The father, being taller could see the entire track all at once, and was able to make an accurate prediction of the outcome.

Likewise, there is an oft repeated story about seven blind men who all try to describe an elephant. The one who touched the elephant's side said it was like a wall. The one who touched the tail said it was like a rope, The one who wrapped his arms around the animal's leg said it was like a tree; etcetera. The point is that they were all convinced that they were right.

You, with your enhanced perception and perspective, have a heightened awareness. Add an additional sense and you understand what a blind man cannot. You can smile sadly and say that they just don't get it. These blind men imbue the essence of pragmatism. They confidently portray the attitude of: "I'll believe it when I see it." While it may be a topic for another discussion, it reveals another timeless truth: "You will see it when you believe it."

Living in the now is a sense that needs to be developed - realized really. Many people believe that they balance on a hairline cross point between the past which is gone and a future which hasn't happened yet. The truth is, nobody experiences reality in real time. The brain must process an event, which means you are always living a microsecond behind an occurrence. You don't know anything until you remember it.

So far, I have stayed away from the term mass delusion because that isn't quite accurate. Mutually agreed to deception would be one explication. Accepted myth would be a more descriptive term. Something we all agree on, like driving on the "right" side of the road. Similar to money and measurements, we've gotten so use to them, we forget that they are just symbols and don't really exist.

Often, in my country, we are accustomed to experiencing a periodic financial blip. There are hungry people, but farmers will slaughter livestock and pour milk into the ground. The money is gone. But this is only a perception. While I will admit the numbers for value of "stuff" may have changed, the final resolution is only perception.

For example, there is the same amount of tangible assets on "Black Friday", as there were on the previous Thursday. As another example, imagine a carpenter shows up for work one day and the boss says. "No work today, we've run out of inches!" "What?", the carpenter says. "We've got wood, we've got nails, and the people still want the house." "No! the boss says. You don't understand, there are no more inches. Everyone says so."

All of these are manufactured realities; the phenomenal reality is quite different. The crops have not spontaneously withered in the ground, nor has the gasoline in transport vehicles suddenly evaporated. The society collectively engages in a delusion that all has ended. From an objective point of view, we have created an alternate reality. If we agree that a symbol has value, then concede that it does not, it is an arbitrary conceptual scheme of value.

And time is such a scheme. In short, time is a perceivable dimension and is subject to our shared delusion. Many may feel that this interpretation is a philosophical position, a ruse to foster an appreciation of the here and now, or a psychological gambit to promote an esoteric world view. But, reason is one's gateway to Nirvana. What is more closer to reality is that Newton and Lao Tzu are two sides of the same coin. One is delivered by the very fact that they can't stop changing. Developing a palpable sense of "now" eliminates anxiety, and is the incentive to stop clinging; the genesis of peace.

In order to experience breakthrough, and mature philosophically, one may have to accept the inconceivable and preposterous idea that there is no time. There is only a perpetual state of now. Because of entropy, things change as the universe seeks equilibrium in dissolution. There are processes, like friction and oxidation, that we observe and document. But these obey entropy; and there are no processes that will allow for the universe to become more ordered. Instead, we become aware of cycles; but there is no time. Our brains are physically hard wired to see patterns and categorize. We think of our mortality, count the days, and calculate what Tennyson calls "that far off divine event towards which all creation moves."

In the case of time, subtlety is important. Remember we were trying to cognate 'the reality of time'. Which is a reality that we create. There is no time. But, before you conclude that this is just semantics, please realize the rational, utilitarian practicality of the realization that "there is no time but there might as well be."

As an absurd, but practical example; let's talk about Bob. Bob has a fantastic wife. She does all the things a good wife should do. But she doesn't love him. It's just like she loves him. The function is there. But this intangible, that the union revolves around, doesn't exist. For all practical purposes, he is calling it something that isn't there. He is not aware of this sad fact, but it is reality non-the-less. In other words, Bob's perception about his reality is limited. But, are we as limited as Bob? To think of time as something that flows or begins and ends is the same as assigning an emotion to Bob's wife that isn't there, Bob is living a lie. And so are you.

All natural creatures live in the now. As Emerson said. "The rose is just the rose. It exists just as it is. With GOD today. Whereas mankind, heedless of the riches that surround him stands on tiptoe to foresee the future or to regret the past."

Time does not exist. This is important because if one is going to fully live their life in reality and not delusion, they need to develop the sense of living in the perpetual state of now. There is only this moment. Time is truly an illusion, but because of the way our brains are wired we feel like there is the passing of time. The past provides reference, the idea of a future provides an awareness of options, and the inevitability of change.

A Zen poem reads "the morning glory lives for only an hour. But differs not from the giant pine that lives a thousand years". To use up any of your now's contemplating the incredible age of the universe is a waste of time that doesn't exist.

Gravity

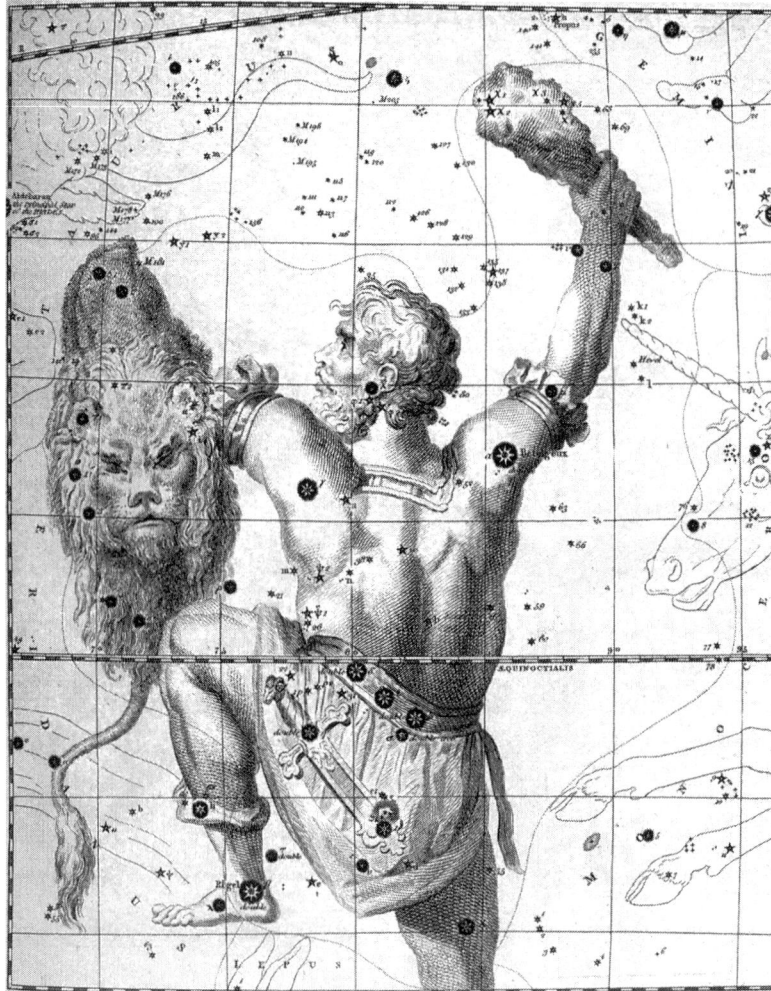

Gravity is a property of mass. Gravity is a consequence of warping space-time. Gravity is a mysterious force that nobody understands. These statements are all true. These statements are all untrue. These statements are an example of Yin and Yang because it has both a mystical and a practical side.

Most people can successfully navigate life using the force of gravity quite adequately; never entreating serious calamity. Even without a deep dive into the theoretical aspects of this enigmatic cosmic element, terrene dwellers can successfully function; even in consequential endeavors like engineering and construction. Likewise, the connate, endemic researchers of the middle kingdom, in ages past, knew nothing of the thought provoking advancements of Isaac Newton or Albert Einstein.

The developers of traditional Chinese medicine and indigenous martial arts were ordained to formulate within the governing precepts of their natural world. A major tenet of the TCM canon is to operate in harmony with the natural environment. Bio-stabilizing and chemistry balancing paradigms, such as; breathing exercises and movements that provide internal organ massage, worked synergistically with weight bearing methods - methods that maximize the added dimension of bending and twisting the bones of the supporting structure, thus producing vital and beneficial mechanical stress.

The results of these benefits have been scientifically verified in our own age by the most sophisticated researches in their fields. For instance, astronauts functioning in a micro-gravity environment can experience up to a twenty percent bone and muscle loss during extended space missions. Academics have used their discoveries to direct both time and resources into developing programs for these space travelers, in an attempt to prevent severe physical atrophy.

Despite critical duties, astronauts must devote two hours a day to resistance training to combat the detrimental effects of zero gravity. Complex machinery has been fabricated to assuage bone and muscle atrophy, such as; the Combined Operational Load Bearing External Resistance Treadmill (COLBERT) and the Advanced Resistance Exercise Device (ARED). Terrestrials fortunate enough to remain earthbound, can simply perform Tai-Chi.

The idea that expensive complex machinery like ARED is necessary for health maintenance on earth is commensurate with the deception that concentrated nutritional supplements must be consumed on a daily basis. These hustles are greed based and are only the repercussion of modern salesmanship. Naturalistic processes, like Tai-Chi, understand that homeostasis is best maintained by living in harmony. And, achieving balance within existing systems; one's that evolved together within the natural world.

In T.C.M. elixirs, medicines, and "superchargers" are administered on an infrequent basis. When administered, they are incorporated for the purpose of nudging natural systems to produce endemic processes and to address a specific, temporary condition. All other perceived aberrations are just the morphing adjustments encountered in the amplitude fluctuations. Regardless, all of these regimens work within the confines of well-established boundaries of natural laws and endemic forces.

Gravity is a constitutional property of the planet on which we live. Recognizing the effects of this phenomenon on the human organism is essential. And, incorporating yet another one of our unlimited natural resources, just as astute as the breathing routines used to foster one's vigor.

Since all principals in Tai-Chi have both a martial and a health aspect, gravity can be utilized to enhance fighting capabilities in a way that reflects the genius of the early pioneers of the art.

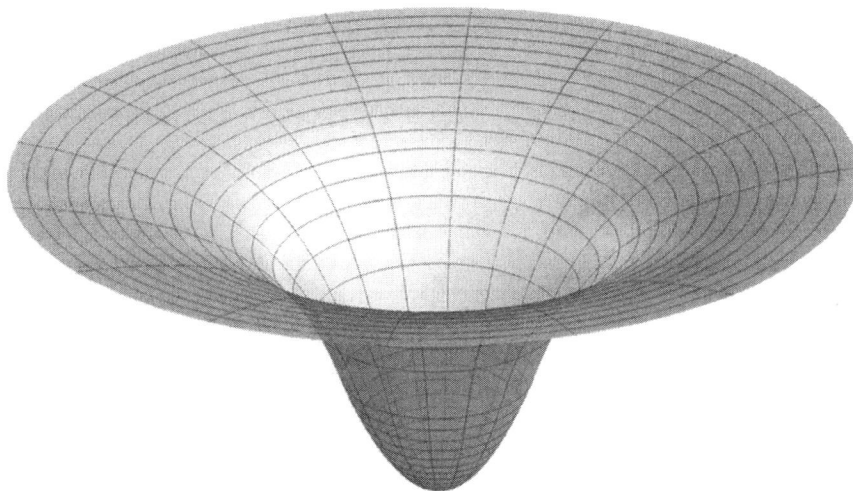

Along with the strong force, the weak force and electromagnetism, gravity rounds out the four fundamental forces of our universe. These are the four known principals of modern physics. Further exploits of these principles have been addressed relative to our purposes in other chapters of this book; i.e., Voltage and Geese and Magnets.

Gravity is called a force due to convention; and for facilitating communication and practical understanding. Gravity, of course, is not a force at all; but a product of space-time dilation. For our purposes, gravity will only be addressed here to refine and improve one's performance of Tai-Chi.

WARPING OF TIME CAUSES GRAVITY

TIME CAUSES GRAVITY

Time is more fundamental than gravity. Time passes at different rates in different places. Time passes faster closer to the earth. Now, suppose there were a terrestrial giant. Really huge. Paul Bunyan huge - only much bigger. Many thousands of feet tall. Floating and suspended above the earth, but with his feet near the ground and his head in the stratosphere. If there were a clock near his feet and another one by his head; the clock at his head would recon time at about 1/100 of a nanosecond faster than the clock at his feet. Admittedly, that's not much, but it is significant enough. If GPS were off by this much it would register one's location arrant by seven miles in just a single day. This is the reason why GPS systems are continuously being adjusted.

Because of this time dilation, if our giant remained motionless, his head would eventually move toward the earth (fall) because time is moving faster near his head. The mass of the earth creates a drag on space-time experienced more as one gets to the ground and less as one moves away from the mass; such as in the stratosphere. What we experience as gravity is the mass of the earth causing a warping of space-time.

MATTER TELLS SPACE-TIME HOW TO CURVE

SPACE-TIME TELLS MATTER HOW TO MOVE

Basic Newtonian physics tells us that our giant will not move unless acted upon by extraneous forces.

1. An object at rest will remain at rest. An object in motion will remain in motion.

2. The change of momentum is proportional to the force applied.

3. Forces between two objects exist in equal magnitude and opposite direction.

The first law tells us that if there are no forces, or forces are balanced, an object will move in a straight line at a steady speed - or not at all. The second law assures that if there are no unbalanced forces, outside of gravity, an object will experience continual acceleration. Newton's third law is well known as each force exerted by one object on another, an equal and opposite force is exerted back.

The comprehension of these principle have very real and practical meaning. Because, if a martial artist expects to gain any advantage and utilize the principals in both a Newtonian and Einsteinian manor, these understandings may provide that edge. Proper execution is, of course, imperative; but internalizing these precepts to a higher level engages both the conscious and subconscious mental aspects that are so meaningful in internal arts.

Understanding that, as a force, gravity doesn't exist will help when it is explained that time doesn't exist either. This is not a theorem or scientific postulation; rather it is a metaphor to facilitate the understanding of and elevate our execution of the physical and intellectual aspects of Tai-Chi. And although flow gradient and time dilation are real, for almost everyone who engages in everyday activities, all of the above information is nothing more than an academic exercise. For anything other than work in a laboratory, calculating rocket launches, or considerations on quantum scales, perceiving the true nature of gravity is baffling and unnecessary.

For the martial artist, gravity can serve as an unseen ally; a hidden covert collaborator that changes the equation from mano-a-mano, to a clandestine two-against-one. So even though we have expended a plethora of words explaining that gravity is not a force, to serve our purposes, we must adopt the tactic of the swindler, gigolo, or flimflam preacher, to exploit agencies that are simultaneously both tangible and intangible; as if it were real.

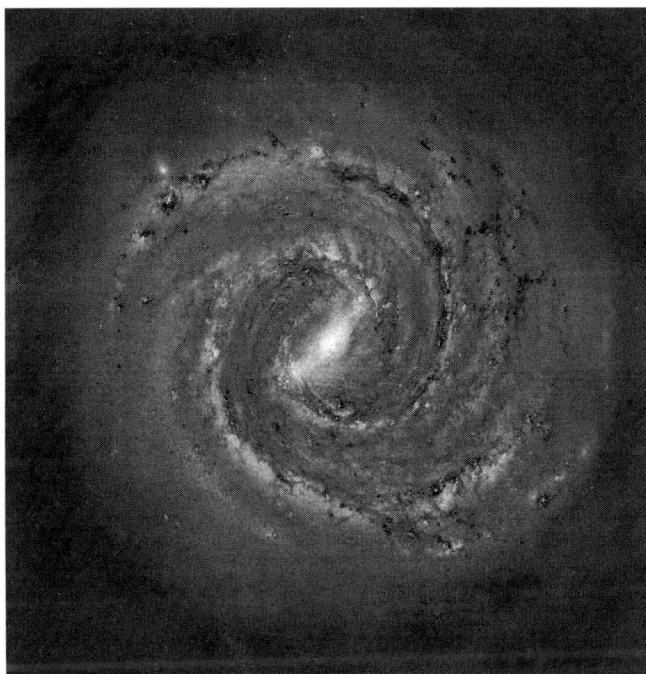

To derive the greatest collaboration from gravity may require an adaptation of technique, but often, it is more a matter of a change in mindset. For example, it may seem to be a needless and subtle difference in perception, but when executing a throw or trip, it can sometimes prove advantageous to differentiate one's perception within technique execution. Instead of redundantly throwing the opponent to the ground, one should learn to think more tactically, shifting their perception to just removing the opponent's base and allowing gravity to participate as an undetected confederate; pulling him toward the earth. A key advantage to this shift is that this new perception does not require one's participation longer than to initiate the maneuver, thus allowing the defender those vital split seconds to adjust quicker and freeing up one's attention to execute a new or follow up maneuver.

When gravity is required to assist in a technique, if the defender drops his weight, then it has proven more effective to simply pick up one's feet; allowing gravity the opportunity to pull the full mass of the executor, In contrast, when most martial artists "drop their weight", their technique usually only provides a partial assist. This is because they employ more of a fast sinking action, utilizing primarily their upper leg muscles (quads). This method of dropping utilizes the legs in a manner similar to a type of shock absorber. This is due to the fact that the muscles of the legs remain in service throughout execution; in a springy, half engaged, compensation of energy.

The lesson here again is one of utilizing a proper understanding of Yin/Yang. It would be easy to be seduced by the superficial idea that more is better. This is like adding just a little more sugar to a cake recipe, or slugging with muscle on a golf swing. Sometimes, just "letting it happen" is the best prescription. Let the regional managers and/or field generals do their jobs.

In this instance, gravity will perform autonomously. No need to micromanage. One only needs to institute the launch sequence and move on to the next task. Although, enthusiasm may prod you to help, it is often advantageous to go around the other way. Trust the process - even give credence to the ludicrous, and unbelievable. In theory, it would be best to possess total understanding; but also know that even the fool who persists in his folly, will become wise.

Undeniably, an in-depth understanding of the effects of mass and its ability to warp space-time provides no real tangible help when buckling someone's leg. In contrast, a simpler and more practical, comprehensive utility of the attributes and "forces" that are part of this world will provide a kind of "street wisdom". Empirical understanding serves the woodsman and the architect alike. Reliance on practical magic and understanding a phenomenon as something that "just is" makes life easier.

However, it is possible to be too intelligent for one's own good, and this can reflect on other examples of our interactions with the real world. Forces and interactions of both the substantial and spiritual dimension may defy what we perceive as logic and tangible. And, being dismissive of explanations that describe "forces" that exert influence in this plane of existence, can diminish attainment in mundane endeavors. Simply "trusting the universe" can allow humans to employ attributes of the unseen world; ones that interface smoothly with functional terrestrial life.

Many of the Chi-Kung health nurturing protocols dismissed as "mystical" simply eclipse a pragmatic, judgmental perception. Gravity, for one, can assist with facilitation of healthful organ function. This is after muscular tension and caustic endogenous stress compounds are removed from interfering with the scrupulous functioning of the organism.

The mere adjustment of mind intent can be quite powerful, although this can be dismissed as doltish by "seeing is believing" pragmatists. But as the improvement in simply "dropping your weight" demonstrates, this is true with many perceived spiritual or inter-dimensional aspects of living. The Yin/Yang of this is the seen working in concert with the unseen. Not accepting this reality diminishes one's full potentiality. Enigmas like luck or the basic animating life force would be coherent; if as quantifiable and dependable as gravity.

This discussion is of course metaphor, and only partially concerned with one of the four fundamental interactions. In linkage with germane topics featured in other essays in this book; half of the common, everyday phenomena experienced are typical of this "force". Use of this demarche in prosaic activities, although trustworthy and constant, is still mystical and not fully understood. Everyday miracles are regularly dismissed; owing to man's bizarre ability to ignore phenomena, only because it is commonplace. When pressed, many physicists will admit that it is amazing that anything is happening at all. Humans who marvel at a newborn, contemplate, or gaze out to sea, share the wonderment of the incomprehensible.

A professional writer would never take the low hanging fruit, or seize the easy and obviously juvenile jape. Since I am not a professional writer, in a final observation on the enigma / riddle of Yin and Yang, our human experience would be a complete celebration; if it weren't for all of life's gravity.

Themis

Because this is a book on Tai-Chi, many references are made to Taoist thought, from which the art derives its philosophical roots. This is as it should be; after all it is a Chinese art. The purpose of this effort however is not a "how to" of a particular martial art, but an attempt to elicit comprehension on the subjects surrounding this genre for the Western mind.

At this point in our discussion, it would seem logical to quote Taoist philosophy about Tai-Chi theory. Yet, even the expression of this statement creates a conundrum; because the Western mind and core method of understanding is engrained in logic, which comes from the Greeks. So, before we even begin to interpret the mysteries of the arts, our starting place is rooted to a divergent culture.

All ancient civilizations, including the Chinese, have greatly contributed to the status of modern man. But to speak broadly, and push towards my conclusion, it can be said, we in the Western world owe it all to the Greeks. Democracy (for one), philosophy, and geometry are not only Greek concepts they are also Greek words.

Many volumes have been written tracing the origins of Western thought and science to Hellenistic culture, so there is no need to belabor that effort in a book about an Eastern fighting style. It may prove elucidating, however, to compare some Chinese concepts to notions already established in Western thought, by merging the two tenuously analogous ideas in a style that may help to explain each in a decidedly unique way.

Themis was a Titaness in ancient Greek culture, more familiar in our modern world as lady justice. In one hand she carries the balance scales, to impartially judge, and in the other a sword which symbolically delivers swift and immediate retribution. The blindfold was only added in modern times.

The name Themis translates as "divine law", which originally implied natural law and divine order. Her attributes were later tweaked to insinuate this quality into the systems of human judicial proceedings. Originally, Themis only made judgments and retribution was dispensed by Nemesis; when Themis was ignored. The wrath of Nemesis is the obverse side of the coin; this is evidenced by the fact that the Nemesion temple was shared by both Themis and Nemesis.

Themis is not a person with a mind, making decisions, but rather a representation of natural law. For our purposes, it may be helpful to think of Themis as one specific illustration of Yin/Yang, where her scales represent the two halves of the Tai-Chi symbol. Themis is in actuality an arbiter. One which provides a natural reaction. One of impartial divine order. The lightning flashes, the thunder sounds. If one walks mindlessly into traffic or steps off a parapet, then natural order delivers an ineludible response. Nemesis.

Whether it's Yin/Yang, the scales of justice, or Maxwell's demon, the idea of a binary transmutation resulting in diametrically opposed outcomes is universal. For example, imagine if each thought and action produced a pellet that weighed one gram and was automatically deposited on either side of your scale of destiny. Positive thoughts and actions would cause the scales to tip towards favorable consequences, while negative would naturally beget darker ones.

Recently, I was accosted by someone bemoaning the fate of a friend who had suffered horribly from a malignancy. She decried, "he a good person, it's not fair". I calmly described how this was someone who had lived recklessly, indulged in toxic behaviors, and nearly always ignored healthful pursuits. I suggested that if you filled one hand with his kindly nature and amiable personality and the other with the noxious pernicious behaviors, one could have made a summary judgment as to which way the scales would tip.

Sometimes appearances may suggest that things are not naturally weighted in your favor. A calamitous childhood or genetic predisposition may appear to weigh heavy against you. Thankfully, we all have the ability to counter-balance nearly every one of these negatives out. Weighting the positive side by modifying behavior, maintaining focus, and staying the course. To aid in your endeavors, in modern times, there is a plethora of useful and valuable information to help deflect or outright avoid many of the potentially unpleasant results.

The Greeks conjured up Themis and Nemesis the same way the Chinese advanced Yin/Yang. One can impart erudition plainly, or by parable, to illustrate that survival is a razor's edge. Savvy apprehension and caution should be our relentless angels, because sometimes the palest wisp of impropriety or fortitude can tip the scales in your favor or against.

Tai-Chi master class: Visualize yourself standing with your arms extended laterally, palms cupped. All of your bad decisions and negative behaviors beget pellets into one palm, while clean living and good intentions fill the other. You are the scales of justice. You are Themis/Nemesis; Yin/Yang. The pellets weigh heavy, fate is in your hands.

Manitou

The Northwest Ordinance was laid out in 1787. Ohio was the first state disseminated from the Northwest Territory and was granted statehood in 1803, or at least that's what everyone thought. Thomas Worthington, a delegate of the Ohio State Convention, personally delivered the Ohio constitution to Washington D.C. for approval in accordance with President Thomas Jefferson's newly signed Enabling Act of 1802. Fun fact: Congress never actually found the time to ratify the Ohio constitution.

Ohio schoolchildren grow up believing that theirs was the 17th state in the union. But this didn't actually happen until 1953 when president Dwight D. Eisenhower retroactively granted Ohio statehood. An action President Jefferson neglected to make.

Prior to 1787, Ohio was the frontier, and my ancestors, like many other invaders, interacted commonly with the native population. Women, like other local resources, were exploited by the marauders; and my great, great grandfather culled a wife from the area tribe. When my great grandfather was born, in the Ohio territory, he was named in the way of the indigenous people. The first thing seen after the birth of a child, produced the name. For the native peoples this would yield; hawk fly overhead or bear runs swiftly through the woods. On his first day, my antecedent presented his son to the world and gazed directly into the impenetrable wilderness. Thus, Western Forest became the name of my great grandfather, who in turn named his son Forrest, likewise my father Forest Jr.

Marriage afforded my great, great grandmother the opportunity to escape the persecution that plagued her domestic sovereigns, and would eventually lead to U.S. polices that produced broken treaties and legislation like the Indian Removal Act, which resulted in the trail of tears. This, along with constitutionally mandated human bondage and the faux pas regarding Ohio's statehood, are examples of government as a work in progress.

Among the abusive institutional policies she was able to avoid was Indian boarding schools. These were where Native American children were kidnapped and raised in government funded, church operated facilities, and where native customs and language were forbidden. Federal laws were actually passed banning traditional practices, such as: the rain dance / sun dance, sweat lodges, and other indigenous religious practices.

As I was made aware of while working in the Dakotas in the early seventies, this persecution continued well into the modern era. An official policy of prosecution continued, unbelievably, until 1978 with the passage of AIRFA (the American Indian Religious Freedom Act). The fact that a repressive situation existed that required legislation to rectify, is particularly notable since religious freedom is officially enshrined in the country's founding documents. Again, a work in progress, I suppose.

Native American religious practices are very broad and may be shamanistic, pantheistic, poly or monotheistic. For the sake of brevity, lets limit this study to the theology of the Algonquian and native peoples around the great lakes, my ancestral lands.

Wakan Tanka is regarded as the Great Spirit, although many scholars prefer the translation "Great Mystery". This type of confusion is very similar to the conundrum of comprehending Chinese words and concepts and converting them to the most equivalent concept in English: it's not an exact science. Nonetheless, Wakan Tanka is probably even better translated into head deity, because Wakan Tanka serves many of the same functions as the Judeo-Christian God.

Wakan Tanka created all that there is and breathed life into the first man. The great spirit is also a unifying life force that flows through all things; be they rocks, trees, animals or people. All things - animate or inanimate. Everything is unified by a life force matrix. This, therefore, means that all things were connected. Sound familiar?

This concept is significant because it merges the idea of a Taoist universal energy matrix with that of a creator god. Other native peoples had other names for the same concept, such as: Manitou or the Iroquois' Orinda (the spiritual life force). Regardless, this concept is of an omnipresent presence manifested in all things, including the environment and event events.

Even more interesting is the fact that the manifestation of Manitou is considered dualistic with the complimentary and opposite component concepts named Aashaa monetoo (good spirit) and monetoo (bad spirit). Furthermore, although separated by thousands of miles and having no opportunity for cultural exchange, the indigenous peoples of the Americas developed an understanding of the binary nature of the manifest universe. In many respects very similar to the Yin/Yang concept found in Sino/Hindi metaphysical practices.

Throughout the world, people who are allowed to evolve spiritually, develop an understanding of the universe as imbued with a life force; often times interpreted as emanating from a loving and just creator. That is, unless, ecclesiastic autocrats prevent the exercise of free will or are place under the yoke of oppressive tyrannical monarchy.

Deep in the subconscious, the human organism innately perceives the cosmic reality. Just like hunger or the will to survive, this understanding is elemental. For instance, one path, which is hindered by ice and frost ridden hardships, may arrive at Valhalla; while another, more moderate and wooded, may lead to the happy hunting grounds. Irrespective of circumstance, sentient beings abhor the same end. Contemplating the mysteries of the hereafter and the here and now are endemic to the human condition.

All human drives serve some progressive purpose; advancing our species towards some unknowable goal. The need to develop spiritually seems at least equally important as corporeal survival. Much human capital has been expended towards these ends. It would seem that through the efforts of both the scholarly and shamanistic approaches; whether an urbanized technologically advanced civilization or a boorish, primitive people; the human soul evolved with our species.

A German trauma surgeon may use different words to describe the same lifesaving procedures and internal structures as one from the Americas. One must understand that the real purpose of the words is just to ease communication with another; to describe, quantify, and clarify. Although the Germans may have named them something different, they are still the same practices and structures.

Likewise, spiritual realities reveled through shamanistic practices or clerics who study books are all documenting the same mysteries. I can discern visions through my Wu-Tai stone while still exercising the faith of my fathers. If the validation of quantum field theory and the religious practices of all peoples, from the brutish to the sophisticated, are to provide us with any instruction, the lesson seems obvious...all are one.

Mind Control

Toxoplasma gondii is an aobligate intercellular parasitic protozoan eukaroyte that is responsible for behavioral changes in mammalian hosts. It is present worldwide and 30% - 50% of the global population may have experienced exposer. The parasite utilizes complex survival mechanisms to infect felid hosts which is the only species in which the organism may reproduce.

Once excreted in cat feces, exposed rats display decreased predator aversion allowing rodents to be consumed by felids and transferring the parasite into the more suitable host for sexual reproduction. Once infected, rat neurons undergo epigenetic remodeling which govern behavior.

Toxoplasma gondii modifies epigenetic methylation in the amygdala through the hypomethylation of argine vasopressin genes. It also effects dopamine levels and exhibits other actions which are complex and confusing to describe. It is a fascinating enquiry and if you enjoy intriguing detective science it makes for a good read.

Although, the alteration of rodent behavior has received, to date, the most examination, the actions exhibited in insects is even more pronounced. Certain wasp species utilize T. gondii to create passive insect slaves for later consumption. In humans, the infection has been linked with subtle behavioral changes and associated with neurological disorders like bipolar and schizophrenia.

Chemical induced mind-control differs from pain and compliance control tactics, yet both are a form of mind control through neurological stimulus. As a simple example; through the application of the arm bar, the subject experiences a change in behavior and becomes cooperative. Similarly, an idea is a targeted mind hit, synonymous to a vital area strike, psychologically.

Throughout the natural and human world, mind control is serious business. Militaristic nations have developed extensive brain washing techniques; pioneered in prisoner of war camps, and on their own populations. Even the United States government engaged in mind-control experimentation; injecting unwitting subjects with LSD, and authorizing programs like M.K. ultra.

Similarly, advertising is a serious science, which utilizes many concepts shared with these standard brainwashing techniques. Repetition, associations with specific stimuli (both good and bad), threat, and promise of reward. Likewise, drug companies induce fear to convince the populace of the need for a remedy to a condition they didn't even know they had.

Salesmen receive extensive training in techniques that produce compliance and agreement. Prepared responses to deal with objections and boxing the prospect into a corner, where the only logical conclusion is to say yes. Leading the customer in a common direction, cultivating agreement, then switching into the close; amounting to a type of psychological judo. Educated professionals, and people vastly smarter than I, are regularly derailed and redirected, merely by employing these mind control techniques, referencing hot button issues and subtly directing human interaction.

I have developed and often employ a type of self-defense mind-control when in social situations; where probing inquires have made me uncomfortable. I know, for example, all I have to do to move the conversation, is to say that the country thrives under Ying administrations, and flounders under Yang ones. Blood pressures elevate, voices rise, phones fly out, producing charts and graphs, and the snarky comments begin. I know that for sure I will be told that president X was directed by a republican congress, or influential bills were of conservative origin. All comments predictably assured, because tribalism will not allow the other team to score. If I say the Yankees won the world series, the person with an ax to grind will defensively say "Yeah, but Micky Mantle was from Oklahoma."

The historic financial records of the country are verifiable by any metric one may choose, This, by the way, is not bias or political opinion, it's just history. Lawmaking is an obtuse, complex business that is fraught with accommodation and compromise. As I try to point out, to hostile partisans who have never worked in government, policy is enacted through manipulation and back room deals. And, even the most astute political observer can never know what's really going on. Add to this political activists with agendas and foreign propaganda machines influencing domestic media, the result being gullible Americans becoming indoctrinated by the use of offshore mind-control techniques.

I have cited the above example because these subjects always produces a predictable result, and at the same time illustrates that mind-control is utilized every day by foreign entities to influence American political outcomes. I have successfully redirected the subject of conversation away from and unconformable line of questioning by touching an emotional pressure point.

Another subject, within my lifetime, that will always produce a guaranteed result is to move the conversation to the American withdrawal from Vietnam. I have a Vietnamese friend who made it onto the last chopper out of Saigon. He and his mom tried to board the next to the last "Huey" out, but got bumped by the mayor's wife and family. The helicopter that carried the mayor's wife wound up going down, killing all aboard. Tuan and his mother landed uneventfully on a US aircraft carrier.

Tuan understood quite well nuances of the Vietnam conflict, having lived through it. He was always able to provide a realistic perspective and input. The last chaotic days of the Vietnam conflict, were stained by the confusion that marked the American withdrawal. When I broached the subject with an American friend, as sure as sunrise, It was pointed out to me that the Americans won every major combat engagement of the entire war. This is true, except my point was not about conventional land battles, but the war of attrition waged successfully by the Viet Cong, who operated in accordance with precepts laid out by Sun Tzsu.

The "hit and run" guerrilla tactics, nocturnal raids, and pernicious booby traps elicited a measurable toll on the better equipped foreigners. My overall objective was to cite guerrilla methodology as an example of Sun Tzsu's teachings as being effective and usable in the modern era. The undeclared tactic, of course, is that I knew exactly the reaction I would get, by leading the conversation in a predictable direction.

Cajoled reactions, like the ones illustrated above, are common, everyday occurrences. They are not mythical nor exotic ideas; yet at the exact same time, studied extensively worldwide. This is very much like breathing. It is at the same time a field of biological study and a normal biological function.

The war of attrition waged by the Viet Cong is only one example of a type of mind-control utilizing many complex pathways - much like the parasite that produces latent toxoplasmosis. A fighter need only to lightly touch an arm or hitch a shoulder to create a coaxed reaction that may change the outcome of the whole fight. Highly trained, experienced defensive players in the NFL are mind-controlled by astute quarterbacks who glance left and throw right.

The Yin/Yang, however, is that individuals can obsess on bad impulses and negative compulsions; and be influenced by subtle interactions with other individuals. But, ideologies can be the most deleterious and insidious forms of destruction. But, can also be innovative and metamorphosing, progressing the human experience. Polarizing ideologies can be exemplified by personalities such, as Hitler and Gandhi, each influencing human history in dramatically, yet opposing trajectories. Both as mentally significant as Toxoplasma Gondii.

The mind creates everything and controls everything. First cause is always mental. Ideas that move nations; a word in a conversation; a look on the football field - each affect outcomes both big and small. Being aware of the influence of the mind is tantamount with survival. Most are aware of the use of mind-control offensively, but it's use defensively (and especially preemptively) is central to the continuity of life. Cultivate this awareness, the parasites are out there.

Mind Intent

YI

You hear it all the time. The mind is very powerful. It has changed the form and function of this planet and soon probably others. It can conceive and execute a plan for a life and a family. Build empires. Destroy nations. And it has actual measurable electrical power. But, can the mind be conditioned and improved, like the body? To be a stronger more capable version of itself. A conditioned body can run a four-minute mile or squat nine hundred pounds. Where a poor physical specimen can't make it around the block. Yet the mind is limitless and not hampered by physical constraints. Trainable yes. Able to make thought processes more focused. But is the mind capable of anything besides executive function?

WILL

It is often said that so-and-so achieved their success through their indomitable will. Someone might denote that one willed a particular situation into existence. Will is something clearly understood by most cultures. So even in the West we appreciate the notion that a focused intention can be an additional element to the achievement of an endeavor. For example: You "will" negotiate this obstacle course, she "will" love me, or I "will" not drown. Co-opting this word is also very useful in helping students to incorporate the idea of mind intent into their martial art.

Determination

Determination is not the same as will. For instance, a determined person is completely committed to achieving their goal. In other words, a determined person is trying really hard. But, the person employing will incorporates an additional element. The force of mind that goes beyond. Someone who is willing an outcome is now touching on the threads of mind intent. In fact, will is an important element of mind intent. However, will is really only fully committed determination.

But, will and determination are not enough. The mechanism that produces a suitable result is a synergistic process. Will and determination are just singular elements in the formula of mind intent. They are components. For instance, charcoal is one element of gunpowder. But, if you don't know the other ingredients, you do not possess the ability to create this incredibly powerful substance. One that can alter outcomes. The formula must be right. Along with these components, there are other elements and techniques. Correct proportions. Sulfur as the stabilizer; saltpeter providing the oxygen.

If one is lost in the mountains, pioneering and survival skills are the major components providing the difference between life and death. Other proficiencies, such as the knowledge of shelter building, are also essential. There is skill, to effect construction; determination, to execute the plan; and will, the ability to persevere under duress. Will is the highway we use to send energy.

Most people's brains are not conditioned for immediate response. Often times individuals will freeze when a car comes out of nowhere, or someone throws a punch. The standard thought/willl/action chain becomes confounded. Rather, our modern society stresses the importance of methodical thinking and planning. An engineer, an accountant, a carpenter, are trained to always be thoughtful. Always, double check the work before proceeding - i.e. "We may need a few meetings to work things out."

Quick thinking and decisive action are relegated to specialized professions. In these professions, one is required to potentially make snap decisions. Which, in fact, are really anything but. Instead, these individuals are instilled with trained responses, when possible, but mostly the process of a cool, agile mind that is capable of computing fast determinations based upon data provided by the situation at hand.

For instance, a quarterback is an executive position with such obligations. The ability to make command adjustments on the fly is a requisite. Demanding lightning quick reflexes and mercurial decision-making skills. Yes, you start with a plan. But a determined opponent will often disrupt even the best strategy.

Teddy Roosevelt said; "In any crisis situation, the best response is the right response. The worst response, is no response." When plans go wrong, as they often will, and even if the standard back up options of the plan have failed; my dad had his own saying; "I'm going to do something, even if it's wrong." My dad, as a solider who landed in Normandy and slogged through France, knew that no military plan survives contact with the enemy.

Making rapid, correct decision training is the Yin/Yang to the methodical type of thinking drilled into modern vassals living in collectives. Civilization demands deliberate, analytical commonality, and discourages instinctive response. Cosmopolitan living requires cooperative team players. However, when societies are being formed, pioneering requires aggressive type A personalities able to adjust, improvise and make usable assets out of available miscellany.

Retraining thought processes to perform in dilemma is no different than preparing the body for the demands of differing athletic challenges. For example, one can be in football shape, and not be in wrestling shape. Similarly, the mind also performs to its specific training. Developing an expansive, resilient mind that that functions on demand in crisis, is a far different form of preparation than one requiring protracted analysis of minutia.

The first step towards a reliable body that responds like a Kung-Fu master, and a mind working in equanimity is analyzing the current mental processes, and committing to retrain them for maxim productivity and function. The mind is a tool, and like the body, can be honed for specificity. Removing the distractions of extraneous inputs and thought. Changing the mind from flipping whim to whim as an imperious dictator, to one that is under control and focused.

Overcoming fear, is not the same as developing fearlessness. Fearlessness is a state of mind. A quality. Brain provisos mandated for command or survival importune a mind conditioned for urgent, applicable riposte. A mind that has control. A mind as component of a unit positioned for survival. But like stated above, accumulated facts and deductive reasoning are only one type of mental conditioning.

If you can train your bowels, then you can train your mind. They share the same contents. Stop and think about thought. If one reaches for a glass, the reach is proceeded by a thought. But even before the thought, there was the desire. First the desire, then the thought. Then the creation. Desire is what brought the world into being.

Desire is the emotional element of the mind intent process. Desire, thought, will. Simple enough so far. But, let's begin to streamline this process further. To start with, if I get mad and desire to hit you; I can cock my hand, step in, then punch. Not a very efficient process. Likewise, with this entire mental aspect that motivates our movement. Desire, thought, will are a chain, but are more efficient if executed as one.

In the same vein as above scenario, when someone reaches for a glass there is a time lag between desire, thought and action. And, sometimes this is a long time. Wow, that ice tea looks good! I think I'll reach for the glass. Then finally, the action.

But, what if your action was one with the stimulus? Yes, like a tiger. Instead, my hand starts reaching as I see the tea. And, that is only if the process isn't confounded or delayed by a plethora of interfering, internal thoughts. "Did I just take a sip?" "Have I had too much?" "Remember aunt Martha's tea?"

Direct action is elemental in Kung-Fu. Animal style is not just about animal type movement. Tiger style fighting implies more than ferocity.

Since this is a book about martial art, it seems appropriate to use fighting as parable. What happens when someone throws a punch at someone else? Within untrained defending individuals, many times all the wrong mental processes begin to manifest. "I'm gonna get hit." "I can't beat this guy." "Look at those forearms." "This isn't happening." To be sure, the intimidation costume and psych are part of the totality of the attack. But one is only helping the attacker by inserting delays in the response chain.

What would it be like if the defending response really was married to the offending action? The second the attack begins the response is blended with the aggressive movement. The proper response manifested; aided by a confidence and a will to win. One that kicked in automatically, without having to think about it.

THE LIGHTING FLASHES
THE THUNDER SOUNDS

Your response is part of his attack. Like dancers moving as one. But if action will always beat reaction, is this something to even aspire to?

Consider Mushin; state of no mind. Sometimes called mirror mind because the mirror takes what it is given and reflects it back undisturbed. But how can you have state of no mind and mind intent? No mind is not an absent mind. Or a vacant mind. It is a still mind. Mind like water. A Zen poem says: "the still lake reflects the image of the geese but cares not." It does so automatically and without involvement. But how do you arrive there? You don't. Your already there.

One needs to just let the training take over. If I'm lucky enough to dodge the first strike, and their chin lights up like high score on a pinball machine. I don't say there it is and go for it. I see my hand already there. If I identify the target, shuffle in, crank back, and throw; my window has already passed.

Johnathan Livingston Seagull achieved perfect flight by already being there. Wane Gretzky was a natural Zen master. He wasn't the biggest player nor the fastest skater, but he was the highest scorer. When interviewed he said. "I can see the puck going into the net."

YOUR MIND LEADS THE ACTION

When executing the Tai-Chi form, don't lift up your hands. Allow them to join where the "mind hands" already are. When performing the Pai-Lum forms, I allow my strikes to explode out from a relaxed state to meet my hands that are already there. This is mind projection. Projecting one's thoughts to the destination. The body then inseparably morphs to conform to the mind's intent.

YOUR BRAIN.

Where is the seat of consciousness? What areas of the brain are thought to be more prominent for exercising voluntary control over the medial temporal lobe neurons? Structures in the hippocampus and para hippocampal cortex control thought, spatial awareness and sensing the passage of time. It is complex and tied in with other structures like the amygdala. The more likely candidate for the origin of conscious thought is the claustrum. A small sheet of neurons just below the cortex. The visual and auditory cortex send axons to the claustrum. I also receives as well. None other than Francis Crick, co-discoverer of D.N.A. strongly promoted a connection between the claustrum and consciousness. Brain science, at least as it applies to the mind, is still an emerging field. Wherever it comes from, our ability to affect outcomes by processes that are started in the brain, is what we refer to as mind intent. First cause is always mental.

A HIGHER AUTHORITY

Changing the fundamental way in which you respond to stimulus is one way to achieve better outcomes in the martial arts. Projecting the mind to already be there. Assuming positively that you have already achieved the desired result.

But are there any broader applications of this idea? By assuming that mind intent is a universal principal, can it have any broader applications? Has anyone other than some obscure martial artists promoted this as a technique? I don't know. But, how about an obscure prophet from Judea. Jesus had something remarkably similar to say, in Mark 11:24.

American Standard Bible: "Therefore I tell you whatever you ask for in prayer. Believe that you have already received it and it will be yours."

King James Bible: "Therefore, I say unto you, whatever things you ask when you pray, believe that you receive them, and you will have them."

If you believe the words of the simple carpenter from Nazareth have any merit, it would seem that in a book that is about him; whatever words he actually said must be important. Although, some scholars count differently, most say that Jesus spoke between 1026 and 2024 words in a book of over 800,000 words. Rarely did he hand out yogic technique. Jesus spoke in parables, giving life lessons and promoting a strong faith in God. But here, he is not talking about a religious doctrine. He did not mention the almighty. Instead, he gave you a technique.

Visualization and manifestation techniques are well documented in Eastern traditions. Usually dismissed in our Western culture, because of fundamentalism and promotion by new age advocates. Affirmations and techniques, such as the one promoted by the sandal wearing, long haired, dissident from Galilee; are not well received by clear thinking realists, who wear shoes. But even they would have to admit that having a positive attitude about outcomes certainly can't hurt.

Meditation

Meditation is a vital component of a properly functioning human life. A healing balm for an over worked mind. A natural sedative allowing the body an opportunity to reset. A conversation with infinitude.

People drawn to endeavors like Tai-Chi and yoga naturally realize that the human animal is body, mind, and spirit. But merely realizing this and engaging in devout ritual does not provide the equilibrium the human organism seeks. Religious practices concern the soul and spirit. Meditation, while a bridge between the mind and the celestial realms, is also a nuts-and-bolts technique to maintain the health of the mind / body unit.

Just as Tai-Chi can be used as a relaxing health maintenance routine or fighting art, depending on the goals and disposition of the practitioner, meditation can serve as health nurturing activity or a gateway to higher consciousness. It is said the when you pray, you talk to God; when you meditate, you listen.

There are voluminous studies and a multiplicity of books describing the many health benefits of meditation. You can research this further or become a practitioner and experience this for yourself. Let me state here, that while all religions incorporate some form of introspection in their practices, it is not inherently a religious act. It is a beneficial routine, and if properly taught should not be offensive nor antithetical to any particular religious path. It is non-dogmatic and nonsectarian. A technique. No different from pushups or breathing exercises. But one for the inner man.

Modern medicine recognizes the importance of meditative practices in which an incredibly divergent set individuals, even ones seemingly contrary to these practices, recognize as an essential act to help improve their focus. One doesn't need to go out and buy any machines, gear, or other aids. Just some guidance and a curiosity for realization. But some individuals do use biofeedback machines to help meter and monitor their brainwave states. Somewhat like training wheels.

Your Tai-Chi, yoga, and meditation are with you always, wherever you go. In contrast, within our mechanistic society, everything requires scads of gear. For instance, in order for any child to play almost any sport in the United States, the parents need to go out and buy a lot of expensive equipment. Helmets, pads, braces, and all kinds of training aids - just so the kid can get in the game. In cultures with a different world view (and yes, economic reality) all a child needs is a ball (and maybe a stick).

Therefore, there is never any legitimate excuse to not meditate, perform Tai-Chi, or engage in other mechanisms of self-improvement. While one can use gym equipment and ride their bike, when schedule permits, but one wakes up every morning - no matter where they are.

The best Yin/Yang balance for a daily routine is one the spends at least equal time on both inner and outer development. One should perform a single or a series of mind/body routines, then arise and follow-up with the Tai-Chi form. As in all things, balance is the key.

Don't worry about not doing all of this perfectly. And, certainly don't use perfection as an excuse for not committing. Without a doubt, it is easier to come up with more excuses to not perform the daily routine than to do it. Don't waste your precious time on this negative energy. By the time you come up with an excuse, you could have accomplished a good deal of the routine. Also, continue this praxis even if you think you're not seeing any improvements. This routine takes time to produce noticeable results. Keep in mind the body builder. It can be months before any discernible development is visible. But if he wants it...he preserves.

Meditation is the most personnel thing that one will ever do. That is why it's called self-realization. Do you really know just who it is that looks out through your eyes? Many people waste an appreciable percentage of their time on this earth becoming obsessed to know more about some love interest, sport, or other external stimuli, than taking the same amount of time to really understand themself. How about you?

Entering the gateway to the internal world is an important, constructive, and valuable enterprise. This endeavor helps us experience a deeper understanding of our perceptual experiences and bodily sensations. So, to aid us in preparation to realizing this distinguished undertaking it might also be helpful to examine some properties ascribed to qualia.

1. Ineffable: cannot be communicated or apprehended by any means other than direct experience.

2. Intrinsic: non-relational properties, which do not change depending on the experience's relation to other things.

3. Private: all interpersonal comparisons of qualia are impossible.

4. Apprehensible: directly or immediately perceivable by one's consciousness. To know everything there is to know about that experience.

Stop to think about the qualia of your most personal bodily functions. Breath, regulation, defecation. No authority required. That is just you being you. No one telling you you're doing it right or wrong. Like these systems, meditation is also a qualia, one of a profoundly personal experience. The only difference is that you are connecting with a part of you that has been hidden mostly behind the smoke and clouds of your consciousness and ego. Meditation is your conscience you detecting your spirit you. Disconnecting from the clutter of your thoughts, which are objects and emotions. Exposing your id. Your Yin reunited with your Yang.

If there is one thing hinted at by quantum inquiry, it's that everything is a part of everything else. It is not egotistical nor profane to comprehend that you are connected to the whole world. If you feel that something is missing, not quite complete, it's because you need to be reunited with your complete self and your environment. You need to remember and appreciate that you are the world.

THE MICRO-COSMIC ORBIT

This highly instructive, beneficial meditation is key to understanding the internal sciences.

It is a life altering experience that can only be described as enlightening.

But before we begin. Let's start to develop an understanding of focused awareness.

FOCUSED ATTENTION - Preamble

The version of the micro-cosmic orbit that I recommend and practice, is physically outlined in the next chapter: Focused Attention.

Understanding about the transformation that manifests when attention is fully focused and the full power of concentration is brought to bear on elevated perception is crucial. In order to place emphasis on this most significant aspect of the meditation practice, the physical formula was placed in the Focused Attention chapter. This was done to emphasize this singular most significant quality that is this chapter's namesake.

The profound internal transformation that occurs during meditation is something that needs to be experienced. Although one may describe it in detail, the experience cannot be fully conveyed using only words. This is true in many aspects of life.

For example, It would almost be considered ridiculous to write a drinking manual. What could it possibly outline? It could, I suppose, contain an explanation of the chemistry and a description of the effects of ethanol on brain function. But, one would be no closer to understanding the sensation and effects; even after thousands of pages.

This idea of a manual to describe the drunken state of consciousness borders on the absurd. Descriptions of cafe life would just be depictions of the environment where the activity took place. To really immerse oneself in barroom culture, hang around beer joints and pool halls may provide the ambiance; but this is not partaking of the internal transformation from normal citizen into reprehensible tool.

Also, people do crave an alternate state of consciousness; and different versions are available for a price. Each with their own pro's and con's, but none as profound as the one produced by meditation.

The beneficial altered state of awareness obtained by meditative practices elevates the practitioner to a state of realization and ultimately union with God. The catch? Only you can enter that door. It must be experientially obtained. It is the difference between taking the medicine, or just reading the label.

Although these are lofty promises, I assure you they are palpable - and deliverable. They require no payment (except this book), and bear none of the deleterious effects of a chemically induced psychotropic state. And, unlike those other venues of alteration, there is every reason to include these practices as part of one's personal genesis; and none to exclude.

As a good comparison to what you may not realize about mediation is: someone trying to function blindfolded. Although they may think they are aware of everything; they literally don't know what they are missing: they just can't see.

Tai-Chi is often referred to as a moving meditation. But, to achieve this advanced form of meditation first requires the precursor of a foundational experience of deep, static meditation. But once obtained, the practitioner will surely find that the movement itself elicits a meditative quality, in and of itself. Tai-Chi movement is the Ying/Yang hum of the universe, the pause between the actions; the space between notes and the notes themself: it is the gap and the non-gap that sparks ellipse.

Focused Attention

In the beginning...of this book I emphasized that the body makes its own medicine. This is an important aspect of Tai-Chi as a healing modality. We then concentrated on three basic precepts to build proper execution. Structure, body energy states and mind intent. While these concepts are most helpful with the martial aspects of the art, proper form contributes to the many health benefits of Tai-Chi. There is another adage to remember that applies more to the internal aspects of the art. A sister concept to mind intent...

ENERGY FLOWS WHERE INTENTION GOES

In this approach we endeavor to identify our energy and move it around. Move it around so it will do you some good. Here is one healing energy routine to hopefully jump start your understanding of internal energy work. I will explain verbally in this chapter, and provide an accompanying diagram in the appendix.

As explained in the chapter on brain wave states. The brain creates an actual electrical current. Which varies depending on which brainwave state you are in. But it is real and measurable. Because it's made by you it is the proper type to promote health within your body. One of the additional benefits of focused attention is that it also increases blood flow and hormonal/nutrient dump to the designated area.

Physics has some pretty strict definitions of energy. In medicine it get a little more murky. Certainly the process that converts food into usable fuel is one definition. Digestion, the Krebs cycle, Then there is brain energy. Electro / biochemical. Hormonal, reaction to neurotransmitters. Epinephrine, dopamine and other process as outlined in chapter two. By focusing laser attention on a particular area , the mind is directing energy to that location. It is simple, but grossly underestimated and overlooked.

WHERE THERE IS THOUGHT..THERE IS ENERGY

Now is all there ever has been. Many unfortunately are constantly projecting into the future or living in the past. Instead of constantly escaping now, begin by training perception. The insights revealed by this simple understanding are real gateways. Building an appreciation for the true nature of reality by expanding awareness begins with not escaping. Enter the present moment by becoming aware of sense perceptions.

The next time you suffer a minor injury, stub your toe or cramp, instead of pulling away and pretending that it is not happening, try focusing attention right at the center of the problem. There are imagining techniques to disperse the sensation, but for now, just concentrate on directing awareness right at the problem. The more you feel, the harder you concentrate. You are master of this ship. By controlling the scenario, you will dial down perception and tune in internally and thus enhance your ability to function.

A MEDITATION TECHNIQUE

Sit comfortably. Half lotus preferably, but seated in a chair is fine. Do several rounds of the complete breath. Effect the Sung state of profound relaxation. Concentrate on the very top of your head. Right in the center. Chinese call this Bai-Hui. It is acupoint GV20. But it doesn't matter. In yogic tradition they call it something else. Just bring your full awareness to this place. Feel this spot intensely. Feel it strongly. And when you feel it as strongly as you can dial it up and feel it more strongly still.

You are going to repeat this intense concentration on each of the energy centers in order. Fully concentrate all of your attention and hold your focus at these energy points. Feel it as strongly as you can.

Four or five minutes would be an admirable goal. But one or two minutes is fine. The important thing is to feel them intensely. Refer to the chart in the appendix for proper location of the energy centers, Focus your mind completely on feeling them strongly. All of your attention. All of your concentration.

ALL OF YOUR AWARENESS

When you have focused your attention as fully as you can, allow your attention to move forward toward the hairline. As your attention moves down the forehead, imagine it flows like dripping honey. Slowly moving down the forehead, coming to rest right between the eyes. Hold your concentration here

FEEL THIS SPOT STRONGLY

Keep concentrating. You are not blanking out. You are not retreating inwardly. You are building internal strength. This is a workout. That's why it doesn't matter if the dog barks or the motorcycle goes by. You are not trying to go blank. You are training your concentration. A distraction may pull you out a little . But go right back. Now let your attention slowly flow down to the throat center.

FOCUS

Your entire being, your whole mind. Fully concentrated at throat hollow. This is more than just acupoint CV22. The entire throat center holds your attention. Concentrate fully. As you move your attention down from the bridge of the nose. feel your nose. philtrum, lips, chin, flow down the throat.

KEEP CONCENTRATING

Allow your attention to move slowly down the sternum. Coming to rest at the heart center. Hold your attention strongly here. Each of the centers should be a challenge to concentrate as fully as you can. Drill your attention deeply into the body. Hold your concentration here.

MAKE THIS REAL

With the unlimited power of the mind. This is real energy. You are doing actual work. A weight lifter starts off light. doesn't see much development at first. Then adds a pound a week. You are making yourself stronger on the inside. Stay the course. Remember the body builder.

METHODICALLY WITH PURPOSE

Slowly move your attention down the high abdomen to a place just behind and below the navel. This is the lower tan-tien. Hara in Japanese. Your center of gravity and collection point for internal energy. Chinese liken the lower tan-tien to a simmering cauldron. Here we collect and store internal energy.

STAY RELAXED

Feel around with your mind till you find this pocket behind the navel. You'll know when you do.

Now move your attention to the sex center. Concentrate fully here. There should be nothing forced or unnatural about your breathing. Forget about it. You should not even be aware of the breath.

RELAX HARDER

Now you really need to concentrate. Turn up your awareness stronger than you ever have before. Focus your awareness on the tip of the tailbone. Light it up. Feel the energetic sensation throughout your entire body. Focus perception in this center more than all the other centers that have been building up to this extreme focused concentration.

ALL OF YOUR ATTENTION

You are now experiencing extreme concentration of focused attention. You are feeling the tip of your tailbone with the power of the sun and a massive electric charge. At this point, you abandon conscious control and you………..

BECOME THE OBSERVER

You now Imagine the spine as a hollow tube and allow your attention to begin to percolate up this hollow tube, moving on its own. You are just an observer to this process.

FOCUSED AND RELAXED

You watch as your concentrated attention bubbles up through the hollow spine. It may move in fits and starts, but this only proves that it is real.

DON'T DRIFT - DON'T PULL OUT

Concentrate fully as you observe your attention continue to rise as it passes the internal organs.

The Stomach: The Lungs: The Heart: You observe as it passes behind the throat center.

ALMOST HOME

Your attention continues to percolate up the spine and begins to empty into the back of the head.

You allow your concentrated attention to flush from the spine and fully collect in the back of the head.

RETURN TO THE SEVENTH

Our awareness travels up the back of the head and returns to the seventh center.

CONCENTRATE ON BAI-HUI

We have returned to where we started. This concludes the microcosmic orbit. Concentrate fully on the very top of your head. Feel it strongly, dial up your awareness. Then relax, take in a deep breath. Exhale. Bask in the complete joy of simply being.

33333333333333

With eyes closed. Dwell momentarily in bliss. Open your eyes and enjoy this Alpha brain wave state.

WHERE THERE IS THOUGHT: THERE IS ENERGY

As you pass through the postures of the Tai-Chi form, It is this sensation of focused awareness you move from one location to another to amplify and augment stimulation of organs, acupoints and problem areas. To not only exercise, massage and condition specific anatomical structures, but to also bathe them with concentrated bio-energy is a maintenance routine tantamount to brushing your teeth, a moisturizing regime or nutritional supplementation. In concert with the benefits of the movement, the saturation of electro / chemical stimulation contributes not only to the longevity of The physical entity, but also heightens awareness, connects to source and confirms oneness and stewardship.

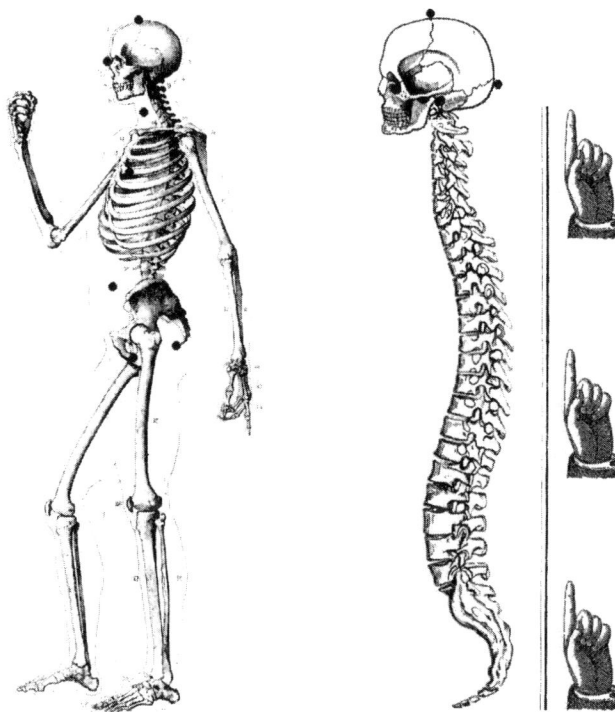

Who's Talking

Performing as a tiki-bar musician on Fort Lauderdale beach may be considered a fantasy by some. And, I do appreciate my life on the beach along with the opportunity to make my living doing something enjoyable. At the time of this writing, I have performed at the pier in Lauderdale-by-the-sea for the past twelve years, and my continued tenure seems secure. A fortunate circumstance for any musician.

Since South Florida is a resort area, there is always a good number of people on vacation. And, I find that people on vacation are usually very relaxed and cordial. This allows me to interact with people outside of their normal atmosphere and have conversations that might not otherwise take place.

Along that vein of thought, one evening, a few years ago, a young man introduced himself as a conservatory trained musician; one who had studied at both Berkeley and Julliard. He was highly complementary of my performance and we talked briefly of art and business. As our conversation wound down, he said: "You should be making thousands doing studio work; it's better than slaving nightly". Then spoke of the "music obsession". And, finally concluded by adding, "Really it's kind of a curse, being driven to live this life." I think of this incident often, and agree that we are both cursed, but maybe my curse includes always winding up singing in some beer joint.

Since this observation is so familiar to me, it can serve as an introduction to explore a vital aspect of the mental apparatus involved with perceived independent thought; or free will, as it is commonly called. I will do this by examining my "curse".

In my younger days, I was a road musician and developed the skills necessary to maintain what was, at the time, an envious position. As the years progressed, I perused other careers; but in the in-between times, I would always revert to playing music. To me, defaulting to a proven alternate resource hardly seems daft, rather a thoughtful conclusion arrived at logically as the most practical way to produce income immediately. After all, I have obtained the requisite abilities and have a good understanding of the business.

During those middle years, I enjoyed my other careers in both business and government service, and was glad to give the music business a rest as my primary career path. But, when I began to play full time again, in my fifties, I took the time to carefully weighed my options. And, being a partial pragmatist, put it my choice to the pencil.

First, making the investment to go to school and acquire a marketable skill would require a loss of income, especially during the training period. This, plus the price of education. Next, I calculated the projected salary and time needed to recoup my investment. Then I amortized against other available options, such as taking a lower paying job. This choice would allow me to keep earning, although at a highly reduced rate. And, although not monetary, job satisfaction was also a consideration. The prospect of working in a T-shirt shop was somewhat less than intriguing. Finally, I concluded that if I went back to work as a musician, I could make twice the pay in half the hours. Also, I already had the investment in equipment, skills, and practical, working knowledge.

On the surface, this all seemed like a logical cost benefit analysis - and not an emotional decision. I thought I was using reason, and intelligently weighing options. Of the competing options, music seemed the cogent choice. After all, I had a pencil.

Or, was it just the curse? And, if it was the curse, how did this curse get inaugurated? As a professional detective and an amateur street philosopher, this analysis provided me with a good opportunity to look for possible catalysts to this dilemma, and consider one avenue that helps to introduce the real subject of this essay.

Like many American kids, of that era, I was enthralled with "The Beatles" when they appeared on the Ed Sullivan show in 1963. I looked at their lifestyle, at their humble beginnings, and saw an escape route. The factory town I grew up in was gray and mean. My dad always came home from work spent and covered with grime. I loved and respected him, but I knew I didn't want anything to do with his world. Yet as a troubled youth, it seemed that congressman or jet pilot was unattainable. Guitar virtuoso, on the other hand, this I could do!

The guy in our neighborhood who was like "Fonzie" acquired a '56 Gibson, Les Paul during one of his B&E's. He sold it to me for eight bucks. Unlike school or organized activities, learning to play was an exercise in intellectual freedom. No tests or requirements. No berating or intimidation. No chastisements for not making the grade. I was only governed by my own drive, commitment, and perseverance. For my specific personality, this was cathartic.

Within me, deep grooves were being cleaved in the fissures of my brain. As local success grew musically, and conflict with authority continued habitually; individualistic and iconoclastic behaviors became even more acutely ingrained. A malcontent was born.

It is true that the above dialogue could be the bohemian, or outsider weltanschauung, from many a life. But, I have ambled through my unique yarn so that one may live in my skin; if only momentarily. To help the reader appreciate the calculus and catalysts of how some of these life-altering determinations were arrived at, and why certain deeds were performed.

Furthermore, while the majority of people function well being directed by organizations, corporations, fraternities, or clubs; those with an entrepreneurial bent, however, tend to crave independence. And, this is a fairly unique characteristic to this personality type. A characteristic that directly effects the decision-making processes of those few, like myself, functioning on the edges or even well outside of the so called "mainstream".

At this juncture, it may seem hard to believe, but I don't really like talking about myself. There are, however, no other exemplars of with which I am more intimately familiar. None more than my own personal experience. So, even though I don't enjoy trying to expound upon myself, understanding the "curse" referenced by a kindly young customer prompted an introspection of events. Acts, resolutions, and conclusions most would dismiss as antisocial, mis-guided, or might even argue as some mental predisposition.

Why is this all relevant? Because understanding thought and reaction is ascendant in getting the most from Tai-Chi. But, just this knowledge is not the only thing that is required. One must also take the time to genuinely understand terms like instinct and conditioning; specifically in relation to maximizing coalition of brain function (an organ whose sole purpose is that of a problem-solving entity).

And for what ultimate aim? The entire above discourse is ad rem to the main proposed thesis of this chapter. To come to the understanding that there is no real free will.

When a human being believes that they are making a decision, the decision has already been made before they are aware that one has been made. Physiologically, the prefrontal cortex and hippocampus are the brain structures involved in this process. A thorough understanding of the role of the ventromedial prefrontal cortex, amygdala, cingulate and dorsolateral cortex is not necessary, even though these areas are credited philologically in the decision-making process.

Psychologically, however, the brain is running a calculation, and it is impossible to know the outcome while processing. Otherwise there would be no need to do the calculation. In the end, the brain will always do what you really want. These processes are wired to serve your preferred interests and never free to override their programming.

The reality is that we all make decisions before we are consciously aware that one has been made. The processing times are so fast that by the time what one perceives a decision has been formulated, the higher mind has obeyed the prime directive. And, this choice complies with one's deepest, innermost desires. Ultimately, the brain, as an administration center, is running a software program to optimize for well-being.

It would seem that decisions are either determined or random (Yin/Yang). But, both the thoughtful and the knee jerk reaction are governed by the same preset. One may indulge in the fantasy that they weighed options, but they didn't. Even chaos is deterministic. One will always choose what they most want to do; even if that is the worst decision. It is still what they most wanted to do.

For example, if confronted by a huge, homicidal monster; one that I know will pulverize me if I take a poke at it; I most want not to be beaten up. But, if I want to "prove" to myself that I have free will and over ride my best interests, then that is what I most wanted to do. Again, it is not free will.

There are always several possible futures from which one may choose. One's programming causes them to choose that which they most want to do. One may choose chaos, but that choice is deterministic. The subconscious shapes the conscious. It is programming: to think otherwise is an illusion.

In martial arts training, one supplants chaotic responses with trained ones. Responses that are so deeply ingrained, that one doesn't know any other way to stand, except in a strong stance. One doesn't know any other way to strike, except with a strong hit. It is not a choice, it is programming.

If the deepest, fixed inclination is to escape, then this compulsion will override training; because this is the thing the brain has selected as predominant. Whichever is the most powerful - flight or fight (Yin/Yang), the processing unit has selected the procedure. The decision was already made. It is not necessarily a response to stimulus.

This is why war fighter training, like the marine corps, is so intense. Selective reprogramming of basic survival instincts, serve to produce only those who pack the gear to become dependable team members. Since no one knows how anyone will perform under highly stressful conditions, the psyche and id are challenged unconditionally. And, an effort is made to build a new man; a fearless man - gung-ho, kill, kill kill. Even when faced with true chaos, deafening ordnance, gore and loss of life, as well as other devastation. The only default ideation is esprit de corps, unit cohesion, duty, and honor. It is hoped that predilections such as these will prevail in the face of mind-numbing catastrophe.

Knowing that ones' will is not their own is meliorism for all aspects of everyday living. One can choose to run a different program, but after all the computations, they will still only choose that which they most want to do. Which means, it's really not a choice. This may seem like semantics, but an understanding that the mind is running a calculation and can only produce one result, eliminates worry and confusion over a phantom decision-making process.

Which leads us once again to the question; just who is it looking out through these eyes? If the brain is just another organ doing its job, who's driving this train? The brain has regions dedicated to management of systems, auditory and visual, maintain circulation, balancing chemistry, and other workaday functions; no more divine than the kidneys or liver. The pancreas dispenses insulin in quantities that are most needed. But the brain, as director of action, is a processing unit and command center.

Relating to the outside environment, is a complex dance. To satisfy other areas of the brain, it must compel actions the way it dispenses insulin. Either organ may malfunction and cause trouble. Mental illness is akin to diabetes of the brain. Through formative experiences and adult trauma, a program is installed; and future calculations are made based on those investitures. Psychological conditions have created a program with only one option. And that is always the same. One does the thing that they most want to do.

To reiterate; the outcome is not a determination between options. The brain makes only one selection, it judges what you most want to do. There is no choice. Free will is a myth.

For reasons well understood by all, the organ most cultures traditionally associate with the soul is the heart. Where people commonly say; "I have kidneys and a brain", and may also assert that they have a soul. The epiphany is manifest when cognized as C.S. Lewis did, "You do not have a soul, you have a body; you are a soul".

According to the determinism of Thomas Aquinas in his best known work, Suma Theologica; things are ordered from eternity by God. Since God is first cause of everything, God is the cause of even the free acts of men through predestination. Nothing in the world is accidental. All is unchangeable. That means predestination is grace, since everything is the will of God.

Our actions should be based on the ever present awareness that human beings in their thinking, feeling, and acting are not free but are just as causally bounds as the stars in their motion.

Albert Einstein

(circa September 22, 1932)

Ethereality

I am an old man now. And I often have old man dreams. I dream of people long dead, and places that no longer exist. Last night I dreamt of my old high school, a magnificent structure built by the W.P.A. during the depression. It was torn down twenty years ago.

There is nothing morbid about this. These are the memories floating around in the brain of a senior citizen. Places and events that are now vanished. If one were to watch these reminiscences unfold, I'm sure it would all seem very macabre.

Because of my yogic practices, I am well (for the time being anyway); and due to the mind element of these pursuits, I am imbued with a buoyant optimism. There have been dark times - some of which are chronicled in this book. My wife was killed in the later part of the 20th century, and my only child passed at 22. I am the last of my linage.

Tragic for them, and like anyone, I mourn and don't fully comprehend. To lose out on life is a cataclysmic injustice. To be denied years in which to experience and grow, not only cheats, but interrupts the arc of a life which was intended to run its full course. As Yogananda says, "to live fully, and fall like ripe fruit from the tree."

When one experiences debilitating catastrophe; loss of a child or spouse, incarceration, violence, abandonment; the natural reaction of the human psyche is to spiral into any one of a variety of isms. Cynicism, alcoholism, defeatism. How does one maintain faith? The departed also trusted, and their gone.

Undeniably, his ways are mysterious. The world is chaotic and random. But if you are lucky enough to somehow survive, you have been given an incredible gift. We all have an obligation to those who didn't make it; to use your perspective, to delve into any possible meaning that may be uncovered from heartbreak or tragedy. To maintain trust in the face of malign forces, requires either an absurd naivete or an implacable faith that transcends the apparent obvious.

Even if you are not naturally possessed of this kind of fortitude; it is possible to behave as if you are. "Fake it 'til you make it" is folk wisdom that obscures and at the same time embodies a genuine eternal truth. Exercising the technique of trust is a type of faith in and of itself. A fairly reliable authority assured us all that one only needs the faith of a mustard seed.

If one were foundering in the middle of a deep lake, the worst course of action would be to panic and clutch wildly at the water. The best course is to relax and lie flat and have faith in the buoyancy of this medium that has supported ships, birds, and swimmers for as long as there has been sentience. Trust in the properties of the water to act in accordance with the laws of physics. It will fulfill its contract with the immutable laws that govern buoyancy.

Let's take that same sojourner and place him in a small vessel, careening through white water rapids. This similar, yet different, situation would now require reliance on a disparate trust. To negotiate the dangerous hazards manifesting at every turn, his faith has now shifted to his highly developed skills. In this case, he is relying on his training, preparation, and experience to produce a successful outcome. His trust is in himself.

Like the kayaker, the Tai-Chi fighter learns to ride the incoming force; skillfully maneuvering any threat or hazard. With the same expert technique as the Tai-Chi fighter, the kayaker learns to hone the needed skills to not unwisely or directly oppose the mighty power before him. The Tai-Chi fighter, like the boatman, learns to avoid hazards, working in concert with the domineering power.

Drawing us directly back to the drowning analogy; the placid lake represents Tai-Chi philosophy, where the rapids represent Tai-Chi in action. One requires abandonment and complete trust in the Tao. But it is also imperative for one to have the ability to draw upon training and skill to persevere when required. Essentially, opposites or reverses. Both go with the flow, but personal wisdom and experiences dictate when to favor one type of trust over the other.

Some situations necessitate an authoritative preponderance, while others demand compliant passivity. In mundane interactions with the universe, like making a life decision, most people employ thoughtful calculations, but then finally wind up making a snap decision in the end. They employ experience and technique, then abandon ultimate outcomes to fate.

Faith and action are unanimity and dichotomy, aspects of Yin and Yang. You as arbiter, toggle back and forth as required. Whether floating on a lake, negotiating rapids, or having surreal wanderings of your old high school; continuity of life may depend on knowing when to row your boat, and when to acknowledge that life is but a dream.

What's the Point

The history of modern science is basically the quest to see of what everything is made. The problem is, things are an illusion. In our Newtonian understanding of the universe, it seemed only logical to begin to take things apart. To divide them into their smallest constituents. This after all is the history of western man's understanding of the universe.

Democritus was a pre-Socratic philosopher who lived from 460 to 370 BC, or thereabouts. He is best remembered for developing an atomic theory of the universe. He postulated that everything in the universe is composed of atoms, a physical structure which is the smallest thing in the universe. An indivisible thing which simply can't be broken down any further. Between the atoms is empty space, and like his mentor Leucippus, he believed atoms were indestructible.

Although the concept of the atom was really more like our idea of the molecule; it was still inspired thinking, which laid the ground work for the advancements of Issac Newton. Let's leave that alone, because here we're more concerned with process than results. The idea that you can keep cutting something into smaller and smaller pieces to reveal its essence is folly.

It's certainly been worth the effort, because this process has revealed that ultimately there are no things at all. The ultimate cosmic joke. And was, of course, known to eastern mystics for millennia. When you begin with the premise that everything is a big machine, you wind up looking in all the wrong places.

There's an old story about a passerby who sees a drunk crawling around under a streetlight. When he offered to help, he was told that the drunk had lost his watch. "Well, where did you lose it?", the passerby asked. "Over there by the trees", the drunk replied. "What are you looking over here for?", he retorted. The drunk said, "Because that's where the light is."

This roughly describes the western discipline known as the scientific method. In our culture, we've decided that the answer lies where the light is, because our method is based on a premise. That the world is made up of things. Like the scholars of old, we kept evaluating and dividing matter into smaller and smaller portions, until we believed we obtained the absolute smallest - the indivisible. We even dedicated an entire field of study to it.

For a longtime, we thought the molecule was the smallest particle. But, as our knowledge and instrumentation advanced, we were eventually able to achieve the ability to even see inside the atom. The idea of the electric universe was becoming apparent. But, there was much resistance. Because it still held that things were made of solid matter.

It was discovered that in the center of the atom was a nucleus, composed of nucleons. These are composite particles made up of smaller particles, organized according to the laws of quantum chromodynamics. A nucleon is either a proton an a neutron. Around this compact bundle whirled energetic particles called electrons. The Greeks were proven right. The atom was mostly empty space. To visualize this, if you stood with your arms extended, the electron's orbit would border your fingers and toes. In the center, the nucleus measures less than a human hair.

Electrons in the outermost orbit, in what was called the valance shell, were sometimes able to give up an electron to a neighboring atom, thus creating new molecules. This understanding led to the science of chemistry.

Scientific inquiry really began to pick up steam. It was discovered that protons, neutrons and electrons were not the smallest things in the universe. Nucleons, it seems, are made up something smaller still, called quarks. Up quarks, down quarks, charm, strange, bottom, and top. Quarks combine to form composite particles called hadrons. The most stable, of which, are protons and neutrons. Quarks possess intrinsic properties such as mass, spin, electric charge, and something called color charge - because scientists were running out of known things from which to compare.

In the standard model of particle physics, quarks are the only elementary particle to experience all four fundamental forces. Gravitation, strong interaction, weak interaction, and electromagnetism. Each quark flavor has a corresponding anti-particle, called an anti-quark.

Because quarks are spin-1/2 particles they qualify as fermions, and are subject to the Pauli exclusion principal; which states that no two identical fermions can occupy the same quantum state simultaneously (more on this later).

Also in this mix are: virtual, sea quarks, anti-quarks, baryons, mesons, and exotic quarks - like tetra-quarks and penta-quarks. And, oh yeah; gluons that act as the exchange particle, or gauge boson, for the strong force. Aptly named because they glue quarks together. If you happen to be a fan of Feynman diagrams, knock yourself out. The visual may foster a greater understanding.

I felt it necessary to illustrate the complexity of particle physics, because it relates directly to our understanding of Tai-Chi theory; in-as-much-as we need to be aware of the current understanding science has of particles. Because particles don't exist.

In our quest to know more and more about less and less, we have discovered that if we qualify these particles as physical things: they are not. Turns out, what is contemporarily thought to be particles are, in actuality, disturbances in fields. What we call a quark is a vibrating ripple in a field. An electron is an excitation in the electron field. A quark is a vibrating ripple in the quark field. What science judged to be mass is rightly understood to be bound up confined energy.

The dichotomy of all this is almost absurdly obvious. In western culture we tore things apart, dissected and developed powerful instruments in an effort to force the universe to reveal its secrets. Whereas in the east, they looked within. Each coming to the same conclusion.

The Guru; the spiritualist; the theoretical physicist; and the stoned out, hippie freak agree: It's all energy man.

Todays scientists have substituted mathematics for experiments. And they wander off through equation after equation. And eventually build a structure which has no relation to reality.

NIKOLA TESLA.

Beginning

On September 11th, 2001 the United States was attacked by radical Islamic militants in a horrific attack that ultimately claimed 2,977 lives. The country was stunned, social order was in chaos, the initial national response was clumsy and hesitant. Scrambling to cover security and investigative needs, while planning an appropriate military response; the government reaction was finally energized after being caught flat-footed by amateur, third-world terrorists.

As in many human endeavors, the thing that makes our country great, is also the thing that makes it vulnerable. An open society is often susceptible to opportunists with malevolent intent. While military assets were being rallied, government facilities and private business needed increased security, urgently. While all this was going on, Immigration policies that allowed the terrorists access to the means and apparatus to affect their evil intent needed to be immediately addressed.

The terrorists entered the country on I-20 student visas, which allowed foreign nationals residence while attending school in the United States. It seemed like a magnanimous program to cultivate future academics and professionals; some of which would become contributing Americans. Since we raided and transplanted European brain trusts after World War II, it seemed natural to cultivate foreign intellectual talent.

This well-intentioned policy proved to provide a loophole for devious enemies with nefarious intent, wishing to harm the United States of America. While the military response was under way, this internal, bureaucratic inadequacy needed to be confronted. The need to plug this loophole and prevent future cataclysms, preventing foreign radicals from gaining deceitful access on I-20 student visas, was of paramount importance.

A cohort of professional investigators was needed immediately to inspect and scrutinize institutions of higher learning, assessing student visa polices; with the objective of preventing future incidents of terrorists exploiting this system. INS became ICE, the student exchange visitor information system (SEVIS) was instituted, and qualified investigators with government experience were suddenly a commodity of high priority.

At the time, I was a private investigator with my own private practice in Florida. This is in the same region of the country where terror mission leader Mohammad Atta attended flight school - again, thanks to our lenient student visa program. I received a call from a friend of mine who had formerly taught at the FBI National Academy. He was often tapped for sensitive government assignments and informed me that he was involved with a contract to provide investigative services for INS, specifically to address this problem. He had a friend (his old CO from Vietnam) who had risen to the number two spot in one of America's clandestine intelligence agencies. His old CO, after retirement, had become an influential K street defense contractor. This individual was ultimately awarded the contract which hired, directed, and managed the cohort created to correct for this defect.

Investigators were needed in the field, immediately, and I was processed post haste. We were now working in support of the freshly minted department of homeland security. There were 800 of us swiftly hired for this new objective. Obviously, this green department wasn't fully organized. And even if it was, the department's permanent agents would have needed to be trained at Langley or Quantico. This would have meant a delay of several months; conferring official status, and administering 800 benefits programs. Finally, what do you do with operatives after the bubble? At that time, no one expected DHS to have any longevity, or equal status with DIA, CIA, or FBI.

Another friend of mine, now departed, was my mentor and was the first CIA agent when the agency was formed from its predecessor, the OSS. I was always awed by the historical significance of his being at the beginning of an important American institution. And yet, here it was, in another era; a new threat and a new response. I feel compelled to add, that while unsung, this individual single-handedly saved the western hemisphere from communism. It is because of his lineage that "The Company" is called "The Company." A national luminary, and a personal hero, I loved him so much, I almost married his daughter.

A beautiful woman and gifted operative in her own right, she was raised among the Washington elite. Because her father was an adviser to four presidential administrations, she was intimate with first families and a playmate of the presidential children. Being representative of traditional Virginia society, she was the product of Southern Culture, cotillions, and what one might envision from this historical culture. As a young woman with her friends, plying the downtown DC bistros; when asked by prospective suitors where they were from, they would reply (in affected southern accents): "We're from Norfolk. We don't smoke, nor drink. Norfolk."

For me it was a personal connection, and homage to this man, to be one of the first people assimilated into the, now venerated, organization. Like all Americans, of that era, I needed to feel I was contributing in some small way to the 9-11 response. Quickly credentialed and dispatched to remedy the new threat, I began calling on institutions of higher learning.

At that time, there were a large magnitude and numerous categories of qualified academic institutions that were authorized to issue student visas. But, the government considered flight schools of paramount importance. This was due to the fact that this type of institution was the venue in which the terrorists gained entrance to the country. The school administrators were always respectful and cooperative. This is directly attributable to two major facts: First, the ability to issue I-20 visas represented a significant portion of enrollment. And second, they could lose this ability to issue visas based solely on the outcome of my investigation.

I interviewed a fine gentleman who ran a flight school in Pompano Beach, Florida. Then, some months later, I re-encountered him as the director of the area's premier training facility in Miami-Dade, Florida. An impressive institution, where all aspects of flight training were state of the art. The flight simulators were space capsule type enclosures supported on stands, which towered twenty five feet off the floor. These pods would dip and spin, as directed by the student pilot contained within.

After I pulled the needed files, interviewed their personal, and inspected the physical structure; the director asked me if I would like to "fly" the 747 simulator. To maintain the decorum of my position, I needed to greatly contain my enthusiasm; and responded with a well-timed and severely muted: "Well...yeah, I guess that would be OK."

We climbed the simulator's ladder, entered, and strapped in. The director assumed the right seat position. It was a technological wonderland with hundreds of gauges and switches. The module is a direct representation of a 747 cockpit, where you can choose any airport in the world. The screens, which are structured to exactly replicate the aircraft windows; are so advanced, and such high resolution, you are left with a feeling that you are not in a simulator - you are landing at Laguardia.

I chose to fly through a mountain pass of Nepal and ultimately landed at Kathmandu. Among my other expeditions were: to made a low altitude pass across the African savanna, skim the Andes, and also land at St. Lucia. Of course, the director had to save the plane several times, and despite his best efforts to intervene, I also managed to crash the "plane" often.

Next, the director offered the opportunity to pilot a 757, followed by a 767. Each of which I gleefully accepted. I finally emerged from the simulator, in complete emotional rapture. I expressed to him that if I were a kid, I would meet whatever challenge and endure any sacrifice to be able to do this for the rest of my life.

Driving home, I pondered over how an opportunity like that was never in the cards for me. I came to the conclusion that even if I had been exposed to such a choice and had garnered the proper enthusiasm; I doubt that I could have guided events to unfold in my favor. That I probably would have manifested the same outcome with my avalanche of poor decisions and even more hard luck that characterized my early life and mindset.

I left home when I was young, dropped out of school, hopped freight trains, and lived in rescue missions. Hitchhiked coast to coast (a couple of times), was almost killed in "the yards", in El Paso, by stupidly standing between two boxcars that were coupling. An fellow traveler shoved me violently from behind, just as the cars were slamming together.

Things did not have to turn out the way they did. I made a lot of irrational decisions, but was somehow eventually set on a corrected course. Like untold numbers of misdirected youth, the many major rescues, and hundreds of minor saves, allowed me to gain my footing and ultimately allowed me to redirect my life. This is a primary reason I am religious today.

It is true that the start of anything can be very critical to forging the remainder of an endeavor. In other words, if you mess something up early on, you've probably screwed up the rest of whatever it is. And, the beginning usually sets the president for what will follow. But worry not - all is not lost.

If bumped off course, it is oft times difficult to recover, but it's never too late. The law of Yin/Yang deems that opportunities cycle back, presenting junctures of fortune, that if taken advantage of provide for corrective measures. Just like a plane, a car, or a freight train; if you miss one, another will come by. While It is also true you can never go back and create a new beginning; you can start now and create a new end.

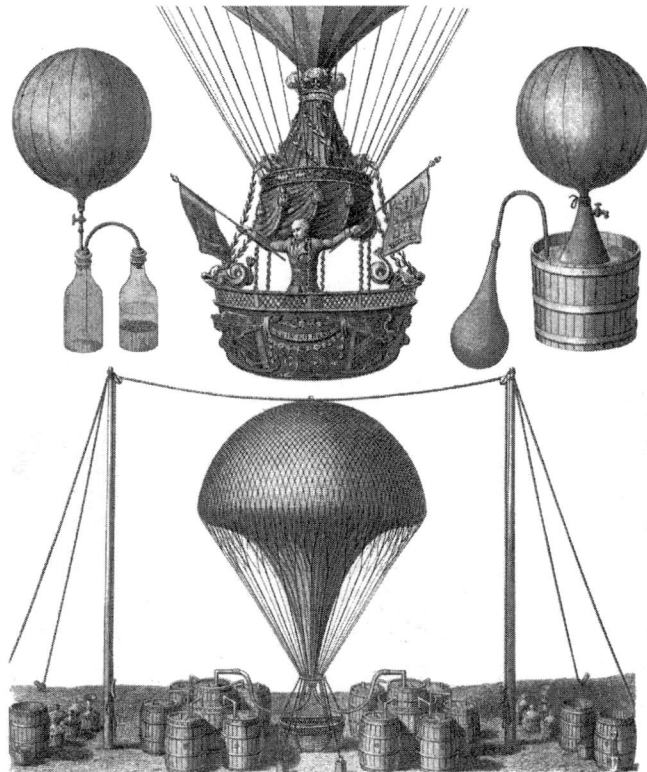

If it were possible to condense a lifetime and compare it to the Tai-Chi form, by metaphor and example, it would prove to follow a pattern observed to be seemingly random and erratic. But, like all things, is actually directed by an intelligent design. Often proving complex and taxing; if one were to adhere to principal and follow the rules, they will complete the sequence fully to the end; and be better for the effort. And, in accordance with universal law and congruence of the cosmic joke, one will wind up right back where they started.

Comparing the Tai-Chi form to the arc and flow of a given human life, or the progression and continuity of the empyrean cosmos, is to recognize the universal patterns common to all events and things. An inter-dimensional arrangement that is ubiquitous.

In Tai-Chi theory, the morning is poetically referred to as "the springtime of the day." That is why it is recommended that one perform the form first thing in the morning. This is considered when the body and the cosmos are most reconciliate and more conducive to receiving maximum benefit from the calibration in both the environment and the body.

To plant a seed in the autumn will not produce the maximal result. It this probable (and if one is lucky) that this action produces only a stunted, withered consequence. Therefore, it is best to operate in harmony with the system as we find it. Plant your seeds in the springtime and perform the solo sequence in the morning. This is when universal energies and biorhythms are most prolific.

The beginning of the form is the most important portion of the entire sequence. Yes, Tai-Chi is all about movement, but the most crucial aspect is set before you even start. While standing in Wu-Gi, prior to even the first hint of movement, this is where the mind and body coalesce. It is here that you set the template for all else that follows. Keep in mind, that once the hands begin to rise, the roller coaster is into the first drop. The form is already unfolding. Dynamics and principals are different once the movement begins.

Yet, even before any of this becomes germane, arises the part of the form called preparation. Stand with feet shoulder width and heels under the shoulder joints. Imagine that you are suspended by a cord from bi wei at the fontanel. One should get the feeling as if this cord is lifting the skull. Feel the vertebrates separate, all muscles hang loose. Affect the Sung state.

This is the vital and decisive moment. The crucial keystone and linchpin governing all movement that follows. This is the all-important beginning. And like one's life, even if this all-crucial event within the form is somehow not correctly accomplished, the form itself has cyclical junctures built into it where corrective measures can be folded in, allowing for a successful final outcome to its completion. This is a universal law. This is Yin/Yang. I can personally attest to the fact that even if you were once panhandling and living in the Salvation Army, one can still end up with a gravy job, wearing a suit and tie.

Regardless, the beginning is an extremely important aspect to the form which one does not need a government ID to investigate. The beginning should not be underestimated nor overlooked. Once the Sung state is achieved, cultivate awareness, feel the energetic body, and begin the complete breath.

Two-fer

Language is symbols. A kind of vocal hieroglyphics. When I say "rock, tree or airplane" you create an image in your mind. This works fine for solid objects, but what about the more conceptual. What does love, altruism or politics evoke?

By convention we say the sun rises in the east. It's just more efficient than describing the precise process every time. We both understand that It's a convenience. People have figured out levers, pulleys, and gears; it just makes things easier.

Because science is a conceptual endeavor with practical ramifications, we sometimes forget about the mental hieroglyphics. This becomes especially relevant with quantum thought. This type of thought is all about concepts and imagery. But, could language and cultural bias exert any appreciable effect on such advanced thought? This all depends on how much power the prevailing culture has had on the process. In such a case, this could be profound, and insidious.

The underlying doctrine of our culture was presaged by Judeo-Christian history and ideology; both influenced by the cultures of Sumeria, Babylon and Mesopotamia. These were all tyrannical, autocratic cultures governed by a succession of imperious rulers wielding absolute authority.

As the religions developed in these areas, it was assumed, logically, that the creator and sustainer of the universe must surly be like an all-powerful king; commanding and dealing harshly with the weakling subjects below.

In the east, religious concepts developed a little differently. More akin to philosophy. It was assumed not that things were commanded into existence, but that they just were. Great thinkers still observed patterns, but assumed a more swirling randomness of things that interact with a powerful unseen matrix.

But this was not the destiny of the west. Deeply embedded in the psyche of even the most learned men was a fundamental understanding of a despotic autocrat who held everything together by an act of divine will.

So when the scientific process eventually emerged from these learned men, we too began to understand the world through the observed principals of regularity. But, because of the deep seated cultural bias of language; the early titans of the scientific method referred to these observations as laws. And, this is where the problem of language and culture arose that persists to this day.

A LAW IS VERY DIFFERENT FROM A PHENOMENON

An edict handed down by an all-powerful lawgiver is something in opposition to a process observed as semi-regular. Observations were completed; studied advanced; comparisons were made and theories, theorems and laws emerged. This continued experimentation produced repeated results. But, more than a deductive theorem, a law is absolute. That is, until, new discoveries bring established laws into question. Science then had to keep creating new laws to account for all the exceptions to some absolute declarations that came before. The concept of the Tao is something quite different:

IT IS NOT MADE TO HAPPEN; IT JUST DOES

The western scientific method dissects everything, it keeps cutting things in half until it can't half them anymore. Or, it throws a grid over everything and qualifies things as they appear in the grid. It is good to know that a retractable claw is part of the thing we call tiger. It is a mistake however to say that this animal is made up of modules called liver; bone; or eye; when, really, they all go together to make up one thing: Tiger. All tiger components arose together. It may seem an obvious, subtle difference, but the idea that this cat is "made up" of parts that collectively function as "tiger"; also informs our understanding of the universe.

If we wish to understand "tiger" by looking through the slot in a fence and watching "tiger" walk by we would say: "there it is", every time I see "tiger" head, it is always followed by "tiger" body. And, you know what? Then comes "tiger" tail. Every time. Conclusion: "head" causes "body" and "body" causes "tail". Empirical observation.

The process "proves" that "tiger" head causes "tiger" body. Happens every time. This is the problem with quantum inquiry. The experimental process produces a conclusion. But the observational methods and prejudicial concepts influence the result.

It benefits our collective knowledge to comprehend the complexities of tiger locomotion. I'm sure machines and people can be helped by having a detailed understanding of synchronized tiger movement. But to forget that the tiger is really one thing, and not made up of parts, is critical to having a complete and thorough comprehension of the universe.

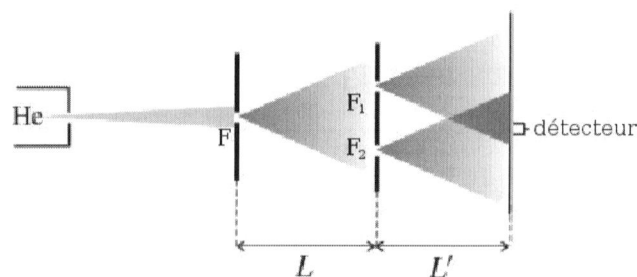

The double slit exeperiment

We have no idea why, but reality is different when you measure it. A particle is what manifests when you measure a wave. As far as we know, particles do not exist. We think they are vibrations in fields, and mass is the energy needed to vibrate in its field. 0.551MeV is the mass of one electron. One electron is created when the electron field is excited by 0.551MeV. We do understand, that all there is ia wave function. Waves resolve into particles when measured. Rest mass energy is the fundamental amount of energy added to a field to create a particle. The material world manifests out of invisible wave function.

Quantum theory states that the basis of the world is non-materialism. This non-materialism is filled with exotic, confusing, and a cryptic reality. This means that quantum theory is a form of mysticism. The unseen world is a virtual state that can actualize. The visible world is an emanation of potentiality.

Here is where the Yin/Yang marriage of science and religion become catalytic.

Eastern mystics perceived the universe as a vast matrix of unseen forces that concurrently could be understood as both a repeatable phenomenon and an understood science, but at the same time random and unpredictable. **Both at the same time.** This presents no problem, as the theory of Yin/Yang provides for both material objects and concepts to be two things at the same time. Or, even in two places.

The Long Game

Years ago, I saw a fascinating special presentation on public television. A two-hour program the purpose of which was to definitively prove just what do women find attractive. There was a panel of experts. One scientist built a convincing case for pheromones. Another was convinced the golden ratio was key. Someone of course was sure that money was the ultimate motivator, nesting instincts and motherhood were given emphasis. Personality and laughter were mentioned. Another expert was sure that physical strength was primary, as women craved protection.

There were several hundred subjects, representing all ages and types. Women interviewed and vetted the men through a speed dating type of scheme. Each female spent two or three minutes with prospective suitors, and completed an evaluation sheet at the conclusion of each encounter.

At the end of the event the data was tabulated, the panel of experts assembled, and the results disseminated. After adjusting for all variables, the definitive conclusion was revealed… If you want to be attractive to women, the single best thing you can do for yourself is to be tall. To be sure, having money, a good physique, or well-balanced features are helpful, but the single most important thing for success with women is out of your control.

Every type of media is awash with innumerable types of health and fitness plans some with merit, some snake oil, but many could prove to be beneficial in the right circumstances. But like our definitive study of sexual attraction, we are all playing with a stacked deck. To paraphrase the conclusion of the above study, if you seek longevity, the single best thing you can do for yourself is to have good genes.

Nutrition, exercise, and yogic technique can contribute, but if you possess a genetic predisposition, you may only be able to alter outcomes by percentage points. This truth can be directly referenced back to a previous chapter on statistics, practices, and procedures. These components can be helpful, but may not significantly alter outcomes for the statistically significant portion of the cohort in genetic jeopardy.

I have known cancer patients who have suffered horribly. Did the poor nutrition, lack of exercise, tobacco, and alcohol cause or contribute? No one can definitively say. It may have happened anyway, but adopting healthful pastimes certainly couldn't hurt. This is especially true if the health practices were joyful and not drudgery.

If the things you do to effect positive health results are enjoyable and create gratifying enhancements to your life, and not time spent in resentment on a treadmill, constantly looking at a heart monitor. But rather, a reciprocal part of life spent hiking, canoeing, or playing tennis - activities that produces a health benefit as a side effect of having fun. If you are spending hours trying to add hours to your life, that's a fool's game. Having passion for an activity that also produces a health benefit is a double win.

What if your recreational activity was healthful, enjoyably, and produced a physiological state that enacted chemical messengers. Messengers that down-regulate the caustic stress response, while simultaneously creating a state of mind that deepens spiritual awareness. Tai-Chi offers all these additional benefits, although it is, by no means, the only path.

One cannot escape the apparent reality that they must play the hand they are dealt. As articulated above, there are things a man may do to enhance his possibilities. He can make money, get in shape, clothes, grooming; they all help. All of the adjunct attributes can be addressed. Statistically, he can improve his chances. He can even achieve his goal by the accumulative effects of the subsidiary enhancements. Collectively, they may be able cancel out his elemental disadvantages, but the key element may already be written.

The Yin/Yang aspect here is, yes, one has to work with the cards they dealt. But through knowledge, understanding, and skillful adaptation; one can shave points and alter outcomes. The quantum universe is often referred to as "a sea of probability", called a wave function. This is because empirical observation has taught to allow for variables in mathematically likely results. The interesting thing about all this uncertainty is that it only takes concrete values after measurement; which, by definition, removes all uncertainty, but also effects the conclusion. My guru once told a devotee, "if you're not careful, another vehicle will hit your car." This statement deliberately allows for the possibility that the amount of care directly effects potential outcome.

Yes, you should take care of yourself; but life is a crap shoot. There are industrial accidents and little kids do get cancer; but Max Schmeling lived to be 100 after being pounded in the head all his life. And, he didn't subscribe to any mystical health practices, that I know of. No one ever said Tony Bennett was a high-level yogi, and I don't believe Betty White is a Tai-Chi master. Yet, they both lived well into their nineties. We are all victims of the genetic lottery.

A poker analogy is apt here. Sometimes you're dealt a good hand and you win. Other times you get bad cards and you're finished. But, the skillful, intelligent player can turn an ostensible disaster into victory, by making wise decisions and understanding the game. We all need to be reminded to keep moving forward, don't curse the darkness, and next time...be born taller.

Internal Arts

Among martial artists there is a generally recognized divide between what are referred to as soft-style and hard-style martial arts.

By definition, hard-style fighting systems consist of what the average person would probably think of as fighting. Tough guy styles with a lot of violence and aggression. Stressing speed, power, and leaving the opponent in a broken heap.

Soft styles, by comparison, feature evasion, and blending with the aggressors incoming force, then redirecting that power away from the defender. This is often completed with a trip or throw. When strikes are utilized, they generally are specifically targeted to vital areas, relying on a highly-developed knowledge of human anatomy.

Admittedly, these are just very broad descriptions of the two main approaches. Most systems are a combination of hard and soft approaches, while favoring emphasis more toward one idea or the other. There have always been hybrid styles, but since the dawn of the modern era there has been an even greater exchange between these two major concepts.

For the Western mind, the division between hard and soft proves to provide the most clarity for distinguishing the major difference between the two. When translators interpreted Chinese (Eastern) concepts of internal and external for the Western practitioner, and began using them as nomenclature for fighting styles; confusion was understandably created.

Because of the comparative effortlessness of the soft styles, and the emphasis on a mind/body synthesis, people generally began to attach mystical, supernatural sources to the abilities of soft style adepts. While these styles certainly can produce astounding feats, and improved physiological function, there is a more meaningful aspect to the internal transformation.

In this book, Yin/Yang metamorphosis has been illustrated many times - summer changing into winter, or a sturdy wooden pole that was once a pliant green branch. These simple examples are the type of conversions believed to occur by the hard style fighter wishing to benefit from internal training. The practices such as iron shirt and muscle tendon change do indeed produce palpable changes in the physiology of the sagacious, but that is not the whole story.

Undeniably, these routines can result in internal transformation. But in contrast, if the internal arts are truly a Yin/Yang activity, then a more substantive type of transformation must actually take place in Shen and Jing. In Chinese cosmology Jing is of the earth. Shen is heavenly, (the spiritual aspect of man is of heaven) originating there, and exerts spiritual influence.

Earth energy (Jing) is associated with the kidneys and heavenly energy (Shen) with the heart. This designation is utilized practically and metaphorically to facilitate internal transformation. The interaction of heaven and earth creates Chi, and is the originator and sustainer of life.

In Chi-Kung health nurturing practices, physical protocols combine with aspects of the mind to produce genuine change within the human organism. Increased vitality, enhanced immune function, and resistance to injury are laudable goals, but an over-emphasis on Jing results in unbalanced consequences.

The more important transformation of the inner man takes place incrementally during the training regimen. Just as the body strengthens by degrees, mind intent practices as well as contemplative philosophical aspects, produce profound changes in the practitioner.

It is a common observation in modern America that a delinquent teenager can be "turned around" by military service. While scouting exerts a similar influence, it is sometimes used as a slur. Someone who is a "boy scout" is one who has been changed forever by exposure to the principals of scouting. In kind, parents will spend thousands to provide a parochial school environment, in an effort to inundate the child with moral codes and positive doctrines.

During formative childhood and teenage years, the constituent of proper coaching in team sports is designed to result with the individual infused with a work ethic and an appreciation for teamwork. Implanted with the realization that one can push through adversity and go much further than they ever thought was capable and the life-long self-confidence and commitment to never let down a team member.

During Tai-Chi style fighting, it is imperative to maintain a relaxed body energy state (Sung). "Dead-hand" blocks and strikes can only be delivered from this Sung state - the state of profound relaxation. If consumed with rage or paralyzed with fear, by definition, this precludes the necessary Sung state and prevents the ability to possess the sedate confidence to remain "in the pocket" (physically adhering and sticking to his coat). And, this proximity is a mandatory prerequisite to having the capacity to execute dramatic discharges.

Unless a practitioner is imbued with a genuine mind/body realization, he is finished. This is where the rubber meets the road. If one's understanding is purely theoretical or conceptual, the intensity and unfamiliarity of a fast exchange will prove overwhelming. In this specific, personal situation soft style mechanics simply will not work. And, any properly motivated slugger will happily provide a practical demonstration of the difference between hard and soft. Actual proprietorship of the mind element is paramount, in any situation. If not, one would only be lucky to survive with highly developed push-hand skills alone.

Taoist concepts of universality, and oneness, are not just platitudes thrown in to fill time, while the instructor is correcting stances and postures. They are a part of the execution. A vital component to enhance the visceral optimization of the routine. An intrinsic element of the Tai-Chi practices. Once recognized as a vital aspect to deriving complete benefit from assimilation, the concepts and their physical outcomes are internalized, apperception attained, and the practitioner is transformed as surely as the Eagle Scout or Marine recruit.

If you allow it, the understanding of an all-pervading matrix of energies, of which you are a part, enhances understanding of your interaction with the universe. Being one with nature and the environment is more than just a mental trick to get you to relax to fluidly execute the form. It is connecting mind to universality and physicality to environment. Shen and Jing in action.

Far from being a disconnected solitary unit, fighting to rip out procuration and preeminence from their time spent on the planet, the idea of being "at one" no longer seems silly and foreign - it is just the way things are. Each practitioner can completely retain their own philosophy and religion, while also absorbing the idea of one's true place in the universe.

It is not dissimilar to denying that gas exchange takes place and believing it is somehow "unnatural" to employ breathing patterns to effect physiological change. This is to employ an obstinate act of will. But this stubbornness to accept reality, ultimately rejects and denigrates the existence of the beneficial modules that contribute to the overall demulcent of the art.

An attempt to explain interconnectedness by using unfamiliar concepts like Shen or Jing almost always creates a barrier to understanding, in the Western mind. Often, a simile more common to the shared Western experience might produce more affinity.

For instance, a body builder who dedicates himself to a program of transformation, becomes something completely different than the person who entered the gym, years earlier. Through continued training of proper technique their body is now functioning at a higher level than the "undeveloped" person.

Likewise, the metamorphosis of understanding and transformation of spirit is also possible with proper direction. The bewildered, scattered, hectic personality (one who need this type of training the most) is in stark contrast to the calm, even demeanor of a fully realized master. One who has put in the time an effort to undergo this holistic transmutation.

Speaking plainly on these matters may alienate some. Then again, plenty of kids quit Scouting. It is just not in them to become straight arrows. If the desire exists to derive maximum benefit from Tai-Chi and the Taoist concepts on which it is based, then it becomes imperative to intellectualize concepts found in the I-Ching. Not because we want to think like the Chinese, but because they edified good ideas.

If one's only interest is improved balance, enhanced immune function, and leg strength; these can all be realized without engaging the heart and mind. But, why only go halfway? Peace of mind and deeper understanding is also readily part of the package, if one so desires. Allow yourself to engage - fully. Wise men don't start out that way. They travel through their experiences with examination and realization. Be like the wise man. Change in outlook and behavior. Become a reliable member of team mankind. Don't only develop like the body builder (Jing). Become a Marine. Become an actual Boy Scout. Emerge transformed in spirit (Shen). This is the internal alchemy.

Geese, Magnets, and Decoherence

A large group of citizens had gathered outside a building in a major metropolitan area. High above, a man on a ledge was threatening suicide. When he would veer toward the edge, the crowd would release a collective gasp. When he veered away, the murmurer would subside. Then, through the hushed silence, a physicist yelled, "Don't do it, you have so much potential."

It has been reported that Richard Feynman said, "If you think you understand quantum mechanics, you don't." In this discussion, we will address some other subjects that people think they understand, and don't. For example, many attempts have been made to explicate the mysteries of physics. This is frequently done by including some relationship with the supernatural or theological. Although this connection may or may not have validity, this book will stop well short of making this same correlation. Instead it will only propose that there are unexplainable phenomena from each group's canon, and that often times these interpretations point in the same direction.

An attempt to explain one mystery by citing another is not only counterproductive, but also a disrespectful misdirection; an intellectual sleight of hand, if you will. By pointing out that there is only one mystery and two feeble attempts at an explanation, positions us with the need to develop a more comprehensive understanding of the situation. In other words, by not being on either "team physics" or "team spirituality" circles us back to the real objective; which is to achieve mental states that constitute an actual sense of contentment and joy, through our interactions with the terrestrial world.

Both science and theology have lengthy histories that postulate answers that fall short of producing concrete proof of any conclusion on the ultimate state of reality. One camp says, "have faith, his ways are mysterious". The other says, "We're not there yet". Since Yin/Yang indicates that there is something to be learned from both the sage and the fool, it is sagacious for the wise aspirant to hew to the advice of the old philosopher; take the middle path. The astute and the wise coalesce their comprehension of these mysteries from a variety of perspectives. But, understanding cosmic mysteries is only a side dish. What, in all reality, we are actually trying to do is meliorate the here and now.

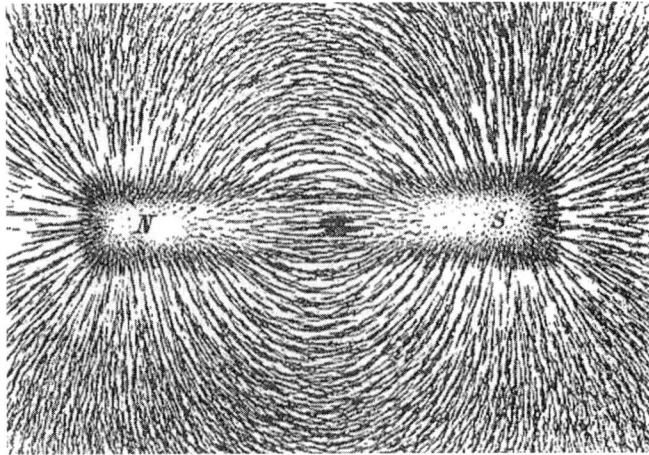

People often cite what an amazing planet this is, and this is true - with beauty and sensations, far beyond what any of us deserve, along with intriguing and mysterious forces, both seen and unseen. This environment give rise to the two main groups of exploration into the wonders of this world, science and matters of spirit. And, the questions that surface from the dichotomy of binary states evolve a perceived conflict between these divergent perceptions. But things weren't always this way. At one point in time, science didn't exist. The term science was first coined in the 14th century, from the original Latin word scientia, which meant knowledge or expertise. Prior to the adoption of this word, people who performed this type of inquiry were referred to as natural philosophers. One of which, William Whewell, is credited with coinage of the term scientist in 1833.

Before this, the polemic was between religion and superstition; which functioned as a sort of ad hoc science placeholder. Superstition served many of the same functions that science does today. It offered an alternative hypothesis to explain phenomenon, from a cause-and-effect perspective. Superstition observed patterns and used logic to assign provenance.

One need only examine medical or cosmological speculations from the Middle Ages to recognize the innate human impulse to engage the "scientific method": only one that builds on a premise that is mistakenly assumptive and not substantial. Though laughable now, many of these theorems followed the scientific method of cogent inquiry. In the face of unexplainable forces, it is only logical to assign perspicuous reason to supernatural forces, or powerful interdimensional entities. If, however, you cut them some slack, and replace words like demon and wind spirit with Higgs field and zero-point energy; their presumptions were not any more far out than some intermediate speculations from the early modern age.

Up to this point, scientific analysis produced results by uniform comparison of observable phenomenon. Empirical observation was the very definition of science. Leaping ahead to the age of enlightenment (a.k.a. the age of reason, experimentation, deduction and the dialectic), pellucid processes and deductive reasoning provide a uniform model from which to launch further inquiry. This quantum advancement provided a model where experimentation of the unseen world begins to preclude trials based on only Newtonian concepts. Also, the coequal analysis of these inquiries begin to coalesce rather than diverge.

Geese, Magnets, and Decoherence

Some systems improved and streamlined over time, such as; transportation and communication. Where others rely on basically the same technology as originally developed, such as; firearms, steam turbines, and audio speakers. Some breakthrough technologies, such as; antibiotics, cell phones, and microwave apparatus were new ways of building on established formulas.

The modern era probably really only began in the late 19th century, where consumer products were made available to the general population. Products produced by revolutions in scientific understanding, building on each other, and reaching critical mass. The standard of living rose in the developed world as more people were consecrated with electricity and the automobile.

Many non-first-world nations did not begin to come online until the late 20th century. Even some western nations did not get phone service or indoor plumbing until relatively late in the era. I was once married to an English girl who grew up using outside community latrines. At the same time, in the United States, I was eating pop tarts and watching Johnny Jupiter on TV.

Subsistence living was the mode of living for most of the world during my formative years. Heartbreaking scenes from China, India, and Africa emanated from the magic box located in the centrally heated living room of a house, in a town and country governed by educated municipal administrators, and protected by professional law enforcement.

As a school kid in the 1950's, it seemed that every day brought some new break through discovery by luminaries, such as, Jonas Saulk or Werner von Braun. Americans felt we had reached a pinnacle; once we launched Telstar, and Eisenhower authorized the first interstate highway system.

Still there were mysteries, breakthroughs were made, declarations pronounced, then withdrawn. Theories postulated as laws were amended, statements retracted, science poked around and made progress and also some mistakes; but religion was always there to plug the holes.

Cavalry was still being used in WWI, and in limited roles by some nations during the early days of WWII. Science changed things dramatically during those later four years and culminated by developing the ultimate technology that finally finished the war and brought to heel the previously unrecondite Japanese. While horses claimed a diminishing role, dogs continued to perform as heroes in many extraordinary circumstances; and almost every aspect of daily life.

During WWII, telephones and field radios provided communication using verbal codes as well as cryptograms for courier dispatch. Transmission of information over longer distances pioneered the use of encryption techniques; exploited most famously by the enigma machine. The imperative to prevent communication intercepts could literally be the difference between defeat and victory. While code breakers and wind talkers evolved sophisticated modes of communication, a natural expression of Yin/Yang manifested. A very essential, yet surprising practice of essential, clandestine communication reemerged; unchanged since the days of Babylon: homing pigeons.

In an attempt to demystify the mechanism of the internal arts, it might prove helpful to explore concepts like physic power and quantum entanglement, as it applies to our purpose. It is a commonly accepted practice in our culture to hijack terms, slang, and technical jargon and apply those words to disparate endeavors. For ease of understanding, let's do that here.

So to more clearly illustrate a point, I would like to explore the concept of spooky action at a distance. It helps our mental picture to utilize the accepted idea of quantum entanglement, which is the idea that two particles can appear to be in two places at once. That really isn't the precise concept, but the commonly accepted one. And, since I'm not making an exact comparison anyway, just having the idea is a good place to start.

Discounting the so-called observer effect, and the Schrodinger equation, and just accepting that it is a quality of our universe and it exists; there are aspects of reality that are so accepted as part of the world in which we live that they are called laws of physics. In other words, this is just the way things work in our world.

The fact that magnets are attracted to ferrous materials could be explained scientifically, but sometimes it's better to just accept the fact that this phenomenon is a property of our environment. Then, we can use that knowledge for practical purposes like navigating the seas. The quantum entanglement analogy provides an opportunity to explore the phenomenon of bonding and connection as it occurs naturally in our world.

Let's consider a betrothed couple. They are so in love that they could be considered the same person. They know each others thoughts, share their world view, and effectively their entire lives. Suppose the man gets called overseas, and during the separation, he receives a package in the mail. He opens it up and finds the engagement ring. He doesn't need a call or a letter, he knows what that means. Or, imagine if he instead opens his parcel and finds a right glove. He would immediately know that his partner has the left one. There is no wire connecting them. He suddenly "just knows", because of the multitude of understandings made through their previous associations.

Along these same lines, migration is a property of certain life forms on this planet. Although unusual to our species, this is not a mystery. Ornithologists are able to precisely explain why geese migrate when they do. These creatures rely upon magnetism, and magnetism occurs because of the properties of the earth's core.

Another law of the universe is decoherence. It is an accepted property of physics. Decoherence can be likened to a drop of ink placed into a pond. It begins to dissipate, losing its coherence, as a unified concentrated drop.

The behavior of Geese, magnets, decoherence, and distant lovers are not mysterious. They are a property of those things, a quality.

Martially, to improve one's chances of winning a fight may seems like a simple matter of acquiring skills and eliminating bad habits. Simple skills, like keeping your hands up and using proper hip rotation. Or, simple mental confidences like: "if only I had enough slick tricks, I could baffle them with my amazing skills." And, while you can certainly alter outcomes by improving skills, and even become amazing, that would be only one side of the Yin/Yang. But what's going on with that other half?

When a musician becomes so adept that the instrument seems to be an extension of his body, nay soul, one feels really connected to the performance. The feelings and expression just flow from the bond: player and instrument are one.

On the other hand there is a type of player who just moves from one riff to another. Stringing together hot licks in a chain of preplanned unrelated amalgams that are more like a musical production line than an artistic performance. The result: a wooden unconvincing listening experience. When someone truly owns their craft, they are able to express themselves extemporaneously. Each note, each second, is as much a surprise to the artist as it is to the audience. They don't know what they're going to do next, but it is always the right thing. Always the best choice. When all combinations and possibilities have been internalized there is no thinking involved. The brain does not need to analyze, interpret, or weigh options. Action is direct. A type of quantum entanglement, if you will.

THE LIGHTNING FLASHES....THE THUNDER SOUNDS

Most martial arts are taught in a "he does this, you do that" fashion. "Here's how you get out of a headlock." "Here's how you handle a straight right." This approach internalizes the technique over time, and one eventually begins to move extemporaneously. In stark contrast, Tai-Chi "flips the script" and approaches extemporaneous movement from the beginning.

From the first move of the form, one is taught to feel and become interactive. This is done to to embed the idea that situations change with each micron and by each nano-second. And, in accordance with the principles of an internal art, first only with the physical environment. But it is not exclusive to only this type of situation. This practice is directly transferable as a fighting skill.

When engaged with an opponent, one attempts to "read" the intent. To "feel" the opposing energy. It is possible to remain one step ahead in the dance if one can tell where the interaction is going; what the opponent is going to do next. But one should not try to guess what the next action will be. Instead, one should ride like a surfer. Not imposing an outcome on the situation. The Japanese have a word for this state: mushin. State of no mind.

Of course, in a fast exchange one relies more on "reading" skills than "feeling" ability. To "read" another's intent is common to tennis, hockey, or other contests where one has lived that competitive scenario a thousand times before. One literally senses, "I see where he's going with that." Tai-Chi adds another dimension to these base skills by also developing what are called "listening" skills. A skill which develops one's internal antenna for otherwise unrecognized signals from the opponent. To be used in situations like when one inevitably becomes engaged at grappling range. In this scenario, the adept practitioner takes on a visceral and almost passive attitude of, "If he withdraws, I follow." "If he presses, I redirect."

Many other martial arts arrive at this same place - eventually. Regardless of time to acquire, practitioners become so familiar and adept that they become like a blank screen, making no notions or preconceived ideas about what the opponent is about to do. It has become...

A QUALITY

Which is the whole point.

Responding appropriately is not a process; it's just something that's always there. In other words, a honed street sense. One in which, that is just the way you are. Not, "I have just been grabbed, apply technique B-27." No, one just responds without any preconceived thoughts. Again, a good street sense. One combined with toughness. This combination is pretty hard to beat.

Of all the attributes a fighter may have, toughness is the one that can be the most outwardly obvious "quality". We have all sat next to a guy at a bar, or passed someone on the street, who just radiated "don't mess". This person may not have the biggest forearms or thickest neck, but everyone just knows this one will go berserk and can't be hurt. Attitude? Certainly! But, this toughness is just in them. Its a quality.

Can this toughness be met and overcome with high level technique? Most certainly! But, the greatest chance in any endeavor is to function naturally, being a part of the flow and state of a particular occurrence. Another way to look at this is that a tiger does not fight with tiger technique - people do. Clawing, biting, charging, etc. are just a tiger quality. We just try to mimic their qualities in an attempt to make them our own. We are unique in the animal world with this ability. And, if done properly one can truly make them their own.

In the Chinese styles, animal movement is not just a pattern or method in which a given animal moves. Each animal possesses a certain number of qualities. In the daily endeavors of human beings, qualities such as honesty and likability allow us to navigate the hundreds of social encounters we experience each day.

We interact and interpret quality constantly. Most everyone has naturally interpreted a genuine or insincerity in quality. One gets the feeling that "There's something not quite right with him." Or, "I trust this guy." To take advantage of this ability, salesmen work hard to develop the qualities that will work in their favor. Some absorb and internalize the needed qualities, others only use them as a technique. One famous salesman adage is: "The secret to success is sincerity; once you learn how to fake that...you've got it made." But one can usually tell genuine from insincere, because its not a quality - it's a performance.

Being honest and being trustworthy are essential for survival in a modern society. Like all social animals, our's is a social structure which requires social skills. Skills that can be used for victory in life, or merely just for social self-defense. If one wants to get along, it's best to be truly trustworthy, goodhearted, and benevolent.

For distinguishing mastership of martial art, become the dragon - possess his essence. He has a quality. Do you? But, not only for fighting skills, but also the inner-man. This can be transformative.

Jieshu

"The book of changes": a volume credited to Lao Tzu in the western Zhou period. In a less important sense, this too is a book of changes, as it has undergone critical alteration many times.

As this book (and the project) has its port in sight, I am filled with a sensation of belletristic release. I am now free to stop dancing around, cease the ambiguity and innuendo, and muse a major thesis of this book. Throughout this work, I have tepidly made the inference that science and religion are, if not synonymous, then kindred.

Although this idea is dismissed, sometimes vehemently, by the scientific community, this is an idea generally acknowledged as practicable among those without academic clutter; if not also felt by the layman on a visceral level. In this concluding essay, I can now "call 'em as I see 'em".

Lastly in this proposal, I suggest a basic flaw in the human psyche. The preposition that these conceits are two sides of the same coin; telling the same story. Each defended by implacable zealots, all in their distinct camps.

Modern physics, in general, and quantum field theory, in particular, offer little conclusive proof of suppositions; except in mathematical calculations. Neither is backed up by material evidence. Therefore, it is fair to ask: "If all of these calculation are correct, why are there so many anomalies in particle physics?" And, while each describes some aspect of the universe with advanced mathematics, one must never forget that these are merely mathematical stories, no better than creation.

Without question, many predictions of quantum field theory are currently being affirmed by experimentation in repeated physical trials. This being said, quantum fields are unobservable in the customary sense. These "observations" are really postulations that agree after multiple calculations. In actuality, it's still mostly math. Similarly, quarks are never directly observed. They are claimed to be "detected" in hadrons. And, even now there is suspicion that quarks may not even be elementary particles. But rather, may be made up of something even smaller, called prions; which are also unseen by normal means.

Displaying the calculations and equations that make up the design of a new model automobile, is an arithmetic estimation... After all, calculations are based on design principals that proved successful in previous model years. But, randomness, bad luck, and Murphy's law have proven historically to produce massive failures. This is despite the multiplicity of meetings, computer reckonings, and executive review. Recalls are commonplace. Likewise; celebrated physicists with impeccable track records have blundered many times. Some examples are:

Einstein's cosmological constant
Kelvin's earth age estimate
Pauling's triple helix
Hoyle's big bang

Coalitions that maintain there is no tangible evidence to support spirit as a legitimate position, conveniently forget that same authority often has to change their position, because the "evidence" has been proven wrong. When "scientists" denounce unexplained miracles, or conduct studies deriding the efficacy of prayer, it would seem both prudent and fair to compare verifiable track records on historical errors and proven inconsistencies. This is in no way a criticism of scholarship, nor a dismissal of the scientific method. Science has given us everything. But looked at from a marginally different angle, so has God.

Both portray themselves as representations of reality. A reality that is obscured, and often defies comprehension. Both approaches use illustrations with equivalent efficacy. To help one comprehend what cannot be seen, and thus requires some degree of faith. Both require the disciple to suspend disbelief, even if only to a small degree. Drawings of electrons orbiting a nucleus are no less honest, or more misleading, than portrayals of a divine king with a white beard on a throne.

Undeniably, religion can be said to have a checkered past. Indulgences, martyrs, witch burnings, and conversion forced at the point of a sword. It was not, however, religion that denounced Copernicus as a heretic, condemned Galileo, nor any of the previously mentioned travesties. But rather, a bureaucracy functioning in religion's name.

Ultimately, it is important to not miss the point. Since science has become our new god, it has been promoted (like God) to be infallible. And yes, without reservation, many of these models are in agreement. But as previously stated, models often require varying degrees of reform when new discoveries invalidate their previous conviction. Also just like religion, science must rely on facsimile and representation. Finally, since the absoluteness of neither can be 100% verified; phenomenon, when experienced, is explained by the requisite authority in terms of adumbration.

For the aspirant who wonders about proper weight distribution when effecting "crane spreads wings", a legitimate question would be: "Why are we talking about this? What does this have to do with a health nurturing fighting art?" Why? Because it is all tied together. Body, mind, spirit - heaven and earth.

The cognizance I would like to manifest is simply that science communicates with mathematical models. Similarly, so does religion; only it communicates with images of God and celestial realms. Regardless, both camps attempt to foster erudition through understandable simulacrum. Since ancient times, alchemists, sages, and philosophers combined use allegory to define paradigm in an effort to direct one scrupulously in search of the archetype. The style of authorship may have changed with the era, culture, and custom; but if you are savvy and look carefully, they each say the exact same thing: There is only one wave function; everything manifests from the mind of God.

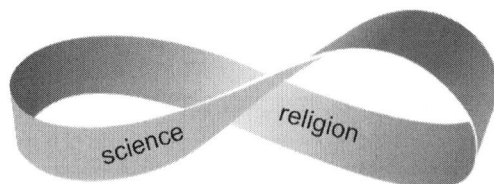

It would be easy to regard this apparent clash as strictly a science vs. religion conflict. Presented in these terms, this seems to be the dichotomy. I propose, however, that there is a deeper issue that is responsible for this loggerhead. One darker, and much more sinister.

I am speculating that as of this writing, the worldview embodied by most readers of this tome is very Euro-centric. After all, history is written by the winners. To date, many Eastern concepts of medicine and cosmology are dismissed in our culture as primitive, undeveloped, and unscientific - all the un's. Because of this, deep in our collective subconscious, "they" are not adequate. They are the godless masses in the far east and the malevolent denizens of the middle east - one's who worship the wrong God.

Historically, within our own nation of the United States; prejudice, and unfounded assumptions regarding the fitness of subgroups to participate in society have been part of our cultural fabric. For instance, when my mother was born, women in this country were not allowed to vote. The official policy regarding this segment of the populations was that they were mentally inferior and emotionally unable to execute the responsibility of thoughtful reason. Likewise, individuals with darker skin tones were similarly tyrannized, and repressed of the constitutionally mandated right to vote.

This situation arose because the rules were made by white men trained in a tradition of dominance and hierarchy. These were beliefs commonly held throughout the society. And, sometimes even held by those most repressed by these very policies. This mindset was rampant throughout the ruling class of the era. "Us" insulated within our own narrative. "We" thrived; convinced that one fraction of humanity was the center of the universe.

Feminists and civil rights activists had to invoke law and appeal to foundational principal before the authority would acquiesce, and pander to their "inferior" fellow citizens. Ultimately, fraternal supremacy succumbed to common decency and relinquished hard-fought conventions. It is this idea of cultural superiority that pervaded the general consciousness and remnants of this attitude persist, even to this very day. What could "other" possibly contribute? After all, "they" are not intellectually or morally equipped.

The cultures of Greece and Rome were dominate not only militarily, but civilizing advancements formed the bedrock of science and mechanics. Because of all their accomplishments, they considered themselves to be obviously superior intellects. And, this cultural dominance held sway through most of the first millennium, although continually degrading until the great world wars of the twentieth century. This century saw these once supreme civilizations reduced to second and third-rate powers and economies. I relate this saga for any arrogant nationalists and advocates of racial superiority as a cautionary example: that history can and will repeat itself.

These arrogantly superior foundations carried forth into other Western style cultures. America, in particular, boasted self-absorbed aggrandizement and unabashedly enacted laws and policies, such as manifest destiny, to justify theft of lands and slavery of fellow creatures, without remorse.

Likewise, arrogantly dismissing the contribution of Asian cultures to mankind's collective advancement is an unwise, foolish, and ludicrous folly. Today, when faced with the well documented success of Asian university students dominating academically, Americans smugly dismiss the culture and ancestry that produced these successes. As previously stated, it is prudent to be reminded of the decadence that contributed to the fall of Rome. In today's American society, ultra-nationalists are flummoxed when soft, spoiled American kids, are routinely bested by "inferior" foreigners from the east.

To assume that no research or advancements have occurred during the past 5,000 years in Eastern culture is pure narcissistic conceit. Many traditions that predate Western science postulated brilliant formulas. Plenty of inquiry has been taking place in China throughout the centuries. And, this investigation is performed by meticulous examiners who do what investigators do; employing the same rigorous testing methods pioneered in the West.

I personally find it fascinating to consider that these Eastern intellects could investigate the same phenomena that the Western intellects examined and arrive at such starkly different conclusions. And, it is important to realize that the intellects and research methods were very similar. What is also important to recognize is that the conclusions varied because inquiry started at a completely different point of view: a view that regarded all things as part of a universal matrix. This shift in perspective about the universe, produced a converse result from the identical inquiry in the West.

CO☪☮♀✡☯†ST

The opposite/reverse (Yin/Yang) can also be illustrated in the fighting aspects of this cultural dichotomy. Plenty of intelligent people devised methods to improve fighting outcomes. Both the West and the East understood anatomy and physics, and yet the West advanced no further than back-up mass; waist rotation; and, of course, the vainglory of enhanced muscular development.

Compare this outcome with the brilliant concept of Dim-Mak's vital area strikes, power generated by Sung state whipping, and powerful Fa-Jin energy release. Also, contrast the elegance of judo throws and Aikido technique to 18th century fisticuffs, and no further elucidation is required.

From a spiritual perspective, Buddhist and Taoist monks refined meditation techniques, while Hindu adepts catapulted the science of God contact. During this same time period, European monastics immersed rites in complex ritual, and relegated introspection to mere reverie and contemplation. In the East, the sophistication, comprehensiveness, and self-reflection of these same pursuits serves as testament to the genius, ingenuity, and earnestness of the minds that conceived them.

Kurt Vonnegut explained European dominance, by saying: "they had the best boats in the world, and they were meaner than anybody else". I would also add that there was a cultural blood lust for conquest which was enforced by the mighty Western military science. Additionally, it would seem that imperialism is hardwired in our genetic code as a species. Similarly, we have a strong predisposition toward colonialism and evangelical tendencies.

Furthermore, where the historically prevalent Western mindset may begrudgingly concede a few inventions and a couple of IQ points to the "other", it has been and continues to be completely wrong about Tao and internal energy.

Finally, in case this seems like a glorification of Chinese history or an expatriation of my own heritage, it is not and I am not. I felt it imperative to address the oft easy dismissal of remarkable discoveries and revelations in medicine and spirituality as primitive, incipient, naive, or stupid due to jingoistic bias. It must be stated that, yes, a different culture can produce a differing and equally compelling theorem, when examining the same data. The primary reason for this, however, is not because of an inchoate method; but like the fate of our universe, the conclusion is determined by the genesis.

成因

You Never Know

Some situations seem definitively Yin/Yang, male/female, black/white, dead/alive. The ball is either in the cup or it's on the green. But, the reason each side of the Yin/Yang symbol is warped and not straight is because often times a thing is on the way to being either one or the other. Sometime things appear to be definitively one thing or the other - positron or neutron. But, electrons can change position and borrow from one valance shell to another, creating a chemical bond and altering the properties of the molecule.

How do we quantify that razor's edge where things metamorphosize? As illustrated in the tip of the tail of one side of the Tai-Chi diagram, that's where the hand-off of the electron is made; right where the point meets the border. In the thick part of either half of the symbol, the person is robust, living in potent vitality. As the section thins out, the person becomes frail and less vital; until nearing the point where attrition becomes obvious - more dead than alive. The ball drops, the electron jumps.

That works fine for tangible, corporeal objects like golf balls and molecules; but what about a nebulous conceptual state, like a situation? This too can be either Yin, Yang, or on the way to one or the other. But knowing that the opposite is surely coming, is the lesson shown in the diagram. To illustrate the point, I will retell an oft repeated story, so stop me if you've heard this one:

There was a villager who loved his son more than anything in the world. One day the son came across some wild horses and was able to capture one. When he arrived home, all the neighbors extolled his good fortune. "How great it is that you now have this fine horse." The father said: "I don't know if it's good or bad, all I know is that we now have a horse."

One day while breaking the animal, the son was thrown and fractured both legs. "How terrible", the neighbors said, "Your son will never be the same." "I don't know if it's bad or not. I only know that he was whole and now he is crippled."

War broke out in the region and the king dispatched his troops to conscript subjects for the army. All young men were taken. The son was rejected because of his legs. Again, the neighbors said: "How lucky you are, the only one to have his son left at home." "I don't know if its lucky or not." said the father. "I only know all the young men were taken and my son is here with me."

A ubiquitous saying in Tai-Chi goes: "I do thus and so...and wait for a change"; which is why this tale is an illustration of Tai-Chi strategy.

The point of course is not that you never know, but that you do know. Yin cycles out - Yang surely is on the way. For you there is, of course, an ultimate end point, and there will be finality even for the universe. But then it all starts up again. Sanskrit sources predicted *big bang/big crunch* cycling long before Einstein, space-time, gravitation or dark energy. Even though *big crunch* has fallen into disfavor, because of the cyclic nature of everything else, It would seem at least a reasonable bet.

Regardless of the astrophysical consequences; here on earth, at least, the laws of physics and the unseen world dictate that smart money is at least aware of these observations compiled over many millennia.

In Tai-Chi fighting, you adhere and stick to your opponent with the objective to read his energy and intent. You attach with authority; like a confident horseman seeming to yield, but controlling through subtlety. An aggressive belligerent can be wildly unpredictable - further bolstering the principle of Yin/Yang and attesting to the fact that "you never know".

In order to have a happy functioning life, the villager has to confidently assume that with attentive management his crops and livestock will produce faithfully, barring unforeseen tragedy. He stays focused, he plans on his son growing whole, and begetting his own family. When the unexpected happens, however, it does not throw him into a tailspin causing further trouble; because exacerbating an already bad situation through panic, is like losing composure when fighting. To waive clear thinking opens the door to seven demons worse than the original one. He rides the situation with an even keel, because he understands the cyclic nature of the world.

At this juncture, another illustrative Tai-Chi saying is warranted: "I am convinced that my situation is 10% what happens to me, and 90% is how I react."

The Yin/Yang aspect of Tai-Chi theory prepares you to expect the unexpected and martial on, continuing to do what needs to be done. The villager is not indifferent, he accepts situations non-judgmentally, You no doubt already realize this, so I don't know if it's good or bad to retell it, I only know that I like the story.

Intermission

If you were to look at the actual history of scientific inquiry, the fact sheet tally clearly reveals that every theory we've had about the universe has been wrong: Starting with the earth as center of the solar system, gravity, subatomic components, the atom, what is the smallest particle, and on and on. We now believe that seventy percent of the universe is dark energy, twenty five percent is dark matter, and only five percent regular matter. This means that ninety five percent of the universe is ruled by forces we can't yet explain.

Scientists are fairly sure that dark matter and dark energy exist. They just can't confirm it. This is because the vibratory frequency of these elements is theorized to be beyond the range of our current instruments. Many known forces exist outside ordinary human perception, such as radio, gamma and ultraviolet. We have developed equipment to detect these vibratory frequencies, but the machines available today simply are not advanced enough to detect dark matter and dark energy, even though we can deduce mathematically and theoretically that they are there.

It would seem logically then, that to definitively state that a spiritual element of the universe is out of the question; runs askance of basic scientific principal, since ninety five percent of the universe is not verifiable. In 1929, when Edwin Hubble identified red shift and confirmed the idea of an expanding universe, the infallible Albert Einstein admitted that his concept of a static universe was wrong, calling it his biggest blunder. The cosmological constant was proposed to create a fudge factor for general relativity. This too, however, fell into disfavor for a while, but has now been revived to plug new holes created by recent advances. Thus, proving that we still have a lot to learn, while further cementing Einstein's original genius. Fun fact: This too may change again by the time you read this.

If you don't make the technical mistakes that Einstein did, it is possible to come up with a different equation - which Alexander Friedman did. This is only half of Einstein's mistake. First, he erred by surmising that we live in a static universe. This theory violates a basic principle of science.

Second, he was a victim of conformation bias. A demonic flaw which occurs in every human activity. When you begin with a conclusion, all further experimentation will skew towards confirming prejudice. This human foible continues to this day; a bane to all endeavors of inquiry. Generations of university-trained minds promulgated with Newtonian physics as a starting point, engaged in research which inevitably produced results to confirm the preconception.

To assume that spirit, thought, or yet undiscovered energies are nonexistent, is to ignore the entire history of science itself. Assumptions, initial conclusions, and strong indicators have a very unreliable profile in scientific inquiry. History has proven that immutable laws are subject to change.

So, when science says "we know" or "we have arrived at a consensus" remember the cautionary tale of most of its history; how often it has had to amend, correct, and back track in its very definitive proclamations. It could even be reasonably postulated that the same is true for religious authority. Or, anyone who says "I know - here is the answer"; has usually, given time, been proven wrong.

It may seem that this book has a prejudicial position implying that science confirms spirit. And, one would be correct in saying that there are many scientific indicators that lead to this conclusion. They could even potentially build a very convincing case. But, this is not only difficult and time consuming to do, it is utterly useless. Furthermore, it isn't even the real question.

The interest in verifying a spiritual dimension is actually the quest for meaning and assurance in life. Religion claims to have answers, but when vigorously challenged, defaults to dogma and principals of faith. Scientific inquiry only creates more questions and will never provide the answers, only an understanding of processes. When people seek out mysticism, or mainstream religion, they are really hoping for protection and resolution of the big questions. Those are: what happens when we die and is there a point to the universe? As unfathomable as it seems, these questions actually do have answers. It may seem dodgy, but the answer, as always, is Yin and Yang. And by understanding fluidity and morphing, as illustrated in the Tai-Chi diagram, we can glean answers to even this most philosophical quandary.

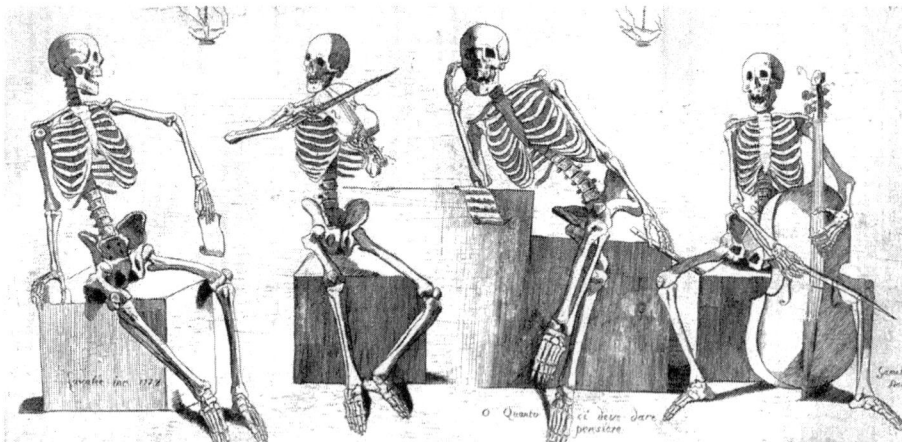

First of all, the universe isn't going anywhere. There is no ultimate destination towards which the universe is moving. Expanding, yes. Possibly collapsing in on itself to begin again, maybe. But going anywhere? No. Here again, the bad news is also the good news. The universe isn't going anywhere because it doesn't need to; just meandering, like a peaceful brook in a sylvan paradise.

The point of dancing isn't to arrive at a particular spot on the dance floor. Not a race to see who gets somewhere first. The point of dancing is to dance. In the moment.

Music, which has been called the highest art form, is even more illustrative. It is ephemeral. It is the definitive pseudonym for existence. It is created, and then it is gone. You can't grab, possess the notes, or hoard them for a latter day. A fleeting pleasure that touches your soul and then is gone.

The point of living is to live. Each breath is inspired and then is gone. Attempting to possess a breath by holding it, violates life's most basic impulse - killing you. Or, knocking you out for being stupid. Releasing exhaust is as imperative as drawing in vitality. Letting go is essential to the cycle. Material objects, relationships, life itself.

"Letting go" and "go with the flow" are not psychobabble. They are the order of the universe. They are also an example of the universe. A universe that is expanding with grand fanfare and magnificent flourish, putting on quite a show; yet ultimately going nowhere.

But one should be able to discern Yin and Yang. Natural order from urgent crisis. Hanging on the edge of a cliff is not a time to let go. Not if one wants to live. Although, letting go at this juncture would most certainly assure a new beginning, it is not natural order.

To truly live in the now is not just a platitude, it is a road map. Yin and Yang dictate that we plan, prepare, advance, and build toward a future utilizing our will and sailing our ship; while at the same time moving in harmony with the Tao. Following the direction of the universe. This is the lesson of the Yi-Ching.

Let us expand our possibilities and temporally forget our western training, considering an alternate hypothesis. One in which the authority can really be trusted; someone who knows you well; someone with the knowledge to reveal life's great mysteries.

"Who am I?" and "Where am I going?" are issues of great importance. Your place in the universe and your ultimate demise is an essential question. To encourage realization, let's conduct a role-playing exercise: Imagine that you had a magic power, and you could have anything that you wanted.

At first, you would no doubt peruse pleasure. Lust and grand palaces. Silk garments and utensils of gold. Everywhere; jewels and beautiful companions. Food, wine, and lavish entertainments. After a while, even your hedonistic pleasures would grow tedious. One gets a glimpse of this very real human frailty in the behavior of certain celebrities. When all one's dreams come true, a loss of ambition sets in. "Is that all there is?"

You would next pursue grand adventures, excitement, danger, A spy, a soldier, a mountain climber. But after you skied every slope and dove every ocean, this luster too would diminish.

You would now "up the game". Since you are the most magical creature in the universe, you would introduce the unexpected, playing the game of surprise. Pretending that you are not omniscient and invulnerable, living with palpable fear and uncertainty. Now the game gets interesting.

Our perception of intensity is a stimulant. Gambling for matchsticks is not the same as betting the rent money or playing for fingers. Wealthy gamblers wager enormous sums, just to keep it interesting. Being lost at sea produces powerful emotions and an appreciation of existence. Not so much when the adventure is on the printed page.

When watching a movie or a stage play with really convincing actors, you may be completely drawn into the experience. Accelerated heart rate, sweaty palms. Enjoying the danger while a sliver of your consciousness knows you're an observer safe in a theater seat.

Using your powers to dial up your reality, actually be the person having the adventure, you would have expanded beyond the paltry magic of enjoying mere illusory phenomenon. You could immerse your entire being in the experience, feel all the emotions, and even actually die. This would be the ultimate use of your supreme ability.

Because of your magic, you can come back and do it again, in another guise. Feeling this new life in its entirety. Unlike the theater goer, who knows it is only a convincing performance, you have made an arrangement with yourself to forget yourself. To not remember who you truly are.

Many sages contend that this is exactly what's going on - God experiencing the world in many guises. As a playboy and a shepherd. As a scoundrel and a saint. Each immersed in his performance, while still being part of the source. Like waves on the ocean. Each one a distinct entity; individual and fully defined. Existing and then reabsorbed back into the whole. To reemerge as a completely different wave and live it all over again.

This idea is common throughout the East. And though not as well known, also in the European mystical tradition. In "Peer Gynt," Henrik Ibsen wrote of the button molder, who melted souls together and poured out a new mix. Whether eternal soul, reincarnation, or the scientific premise that; "energy cannot be created or destroyed", the concept of cycling back around within a closed system has a long tradition.

Ultimately, however, all roads lead to Rome. And, apprehending the universe, and our place in it, dwarfs any lesser concern; there is no bigger deal. Those immersed in a code, religion, or philosophy; garner strength and assurance from a strongly held conviction. To be sure, there are many ideas and concepts.

But, which of these possibilities are worth considering? To feel lost and alone in a pointless and hostile universe; or cowering under the yoke of an omnipotent tyrant. Each is a choice every individual must make deep in his innermost soul. Alternatively, you may feel like many on this planet, those who trust in a god who, of course, will love and protect you; because he is you.

An absolute, by definition, should be just that. When science and religion make definitive proclamations and then amend them, even a little bit; that means they do not have the final answers. Times change and history has taught us that so do convictions; no matter how strongly held. Rules, principals, and opinions promoted as implacable are always, given time, found to be fluid and malleable. This seems to be the only true universal law. Hey, everything changes.

Why Don't You Just Say So

Like many of life's seemingly mysterious or occult practices, Tai-Chi really is neither. It is a rational, scientific, mundane practice that will perform as advertised. Again, just like many other things in life, it only delivers a return on proper investment. Not a religion or a cult, it is a non-sectarian, non-dogmatic health practice that also happens to be a devastating martial art.

In the following chapters, I will expand on some themes, certainly martial art, but also the other things that the internal search implies on the path to self-realization. Points of focus will include the pedestrian, but also delve into more lofty subjects, such as: enlightenment, ultimate reality, the electric universe, and the impact of consciousness on reality.

Most people's curiosity regarding this art usually concern matters of health maintenance or remedies for specific conditions. Fighting technique is generally of a secondary concern, as anyone interested in such matters generally practice a more combative form of pugilism. We will address both, and offer a perspective on all relevant aspects. Here we will begin to offer a summary of the contents of this book.

Your body is a miracle. It knows how to maintain health and provide healing, the same way it knows how to pump blood and digest food. No outside help required, except in extreme circumstances. The body makes its own medicine most of the time. The mind can generate incredible powers to heal. And you're doing it all the time. Every day. Unexplained health restoration is referred to as spontaneous remission, instantaneous healing, miracles, and/or faith healing. When science can't account for it, but still must acknowledges that it happens, they call it the placebo effect.

Yogic traditions, folk medicine, and traditional structured approaches, like Chi-Kung, harness and direct the chemistry and innate healing responses of the body to provide first line remedies for distress that the body encounters interacting with the environment. You have not only evolved natural defenses, but also possess an ability to self-heal to a certain degree. This ability can be enhanced and developed in much the same way as one develops their music prowess or athleticism. With proper instruction, by a competent guide, these inherent abilities can be discovered and strengthened, for the benefit of the human organism.

Tai-Chi is a Yin/Yang art. As far as health concerns go, anyone can have one of two attitudes: They can provide for their own well-being, or they can pay someone else to do it for them. Because we live in an age of specialization, we have all become comfortable deferring to a specialist for every little thing.

It is almost a parable that no one knows how to do anything anymore - except make money. Concentrate on that one skill and when one needs to, they call in a plumber, carpenter, or handyman to perform tasks they should be able to do for themself. This has become standard operating procedure in the modern western culture. The attitude could be surmised by the following attitude: "Well I guess I should be able to snake out a drain line, but for matters of health, don't you need a white coat?"

The answer is attitude is both yes and no. One should be self-reliant in all things including matters of health. Yet, Yin/Yang dictates one also need to know when to call in the white coats. This does not mean to foolishly ignore symptoms or self-prescribe western medicines, only developing an awareness of one's body and performing maintenance functions, thus providing an optimal chance for survival.

Most people outside of the health culture treat their bodies as they would a car they don't maintain. They run it low on oil, slam it through the gears, and recklessly bang it into curbs. In contrast, someone who cares for their vehicle accelerates slowly, brakes gradually, and garage keeps their car. One may sometimes see a car driven dependably for over thirty years. It can be done. But, what happened to all the others of the same make and year? How were they treated? And, of course, it must be stated that there are people who maintain their cars better than they do the body they take for granted. Commonly, they also curse the stars or other outside agency when either one breaks down.

People who exercise, study nutrition, and have developed an awareness of internal culture are hosing down their car and maintaining its fluids. If one has an interest in health it might add to their pool of knowledge to understand how people addressed health concerns before the advent of modern medicine. And surely, we are lucky to have available the miracle of modern allopathic healing. Without question, doctors can save your life. But, Yin/Yang demands, however, that you share equal responsibility and provide for maintenance of your biological vehicle. How did they do this before the modern era? I hope the following pages offer some insights.

Yin/Yang - Manifestation

One may be so inclined to ask: Why should the Tai-Chi symbol be emblematic of harmony and balance? And, what's with the half black / half white swirl? These are both very intelligent and insightful questions. Let's examine a few possibilities. But, before we discuss the swirl or the dot, Let's look at the outside boundaries. THE CIRCLE signifies the universe. Some Chinese coins have a square hole in the middle. Why? This symbolizes the earth within the circle that is the universe. From this perspective, there exist two polar energies. Opposite and inverse furies supplying motivation for all activities within.

The Tai-Chi symbol, simple, elegant. Primitive, timeless yet encompassing the most advanced scientific concepts. Our method of understanding the world involves tearing things apart, cataloging, and inventorying for comparison. Eastern cultures also did this, but there was an additional dimension of introspection and personal connection to the inquiry.

In ground fighting, it is said that we have an advantage because it's two against one. The ground and me against you. In trying to experience revelation, it also is two against one, or five against one, or a million against one, etc.; because it's the whole universe working on the problem. And, notice it was not said that one is extracting knowledge from the situation. This is because you are a component, working in harmony with all the forces that exist.

A radio may be broadcasting lifesaving information. A hurricane is coming. But if one is not tuned into that specific frequency, they simply cannot receive that information. Now, someone who knows all about radios, smiles and says, "it's this frequency right here. See...now the information can flow in."

Experienced guides who know the wilderness area you wish to explore, can lead you safely past obstacles and inherent dangers; because they have trod that path many times before. You may think of your guide, "How does he know that? He ain't got no book learnin'." But they are intimately familiar with the environment. Not because they mapped it or studied it. They are part of it. They are just the part that transverses the environment and remembers things, while also drawing life from it.

Many western doctors and physiologists have been amazed at the accuracy of the ancient anatomical texts which were formulated without the assistance of modern equipment. A genius level thinker will always find a way, even if they are hamstrung by the era or environment in which one lives. Through research, guesswork, and extrapolation they were able to form complex theories and derive multifactorial conclusions. But there was another element at work here.

A large number of these discoveries can be attributed to be revealed through meditation. By connecting to the universal mind. And if I were to be completely forthright, it's only because it's really not in any dispute. In our western traditions, we credit scientific / technical advancement to genius and inspiration. I personally don't really see any tangible differences. Even, notables like Tesla or William James as much as said so. Einstein is accredited with saying. "I did not arrive at my understanding of the fundamental laws of the universe through my rational mind." In other words, he transcended ordinary consciousness.

It's all a part of feeling the interconnectedness of life. You're not some isolated organism trying to rip out the revelations. You are part of the equation. I once had a motorcycle racer tell me, "You become a part of the machine. You are just the part that controls it." In inquiry, you are part of the equation. You are just the part to whom the understanding is revealed.

氣

Every elementary particle is a vibration in its own field. Fields interact with each other transferring charge, energy and momentum between particles and fields.

Most of the mass of anything is made up of atoms. But the atom's mass doesn't come from elementary particles, most of the atom's mass is in the confined kinetic and binding energy of quarks. As presented in the graphics below, one can see that the neutron has no charge, the electron has a negative charge, and the proton has positive charge; which are composed of quarks. Yin and Yang. Even if you disregard the intrinsic mass of elementary particles and just consider the electric properties of atoms, it is the electron that provides the excitation in the field. Quantum field fluctuation is a feature of space-time.

LIKE AND UNLIKE ARE THE SAME; OPPOSITES ARE IDENTICAL IN NATURE. BUT DIFFERENT IN DEGREE. EXTREMES MEET; ALL TRUTHS ARE BUT HALF TRUTHS; ALL PARADOXES MAY BE RECONCILED.

THE KYBALION

Building Blocks of the Elements

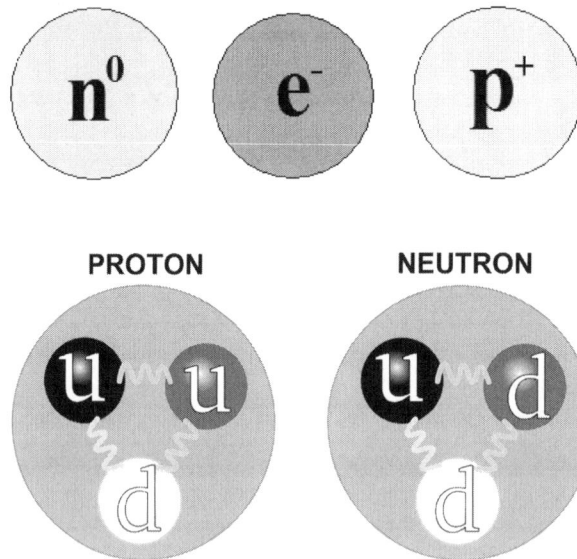

It is this positive/negative energy balance that is responsible for everything in the universe, i.e. everything within the field of the Yin/Yang. True that the above diagrams did not represent the atomic structure of the atom. The idea wasn't to illustrate that point. But rather, to impart the concept of opposing energies in everything. Starting with excitation in the electron field; Yin/Yang, on/off, one/zero. The square root of a positive number always has two answers.

One reason the Yin/Yang diagram has the swirls is to indicate energy interdependence. The opposing colors demonstrate how the complimentary, yet opposing furies manifest within the macro world. Yet, each has an element of the other, just like the composition of the elementary particles.

Positive/negative, light/dark, day/night. Active during the day, but life would die without rest and repair at night. Or vice-versa. If you worked your body 24/7 you would die. Yet, if you never moved, your body would atrophy. Day/night and sun/rain are and are not antagonistic simultaneously, although they work in harmony. Man and woman are individuals (and antagonistic), opposites but mutual halves of a union. It is this fundamental structure that binds, perpetuates, and makes the universe possible; all beginning with the elementary particles (i.e. disturbances in the energy fields).

Understanding Yin and Yang is not just awareness of opposites in the observable universe. It should be a mindfulness that is infused within your whole being. A quality of your personality. Parenthetically, I have been advised to present this material in an exclusively scholarly manner; but that would not be Yin and Yang. A dry academic rendering would be like a duck in the desert, in search of another duck. I've included the flippant and irreverent right alongside the scientific and collegiate, because I can't function any other way. The humor is right there with the somber. Like two sides of a snake swimming. Baked in - it's a quality of all things.

If you choose to live in the natural, then you are on your own. But existing right alongside that, just behind the screen, is the supernatural. Now you are no longer on your own. Literally the whole power of the universe is available. Of course there are laws and formulas that govern access and understanding, But the first step to living in harmony with the spiritual universe is to realize that there is one.

THE WAR OF GOOD AND EVIL

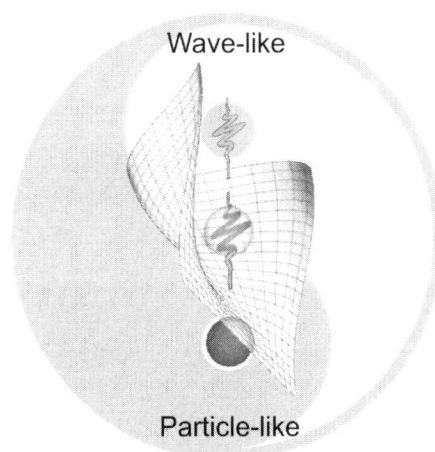

If you fly over a mountain forest or tropical jungle, you may ruminate on the beauty and order you see there. An ecosystem functioning in harmony to produce a balanced natural environment that is cooperative and self-sustaining.

But on closer examination, it ain't nothin' but conflict. Every organism fighting for survival. Predation. Burrows and nests hijacked, gangs of organized predators raiding and pillaging. innocent victims who are sometimes juveniles. A hostile, dangerous place.

A microcosm of the jungle would be your body. A constant battle to repel invaders. This system fighting that system. When describing the immune system medical writers often compare pathogens to invaders and the immune response to your army. The human gut is a bacterial war, raging with conflict in order to produce a harmonious result.

Everywhere I look I see conflict. If Yin and Yang is harmony, then it also represents energies physical and emotional fighting to produce the movement of the universe. A machine requires fuel to create an electromagnetic conflict (Yin/Yang) or in the case of the internal combustion engine this violent explosion to produce the resulting controlled tumult that ultimately proves beneficial.

The universe was born in extreme violence then settled down into more passive functioning. Order out of chaos. The grass grows is consumed by the rabbit, the rabbit is eaten by the lion. The lion rests.

And of course the Lion defecates and ultimately dies and is absorbed by the earth producing more grass. Everyone understands this cycle but for perspective on Yin and Yang it's important to not forget that Yin/Yang recognizes the extremes, the violent death of the rabbit, the lions peaceful return to the earth.

Just being aware of Yin and Yang is one step in the realization process. Understanding that everything you encounter has opposites and reverses promotes a more comprehensive understanding of the world in which you live. But it is just a one dimensional appreciation of Yin and Yang. Flat like the paper it is drawn on. It is an entry level gateway to appreciating the multi-dimensional interconnectedness of every level of reality.

A friend of mine once took a job delivering pizzas. After the rush, he went in the back room and sat down. The manager told him to get up and start chopping vegetables. He said; "I'm the delivery driver."

The manager said; "It's part of the job." Jim replied; "I'm the delivery driver." Again the manager said; "Everybody chops veggies." Jim said; "That's not the ad I answered." So he quit.

Usually the Yin/Yang symbol is shown vertically. If you turn it on its side it resembles an ocean wave. Reminding us to ride experience like a surfer. You may hire on as a delivery driver but be prepared for Yin to surge and whip you around the curve. A job , a marriage, can cause upset because all situations have a Yin/Yang aspect. Being unaware of this can cause trouble because you think that it is something that it is not. Believing it has only one aspect. "She will always be sweet and kind!"

Another friend recently mentioned something about his feminine side. We both understood what was meant. However hardly definitively accurate. Traits like kindness, compassion and understanding are components of a fully developed personality regardless of whether it's a man or a woman. But because of our clumsy language, We poetically assign these traits to the fairer sex for ease of communication. This is an example of already using symbols (male/female) to facilitate understanding.

Night does not suddenly become day. It is a gradual intensification like the swelling of Yang in the Tai-Chi diagram. And to someone standing 500 miles west of you, to a different degree. A matter of perspective.

Yin/Yang in Tai-Chi health applications swells and diminishes circulating body fluids and massaging internal organs in a pulsating surge like ocean waves. Tai-Chi fighting whips from nothing into a crescendo of ballistic power. Di solving potentially violent situations and manipulating conflict as illustrated in the Tai-Chi symbol is part of the Yin/Yang nature of the art.

Tough guy fighters who feel that dominance in single combat is the totality of martial art are ignoring the obvious balance promoted by generations of thoughtful, inspired men who trod more difficult paths than yours and still concluded that a martial artist or any human being would benefit from the example of Yin and Yang demonstrated at every level of the cosmos.

Not taking dangerous medicines to enhance physical strength. Glaring, swaggering and challenging everyone you meet. And not Passively being bounced around by the inequities of the universe and other peoples wills. But a balance, riding life and situations like a surfer. The dark side swells and tappers off ultimately becoming light. Electron, positron. Quantum field fluctuation. Yin and Yang.

If you were to encounter a Zen master, you would not find a passive renunciant, someone sitting quietly on the edge, dipping his toe in the pool of life. Instead it's someone aware of Yin and Yang, richly living the ups and downs of human experience. Expect to observe the full range of human emotion. Swearing, throwing tools. Prayer and contemplation. The difference is he is not completely taken over by the drama, a part of him is observing and probably laughing, the circle surrounding the opposing furies. He knows it's only a play. We the players? The fuel for the engine that produces turmoil/benefit. Your contribution keeps the machine running.

Addendum: Because there are now systems that can detect fluctuating zero point fields, this has caused scientists to reintroduce the antediluvian concept of aether in physics. Due to the Lorentz invariant, it should not, however, be considered as a physical medium. Classical and quantum mechanics are Yin/Yang in nature, as different governing principals apply. Indicated by the Heisenberg uncertainty principal, quantum systems fluctuate in zero point energy fields; their lowest energy state. It would be a mistake to think of particles as isolated things, but more appropriately as continuous energy fields; always in fluctuation. The dichotomy of energy fields, whose quanta are fermions; and matter fields, whose quanta are bosons, seems to me to be one of tomato/ tomatoe. Or, more fittingly for our purposes, Yin/Yang; as matter certainly does manifest from these energy fields. The reintroduction of the classical aether only serves to legitimize the original wisdom of the concept of Tao.

A Brief History of Rhyme

There once was a theorist named Hawking, who was famous for thinking not talking, his theory of black holes, radiated and extolled, his ability to overcome walking.	A Swiss patent clerk wouldn't be, if he exceeded the velocity of C, his M disappeared, amidst a span so weird, in this instance there just wasn't E.	Philosophiæ Naturalis Principia Mathematica, the conclusions proved quite dramatica, the theories came to be, as he sat under a tree, but replaced by the quanta systematica.
Comparing an acid and base, $PH = -\log[+H]$, a 15 point range based on electron exchange makes voltage and PH same case.		

Before the scientific era, in the western world at least, it was concluded that all things were brought into existence by an omnipotent conjurer who willed planets, environmental systems, and microbes into existence by divine fiat. With the enlightenment and the discoveries of the eighteenth century, It became fashionable for intelligent people to suppose that the universe was a big machine running on automatic.

With the continuing scientific breakthroughs of the nineteenth and twentieth century, a universal neurosis began to develop, because human beings who once were convinced that they were answerable to an infallible creator, were so saturated with science, that they felt overwhelmed by astronomic observations and atomic theory.

Then a game changer came along. This game changer dramatically altered western scientist's manner of speech to the point that they started to sound like eastern mystics. What was this transformational conception? It is called quantum field theory.

The Tao.. An all pervading matrix in which all things are contained... One contiguous membrane to which everything is connected. The very definition of quantum field theory. Everything is a wave; a wave in the field. Similar to casting a rock into a pond, a disturbance in the field creates an energy wave. Fields are continuous, not discrete. According to Heisenberg's uncertainty principal, fields are never still.

Everything is energy vibrating at a different frequency. Every elementary particle is vibrating in its own field. Fields interact with each other; transferring charge, energy, and momentum between particles and fields. Every point in the universe has a varying degree of "electronness" to it. Every point is its own field.

A scalar field assigns a value to any given point in space, like temperatures on a weather map. A vector field would be wind speed and direction on the same map - i.e. direction and magnitude.

Even in a vacuum, a field is there. When a field is perturbed, it's like plucking a guitar string. A wave is energy in a field - a jittering type of action; a vibration. This blanket of energy pervades the universe. A sea of probability. What is currently (as of this writing) being called quantum foam.

Isaac Newton said, "All are one. Everything in the field is connected. It is inconceivable that inanimate brute matter should, without the mediation of something else which is not material, operate upon and effect other matter without mutual contact."

NEWTON

Since the time of Newton, theories have been advanced, laws made and rescinded, with new technologies producing ever greater insight. Energy waves? Particles? A brief chronology of the particle paradigm as an example.

	STANDARD MODEL PARTICLES	
THEORIZED		DISCOVERED
1874	ELECTRON	1897
N/A	PHOTON	1899
1930	NO CHARGE NEUTRINO	1956
1964	QUARK	1968
	UP, DOWN, CHARM, STRANGE	THRU 1970'S
1962	GLUON	1978
1968	W&Z BOSON	1983
1970'S	TAU NEUTRINO	2000

It became apparent that space was saturated with energetic particles of many varieties and therefore permeated with energy fields. Not empty space, but an ether unto itself. The energy of the ground state; the lowest possible energy that a quantum mechanical system may have - zero point energy.

When religionists proclaim: "all things are God", "God is everywhere", or "all things are in God", It is only using different words to express the same thing. Essentially a different means of stating field theory. If spacey, American yoga types say: "all are one", or a legitimate mystic of the ancient world speaks of moving in the vibrational field; they are all trying to communicate the same general implication. Even mainline denominations say "God, in whom we live, move and have our being."

In the well-loved book, *"The little prince"*, Antoine de Saint Exupery wrote: "words are the source of much misunderstanding." People define themselves as more aligned with science or spirituality, as if they were political parties. That may have been true in the mid-20th century, but when someone who regards themself as a hard-headed realist says they only trust science, and can't believe in what they can't see, they may be forgetting that no one sees the quantum world, not even the scientists.

Throughout the history of science, all conclusions were arrived at by empirical observation. People dropped balls, dissected squirrels, or shot projectiles into ballistic gel. But, sub-atomic theory is just that, theory. We don't really see a lot of this stuff, we see the evidence and develop a theory. To date, wormholes have never been observed, they are predicted through models. It's math.

Before the age of science, there was only superstition, which, interestingly, also employed the scientific method of observing patterns and arriving at a conclusion. The age of Newton ushered in a mechanistic understanding of the universe which held sway for centuries.

As equipment, methods, and modeling improved, we began to unveil the quantum world; and science itself began to sway into an arcane, fantastical realm. Mathematical discoveries, experimental feedback, coupled with evolving theories, produced statements more suggestive of mysticism than Newtonian physics. This shifted the science to a point in which theories and explanations were more analogous to the earlier age of superstition.

From a tangential, but equally compelling view point, a biologist and an aboriginal hunter who encounter the same creature, construe the animal in very different ways. Each is correct as culture and training dictate definition and annotation through his indoctrination, in his own world.

In a bygone era, there were a proliferation of minister, priest, and rabbi jokes. The humor came from the confusion of a shared experience, interpreted from different perspectives.

Tao and field theory are not the same, but, if not synonymous, then at the least, they certainly do rhyme. There is still much to learn from the ancient way.

I'm glad that I live in the age of science and not superstition. We now are starting to understand much of the mechanics of nature and the cosmos. Science is currently looking for the intelligence behind the creative force. It appears that this intelligence is already there; In everything. Given opportunity, a further understanding will develop. A perfect system of comprehension. Hidden in plain sight. In everything.

It would seem that life creates itself. From the smallest constituents. Energies clump together, manifest tangibility, become mesons, hadrons, and gluons; real and virtual, irresistible processes form, become atoms and molecules. But what happens if, in the incomprehensible expanses of time, random energies coalesce driven by this universal dynamic process and manifest the unbelievable.

The One and The Other One

A Gentle Proposition on Second Emanation

The Genesis creation story shares many affinities with Mesopotamian mythology; on whose themes much of it is based. The Pentateuch, composed in the sixth or seventh century B.C., edited and revised many times, begins with Genesis. The original source was Jahwist, which was later expanded by other authors, and became the priestly source recognizable as the Genesis we know today. In reality, it is a composite work, although tradition dictates that we attribute authorship to Moses.

The creation stories differ greatly in genesis one and genesis two. The former features the accepted seven-day creation, and the latter, creation in one day. Some sources suggest the two divergent themes were combined by the urging of a strong Persian authority. Things changed again when Greek ideas were assimilated. Regardless, the obvious Mesopotamian influence is undeniable.

I have no denunciatory reason for comparing the differences in Genesis one and two: seven-day creation or one day creation; simultaneous creation of man and woman (gen1), or the Adams rib version (gen2). Furthermore, I would never claim to be a translator of Hebrew. My only point is to call out that there are contradictions within the same document - depending upon version. I do this to build the case for offering an idea regarding the creation of the creator, not an alternative narrative to Genesis; rather a possible understanding of the time before the Pentateuch.

Plotinus had a concept developed in Greece and adopted and promoted by the Gnostics (and others). That is the idea of second emanation. That the entity that we regard as the creator god was himself in fact created.

This fits logically with the concept of the Tao, the primordial universal energy that permeates every corner of the cosmos. An idea shared by quantum field theory; that space, far from empty, is a matrix of active energy fields. An electric universe whose province is the business of creation.

Many have suggested that out of this elemental domain of continuous formation, developed the powerful cosmic being who created what we experience as the material world. It would be an intriguing exercise to address the perplexing, unfathomable quandary of all time. Where did the big guy come from and who is this GOD?

Who created man from the dust (Afar / Efer?) of the earth? Who breathed life into man (gen1-2)? Mystifying and ambiguous though it may be, let's peer through the murky glass and synthesize what some great thinkers and very devout adherents have conjectured over the eons. For your consideration, human thoughts valid as any other. Seekers only. Ideologues need not apply.

There is a power in the universe. An awesome power. A ubiquitous power. Raw and unmanifested. Learned Greeks knew this, and so did the Gnostics, along with many others. The Kabbalah speaks of a raw energy so powerful that they needed a ten step-down transformer to dilute, divide and categorize it. A raw energy from which all things are made.

So we can get started, bear in mind that I am purposely using nonspecific, everyday language, throughout, in an effort to avoid offending any regimented theory, and simply to convey general ideas.

Tao is nonjudgmental and nurtures all. but does not lord it over them.

The universe in which we live is so unfathomably vast that it is not only possible that anything could happen - it is inevitable that everything "will" happen. What I offer here is not a theory and not something that I believe, rather a postulation, a thought problem, a koan. A way for the human mind to analyze and understand the ultimate power in the world as traditionally defined by people who made the assumption that this was so. A possible explanation, stated as metaphor, to illustrate how an original creative force, with personality, may have come to be.

Imagine, before the big bang, gravity, electromagnetism, the strong and weak forces were unified into one super force. Photons were appearing in and out of existence in a material stew, just before the inflationary period began. It is possible that dark energy and dark matter are echoes from the initial pre-plank second in the creation of our universe as we know it today.

Now, imagine a universal substance, a ubiquitous material; one from which all things are made. Undetectable because it is unmanifested. A raw power that contains every kind of energy at the same time; light, heat, nuclear, chemical, spiritual, emotional, and of extreme intelligence.

Only, this power simply can't contain itself. It keeps spewing out creations like a volcano or a sweet tart in a soda bottle. Manifestations of all kinds. Some just globs of energy. Some tangible molecular structures that exist in our dimensional plane and in other dimensions, where the laws of physics may be different. Sometimes, unimaginable combinations of materials that can't even exist in our manifest universe.

Trillions of gazillions of things and non-things; in ways, combinations, and places we could never comprehend. Sometimes, a concentration of emotion, creative power and some intelligence; but a moron. Creativity, but low intelligence. An idiot spewing out blobs of incomplete matter. A failure, by our standards. And, even sometimes a glob would manifest that we could imagine and even understand. A glob of chemical energy with emotion. But, also a failure - again, by our standards.

Then after the quadrillionth roll of the dice, a combination of intelligence and creative power with all the raw materials to produce this manifestation. And ultimately, our universe was created; one where atoms and molecules are subject to the laws of physics within this specific realm.

This outcome is known as the Demiurge within the Platonic, Neo Pythagorean, Middle Platonic, and Neo Platonic schools of philosophy. The Demiurge is the artisan who makes and sustains the universe. The Gnostics adopted this term from the Greeks, sharing the concept that the Demiurge was the creator sustainer, but itself a product of a higher power.

In my last few laps here on the planet, I seek peace. Peace in my environment, peace in my relationships, peace in my mind and soul. The questions of who is God and where did he come from seared into my very being. I personally needed an answer that made some kind of logical sense.

The concept of the Demiurge resolves much of this confusion. When the bible states that God says, "I am a jealous god"; we think that doesn't seem very godlike - destroying nations, taking sides, picking favorites. But now it makes sense. The Bible is accurate. Our creator has a personality because he himself is an imperfect creation. He is not the one.

I quote Seneca often, but I find it difficult to pick a favorite ancient Greek philosopher. A perennial favorite, but by far my favorite personage of the ancient world, is Plotinus. Plotinus was a Hellenistic philosopher, and subject of Rome, who lived probably from 205-270. His ideas are the impetus to developing these concepts as I understand them. Plotinus was clear: there is a molder, a fashioner, a mechanic - but he is not the one.

If one is confounded by the question, "who created God?" - here is an answer. What Plotinus refers to as the one, is the ultimate power in the universe. A power above that of the creator god. And, many mystery religions believed this; including the Gnostics.

Ultimately, the universe creates itself. There is an endless stream of creation manifesting as quantum possibility in the energetic fields. And, because the observation that energy cannot be destroyed seems to be a settled question; if, by chance, it does all end; then it circles around on itself and begins again.

But, is there a spiritual world? Does anything live on? Who listens? I say that there must be a spiritual world. That there is just too much evidence to dismiss this possibility. Something must be going on. Surely with the energy of intense emotion, physic, mental capability, measurable brain waves, some kind of presence must carry on. It's probably just as the holy men say.

The empirical experience of millions seems to substantiate overwhelmingly that saints and angels are real. If someone develops spiritually, with strong will and the mental vitality enough to produce easily measurable brain energy, then where does this energy dissipate to? It may carry over into the next realm, but I am also willing to admit that it is possible that it's just us. Who knows?

Undeniably, there is an incredible world of physical beauty; but if one closes their eyes, they can still deny that it is there. Still, most people feel a strong spiritual connection, and a few may have been the recipient of seemingly unexplainable miracles. Some of which are chronicled in this volume.

Legion are the seekers who have trod many paths seeking revelation; and there have been many who have been duped, deluded and conned. I have seen the gullible, the desperate and the well-intentioned fall prey, succumb, or just surrender. I would be wary of anyone who says they know for sure. No one does.

This is by no means an endorsement of the ideas of Valentinus or Gnostic theology. I have deliberately avoided the use of words such as pleroma and metanoia as the intention was to suggest a general alternate cosmology and not challenge any established orthodoxy.

There is definitely something going on, but I don't know what it is. There is, without question, a spiritual world. It is a part of this one, yet has many entities that are hard to define. And somewhere, pervading the energetic matrix of quantum fields - The ONE.

Quantum Chromodynamics

Writing this book has been a great experience. I have enjoyed the process. I'm so glad my friend talked me into it. But in order to experience this process. There was a lot of training and preparation. I had to go to school as a boy and learn the language, the alphabet, and so on. Then had to make the conscious decision to peruse training in the martial arts.

After a series of experiences that formed a perspective and gathering expertise on fighting and the arcane aspects of the martial arts, I was in a position to have the experience of writing a book. A spy or a politician may have a similar path and we can learn from both of their experiences.

When you see someone with a guitar or playing tennis you say, "I would like to have that experience. That must feel great to be able to do that." You see someone who is in good shape and you think, that looks so cool, I would like to be that guy, and you set about putting in the time and effort to develop the physical form to match the image in your mind.

This is understandable and normal for things like guitars and tennis rackets, But what kind of person peruses the esoteric arts. Most people feel it is too intangible or not even real and seek to master things with direct interaction with the material world, like guitars and tennis rackets. It is one thing to gain practical knowledge like baking or math, but why waste your time on something that isn't even real?

If it so happens that esoteric knowledge is an outgrowth of some more practical endeavor attached to it, like two halves of the same coin, one may find them self-immersed in arcane practice and experiences that they didn't think integrated to the practical endeavor. This can produce adepts who began with a very different expectation such as some of the heroes of Christian mysticism.

Most lay people and even some clergy are mostly concerned with the nuts and bolts of practical faith and forming a strong union with the almighty. Some, however, due to an innate ability or exposure to enigmatic thought and technique travel down a more enlightened path and become aware of other levels of reality.

Imagine a father and son are both watching a horse race. They can't get into the track, so instead, they watch the action through a fence. The boy can only peek through a crack and see the horses go by one by one. He looks through the fence and can see that the white horse has passed well ahead of the black and brown. The boy stops watching because he can see that the white horse was leading by several lengths.

The father says, "the black horse is going to win." "How can you say that", the boy says, "the white horse was leading by three." The son has made a logical conclusion based upon observation. Reality, from the son's perspective, demonstrated that the white horse was leading and would obviously come in first.

The father, however, being taller could view the entire track and see that the black horse was gaining rapidly on the other animals. Because the father was physically more developed than his son, he literally had a more complete perspective than the boy, who was hampered by his underdeveloped stature.

This is a good example because there is nothing mystical or occult about this illustration. The father is not clairvoyant, he can simply see the whole track. He cannot predict the future, the horses may stumble, or the brown horse may rally and pull it out at the last minute.

The father has simply developed an ability, in this case physical stature that enables him to do something the son cannot. If the son grows properly, then he too can see things as they really are. Not hindered by a limited perspective. It is possible to see the complete picture if you are fully developed.

I received my shaktipat from Harri Harinanda but did most of my training with his lieutenant, swami Atmananda. I was his driver whenever he was in town. On one occasion, I was not driving but was in the car when one of the other Kriabans picked him up from the airport. In front of the car-full of people swami said, "if you're not careful, you're going to get hit right here", pointing to the passenger side door. Sure enough, two days later the student got hit right where swami indicated.

As a vigilant observer of such phenomenon, I noticed that like the father in the horse race story, Swami didn't say, "you WILL get hit"; he said, "if you're NOT CAREFUL". He understood that there are many potential variables; but being able to see the entire track, he warned of the most dire.

I have no special abilities myself, but have been around it all my life. I have seen people make predictions with uncanny accuracy. Countless times I have witnessed adepts start cars and produce parking places. I knew a guy in California who could blow out light bulbs, at will. I have had psychics and mediums tell me things they could not possibly have known.

If someone has a talent for playing the piano, this ability should definitely be developed; even though few people are true proteges. Uncommon talent is a rarity. But, everyone could develop some ability and at least have the experience of knowing that inside them somewhere is the capacity to produce in this medium and communicate in this wordless language that speaks to the emotions and the heart.

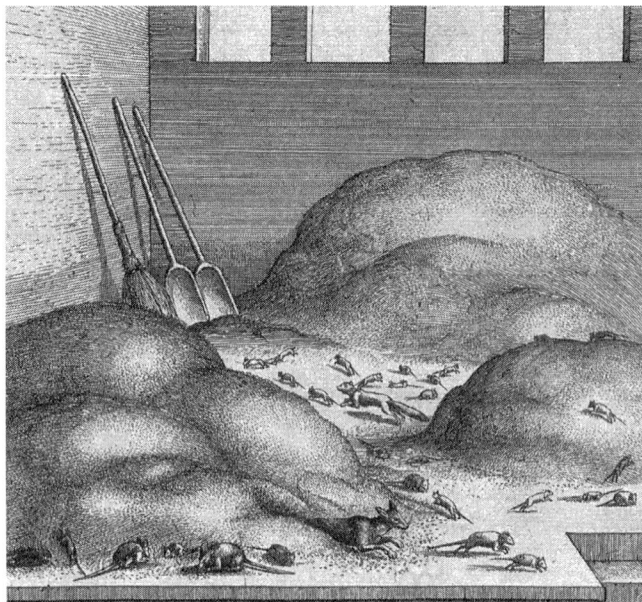

"There are more in things in heaven and earth than are dreamt of in your philosophy", Hamlet said to Horatio. But Shakespeare's intent was for us to realize there is much outside the mundane tangible realm. Organized business operations and western society, in general, places a taboo on inquiry into existence. But, much like society's repression of sexuality, it is very much there; a part of everyone who draws breath. People get hunches or inklings, but sanitize them, relegating the perception to brain chemistry or emotions, while deferring to statistical odds.

Premonition, foreboding, and intuition are accepted phenomena of the human experience; but again, like sex, a powerful biological component we are obliged to downplay as a quirk of corporeal existence.

EMPIRICISM IN THE HUMAN EXPERIENCE

"Liars, damn liars and statisticians." This phrase has been attributed to many from A.J. Balfour to Benjamin Disraeli; though most of us give credit to Mark Twain. Figures don't lie, but liars can sure figure; is an observation often used to describe the practice of using real numbers to lead to a false conclusion.

If someone has an agenda, or even an unintentional bias, they know statistics build a convincing case. There are entire professions dedicated to numerical sleight of hand. Investment adviser is one glaring example, and many studies reveal that while some recommendations are science driven, although overall performance is barely better than a coin flip.

My favorite is the often repeated university study where the class is divided into three groups. The first group is told to make investment choices based on science. The students do research, make comparisons, and choose wisely. The second group is told to invest emotionally. They select companies because they like the name or who they feel about the product. The third group literally flips a coin.

This scenario has been repeated at different times and in various places with the results of all three groups usually scoring within percentage points of the professionals. I'm sure someone somewhere is tearing my book in half right now; and I, by no means, intend to disparage the profession. But hey, the numbers don't lie.

Science deals with repeatable facts. But companies, like the ones mentioned above, can experience internal turmoil, natural disaster, or succumb to political whim and manipulation. Unknown factors, like these, can affect an otherwise sound recommendation. An examination of palpable systems, however, produces repeatable results. Hypothesis, theorem, research, conclusion.

That is, until, you insert the word theoretical in front of your branch of science. Newtonian mechanics held sway through the dawn of the modern era; because in the world of rolling balls and calculating airfoils, the solid world needed only to be observed and cataloged.

If one side of your Yin/Yang symbol is labeled mysticism and the other quantum theory, you can see how one leads into and becomes the other. You may choose sides, however this is only due to bias. Not only does the observer affect the outcome - the observer produces the conclusion.

If someone's history and brain chemistry predisposes them towards mysticism, then the confusing, the obtuse, and the obscure seem to logically indicate the supernatural. In contrast, If another mind is heavily biased towards billiard balls banging into each other, he sees what he expects.

As long as western science paralleled Yin/Yang theory, only two of anything were ever needed. It's either positive or negative, attract or repel, clockwise or counter-clockwise, etc. For instance, a dipole magnet only has two fields - North and South. And, although the atom can have many electrons, the entire composition is either electron or nucleus. Examining the nucleus exposes the proton and neutron.

When science advanced sufficiently to tear apart the nucleus, E plurbus unum. Each nucleon revealed more components. Of major interest were the newly discovered Quarks. Quarks came in several varieties so the previously binary naming system was now outmoded. Up, down, charm and strange were chosen arbitrarily. In the same way, biologists differentiate between sub types within a species. Deer, Moose, Caribou. They chose a familiar comparison to describe the triune nature of color charge.

Just like the way meteorologists ran out of female names for hurricanes; to accommodate even more diverse species of sub-atomic particles, colors were assigned. The branch of science dedicated to the study of these elements was named chromodynamics, from the Greek chromo; color. Closer examination would reveal that quarks were really disturbances in the quark field, the same way electrons are an energy fluctuation in the electron field. Revealing once again...

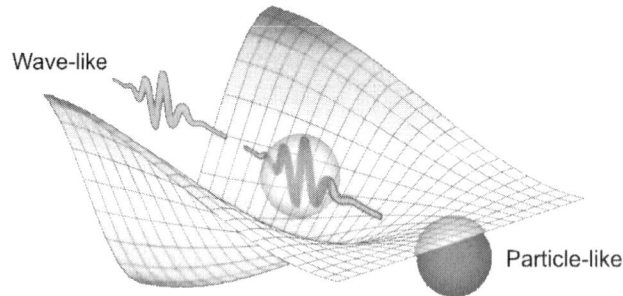

Wave-like

Particle-like

THE UNIVERSAL ENERGY MATRIX

A concept known and understood by mystics and all thoughtful people throughout the east.

The visionaries of the East and scientists of the West are both describing the same process in different terms. Like John Smith and Powhatan discussing the turkey. They are both examining the same bird. The Englishman wants to classify and quantify something new. The Indian, who is intimately familiar with the animal, is trying to explain something he has always known quite well, but can't convey his knowledge only because he is speaking another language.

The ancient Greeks believed atoms of solid material were composed of little cubes because cubes can be stacked. Atoms of water were balls because they slipped around each other. Air atoms were like pyramids. They assigned a shape as a best guess because they had no way to see inside an atom. The cutting edge science of quantum chromodynamics chose color for the same reason.

Statisticians, like all westerners immersed a lifetime in a worldview dominated by Newtonian physics, assemble numbers in order to support observation and research. When at home in his village, I like to imagine the wife of Powhatan asking his impression of the English. "Damn liars and statisticians."

Let's suppose that a group of scientists want to explore the unseen universe of romantic love. I suppose it is possible to quantify the various elements and phases of this condition. Using established research methods let's see what this might look like.

Well, the process initiates with the loneliness/desire phase, which triggers the attraction phase, which becomes the excitement phase, and that naturally morphs into the complacency phase, and then degrades into destruction/annihilation.

It has been determined that each phase consists of a various number of units of time. Now these time units may be two days each or three weeks, depending on variables. For example, the excitement phase has a duration of 340 units, after which the complacency phase emerges. We know this because oxytocin levels drop by 27 percent and cortisol rises by 16 ppb.

This could be done. There could be a scientific examination of romantic process and assign numbers to a natural phenomenon that everyone on the planet is living every day. Well, to do all this work you would probably need an anthropologist; a psychologist; a physiologist; and at the end, of course, a psychiatrist and a lawyer.

Does it matter? Do I really need to comprehend micro-processes every time I look at the ocean or start my car. It is good and necessary that a metallurgist understands the molecular composition of my engine block. But do I?

Automobile ownership enhances my life. But maintaining my vehicle and driving safely is about all I need to know. Likewise, the processes and enhancement of biological systems that take place during Tai-Chi are happening whether I understand them or not.

Tai-Chi and other yogic endeavors can be a profound enrichment of the human experience as well as a gateway to unseen mysteries. I have included some examples of biologic activity that take place during Tai-Chi, and that's good to know, but like the romantic love example, is it necessary or even possible to reduce the experience to scientific equations? As always the answer is Yin and Yang. It both matters and it doesn't.

Addendum: Trends in science change over time, as do religions. Like the Kabalistic concept of Ein Sof, dark energy is just a placeholder for an, as of yet, undiscovered power; one perhaps describing some unknown anti-gravity substance. It is here where not looking too closely may prove prescriptive. Rather than disagreeing over minutia and detailed specifics, in some way it may prove advantageous to become a spiritual generalist, adopting a more universalist connection with the ultimate reality. It is not faith to try and "hedge your bet" regarding the destination of your soul. Nor is it trust to bemoan the inevitable calamities encountered by earthbound terrestrials. It is a fools errand to think that having complete information will somehow safeguard anyone from the laws of chance. To live is to never be 100% safe and secure. This is why the first element taught in Tai-Chi is the mechanism sung - calm, tranquil, quiet. To mollify and pacify a frightened, unsure, agitated mind. Faith is trust. To relax and experience the joy of physical existence and convey one's soul through tumultuous life experience requires the peace of mind brought about by a simpler type of faith. True, today as always: those who believe, enter into rest.

Titivations

The Ubiquity of Tai-Chi Principles

For us believing physicists, this separation between past, present, and future has the value of mere illusion.

Albert Einstein

Who Says So

There are two reasons to include an author bio in any publication.

Number one: curiosity. Who is this person, and how did they form their opinions?

Number two: what are their qualifications? Is this person even entitled to have an opinion, and is it worth listening to?

These questions are both valid and deserve an answer.

First: I am well-seasoned martial arts stylist with over sixty years' experience as both a practitioner and an instructor. My experiences include the Chinese, Japanese Indonesian, and American (both types of martial) styles; with a heavy emphasis on the Chinese Arts – specifically Tai-Chi.

Second: I will rely on the well-worn adage of Chinese origin; "a picture is worth a thousand words". I believe it is auspicious and opportune to follow this sage advice.

Finally, the photographs included in this book not only establish a history and timeline, but many also serve as bi-sifu pictures, acceding both authority and linage.

Historical fun fact: In the late nineteenth century, many aspirants and neophytes sought to be photographed with renowned Chinese masters. To avoid implied sanction, these wily adepts ratified a subtle, yet visually verifiable tradition, a.k.a. the bi-sifu photograph. This tradition played into the western custom of being photographed with a person of gravitas, but also preserved their right of indicating disavowal and/or repudiation. This was done by the crossing of any appendages; often blatantly (with arms akimbo), but sometimes surreptitiously (with a leg or foot).

This was the visual equivalent of them saying: "I do not certify nor endorse this person." On the other hand, if this physical indicator was not present, this was to mean that the adept agreed to be photographed and respected and/or avowed some sort of affiliation with the others in the photograph. And, the more physically open the adept was within the photograph, the greater indicated degree of endorsement is implied to be stated.

Tableau

Circa 1988

Circa 2009

Circa 1991

Circa 2017

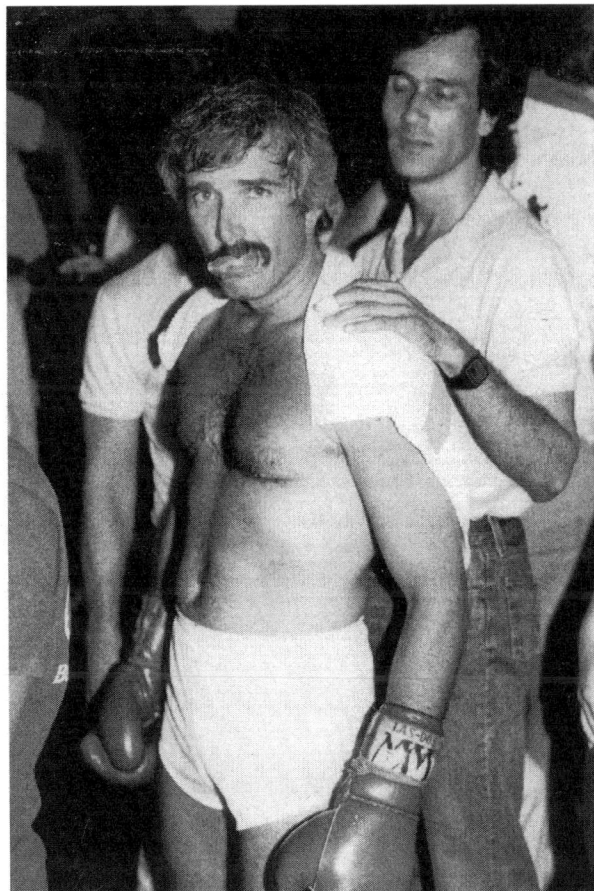

Circa 1987

Circa 1991

Circa 2011

Circa 1994

Circa 2018

Circa 1988

Circa 1979

Circa 1986

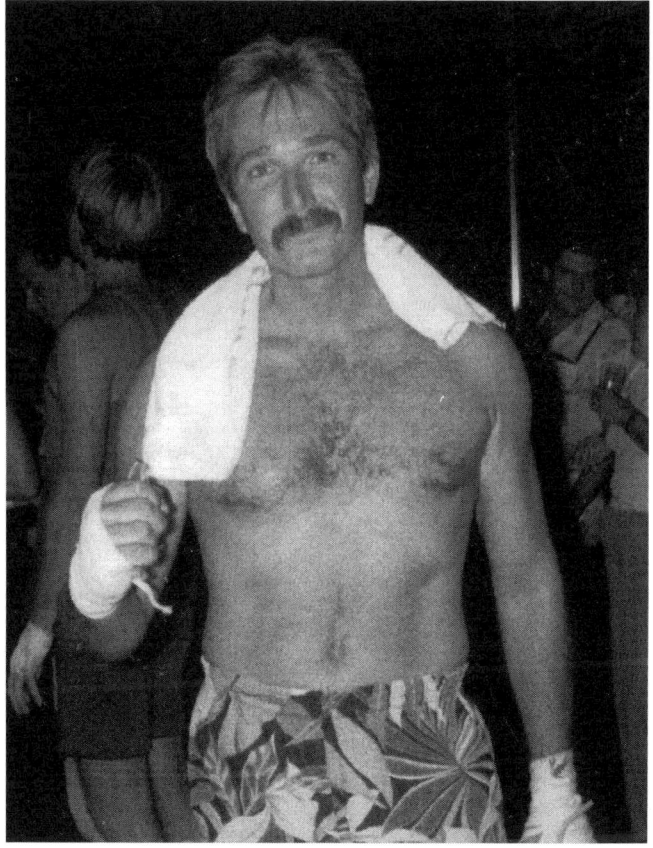

Kukri Seminar 2007 with Dr. Gyi

What They're Saying

What follows are professional observations from highly respected and accredited individuals on the subject matter. It is hoped that these varied personal perspectives and germane experiences will help to assure those who are not yet fully swayed as to the holistic benefits of the art. Their educated input is both indefensible and appreciated.

Dr. Bonell

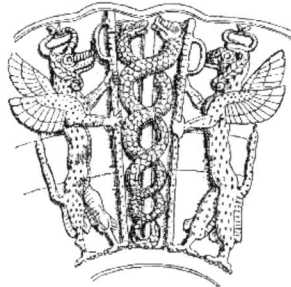

Josephine Bonell, M.D.

**Internal Medicine/Preventative Medicine
Bachelor Degree in Chemistry
University of San Diego
Medical Doctor M.D.
University of Miami School of Medicine
Internship Medicine/Psychiatry
Jackson Memorial Hospital Miami FL
Internal Medicine Residency
Cleveland Clinic Hospital**

The Complete Book of Thai-Chi illustrates why both the art of Thai-Chi and the art of Medicine make a beautiful marriage: East meets West. They perfectly complement each other and work synergistically to provide a platform of wellness and healing.

Just as the human body is both extremely complex, intricate, and delicately balanced; so do these two modalities of healing work together to create a complimentary world.

I have seen the gradual change in mind set of allopathic medicine accepting and thus integrating eastern medicine in the span of my own career. This is a long awaited and warmly welcomed change. In my own practice of internal medicine and preventative health, I have incorporated the art of Thai-Chi by recommending Professor Brubaker to several of my patients. He not only teaches the art of meditation, physical movement of flowing forms, but concomitantly educates people on the theory behind its healing powers and how they work together in perfect harmony.

His years of knowledge, experience, appreciation, and passion for this beautiful art are inherently authentic. Professor Brubaker is the quintessential master. Practicing with him is a both a valuable lesson and a life changing experience to all who partake.

As a very traditionally trained western medical doctor, I wholeheartedly believe and accept this art of Thai-Chi as a valid modality of healing whose time has come.

Dr. Burack

Steven Burack D.O.

Pysical Medicine and Rehabilitation

As a physician who has dealt with pain and musculo-skeletal maladies, disorders, and complications for over 15 years, I commonly recommend Tai-Chi to my patients as a part of their treatment and/or recovery plan. This centuries old art is commonly and justly known to improve aerobic capacity, increase energy, and improve flexibility and balance. Each of these benefits are helpful assets to dealing with patients suffering from chronic pain. Also, I consider Tai-Chi to have a remarkable therapeutic benefit - helping to decrease stress levels; which can often be a substantial contributing factor to chronic pain. I am such a confident advocate in my statements, that I, myself, have been episodically training in various martial arts since I was 16 years old.

I have been studying Tai-Chi with Professor Brubaker for over 3 years. During this time, Professor Brubaker has exposed me to the diverse, beneficial aspects of Tai-Chi. When I witness a Tai-Chi practitioner, such as Professor Brubaker, 20 years my senior, that can attain and maintain some of the more difficult postures; ones that most people 20 years old cannot even dream to accomplish; that is the power and draw to Tai Chi. By studying with Professor Brubaker, my eyes have been opened to the invaluable concepts of hard and soft, and how the Yin/Yang of them both are required to maintain a strong, well-balanced, and healthy body.

Dr. Laura

Laura Haughie P.P.T

Health.Harvard.edu
Meditation In Motion
Mayo Clinic
Tai-Chi and Qi Gong
nccih.gov

Art Of Embracing The Mind, Body and Spirits

NIH: Research finding suggest that practicing Tai-Chi may improve balance and stability in older people and those with Parkinson's, reduce pain from knee O.A, helping people cope with fibromyalgia and back pain and promote quality of life and mood in people with heart failure and cancer. Tai-Chi may also offer psychological benefits such as reducing anxiety.

MAYO: Cardiac Rehab Cultivate Tranquility
Harvard.edu

Decreased Falls Research has found that people who do Tai-Chi see a 20% to 40% reduction in the risk of falling even after as little as 6 months.

In 2017 Journal of the American Geriatrics Society found that older adults who participated in 1 to 3 hour long Tai-Chi sessions each week for up to 26 weeks lowered their fall risk by 43% and cut in 1/2 their likelihood of injuring themselves as a result of the fall. As we age our muscles weaken, we develop sensory deficits, slower reaction times and osteoporoispenia and loss of focus. Tai-Chi appears to help with these multiple risk factors. Tai-Chi is a weight bearing activity that helps strengthen bone and muscle. It is particularly a good exercise for the ankles knees and hips, where it is needed for good balance and flexibility. Professor Brubaker is able to modify certain movements if one has a disability. I myself trained with Professor Brubaker with a congenital foot and ankle injury and after recovery from life threatening injuries.

As we age sensory deficits increase due to medical conditions such as peripheral neuropathies that causes weakness, tingling, and numbness, most often in the hand and feet making it harder to balance.

"There are several studies that show Tai-Chi improves plantar sensation (Feet)." This improvement in sensory deficits can help the person tell if they are leaning too far forward or back and to make adjustments so you don't have loss of balance.

The research has also shown that people who practice Tai-Chi have better muscle reaction time. In one experiment while walking on the treadmill people (wearing a harness) were exposed to a small shift underfoot. Those who practiced Tai-Chi had much better muscle reaction time and were less likely to lose their balance than people who didn't do Tai-Chi.

It has also been proven that people that people sometimes fall because they were distracted. Tai-Chi helps people mentally focus and more readily shift their attention between tasks. It helps them be aware of multiple things at the same time.

Once someone has fallen and sustained an injury they usually become fearful that it will happen again. Poor posture and guarding usually pursue. The person may hold their breath, change the way they walk, tightening muscles groups which unfortunately makes it more likely that they will fall again. Tai-Chi helps the person gain strategies to reduce improper posture, gait and muscle posture.

Some research suggests that Tai-Chi can help make your bones stronger as we age there is bone loss. Many women see a steep reduction in bone density due to menopause whether surgically or naturally. Osteopenia and or osteoporosis is caused by reductions in the amount of circulating estrogen. The evidence suggests that practicing Tai-Chi works to slow down the rate of bone loss because it's a weight-bearing exercises which stimulates bone growth.

Professor Brubaker explains how everyone can benefit from the practice no matter what your age or fitness level.

Dr. Falck

Carol L. Falck

V.M.D., M.S.

Tai-Chi is my daily supplement, my coach and my religion. After 30 years of practice, it enhances both my personal well-being and my professional successes as an integrative medicine practitioner. As one of the five branches of Traditional Chinese Medicine (TCM), it provides unimaginable benefits as a solo exercise, and works seamlessly and synergistically with acupuncture, Chinese herbal medicine, food therapy, and Tui Na manipulative therapy.

Sifu Brubaker is an accomplished and masterful Tai Chi instructor. He provides a unique style of instruction, catering to individual learning styles. Classes combine meditative and self-defense aspects of Tai Chi, challenging one to study and develop a life-altering, health-boosting practice.

What Else They're Saying

If you can have only one book on Tai-Chi buy it.	...Lawn and Tractor
Then get this one	
An incredible mix of Yoga, Kabbalah and bullshit	...Yoga review
If you use a thesaurus, is it still plagiarism?	...Newsthing
None of this is right	Tai-Chi monthly
A book by someone who really understands their subject matter...	....Writers journal
would be nice to read, this unfortunately is not one.	
Perfect for the toilet	Harvard Law Review
This author is 100 % correct. He knows very little.	International journal of internet trolls

Sea Stories

What people commonly call fate is mostly their own stupidity.

Arthur Schopenhauer

The difference between genius and stupidity is that genius has its limits.

Albert Einstein

Introduction

Anecdotal accounts can provide a colorful and instructive example for many people. That is primarily why humans are enthralled by tales of strife and conflict. While these yarns are educational, the best lessons one can relate are epics that are not only true, but also purchased with a deep degree of personal cost. Therefore, I have decided to recount occurrences from which I have the best experience, culling from my own personal history.

When one inhabits a world rife with conflict, one will, on occasion, come in contact with such conflict - it is almost unavoidable. Unfortunately, for a good portion of my life, I resided in such environments. What is even more unfortunate, and all too common, sometimes I found it necessary and sometimes I just found myself existing and trans versing through these less-than-desirable ecosystems. To paraphrase some famous philosopher: "some are born to ass-beatings, others have them thrust upon them."

In my adult life, amazingly, I have encountered many people who had never been in any violent physical altercations; some of them martial artists. I can see how this can happen to normal people in normal situations, but as previously stated, sometimes normality is only a misty vision through the veil. So, for those fortunate enough to have only needed to deal with escapades of a more pedestrian nature, here is a sampling of what can happen to an ordinary person confronted with varying degrees of extraordinary inter-personal challenges.

These are not riveting, breath taking fight stories. Just the kind of thing that occurs sometimes in life - if you happen to be a complete asshole.

The Boatyard

When I was a private investigator, I once had a client who owned a shipyard. A very colorful character, well known and respected in the shipbuilding business. He was building a yacht for a customer, and there was some type of intrigue between him and a rival ship builder in Miami. He needed me to go to the Miami shipyard and pose as a wealthy client with some particular specifications for a custom yacht build. It's always less suspicious if you pose as a couple, so I took my girlfriend along as a decoy.

After the interview. We left the shipyard and had to cross a deserted side street. It was mid-afternoon with no cars to be seen. Directly across the street was a vacant lot about half the size of a football field, where a large building had been torn down. I did notice two taxi cabs on the far side of the lot. They were not at all in my radar, as they were quite a distance from us. Evidently, one of them received a call, because he blasted in a side-drift, racing to get out of the lot. Just as we stepped into the street, the cab came careening out of the lot, and attempted to straighten out, now not far from us. It was so odd. He was half-hanging out the driver's window looking left. We were on the other side of the car, two steps into the street. For some reason, known only to lunatics and whoever is the patron saint of detectives, he accelerated; heading right toward us.

There is a common phenomenon which occurs during highly stressful situations. Often, people experience tunnel vision; auditory exclusion; and slow motion time. This began to happen to me. I grasped my girlfriend's arm and began to tug. Even though, in reality, it was only a split second; I seemed to have all of the time in the world. The taxi was now within about two inches from impacting her. I had her in motion, yet I could see that it still wasn't going to be enough. So I really cranked her arm - pulling her clear. Accelerating rapidly, the cab practically grazed her, avoiding impact by a hairs breadth.

The movement I used to pull her clear is from an old Tai-Chi form that I no longer practice, called deflect downward. Of course, it is a self-defense move, so there is plenty of juice. Because of my necessity to execute this maneuver fast and powerfully, my girlfriend's leg was broken at the moment she met the concrete. The cab never stopped.

With the cab traveling at over forty miles per hour, this could have been a horrible disaster. I take credit for the save, but clearly I see the hand of god. I firmly believe, M.M.A and tough guy fight training would have left me ill equipped to provide the type of response required to successfully resolve this situation. If I never have any other encounters the rest of my days, all the classic martial arts training was worth it, to be able to save this one life.

WHAT I LEARNED

Always be aware. Never allow yourself to be absorbed into mundane reverie. Even on a quiet street, things can come out of nowhere. And, oh yeah….you're lucky if you have a good angel.

Happy Halloween

I should probably relate this saga next as it involves the same person who was almost struck by the taxi cab. Her leg took a long time to recover, as it was a very bad break. Because she twisted when she went down, there was connective tissue damage and, of course, the femur takes a long time to heal. So, about a year and a half later, we were downtown for Halloween night.

My girlfriend was dressed as a butterfly and I as a butterfly catcher. I had just read the book "How to Get Your Ass Kicked on Halloween", and was wearing a pith helmet. I guess this made an irresistible target, because out of nowhere, I was struck from behind. I wasn't fast enough to processes it, but a half second before I was hit, I did sense motion. This guy leapt up from behind, and came down with his full weight - double palm striking me on the top of the head. Suddenly we were surrounded. I was stunned, but wasn't dazed. My focus was on the 4 or 5 punks circling. One of them tried to take the butterfly net I was carrying, but he let go when I threatened him. By that time the one who hit me, obviously the leader, came to the front, so the real fun could begin.

I was very concerned about my companion. Not only was she limping and walking with a cane, from our last misadventure, but she also suffered from other health issues. I didn't want her get further injured, especially in a street may-lay on Halloween night. Can't really remember exactly how I unraveled the situation. But, I believe I told them to try something, now. They made with some tough talk and wandered off.

Well, that's not much of a story. But actually, it is. I did so many things wrong. Starting with a failure to act. I say I didn't want her injured, and that's true...but it's also true that I simply didn't know what to do. With all this training I've had, unless they grabbed me or threw a punch, I was left waiting to respond. I could have put up my hands and gone after them, but that's not really scientific martial arts. Is it? Also, it's not remaining clear headed. Plus, we had just finished talking to Sergeant Laginager only two minutes earlier. He couldn't have been more than about twenty yards away. I could have yelled for him.

But the most concerning issue is that I missed my window of opportunity. I had the element of surprise. You can move into action first, and still be the defending man.

WHAT I LEARNED

My karate system sucked.

I immediately went home and developed preemptive techniques, which I teach to this day. Like Bojangles told me...whoever gets in the first lick...usually wins. If your system doesn't have "obvious" preemptive techniques and multiple attacker scenarios, it is far from complete.

This incident lingered with me for months, resulting with incessant pain in my traps and cervical vertebra. But, I did eventually physically heal. Frankly, the thing that I never truly got over was being considered a high level black belt, and not having an answer.

Johnny B

In '76 I was on the road with a new York show band. On this particular occasion, we were working the quad cities; more specifically, Bettendorf, Iowa. Several notable incidents occurred at this engagement, including getting fired, which was a direct result of this kerfuffle. Everyone in the band was married, except for me and Johnny B. So, we had to be roommates. Johnny was a psychotic, pot smoking, half trained, ex-boxer from Atlanta, who had played with some well-known acts, even on the tonight show.

I was trying to get over a divorce, and after work, all I wanted to do was go back to the room and read. Now, johnny and I were fine during the day. But, at night, he would start drinking and turn mean. He hated white people and resented everyone in the band. Every night it was the same thing. After two joints and half a bottle of gin he would hatefully look at me and say: "Take those G.D., M.F.'ing glasses off." I would say: "John...I really don't feel like mixing it up tonight." So, he would come around to the bed, where I was lying, and start pounding on me.

Often, it wasn't enough just to beat me up. He wanted someone else to enjoy it too. Once, about four in the mourning; Johnny went next door, woke up the bandleader, and brought him I in; so he could watch.

Paul sat on the edge of the bed and started playing my guitar. Johnny stood over me, while I was reading, and started dropping body shots from above. After he unloaded about fifteen punches, I pushed him away.

Well, Johnny was so drunk that he stumbled backward, fell, hit his head on a table, and hit the floor motionless. Paul and I looked at each other for a long moment, and Johnny hadn't moved. So, I continued reading, while Paul went back to strumming away, We both hoped he was dead.

Everyone ought to know that you shouldn't leave someone knocked unconscious for more than a few minutes. The reading and strumming casually continued. But after about five or six minutes, the suddenly conscience Johnny jumped up into a fighting stance and said: "what did you say about my wife?"

This torrid event is just one example of many of the same. And believe me, this was a nightly occurrence. I'm, not exactly sure how many times similar stories to this were repeated. But, I lived in this pugilistic twilight zone for a couple of months.

So, back to Iowa...One night, I guess I just had enough. Johnny started into his act, but this time, I went after him. This was just like a cowboy movie. We were up and down the hall; fighting, knocking over tables, absolute mayhem. Every motel door on the entire floor flung open. Don't really know how long this went on; but it was long enough for the guests to call the front desk, have the night clerk call Cliff and Paul in their rooms, and have them break it up.

By the time Cliff and Paul got to us, we had fought to the edge of the stairs, tumbling down the long flight, in a death embrace. When we finally landed at the bottom, just in front of the lobby desk, I just so happened to be on top and was able to land a few telling shots. The night man and our band mates were eventually able to separate us, and needless to say, that was our last performance in Bettendorf.

WHAT I LEARNED

I had never been in a fight that lasted that long before - nor since. Conservatively, there must have been well over two hundred punches thrown. The surprising detail is that neither one of us was seriously injured.

The moral of the story is - I guess some things are just unavoidable. The months of reasoning and psychology were to no avail. I should have addressed this earlier.

Shattered Expectations

I can tell this story because the principal has passed on, as I believe have the other subjects in the tale. I once had a client who was a very interesting guy, well known in his field. For this story I'll just call him Bob. Bob trusted and liked me. I had done some investigative work for him, and one day he approached me with a disturbing request. He politely asked if I could neutralize one of his business rivals.

Of course, I told him I don't do anything like that; to which he replied: "it's done all the time". He continued: "I'm sure you have contacts. Fly someone in from Iran and there gone the same day". Sounds like you've done this before, was my answer. So he proceeded to tell me a couple of stories of which only this one has a funny ending.

It seems he had a business rival who was causing complications. I guess he had tried a couple of attempts at resolution, but the impasse was insoluble. So, as was his custom, he decided to have this competitor eliminated. According to him, he had done this a couple of times before, so it seemed a natural solution to just have the complication removed from the equation.

Bob was ruthless and cruel, but he was also cheap. Because of this, Bob decided to hire a young man who was just trying to break into the murder for hire industry. This being the lad's first engagement, and wanting to make a good impression; he procured a top of the line, high powered rifle. The arrangement was topped off with great optics and jacketed hollow points, filled with mercury.

Just for general information; the longest sniper kill officially confirmed (as of this writing) was performed by a Canadian Special Forces JTF2 sniper in June of 2017 - at an incredible 3,871 yards. At such distances a projectile would have a flight time of 5 or 6 seconds and lose 90% of its kinetic energy.

I don't know how far away Bob's shooter was, but I'm sure it was nothing like that. Anyway, the story goes that because this target had experienced threats and incidents in the past, he had sniper-proofed his home; by installing bullet proof glass in all the windows. On this particular night, the target was in his underwear watching TV, not knowing what was about to happen next.

The youth set up in his nest, gained target acquisition, calculated range and windage, and fired. I'll give the kid this: It was an accurate shot. His bullet struck the mark right on the chin. Due to the energy dispersing properties of the window, the glass took a lot of the starch out of the projectile. When it impacted the quarry it had no more power than a strong punch. It did however knock the man right out of his chair.

What happened after, or how Bob resolved his issues with the competitor, I don't remember. But, I do like telling the story. I realize that, technically, this is not a story about fighting. But, it is about violence; so it does qualify for a partial credit. To maintain continuity, however, I am writing this while standing in a horse stance.

Time's Up

When I first opened my little school in Pompano, I was living in half a duplex near the beach. I had been living with someone, but she experienced a family tragedy and had to move out. I eventually left too, but for a couple of months I remained in the property and continued to pursue the island escapist lifestyle.

I was now alone in the back half of the duplex and in the front half lived a single man named Robert, who I only knew well enough to speak to in passing. Robert had a part time girlfriend who I would see occasionally, but didn't know at all. I had acquired a Lab/Rottie mix who was mildly retarded but a really good friend. This proved valuable when I lived in my school.

So it was one evening, I was walking the dog near the beach, and a woman who was also out walking began talking to me. Turns out it was Robert's girlfriend. She was a nice girl, but I have to tell you, in the intellectual Olympics she made my dog look like John Bell.

While I was letting the dog sniff around, she began to tell me how she and Robert had a big disagreement and he left to stay with a friend. She went on to explain that she rented a room at a hotel on the beach, and it would probably be a good idea if I were to join her there. I have always had a long standing policy to not mess around with a buddy's wife or girlfriend. But, hey, he wasn't that good of a buddy - actually I hardly knew him.

It was a great night with a tropical breeze, a warm invitation, the excitement of novelty, and the challenge of trying to prove that you're Superman. You know the usual. I never saw her again, though I made a few feeble attempts to find her around town. Applying Occam's Razor it would seem that the Superman hypothesis was inaccurate.

The next day I was sitting in a lawn chair on the side of the house, sunning. It was about two in the afternoon and very still. I sensed some movement to my left, at the front of the house, and half opened my eyes. From about fifty feet away I could see that it was Robert approaching in my direction. I pretended to be unaware, but through half-closed eyes I could see his left hand balled up into a fist.

I don't know why I made this decision, but I decided to let him hit me. I think I really did feel bad after all. He was a little bigger than me, but for some reason I had him pegged as not much of a threat. I know, I know - but that was the overwhelming emotion at the time. I sat there, ready for anything.

What happened next took place curiously swift. He snatched my left wrist with his right hand, quickly raised his balled up left fist and...and placed my watch in the palm of my hand. "Here, you forgot this last night." He turned and walked away.

WHAT I LEARNED

Maybe Robert was a really good buddy...

Merry Christmas

The firefighter's union once had a magazine called "The Code Three", connected to a fund-raising operation in Broward County. For a period of time, I sold advertising for this publication. The way the scheme worked was that a salesperson would sell an ad, and a collector would then drive out to pick up the check. I believe I can say that, without question, some of these collectors were of dubious character and backgrounds. One day, a new collector hired on named Steve. The first time I laid eyes on Steve, I wanted to punch him in the face - hard. Covered in tattoos, bragging that he beat up six cops, etc. You know the type.

One day, I sold an ad to a local restaurant and Steve was the man selected to make the collection. Evidently, the restaurant owner really liked firefighters, because he invited Steve to have he and I come to dinner with our wives. I was not married at the time, so I took our secretary.

Owning to the restauranteur's reverence for the firefighters, we all celebrated an indulgent and almost decadent dinner. Afterward, it was suggested that both couples retire to Steve's condo for drinks. Since it was the holidays, and I never turn down a celebratory imbibe; it was agreed. Before long, we had consumed two bottles of wine, and Steve, who had been acting antsy all evening, offered to go out and purchase more. His wife immediately shot me an ominous look. I did not understand why at the time, but its meaning became clear as the events of the night unfolded. Steve volunteered to physically execute the transaction, but he had no cash. So, I produced a twenty.

At that time, my date, and my ride, decided it was time for her to call it an evening. She offered to bring me home, but Steve interjected and insisted that he could give me a ride later. So, I decided to stay. And, both Steve and my date departed.

Two or three hours passed and Steve was still nowhere to be seen. During his absence, his wife took it upon herself to regal me with horror stories of how terrible Steve was. His proclivity for drugs and alcohol, and his general mistreatment within the relationship. I don't think I need to stress this, but the whole situation was extremely uncomfortable, with the night languishing on and on.

When Steve finally came in the door, about five in the morning, I was steaming. He let me sit for over six hours... sober!... And nobody does that to me! I calmly asked: "where's the wine?" His responded by insisting that he had been looking for it the whole time. I shot back: "well then, where's my twenty bucks?" He shrugged his shoulders, smiled sarcastically, and with a disdaining inflection, sheepishly drawled my name: "Bru........." I was livid! I kissed his wife goodbye; he and I both stepped into the hall; the door closed...and I threw a heavy hay-maker directly into his face. I must say, It really wasn't my best shot. But, I had pretty good rotation, so it connected well and knocked out two teeth.

What I didn't realize was that Steve was a crack addict and had invested the past five hours and my twenty bucks in pursuit thereof. I'm assuming that crack cocaine has an analgesic effect, because when the punch landed his head rotated sharply and snapped back looking at me. As I was throwing the punch, in my mind, I imagined he would slam into the wall, slide down to the floor dazed or unconscious. This did not happen. Not even close. So, I stepped back into a fighting stance, ready for anything. Then the unexpected happened...

He spit one tooth into his hand; wiggled the other one out with his fingers; shook the blood onto the floor; smiled like a jack-o-lantern and said: "Come on Bru.. I'll take you home."

Down the elevator, through the parking garage, and all during the ride home, it was all pretty normal. Small talk. Sports. Weather. When the car finally came to a stop in front of my trailer, I said to him: "So you want to come in for a beer?" Which he did.

The trailer I lived in at the time had an external, ground floor extension, with a couch in the middle, facing the TV on the far side of the room. Steve stood near the door, drinking his beer. I sat on the couch with my back to him. It was probably around six in the morning and It had been a pretty long day for me. So, I slipped quickly and quietly into that deep, dreamless slumber known only to aficionados of cheap spirits. What I failed to mention up to now, was that next to Steve, by the external door, was an umbrella stand containing bats, swords, and assorted tools of mayhem ready for quick home defense. All of these immediately within his reach. And then...as he saw me unconscious, this depraved bastard... finished his beer, let himself out, and went home.

The next day in the office, Steve told the tale as a rollicking good time. When I related this story to my Blackwater mercenary friend, his only comment was: "someone was looking out for you that night."

WHAT I LEARNED

Again...my situation is ten percent what happens to me and ninety percent how I react to it. I always criticized the tattoo crowd for living so far in their comic book fantasies that they create a majority of their own problems. But, I must admit, that I'm guilty of that too. Nobody screws me around...leaves me sitting there all night! But, if I really lived the Zen philosophy, I would have just accepted that these events were just what happened on this particular night, that there was some explanation, and tomorrow is another day in this wonderful life.

So one more time....thanks Clarence. Merry Christmas.

Friends

Rob….Rob was my buddy and partner in crime. We worked security together at the hospital and hung out almost all the time. When I finally couldn't take it anymore and had to get away from the shrew I was married to, I moved into the back room of a karate studio. My plan was to get the most meaningless, banal job I could find, and just party. Therefore, I became the parking lot guard at the local hospital. Because I would often come to work with only twenty minutes sleep, I would sit in the patrol car wearing a cervical collar and sunglasses staring at the entrance to the E. R. - except I was asleep. Also, while on that job, I became a master of the "Slim Jim". At that complex, there were 1500 nurses employed. So, if each one locked her keys in the car once a year, that meant I had to "Slim Jim" about 4 cars a day.

Rob, on the other hand, was what we call a "good" employee. Conscientious, dependable, always on time. He came from Wilkes Barr, PA. This was a very rough coal mining town, where Rob had been a high school football star. There was a club near the beach we went to almost every night. We were 2 guys, in their early 30's, in 1982 Fort Lauderdale; not bad duty.

We would operate independently in the club, and cross paths a few times a night. On this particular occasion, Rob had been engaged with 2 girls most of the night, and I was circulating. Although Rob had all of their attention, a group of aggressive guys, from some foreign country, kept bothering the girls.

There was something very sinister about this bunch and Rob had to intervene several times to protect the girls. Rob was a real nice guy and although he could handle himself, a total peacenik.

I met a tourist from New Jersey and left to follow her back to Hollywood. Rob had become closer to these girls and they all decided to go to another club. They were waiting by the valet stand for the car to be brought around and out comes these scary dudes, now very drunk. The guys started getting really aggressive with the girls and at one point Rob had to step in, because one of them had put his hands on one of the girls. So this guy goes into the standard tough talk: "you don't know who your messin' with", and all that. So Rob says: "don't you think you're a little light in the ass to be fooling with me?" This guy really gets in Rob's face and says: "so, I'm too small..I'm too small...?". So, Rob pushes him. Not hard, but just to get him away. It turns out that the guy really was so small, and he goes flying. Hell breaks loose and they all attack him. Rob was a rough guy, but totally untrained. He was all right hand. Putting them down one at a time. Real John Wane stuff. Even though it was 4 against 1; if you are the valets, what are you going to do? They grab the guy that's doing all the damage. So, each valet grabs an arm and slams Rob against a car. During the moment Rob was being restrained, the small guy, he had originally pushed, springs up and stabs Rob….in the heart.

Now an American would have cut him, or stabbed him in the gut. But these guys were killers. Palestinian terrorists from Israel. We know this because of really good police work. There was an officer working the detail who radioed it in. Even though the guys immediately jumped into a new Corvette and took off; there just happened to be 2 cruisers close by, and they nabbed the guys a few blocks away.

It was touch and go for Rob. The story goes that the doctor said the blade entered while the heart was on a contraction and just grazed the it. Still serious, but not a puncture. There were no real consequences for the Palestinians. They got deported. Rob refused to press charges, because he was afraid.

WHAT I LEARNED

The night life is inherently risky. Especially in a resort area. People from all over the world - competition...alcohol. This is a lesson in taking every encounter seriously. Rob came from a town where Saturday night fisticuffs was common. He later said that he was actually having a good time...until he got stabbed. He believed that they were just brawling. Terrorists from another culture, where every conflict is life or death, thought something different. Maybe, if I had been there, It would have ended some other way. Maybe, the knife man wouldn't have gotten up. I'll never know. But certainly, the rhythm would have been different.

Tiger Joe

When my time was up in the Marines, I was discharged from a Navel installation on the East Coast. I could have gotten a plane or a bus ticket to anywhere. Or, could have gone back to California. But, there was really nowhere to go. So I went home.

Most people would have chosen the expediency of flying, but I was a little lost and had a lot to process; so I took the bus ride. The first night I got "black out" drunk at a downtown bar, behind the bus station in Buffalo. Everybody was buying me drinks; and it was a real release. For some reason, it took another whole day to get from Buffalo to Cleveland. I know this because I distinctly remember buying a watch from a hustler in a parking lot, behind the bus station in Cleveland. Almost immediately, I hurled the watch over the parking lot fence, because I realized I had just received stolen property - my second night out.

Turns out, the bus ride was the right decision, taking the long way home. As the ride through PA and Ohio was scenic, and it provided needed time to reflect.

I never really liked Toledo, or felt like I belonged there. But, it was where I was raised. It was gratifying to recognize the city when the bus pulled in. And, it satisfied that very human need for familiarity. Even though my neighborhood was still about five miles away, I decided to walk. I found it comforting to drink in the familiar sights, but I was still carrying my heavy sea bag. So, I eventually caught a city bus out to Point Place.

It was kind of crazy going to Toledo because, at the time, I was estranged from my parents, and really had nowhere to go. So, I called my buddy Joe, and of course, he let me stay with him till I got settled.

Joe was the toughest guy in our crowd. Whenever there was trouble, when we were young, we would always say: "yeah, but we got Joe." And he would always reply: "I'm not tough." But he was. Plenty. Joe was 260lbs in high school and, although he really didn't need it, picked up a few fighting tips from a local boxer. To know some angles and keep his hands up made Joe a force to be reckoned with.

That afternoon, we sat around his place reminiscing, and in the early evening went to the local bar. Our neighborhood picked up a lot of "rough trade", because we were right on the Ohio, Michigan line. In

Ohio, you could drink at age 18, but Michigan it was 21. So, all the young trouble makers from Michigan would flood the bars in our end of town.

The drinking establishment Joe and I were patronizing was a tavern called "The New Barge Inn." It was across the street from the local deli. The deli happened to be in a 100 year old building, that used to be bank. This deli was owned by a very colorful character named Fred Lebis.

In my high school years, Fred would allow me to take girls down to the basement and into the abandoned bank vault. Also, I was also able to supply all the high school social functions with booze, because I had forged such a position of trust with Fred. I was the only minor in town Fred trusted enough to sell liquor to. Even the cliques and crowds that didn't particularly like me bought alcohol from me, because I was the only one who could get it.

It was sometime after dark when Joe and I decided to call it a night. We got in his car behind "The Barge". And, even though it was only a couple hundred feet to our new destination, we drove and parked behind the deli building. As, Joe wanted to go in to buy some cigarettes. Just seconds after Joe went in the back door, a carload of drunken Michiganders pulled into the parking lot.

Before they made it to the door, Joe comes walking out. This was early 1970 and Joe had long hair. Seeing Joe, they started verbally accosting him, hurling epitaphs. Then, one of them tried to punch Joe. Joe easily dismissed the punch and knocked him out. Immediately, Joe grabbed another one by the belt and collar, and ran his head into a tree. By that time, the third one was backing up with his hands in the "don't hit me" position, running as Joe advanced. A fourth one started their vehicle and took off, leaving his companion running behind. All this happened before I could even get out of the car.

I ran around the back of Joe's station wagon and stopped in front of him. We both took a moment to survey the mayhem. Two unconscious bodies, the escape vehicle idling down the street, tepidly waiting. His compatriot running frantically to reach the car. Joe looked around and said: "the Pepsi generation."

I asked Joe what had happened, and Joe explained that the closest person called him a "hippy queer." I retorted: "Is that when you let him have it?" Joe replied: "No. I figure if it made him happy to call me a queer, I like nothing better than to make people happy! But, then the punch came."

Now this accordance was not that unusual. I've seen Joe in similar circumstances, many times. I once saw a movie where the hero was surrounded by some threatening thugs. He told them: "I only have to fight two of you. First I'll take out your leader; the second toughest will try; and after I knock him out, you other three will run away."

That is pretty much what happened here. Joe was a legend in our end of town. When we first met, he and I got into it. But fortunately for me, the altercation was quickly broken up. Joe was my best friend through my teen years. He did eventually settle down, and had a nice family. But sadly, Joe passed at a young age.

For those of us who shared that slice of time in that backwater peninsula into lake Erie; we will always remember Tiger Joe.

WHAT I LEARNED

You don't have to fight everybody in the crowd. Probably, never more than two. And, size does matter.

Bill Boggs

There is an illustrative story regarding Bill, but first a little background may be in order. If the purpose of this book is knowledge, then it is worthwhile to learn a few things about Bill. Boggs is not his real name surname. Because of the many questionable incidents, only some of which are illustrated in this chapter, I'm sure he would prefer to remain nameless.

Bill was quite a guy: erudite, hugely successful, and my mentor in all manner of dissipation. I would drive his Rolls Royce when we went out clubbing. But before we get into all that, it might be illuminating to relate a couple of incidents from his past.

Bill was from an aristocratic family and had been raised in boarding schools. When he was about nine years old, he attended a prep school either in Canada or in England; I'm not really sure. But, what I am sure of, is that during his attendance in said prep school he created a "little" controversy which led to his dismissal.

Evidently, the prep school was situated next to a sheep ranch. And, being both a curious and exceeding, horny young man, Bill uncovered a secret passage into the sheep farm, providing him the ability to commit bestiality with the unfortunate ruminants. Being the enterprising lad that he was, and a portent of his future success in business, Bill began to sell tickets to other male attendees of the prep school. For a sizable fee, Bill would disclose the location of his hidden passage, so that the other boys would most assuredly be requiring therapy in their adult years.

It wasn't long before his little enterprise was revealed and Bill was hauled before the headmaster. You can imagine the conversation. At the end of the harangue, the headmaster said: "Boggs, you've got a real problem." Undaunted, Bill snapped back: "I'm just a businessman. You've got 40 young boys who are paying to fuck sheep. I'd say you were the one with the problem." That was when he was nine years old.

I'd like to provide an illustration of why he always prevailed in business and pretty much everything else. Flash forward forty years and many adventures later, in the years prior to the internet; personal ads were "a thing" in almost all American newspapers. It was commonplace for people to meet this way. One may recall the famous song, "The Pina Colada song" which detailed this very subject.

Bill, of course, had to supercharge the concept. He had two friends which would run a personal add which went something like this: "Multi-millionaire, loves cats and dancing. Tom Selleck look alike. Seeks companion to travel the world on luxury yacht."

They received letters by the hundreds. It was amazing. Women would offer to leave their children or quit their jobs. They received innumerable, unbelievable responses. I have personally stood there, watching them trade their letters back and forth. Bill would throw a letter at one of his co-conspirators and say: "Here, you like redheads. Answer this one." Now, anyone could take out a personal ad and lie to women, But here's the genius part!

When they answered, they would always say something like: Look, I'm not the guy. I'm the friend of the guy. He winnowed it down to two letters, and unfortunately, he met the other girl first and they really hit it off. He handed me your letter, and said: "This girl is really special. I wish I could have met her, but I've fallen in love with Shirly. I know you're alone, so maybe you two should meet. Be good to her."

Well, most women would figure that if they were friends, this guy might be a millionaire too! So, through this ruse, they would meet tons of girls and be off-the-hook for the yacht and world travel. You're not the guy who ran the ad; you're only the friend.

I could go on, but I should probably get back on track and tell the fight story.

One evening, Bill decided to go out on the town and drove alone to a disco. The place was packed, so he needed to park a good distance from the building. As he opened the trunk of his car to retrieve his jacket, a young man came up to Bill and said, "give me your wallet." Bill retorted: "why you little shit, I'll backhand you out of this parking lot", and turned away from the individual.

Out of the corner of his eye, Bill saw a foot rapidly approaching his face. Now, bill was a tough guy. Throughout his career, he had both boxed and played professional football. These experiences also made him quicker than your average man. Because of his training, Bill managed to catch the guys foot, before impact. With the man's foot in his hand, Bill queried: "now what you gonna do?", and threw him to the ground.

Supremely self-confident, Bill turned his attention back to the trunk. Taking advantage of Bill's diverted attention, the kid quickly sprang up and stabbed Bill in the leg. Almost immediately Bill's boot began to fill with blood. Undeterred, Bill grabbed the assailant, knocked him silly, and tossed him into his trunk. He then slammed the lid and used his tie as a tourniquet for his leg. With that taken care of, he called the police. This situation resulted in a trip to the hospital, a tetanus shot, and a spell of limping. I ask, was all that necessary? Let's look at a similar story and compare.

JOHN

I had another friend, far less colorful, but still a great guy An electrical engineer who held several patents and was a friend and student for many years. John had an almost identical experience, but handled it in an opposite manner to Bill.

John was also alone in the parking lot of a night club when he was similarly approached by a street thug. John was a capable guy. Highly trained religiously and was in great shape. John's main disadvantage was that he looked like a suburban yuppie.

John's potential assailant was very low key. During his entire career, this goon had probably never met any resistance to his robberies. He must have just been used to, and targeted guys, that looked like John. And, they probably all just handed over their lunch money.

This perpetrator approached John at his car, and said: "You got any money?" John replied: "no." Then the mugger said to John: "give me your wallet." Without hesitation, John drilled the guy with a front kick to the gut and finished up with repeated strikes until the man stopped moving. The guy never saw it coming.

The addendum to this story is something that has also happened to me on several occasions. The style we both studied at the time had a large number of preset responses to many self-defense situations; some of which we absolutely hated and swore we would never use in a real situation. But in this specific scenario, there was just something about the way the attacker bent over from the kick that moved John finish off this criminal with a series of maneuvers he swore he would never use in a real scenario. Never-the-less, John left him in a motionless heap on the ground.

WHAT I LEARNED

Hubris is a martial artist's greatest downfall. Bill was so over confident, he dismissed the danger. He completely misjudged his assailant, and over-estimated his ability to handle anything. And, it could have turned out much worse. Regardless, there was a high price to pay for Bill's complacency.

John, on the other hand, moved into action immediately. Once the attacker announced his intention, the kick was on its way. He then followed up, repeatedly, until the attacker stopped moving. John assigned the appropriate gravitas to the attackers words, and deployed without hesitation.

To quote the father of American Karate: "He who hesitates, meditates in horizontal position."

Big Boyz

When I had my nondescript and modest school in Pompano, among my students happened to be two individuals, both 6'6" 280 lbs. Nick was a med student. The other, a local cop named Mike. Mike was employed by the county sheriff's office. I found that it was instructive to have two massive bodies to work with because this tactile exposure can keep one grounded in the reality of physics.

The officer related to me that he felt that many of the things I was trying to teach him were unworkable while on-duty, because he was encumbered by the equipment that he was required to wear. In order to help me understand and have firsthand knowledge of his situation, one day, he brought in all his gear and had me don the vest and belt. This was very instructive and gave me a more definitive appreciation of the confinements resulting from having to always wear this bulky and somewhat cumbersome equipment. It was an illuminating experience for me as an instructor to have to adapt principals that are primarily based on the assumption that there is always an unencumbered degree of freedom of movement.

The other behemoth was a medical student who was also a black belt in Tomiki Aikido. It was always edifying having these two individuals to work with, continually and doggedly reminding me that size and strength is always a factor and that big guys can be just as quick as smaller ones.

In a previous essay, I had referenced my Vietnamese friend who made it onto the last chopper out of Saigon. This incident was worth relating but, by far, not the only notable thing about Tuan. Tuan was also 6'6" 240lbs. And, although it had always been gnawing on me, out of politeness I would never ask the obvious question.

One day at lunch, there developed an opportunity to ask; "how did you manage to become so big?" I was accustomed to Americans just towering over the Vietnamese, and it was highly unusual to observe this example of opposites and reverses. It would probably be instructive to mention that Tuan was six years old when he escaped Vietnam and, since then, had been raised in America. He was also a molecular biologist and involved in research into children's diseases. This gave him an authority to speak on matters related to human biology. Always the consummate social adroit, he looked thoughtfully across the table and said; "well, every oriental has the capacity for size, but because of the lack of protein in the diet, the entire population is stunted."

At the time I was working at a shipyard which had an international crew. After my engagement with Tuan, I went back to work, observing anew, our employees from all over the world. And, yes, workers from third world countries were indeed diminutive by comparison. The individuals from New Zealand, England, or France tall and robust; those from Cuba, Thailand, or the Philippines, not so much.

Through these and a vast array other experiences, my appreciation for the power and inertia of increased mass was elevated by my considerable training involvements with larger individuals. Unfortunately, further comprehension was gleaned empirically through one such encounter; I was knocked out twice in one day by a maniacal gunnery sergeant of like proportions.

For my first trip to theta brain wave state; evidently I said something that the sergeant took as a challenge. Because, he grabbed me with both hands around the throat and slammed me on top of the oil heater in the middle of the Quonset hut. I was choked into unconsciousness and don't even remember what transpired after.

Later that day, something else was done that offended the sergeant, because he grabbed me again in a two-hand front choke, lifted me off the ground, and pinned me to the wall; until I choked out. Only, this time, he began kicking my motionless body with all 280 lbs. The intense pain actually helped to wake me up, because I was able to get to my feet and stagger into formation. I know I was severely banged-up. And, I'm sure I had sustained a couple of cracked ribs, as well as severe bruises and contusions. These injuries made execution of any normal duties debilitatingly painful for a couple of weeks, serving as a constant reminder of the kinetic energy generated by increased mass. If sick bay was possible, I unquestionably should have received treatment. But in this instance, this was not an option.

I suppose, if I were to encounter Sgt. Rickets today, the confrontation would have a vastly different outcome. For one thing, my skill level has crested with my age, and I'm also assuming that I would have an advantage in vitality and mobility. I was 17, in 1968, and Rickets was at least 15 years older. This would place him in his mid-to-late 80's, as of this writing. My collection of slick tricks and power striking might provide a very different outcome.

The glaringly obvious reality, of course, is that if we were to meet today, there most likely would be no conflict. I certainly have changed in these odd 55 years; as I am sure has he. The perspective of time and introspection heals souls and attitudes. Being removed from that highly stressful situation and also distanced from the macho death culture, the encounter would be an interaction between two very different persons. I knew another Vietnamese in a position of authority and control, who said to me and some other incorrigibles; "in different circumstances, we would probably be friends."

Over time, the big cop went on to run the bomb squad at the sheriff's office. He eventually stopped training with me, but I did run into him a few years later. In that time, he earned his Master's Degree and was now running the Financial Crimes Unit for the entire department. Turns out, he was working a detail at the hospital when I happened to be dropping off a friend. At that time, I was doing a lot of financial work as a private investigator and mentioned to him my frequent successes with my clients. He looked quizzically at me, and said; "oh….we never get anybody's money back." And so it goes.

What about the big med student? He became a prominent O.B.G.Y.N. in another city. I remember him fondly, because of a kind gesture on Christmas day, during the time he was under my tutelage.

But first, I need to disclose a few facts and details. My school and my office were on the second floor of a building about a mile from the beach. One exercise I really enjoyed having prospective new students participate in, was to stand on a milk crate and peer out the corner of the last window in the room. From there, they were able to see between two buildings, and on a clear day they could see a small sliver of beach. I offer this visage because I advertised the school as; "ocean view karate and fitness."

At one point during my school's operation, I was living out of it. This was due to a family tragedy that caused my girlfriend, at the time, to move out in order to provide care. As I could no longer afford our rented duplex on the beach, I was forced to temporarily move in to my studio. If you can call two years temporary. It wasn't that bad. I slept on the mats with my big black dog, and showered at the beach.

But, the first Christmas in the studio was emotionally debilitating. I had no TV, so I just stared out the window at the empty streets, mulling warmer Christmas memories. The day dragged on. Then, suddenly, a knock on the door! No, it wasn't Heather Locklear (or Santa), but much better. It was my student (saint) Nick. His mother had prepared a heaping plate of turkey dinner and the big galoot delivered it.

WHAT I LEARNED

Tapestry of life, I suppose. I learned some Tomiki Aikido from Nick and received a new perspective on teaching police from Mike. The back and forth of human interactions: equitable. The severe beating I received from the homicidal marine is probably just another reason for my unending determination to stay in the martial arts. If only I had blended in and stayed off his radar, there may never have been an incident at all. But then, later in life, as an effective surveillance agent, I would not have been able to appreciate the importance of "gray man" skills.

The Bell Telephone Hour

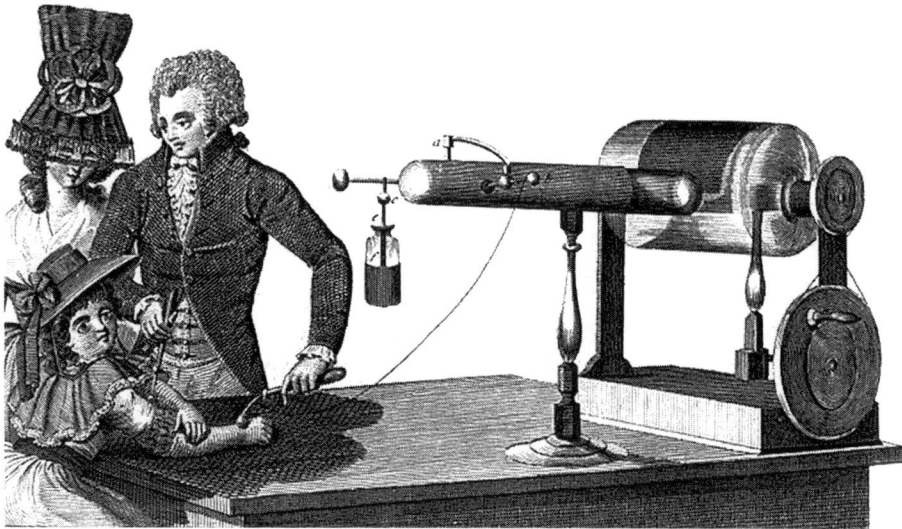

When one is deemed incorrigible in the Marine Corps, and is of sufficiently low rank, you may be remanded to an attitude modification process known as - motivation platoon. It is the purpose of this experience to prove so uncomfortable that you, at once, realize the complete authority of command; and never wish to compromise your position, by showing any dignity, self-respect, or personal moral standards.

A typical day in this troupe begins with lights on at 3 a.m. and the Sargent pounding a trash can with a night stick. "Detainees" have 5 seconds to snap to attention on the yellow line, with a bed sheet in each hand, held high overhead. Anyone who is less than perfect rewards the platoon with additional missions of morning exercise.

One mission consists of 25 repetitions of standard physical training exercises, such as: pushups, squat thrusts, or side straddle hops. If all members perform satisfactorily, and it's a particularity easy morning, you may be allowed to slide with 10 missions of each. But, of course, there is always a screw up; resulting in additional missions, so the real number could be who knows what.

After 2 minutes to shit, shower, and shave; the platoon runs to chow. As motivation platoon is the last to eat, the remaining gruel winds up being the usual, miserably grim fare. After 10 minutes to eat, we are required to run back to the barracks; to be issued tools for the work day.

On alternate days, the work schedule switched between digging and working at the dump. Although there were some days of double-timing to the quarry with sledge hammers carried at port arms, then breaking rocks - just for nostalgia, I suppose. But the digging/dump swop is the most vivid in my mind.

The dump detail was the easy day. I guess the stench/gross factor was supposed to make some kind of impression. I'm sure the routine was devised by psychological professionals, but in the totality of the experience, feted garbage and hospital waste were just not that intimidating to me.

The digging day routine went like this: 15 of us in a large circle with shovels. We begin a digging cadence count and if anyone breaks the cadence, we all jump down into the circular hole and run laps. The laps are increased incrementally with each error. As such, the depth of the hole and the number of laps increased rapidly.

There was one individual who cost the group many orbits. He kept complaining about his asthma, and breaking cadence. When he would falter, he was punched out and throw him the hole. Well; then we would have to jump into the hole and run on top of him. When begging for respite, he was only told: "fuck you and the horse your asthma rode in on."

I have to admit that after about the third time, I too kicked and ground my heels as I ran over him. He was costing us all so much. There came a time when he just stopped moving. We stopped too and dragged him out of the hole. He was unresponsive.

An ambulance did arrive, but not in time. We were sworn to a code of silence; with most dire threats. I did receive conformation later of unfortunate news. The family was notified of an unfortunate training death, which was not entirely uncommon. I was threatened with similar results many times, myself.

Let's not forget that this assignment was not punishment. It was specialized training for minds that were too independent, and incorrigible attitudes - yet not beyond saving. Marines which needed to be molded just a little more to ensure proper functioning. After all, it was the motivation platoon.

The above experience served as a modifier to what I had perceived as an acceptable standard of cruelty, and an introduction to specialized intel practices; like enhanced interrogation techniques. One such technique was named the Bell Telephone Hour, and it was an effective procedure involving electric current generated by a field radio. Among the problems with such procedures is that they produce unreliable results and are almost always applied to the wrong people.

When a well-adjusted citizen encounters a veteran who is reluctant to talk about military experiences, they usually assume it is due to a scarred psyche, which is the result of normal combat operations. Reticence to elaborate is, often times, because of involvement with things like enhanced interrogation practices, such as: the Bell Telephone Hour, beatings, forced stress positions, food, sleep, or light deprivation. Along with rape and selling prisoners to comrades just for the thrill of eliminating them.

The Bell Telephone Hour was an American television series which was popular during my childhood. In 1958, Frank Capra produced a segment on global warming, in hopes exposure on the popular show would serve to give an early start to environmentalism. There were many fine dramatic offerings presented in that sanitized style, prevalent in the 50's. Oscar Levant was terminated for making remarks, such as, noting that Marilyn Monroe had converted to Judaism; which made her Kosher and now Arthur Miller could eat her.

Because the technique involved electricity generated by a telephone, and because the show was so schmaltzy and puritanical; It seemed in keeping with the sarcastic dark humor of the teenaged mind to name the procedure after the beloved television production.

In my lonely hours between coffee and alcohol, I sometimes think of such things as the loss of life in motivation platoon and experiences that followed. As a comedian, I have retained a special appreciation for the Bell Telephone Hour, while completely writing off any resultant human misery. The naming of this incentive, while meant to be sarcastic, is yet another illustration of the natural balance of opposites and reverses, Yin and Yang.

Anchors Away

It seems as though everyone who retires from the fire department in Cleveland dreams of moving to South Florida and becoming a restaurateur. A near guaranteed route to a successful commercial endeavor is to do anything that has something to do with new businesses. Carpeting, office furniture, painting - to name a few. I once knew someone who became a millionaire dealing in used restaurant equipment. Just kept reselling it to the endless supply of new hopefuls from the Great White North, with dreams of opening a yogurt shop in Fort Lauderdale.

I had the honor of working for one such specimen in the late '70's - Dave. Dave started as an electrical engineer in Boston, and upon his retirement; wait for it...had fulfilled his dream of opening a bar in Fort Lauderdale. I was working a duo with a drummer; and we had just finished a six month tour of the state. This left us looking for steady local employment. So, we accepted the engagement at this new venue in the biker bar district, and began a grueling 12 hour daily schedule; providing music and laughs to South Florida's finest tattoo enthusiasts. We worked 2 pm. to 2 am. Frequently, Dave would host after-hour parties, 'til sunrise. It was during one of such soirees that an incident occurred that, once again, resulted in termination.

When last call is made, in establishments such as this, and the doors are closed; it's kind of like throwing a cast net for society's lost and confused. On one such occasion, we were left with the usual collection of regulars, plus strippers and bartenders, who finished at 2 am, but knew we were an after-hours destination.

Among the residue, on this particular after-hours, evening; was a young sailor who had been drinking since early afternoon. He played a lot of pool and seemed to have lost every game. Dave took him for a few $100, and at one point, I stated that I had never won a pool game for money in my life. So, I got in on it too. When I finally sank the eight, the sailor reached in his pockets and had no money. Several other players began demanding payment, the most vocal of which was Dave.

The sailor could have handled it more diplomatically. Instead, he got cocky and started on a "so what" diatribe. His smug tirade was not well received by the tattooed, select of Dixie Highway. So, Dave picked him up, slammed him onto the pool table, and began going to work on him. But, the kid pulled a nifty move - he rolled off the table and flew out the back door. Unbeknownst to the sailor, the back lot was secured by a high fence; and Dave was right behind him. In an attempt to escape, the sailor stepped on a crate and tried to scale the fence; but Dave snared him by the collar and belt, and slammed him into the side of a dumpster. I watched for a few seconds in a kind of "get him Dave" attitude, but after a few big hits I tried to pull Dave off of the poor man. I didn't want to seem too aggressive towards Dave, so I fish hooked him from behind and tried to pull him off. He half-elbowed me in the ribs, wriggled out of my grasp, and resumed pounding on the sailor.

The pounding really was becoming too much. The kid wasn't looking very pretty. Enough! I drilled a right knee into Dave's tailbone and slipped on a figure four choke. Dave peeled back like butter. Although Dave was a relatively massive guy, I successfully got him onto his knees, while the sailor vaulted over the fence leaving a bloody trail.

WHAT I LEARNED

Expect nothing less if you're sequestered after-hours in a questionable beer joint. Make sound decisions; chose your associates wisely; stay in school. If you don't, the figure four choke always works well.

Punch-Pourri

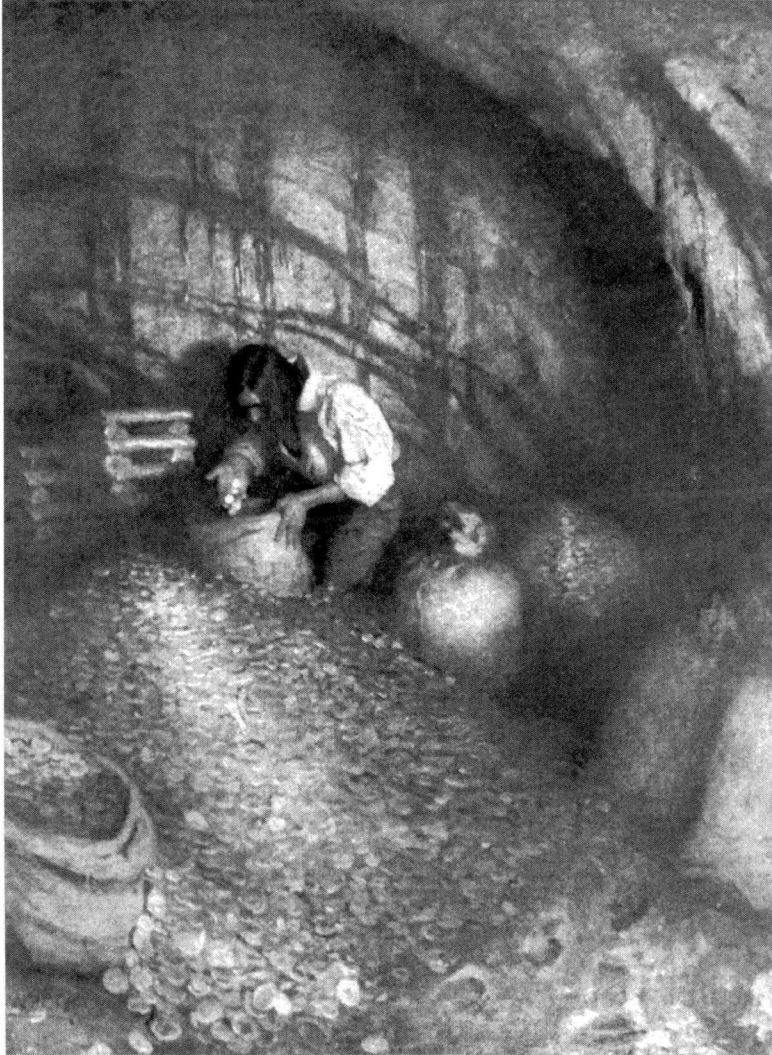

I was playing music in a hotel in Central Florida, not far from Disney World. There was a young desk clerk who came from somewhere outside the USA. I have no idea why, but this fellow just hated me. Every time he passed me, he had something to say. I tolerated this tripe for a couple of weeks. Then, one day I was walking down the stairs on my way to my gig, and there he was again. This wise-ass and one of his associates were both standing to my right, as I came off the stairs at the entrance to the courtyard that surrounded the pool area.

I happened to be carrying my guitar case, in my right hand, a cup of coffee in my left, as I passed by them. He must have said abra cadabra, because the genie leapt from the bottle. I hurled the coffee in his face and lobed the guitar case in his direction. Before the case could touch the ground, I kicked it into his legs. He just didn't have time to think or react. I flew over the case and pushed him hard onto the ground. I had peace for the rest of my engagement.

I was living in a small four unit apartment on the beach. My girlfriend and I just turned into the driveway when a car screeched to a halt in the middle of the street. Some bozo gets out and starts advancing with blood in his eye. Had I cut him off? I got out and advanced to meet him. When we were about twenty feet apart, he turns around gets back in his car and leaves. I said to my girlfriend, what the hell? She said, Well he saw your ponytail and figured you were a bad-ass. Really? Is that true. I knew guys got tattoos and leather jackets to elicit intimidation, but is that true? She thought so. Really?

One night during marine boot camp I got hauled out of my rack and dragged into the head by eight or ten guys. Blanket parties are not that uncommon. Happens all the time. They started to go to work on me and I completely freaked out. I started doing all this long-fist dragon movement. Which was great, except I didn't know any longfist dragon movement. I channeled it. I managed to keep them off me for a really long time. Maybe 30 or 40 seconds. They finally got me down. The D.I. broke it up.

When I was I guess fifteen. I was at a C.Y.O. dance in west Toledo. I pulled out a pack of cigarettes. And drew one. My friend Rick, The great quarterback, student council president, Didn't like that for some reason. He grabbed the cigarettes out of my hand, threw them on the floor and stomped them. I delivered an uppercut to his solar plexus. He dropped to his knees. Clutching his stomach he said. "you better get outta here". I did.

At the same function a few weeks later I got into a confrontation with some monster wrestler from another school. He tapped me with a hammer fist to the forehead, just enough to buckle my knees. I staggered away.

There was this six foot six, two hundred eighty pound gunnery Sargent who knocked me out twice in twenty four hours.

I had hopped a fright in the yards at El Paso. It was bitterly cold. When the train passed closer to the Rio Grande, about sixteen Mexican wetbacks jumped into our boxcar. There was a skinny Mexican kid wearing a leather jacket. I was willing to commit mayhem to get that jacket. I thank my better angels.

The bouncers at Art Stocks playpen in Fort Lauder dale, worked me over really good. I was bruised and limping for weeks. Not sure of the circumstances.

One of the occurrences that prompted my travels was an incident where my dad tuned me up. It wasn't bad, but it wasn't good either. I was about 16 and defied his order to not go outside. He got me in a corner and started throwing body shots till I was down and sobbing. Can't remember if he kicked me, But every authority figure whoever beat me up would always kick me until I got up. Usually when you get beat up in the street, when their finished with you they walk away. Conclusion: It's better to get beat up by strangers.

I was performing in Roanoke Va. And had had a long running dispute with the manager. He had propositioned my wife. And had been a general dweeb in all interactions. One night after the first set. He and I got into it over the price of a beer. I blew up and challenged him about my wife. He said "that's it...You're fired!" I grabbed him by the throat and the belt and slammed him into the wall. I pinned him with my forearm to his throat and just started throwing uppercuts to the ribs. It was so weird. There was just this look of shock and disbelief on his face. Like nothing like that had ever happened to him before. My trumpet player was a 250 pound Tae-Kwan-Do black belt from Chicago. Also one of the local musicians who was a body builder was in the front row. Together they pulled me off him. We did get fired.

About 35 years ago I was sitting at the bar called the quest off prospect. It was mid-afternoon and there were just a few people in there. Then I decided to do something so embarrassing and stupid I won't even relate it here. Alright, alright. There was a girl sitting on the other side of the bar directly across from me. And I got the bright idea that it would be cute to shoot a spit wad to get her attention. Well once a stone is cast...you can't call it back. I'm embarrassed to say it hits her square in the forehead. And she says " If I were a man I would kick your ass". So of course every man in the place has to defend her honor. They all start yelling at me. I thought I could deflect it and laugh it off, but they were having none of it. Things got more heated by the second, so I threw down a twenty and made a hasty exit. One guy felt it was necessary to follow me out. And catches me in the parking lot. Like I said it was the middle of the afternoon and there were only a few cars in the lot. After the obligatory threats and tough talk, he starts to go after me. Something about that day or that person I just didn't feel like engaging. With all that room to work, he couldn't get near me. It was all footwork, I didn't even put my hands up. He made a few runs at me and chased me with a couple of overhands, but never even came close. After a while he says "Well if you're going to do that shit". And walked away winded.

Almost the exact same thing happened to me a few years before. I traveled with the circus for a short time and we were playing in Hartford Conn. In about 71. I was in a convenience store buying beer and they had the lottery which I had never seen before. So I start asking questions of the clerk, jawing with other customers and I guess I said something wrong, because one guy follows me out. Same thing...I danced around the parking lot till he got tired. That one almost got me Maybe he had some sort of training. I certainly was not very skilled. My youth may have made up for it.

The co-owner of the karate school was also my roommate. We were watching movies one night with my girlfriend and a buddy of ours in the trailer that we shared. We decided to go for pizza, so the girl, the friend and I drive to the local plaza. No one was around and seemingly for no reason there was a podium halfway into the parking lot with some muscle head seated behind. It seemed oddly out of place. I just walked passed. The muscle guy grabs my right arm. Evidently that was the check in for the restaurant, I thought he was the valet.

I deftly dissolved his grip, tapped him on the forehead with my fingertips and kept walking. He leaps out of his chair and steps in front of me. He says "don't flip your hand in my face". I say, "You don't grab a man". And continue to walk around him and went through the door. A long minute passed. I was ordering at the counter and he comes in. This meat-head then did something very unexpected. He extends his hand and apologized, saying he was wrong. He was the Zen master and the bigger man in more ways than one. I should have differed and laughed it off when he grabbed me. He also beat me to the punch by being the peacemaker. Lesson learned.

The first few days of boot camp are orientation, organizing and issuing gear. It is at this time that you also receive inoculations and physical exams. While I was seated in the optometrists chair I evidently said the wrong thing, because the optometrist plowed me in the chest with a very powerful left and knocked the wind out of me. I can only assume that it was an E and not a B.

At one time I was in business with this 260 pound bully. I had to confront him because he had cheated someone I knew. As things got more heated he started to come at me. I dropped down into a stance and he stopped dead in his tracks. Just the fact that he knew that I trained was a psychological defeat. When I used to run, many times dogs would rush into the street at me. Same thing. I would turn aggressively towards them and they would back down every time. I suppose that just like people, you can rely on that strategy until you meet a dog that's a real killer. Like a lot of things, It will work until it won't.

I was in a casual company in this huge dormitory that held about fifty guys. Everyone killed time in this big day room. I was on the floor wrestling with a buddy of mine and I happened to bump against this guy named Jefferson who was playing pool. He cranked the stick back and started kicking me all around the room. Everyone was yelling "get up, get up", but every time I tried I'd meet a massive foot. So I just rolled up into a ball until it was over.

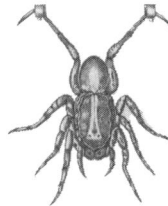

I was at a friend's house and a dispute arose over money. This person was always known to be little unhinged; so he jumped up, ran to the kitchen, quickly returned, and attacked me - with a knife. The strangeness of the situation caused me to be a little dumbfounded, which cost me valuable seconds in my response, because he almost got me with the knife. I barely made it out the door and vaulted over the porch railing. While running, I looked over my shoulder to see he was under the streetlight, slashing the air and yelling: "I'm not crazy! I'm not crazy!" Interesting aside: this guy went on to become a CIA super, black ops. specialist. Real James Bond stuff. Not some bullshit analyst. A real field guy.

I have been bit by dogs, but never one I didn't know. I have been mauled by squirrels, which sounds funny, but was no joke. I have even been charged by a tiger, which turned out to be a joke. But, I digress - I should probably wrap up the story about the CIA guy. For one of his undercover ops., his cover was to be an owner of a strip club in China. What a gig. Who wouldn't want that one. But, I digress again... He was a tall good looking guy who never wanted for company. My guess; he probably was with well over a thousand women in his lifetime. But while he had the bar as a front, he was having sex with all the strippers. He later died of HPV induced throat cancer.

Bunch-O-Nuttin'

It has occurred to me that if this is truly to be the comprehensive book of Tai-Chi, it would be incomplete without a section on almost fighting. As stated elsewhere in this manual, most altercations never develop into full blown physical violence. Therefore, it is helpful, and entertaining, to include some examples of hostile situations that were arrested in the developmental stage. Since this is a manifesto with a bent toward theater, it might be amusing to relate some incidents that never quite erupted into a story worthy of the sea. Tales that qualify only as an "almost fight". These yarns are not exciting, but can prove illustrative for those of a non-confrontational demeanor. With an eye toward true Yin/Yang, allow me the privilege to relate how these scenarios unfolded, ending just short of violence.

ON THE WATERFRONT

In the mid-'80's, I accepted a position as the head disc jockey at a resort on Singer Island, which is the sister cay to the island of Palm Beach in Florida. While this particular spinning job was short lived, I did get the opportunity to meet the husband of one of the bartenders. He was a drummer and knew the area. With almost no downtime from the gig, we started working steadily together in the West Palm area.

On one of our off nights, we were drinking at the waterfront bars in Riviera Beach (just south of West Palm Beach), and eventually became separated, He assumed I got lucky, leaving me stranded in unfamiliar territory. Totally lost and intoxicated, I began walking home; even though I had no idea where that might be. At one point, I was following a fence along a dirt road which surrounded a marine repair facility, far from both lights and people. I quickly became disoriented in the darkness and uneven terrain.

Out of nowhere, a flashy convertible screeched up to me, kicking up a thick cloud of dirt and spinning around me in doughnut. The car then stopped and a half dozen preppie types jumped out of every car door, and they immediately encircled me. As they circled around me, they started with their drunken collegiate tough talk. A tongue of which I happen to be very fluent, only of a different dialect. My verbal offensive seemed to attenuate their savagery, and buy me some time.

Soon, two of the preppies tried to close in on me, but I rushed them and they backed off. More began to envelope me from behind. I quickly spun and advanced toward them with long-fist. They too backed off. The leader, who was leaning against the car, called them all back to the vehicle. Luckily, blows were never exchanged. I must say that the way I remember and relate this scenario, it sounds like I just outclassed them. But I'm sure, here again... angels.

UP WITH PEOPLE

In the '60's there was a traveling troupe of clean-cut young performers called "up with people". They were a folk music minstrel show which was comprised of student council and ROTC types. I describe them in this manner not to be derogatory, but rather to just establish a contrast between this group and the rock band I was incumbent at the time; which of course any such elucidating descriptions would be redundant.

We were contracted to perform as part of a Cavalcade Holiday Show at a big county recreational facility in northwestern Ohio. The show included soloists, bell ringers, a kid's choir, "up with people", and us. We were the rock act (hold it down kids).

The "up with people" show was a stage presentation, with each performer dressed as a different Rockwell painting type. There was a plumber, a mailman, a nurse, etc. Backstage, during the set change, I made a totally unnecessary and smart remark to the milkman. Obviously, it was all my fault, and I don't blame the milkman for what happened next. What made my actions even more stupid was that the guy was far bigger than me, a couple years older; and once in his grasp, I realized, also probably a jock.

As soon as the comment was made, the milkman grabbed me by the shirt. My reaction was to wrap my hands around his throat and dig my thumbs into his windpipe. Immediately, our drummer "Tiger Joe" came between us. Joe was always a big guy; in high school he was 260 lbs. And, although Joe physically separated us, he didn't intervene any further; I believe because he knew I was wrong. He simply pushed the milkman back with one hand, and said, "I'm sorry, I'll keep him under control". As Joe dragged me away in protest the milkman said, "put a leash on him".

TIGER TALES

There once was a successful television show about teenagers living in the 1970's. It was set in a mythical town in Wisconsin called Point Place.

Fun fact: Point Place in a very real place, only it is in Ohio, I know, because I grew up there.

Evidently, one of the writers was from the Point because many references were made of familiar circumstances, and several characters were patterned after real people in my circle of friends. A circle that was legendary. This person was a few years younger than us, so I don't doubt the writer was privy to our many famous exploits.

Fun fact #2: The CIA operative indicated in a previous sea story was the youth they patterned the character Kelso after. I say this because the character is, without doubt, this guy. Tall, goofy, good looking, and girls, girls, girls. Only the show changed all the names around, assigning the name Kelso to our future covert opps. guy. In reality, there was a person named Kelso, but he was a singer in a local rock band. I know this because I was also in this same band. I wound up replacing Kelso in the winter of

'66. And, one of the first shows I played with this outfit was the Holiday Cavalcade mentioned in the previous narrative.

Before the infamous "up the people" incident, there occurred a very similar event at a local teen dance. Parks and recreation in our town, sponsored Friday night dances called "teen town". These dances were held at the shelter houses in the area parks. This venue proved constructive, providing a local circuit for adolescent rock groups to perform. The week before the holiday show, we were playing the teen town at Riverside Park in the city's north end.

While setting up, surprisingly, an altercation arose between me and the drummer. At the time, I had no idea that this was the renowned "tiger Joe". Out of ignorance, I just assumed he was some big fat guy. I guess he said the wrong thing, because in a harbinger of what would happen the following week at the Christmas show, I grabbed Joe by the lapels. He returned the gesture, mimicking me in kind. And, for a very brief second, we jostled for dominance.

Joe attended Central Catholic High School in the old west end. I, however, attended the public menagerie in the north end; which happened to be where this event took place. Each side of town had its own reputation, and north end guys were as storied as anyone else. In this situation, mine was a known face; Joe was unfamiliar, and thus suspect. Before things got out of hand, my friend Smitty jumped in with a few of the boys. I tried to assert my advantageous position, but Smitty would have none of it. Like a mature Solomon, he put me in my place.

Time would make Joe and I the best of friends. Often, it would prove that it was far better to have Tiger Joe on your side, than not. When Joe passed, everyone in town came out to give him the big send off, Years earlier, I had re-calibrated for greener climes, but Tiger Joe stayed in town. He cemented his position in lore and legend of the real Point Place.

TROPIC NIGHTS

Like everyone else who lives in South Florida, the archipelago known as the keys is always a preferred destination. Together, my girlfriend and I drove down to the keys to celebrate my birthday, and did not have the forethought to book a decent room. But we were lucky enough to wrangle a literally rat and bug infested dump in Key Largo, behind the Goodwill store. For those who may not know, there are places on Key Largo that don't rise to the description of a resort destination. There are many decrepit, decaying locations. And, although this particular auberge was located on US1, it also came complete with the felicitous denizens one would expect from an accommodation of such quality. The one thing it had going for it, was it was not far from a more appurtenant location; directly on, and overlooking the gulf. This was a very nice Nuevo cuisine destination, both of more recent construction and higher quality of resident.

It was still daylight when we decided to walk to dinner. We sat at the bar and talked to a nice couple vacationing from the Midwest, and partook of decent selections from the obligatory sea fare. It was well after dark when we began to wend our way back to the location which room we patronized. The path between the back of the restaurant and our motel ran through a woodlot and behind a commercial building on US 1. At the same time that we left the establishment, also exiting were two drunken young men; or at least they seemed to be. My radar went up, just a little, as these individuals passed us. But typically one's guard is down when on vacation. A fact professional robbers are well aware.

They passed us on an adjacent path and were talking animatedly. As they proceeded to travel to the back of the Goodwill store, they stopped and began urinating on the wall, or so it seemed. Once we passed them, they separated, and rapidly approached us from behind. We both felt something was up, so we stopped walking and I turned to face her; as if we were talking. Without drawing any attention, I slipped my knife out from my belt.

That particular evening I was carrying a spring assisted Kershaw. With the knife in my hand at my side, I attempted to quietly click it open. And, although I was hiding the blade, in the still of the night, there was a discernible resonance as the lock engaged. Immediately, the potential muggers stopped and turned in unison, withdrawing.

My girlfriend maintains that it was the appearance of another couple from around the corner that spooked them. But my Spiderco sense says that they aborted when the audible snap revealed that something might be up. Some may wonder if people really do get jumped in dark alleys. If you are less than fully aware at all times, and not lulled into a false sense of security, or seduced by perceived environmental factors, well… yeah.

Hogan's Alley

Now that I have told the almost mugging story, I might as well include an incident that actually took place.

In 1970 I received an opportunity to relocate to Washington D.C. for a propitious employment opportunity. At that time, things were a little thin and I had no transport, but I did have a friend who just purchased a car and was looking for any excuse to travel. So, arrangements were made to give me a lift to DC.

In that era, my older brother just so happened to also be stationed in Washington, and was experiencing huge success as the top writer/arranger for the Air Force band. While he certainly had played his fair share of state functions all around the world, this was his gravy gig. He never had to wear a uniform and never stood muster; he just stayed at home writing music. The Air Force had a company runner who would collect his manuscripts and transport them to the base.

My brother's father-in-law was a slumlord in a rough and diverse neighborhood in the area. This was a big benefit for me, because once I arrived, he arranged for me to live temperately in one of his properties. I moved into this expansive abandoned domicile with only my sleeping bag and one pot. And, while I was slogging through the excruciatingly lengthy government application process, I amused myself with a few books. Also, there was plenty of time for contemplation and dreams of better days.

When I was not involved in the long trek out to Dolly Madison Blvd. for the torturous interview procedure, the highlight of my week was to walk to a payphone to call my parents. This walk traversed through the sketchier part of an already sketchy neighborhood.

At that point in time, my amassed fortune was about 500 dollars, in cash. And, even though there were travelers checks and wire transfers, cash was king in my microcosm world. I debated with myself whether or not to hide the money in the house when in transit, but I finally concluded that I would keep it on me; that way I could "protect" it.

Fun fact: I never had a bank account until I was in my mid-thirties.

On one particular day, at about four in the afternoon, I was on my way to the payphone and was traveling the few blocks to scout the closest main road. It turns out that this road was Constitution Ave.; a central thoroughfare through our nation's capital which is a multi-lane highway that was widened to 80 feet back in the '30's. Traffic was light, and had no other visible pedestrians, except for a group of young kids ahead, traveling toward me, on the other side of the street. Immediately, my radar went up a little because they started crossing the street, seemingly to meet me. I wasn't overly concerned, after all, they were just kids. But out of an abundance of caution, I crossed at the same time they did, in an effort to avoid interacting.

Soon, they began crossing again, to intercept me, and I knew something was up. So, once again I traversed to the other side in unison with the kids. Again they spanned the avenue, and now contact was becoming unavoidable. At this point we were both on the same side of the street and rapidly approaching each other. As we got even closer, I took a better look at the group and saw that they were composed of only 11-13 year olds. Although there were five or six of them, I towered over them all, including the leader.

Still, in my unwillingness to engage in paranoia or racial profiling, I tamped down my concern and stepped off the sidewalk, walking around them. En-mass, the group switched back and passed back in front of me in a fairly confrontational manner. I juke-stepped, and again slipped around the group. They too adjusted with me, but this time they surrounded me.

For a brief second there was a pause, then the leader said, "gimme what you got". I actually laughed in response, for I could have easily tossed any one of them with one hand. Still, once more I attempted to walk around them. But this time the leader jumped in front of me and produced a small revolver. The then repeated, "I said gimme what you got". For a brief second, I debated whether I should charge and overpower him, but in my equivocation, he cocked back the hammer.

Fun fact: As I twitched to extract my wallet, they all snapped to the ready, and one actually said, "don't' you try no karate shit on us". This reminiscence would provide me with much amusement over the years, as at the time I knew very little karate.

I'll give my main assailant this, he was wise enough to stay three feet back. But like all recreants who feel that a gun is their power, extended his arm and pointed the weapon in my face. For a moment, I still considered blitzing the kid, but he judiciously stayed just out of range. Also, within the brilliance of the halcyon, afternoon sun, I could now identify the revolver as a cheap, blued 22 and clearly see the bullets in the chamber.

I slowly produced my wallet, and very deliberately, with two fingers, handed over my entire grubstake. They saw all of the bills, and couldn't believe their luck. Like I said, they were just kids, and one of the smaller ones covered his mouth with both hands and giggled. The leader snatched the cash from my hand and they all ran away laughing.

The film, *Full Metal Jacket* was the greatest war movie ever made. In the film, competent leadership gets wiped out, and an ill prepared N.C.O. winds up in charge. He unnecessarily sends his best man into certain death, overestimates enemy resistance, and very stupidly gets zapped himself.

When the squad finally confronts the sniper, it turns out to be a 14-year-old girl. The most unlikely team member "takes her out", indeed saving the platoon. A well-crafted, ludicrous lesson in absurd waste. Kubrick eliminated the macho "death or dishonor" vindication of violence, and exposes a wretched, melancholy. A juvenile with a rifle wreaks havoc, and a silly screwball makes the kill.

A Yin/Yang theatrical expression, to accentuate that: at once, a situation can be both frivolous and senseless, yet still be deadly serious.

Vastness of the Sea

Before we leave the motif of the ocean, please indulge me with one final personal observation. One may consider this prose, as an interesting Segway into the next section of the book – philosophy.

As someone who grew up around boats and the water, thalassic images figured prominently throughout my formative years. To this day, they dominate my hopes and aspirational endeavors. So, it was not remarkable that I found myself, for a time, working aboard cruise ships. Although it may seem like a romantic fantasy, in reality the boat just keeps going 'round and 'round.

On one particular excursion, my cabin was located right next to the engine room. At times this location proved hypnotic and soothing. But on other occasions, it was just disturbing. Resultantly, in my solitude, I would often find it mollifying to just stand at the rail looking out to sea, contemplating the impressiveness of existence and revealing all the ardor an experience such as this evokes in the human psyche.

Also, accompanying these wondering ruminations, I often found it propitious to equate the arc of an individual life with one circumvolution of a cruise liner. If a lifetime were condensed down into a two-week cruise, then old age would be synonyms for when port becomes visible on the horizon.

One would, no doubt, reflect upon what a disparate collection of experiences and sensations the trip had been. Yet, no matter how nice the trip may be, one will be unquestionably pulling up to the dock soon. One knows the end of the trip is coming - nearer every minute - nothing can be done - it's almost over.

What a trip! Yes, there were some troubling times down there on Lido deck, and you definitely did have to pass through some of them. But for the most part, you were on the party boat. In short, the good times vastly outnumber the bad. After all, it was a cruise. But regardless, the ship will be tying up soon. Sure, you hate to leave, but there is also a sense of relief; because you are only going home.

Ghost ship

At this time, it may be remedial to ruminate on a tale of woe and the two "vessels" of mindset and an allegory to the "cruise" of life and the hereafter.

Suppose you were offered a great deal on a small boat. The one caveat, however, is that the seller insists upon a cash payment. So, you place the ten thousand dollar asking price in your front pocket. But somehow, during transit, a calamity befalls you and you lose the money.

In the first mindset, a wave of negative emotions overtakes you. You are consumed by a sense of anger and loss. You contemplate a variety of self-destructive behaviors to console your loss. But it can get worse; you can always make it worse. In this vein, you get drunk and drive; and because of your continued distracting rage, you injure someone with your car. What was, in and of itself a tragedy, develops into a far more intense and serious drama. And this is a short-sighted view.

Let's take the exact same situation. The money is missing – a seemingly major loss to be sure. This time, however, you remain unfazed and return home to your wife. As you pass through the threshold, your wife informs you that you have just won the lottery for eighty-two million.

Now, the loss of the ten thousand. which seemed so disastrous at the time, is rendered as inconsequential. What was waiting for you at home was so much more remunerative; far beyond anything you ever dared to hope. The experiences on the way home are now revealed to be just that, experiences.

Admittedly, it is difficult to always be possessed of the second kind of mindset. One of hope, optimism and promise. This however is exactly the appropriate attitude one should possess when experiencing a material loss or contemplating the ultimate destination of their consciousness.

The boat is docking anyway, one might as well have faith and courage.

BON VOYAGE

Final Thoughts
最後的思考

If the whole universe has no meaning, we should never have found out that it has no meaning: just as, if there were no light in the universe and therefore no creatures with eyes, we should never know it was dark. Dark would be without meaning.

C.S. Lewis

Fini

When I was very young, I returned to my hometown from my initial youthful misadventures. Since music has always been a big part of my life, I decide to put together a musical combination. Things went really well for the band, and after a short period of time we were working six nights at one of the area hotels. In those days, my confidence in myself alone, was not high, so I hired an old friend from high school and his girlfriend, to front the band.

This was a rare example of where my wacky vision paid off. I named the band "the clean American version", which came from a line I "appropriated" from the liner notes of a Frank Zappa album.

Fun fact: years later, Frank would call me crazy after hearing another one of my acts. In our end of the business, this was a real compliment. And even more so, since Frank built his own career on his renowned eccentricity.

The hometown band was successful beyond my wildest dreams, and we wound up being the biggest thing in town. We were sponsored by the largest food corporation in the area. We also had our own radio show and band memorabilia. Everyone came out to see the hippies in the Uncle Sam outfits playing this weird mix of standards and rock and roll.

The main band members were all hardened road musicians. In contrast, the front people, Ric and his girlfriend, were strait laced "up with people" types. Ric, in his high school years, was the student council president and captain of the football team. And, the girlfriend taught at a catholic high school. This was a clear Yin/Yang to the backing band.

Fun fact: "up with people" was a touring act of 30 or 40 young performers. They were offered as a clean-cut alternative to the counter culture hippies; who seemed to be everywhere. They were kind of a cross between the *New Christy* minstrels, and the *Young Republicans*.

Things were going great for the band. That was until Ric was called out of town and I became romantically involved with the girlfriend. She was an irresistible blonde and I really couldn't be blamed; everyone in the band was smitten with her. Upon his return, the relationship came out, causing no end of trouble within the band; as well as jeopardizing the three friendships.

Ultimately, Ric and I decided that maybe we should talk to someone. We booked an appointment with Father Kevin. Father Kevin was a young priest at the church school where the girlfriend was employed. At the time, this seemed to be a logical decision, because her and Father Kevin were close personal friends. Also, he had been out to see our show several times with a group of nuns, all in civilian clothes; which proved to be a form of enlightenment in itself.

Ric and I met informally at the rectory. We shared wine with Father Kevin as we tried to sort through the emotional conundrum. This love triangle that impacted both our relationship and our livelihood. The session progressed well. That was until it was disclosed that Father Kevin had been sleeping with the girlfriend also. This caused an abrupt switch in the focus of the difficulty. The dilemma was no longer just between the girlfriend, Ric, and I. It now included the Father Kevin.

Needless to say, this was a very disturbing revelation, and I soon became very drunk on the sacramental wine. But not before I was able to press our good Father for explanations of deeper theological mysteries. It turns out that this young priest was more of a humanist and not particularly religious (ya think?). He confided to me that he had entered the pastorate because he wanted to help people; and had no strong convictions regarding his boss. In the end, he proved unable to answer the great mysteries, and was wholly unsure about the state of the hereafter.

Years later I was driving an acclaimed swami en route to a yoga retreat and had the opportunity to make the same queries respecting the afterlife. I really can't even remember the answers he gave, but what I do remember is that the answers were evasive, and frankly, just as big a dodge as the ones I got from the philandering priest.

There are ideologs who, from the prominence of the pulpit, are willing to state authoritatively the state of the hereafter. All while making sure they stay well this side of any crossing over. And, those who have survived a near-death experience are convinced of their sensations. However, no one has ever come back from a full death experience. It is undeniable that a skydiver is different from someone who just walks past an airplane and dreams of the jump. And, our local panhandler almost went to dental school.

For sure, one function of religion is to provide courage and comfort to the dying. The loss of control, tellurian connection, and the threat of oblivion, is disturbing to our deepest visceral instincts. In an effort to avoid debilitating anxiety, most human minds crave a calming balm respecting a destination in eternity.

The customary proletarian concept of heaven is one of golden palaces and endless pleasure. But stop and consider what heaven would be like in reality? Could one be drunk twenty-four hours a day? Have sex constantly? Maybe. But, then one would never be able to fish or go to the movies. Instead, what if there were a place where one could split their time between all these activities, and not miss out on any satisfying experience.

Wouldn't it be heavenly to be able to do anything, whenever you wanted, and yet still have some mystery and uncertainty? Fortunately for us there is such a situation. It's called life. We can do all everything and more. We can look at sunsets, smell flowers, and all the countless other mundane sensations that comprise everyday living.

Since no one has ever come back from the beyond; its best to call it on a technical, and bet on the sure thing we all have - the life we are already living. Without question, there are disasters and very real dangers. Yet, this doesn't happen constantly; and not to everyone. Sure, we must execute our duties, humble though they may be. And, if we are lucky enough to avoid major tragedy, enjoy our one turn on the carousel. But sowing doubt or confusion only diminishes our appreciation for the wonder of this cosmic ride, which is our life.

One rational conclusion from this perspective could be that the main focal point is survival. To hang on as long as possible. Drawing as many breaths as one can before they leave this realm. There is, however, a Yin/Yang to this point of view. Yogananda said that there is really only one reason for human existence - union with God. This statement is based on the belief that the longer one has to work on perfecting the understanding of their existence, the deeper one's understanding becomes. And therefore, their full unification with God becomes ever closer. There is of course a Yin/Yang to even this conviction. And, that is grace. This is where some receive enlightenment in the twinkling of an eye.

Is there a soul in the conventional sense? I think the answer is: yes, no, and what difference does it make. If the idea of the soul as an individualized personality continues on, then: possibly. That reality would be great and has become the evolved dogma for which we all hope. But his ways are mysterious.

The original Hebrew doctrine held that, when your dead, you're dead. The ancient Jews believed that the soul could not exist apart from the body. In the old Hebrew tradition, the soul was synonymous with breath, which God breathed in to the first man. When breath stopped, so did life.

But, Hebrew cosmology changed through the years. And just before the time of Jesus, the Hebrew party line had concluded that resurrection was not a paradise, but a second chance. God will breathe life back into the departed. Both the good and the bad. Then everyone will be judged. The righteous will dwell with God in this new earthly paradise, and those who defied God's law will be annihilated.

As evidenced in; Love of God (Deuteronomy 5:4-6.) and brotherly love (Leviticus 19:18.), this is a principle Jesus most likely accepted as intrinsic. Jesus placed little emphasis on the stringent rules of worship, streamlined the ritualistic requirements, and returned to Jewish tradition; placing the priority on loving God and helping others. In all probability, Jesus did not believe in an ethereal heaven in the clouds. But, as always promised in Jewish tradition, a return to eternal life on earth.

Fun fact: Jesus also probably didn't believe in hell as a place of eternal torment. When Gehenna is referenced in (Matthew 5:22,29-30), the allusion is to the city dump. This was the place where the ancient Israelites conducted child sacrifice. This inference is to the abhorrent fate of having a body dropped, left there, and forgotten forever.

Furthermore, and despite the twisting of scripture by Sunday preachers; Jesus most likely did not believe that a good god would torment his own creation. This idea, where souls were considered immortal, was introduced by later gentile converts from the Greek world.

Plato records that Socrates held no fear of death; for death was accepted in the Greek tradition. This passing meant either a deep sleep or an ecstatic conscious existence. And, Socrates often stated that the soul survived death. Christians who converted from the Hellenistic world morphed this idea, from their tradition, into the canon of their new religion. They reasoned that those incorruptible souls must abide an equal fate; fate good or bad. This amalgamation of the speculations of original Christians and Greek thinkers produced passages cited today as... well... gospel.

Torture was a foundational dictum in European feudal society. And, once this religion was infused into their traditions, torture seemed the likely ultimate destination for souls. This founded the lasting convention of fire and brimstone rhetoric and imagery we witness today. Once established, renaissance painters began to delineate the tortures of hell. Much later, American preachers, pounded the "good book", proclaiming what miserable hopeless sinners were we all.

It's not surprising that the cultural revolution of the 1960's unshackled free-thinking minds from ecclesiastical tyranny. And, that people, once released from religious despotism, sought out and adopted kinder, gentler paths. Paths like those of the Buddhist and yogic traditions. A new mythos of "spirituality" bloomed.

Throughout the modern era there have been many attempts to develop media with a positive twist. Efforts like *happy times* newspapers or *good news* cable channels. Also, a few evangelical preachers have tried to promote a positive message. Some to great success. But despite the best of intentions, the vast majority have all failed miserably. Yet sensational news channels filled with violence, disaster, and tragedy continue to prosper. Without question, the monopolistic bulk of the market responds to fire, brimstone, the tortures of hell and everlasting damnation.

My personal intuition has always been that it would be senseless to volunteer for unnecessary abuse, just because it happens to be the current mass delusion. That there are enough entities threatening me and trying to push me around in the manifest world. And, since I am fortunate enough to live in a country where I can pursue any spiritual path I want; I am more attracted to the gentler, uncorrupted message originally advanced by Jesus. Or, even the Hellenized hybrid of the 1st and 2nd Centuries.

Comfort is offered by great thinkers like Socrates. According to him, and stated affirmatively before the administration of hemlock, he pronounced that death is either complete oblivion and the end of pain and suffering, or the hope of paradise. Either way, there is nothing to fear.

But there exists another idea; one understood by billions of clear-thinking individuals around the planet. The idea that your truest essence will be reborn and recirculate as long as life exits. That one can never really die; because their most fundamental substance and energy must conform to universal laws of physics.

What if an all-powerful entity promised you that your essence would live on forever? Then went on to explain that it would be you, but you wouldn't retain your memories or personality. That your energy, your soul would live on throughout all eternity, but with none of the things that make you, you. It would be the immortal part of you, as promised, but you wouldn't know it was you. You would be transferred into another life. Your essence would live on in a new baby.

What if all this were absolutely true, only your life force was distributed between a thousand babies, or a million other lives...

Yet, if you had no recollection of who you are now, what difference would it make? The breath that I have exhaled over my lifetime is out there, mixing and redistributing - recycled through an untold number of plants and animals. Once a part of me, now a part of everything. A part of me continues on eternally. And, how much more so if one has children. One's essence recirculates continually - forever. Which begs the question, "who where you before you were conceived?"

Then there are those who contend that an embryonic soul is brought fully into existence through a process of self-discovery and examination, guided by a realized master. Through this process, one's default living transforms and they become something new.

Hua is transformation. Everything changes. Your essence, like a caterpillar emerging from the chrysalis, will surely become something else. Your chemistry will be redistributed throughout the environment. But, what of you as a personality?

The bible says, "it is appointed to each man once to die".

Jake the bartender says, "you only go around once".

Tai-Chi says, "relax, It's all transformation".

Laeta Finis

This book is planned as a beginner's guide. And as such, it's commission is intended to be only one of preparation. Also, rather than provide a detailed tutorial on execution of the form, it is a precursor envisioned to instill a Tai-Chi mindset; one receptive to intellection. If one is intent on this type of a tutorial, there is an abundant amount literature and video that may provide one with such step-by-step instruction. Furthermore, an in-depth study is best left for a later day and would only prove confusing and premature; highlighting and characterizing extraneous issues.

Instead, one of the major purposes of this primer is to provide a rooted foundation, one that is not only conceptual, but physical. This is accomplished by emphasizing the importance of Sung and Hua. There has been a deliberate avoidance of various Tai-Chi energies, whose exploration at this time would prove superfluous and peripheral, so this advanced curriculum will be left for another day. Rather than layering on difficult, complicated mind/body protocols, three nails rooting, and/or kua dantian coordination, which will only serve to scatter one's attention on advanced complexities and impede a beginner's progress, this book will bypass such detailed emphasis.

While these complex interactions, modular associations, and precise movements are important and required to function synergistically, they would only confound the objective of this book; which is deliberately designed to get one off to a good start. It is for this reason a gratuitous dive into advanced concepts is exorbitant. This mention should serve only as a bellwether of future areas of focus, no more than just an awareness of Peng, Liu, Ji, and An. Passing references made in this book are necessary for one's later development, and are provided as a preparation for instruction of these energies, and others. Instead of concentrating on these energies, it is felt that the most efficient action for this book is to help one develop an acute understanding of relaxation (Sung), and a comprehension of transformation (Hua).

For the beginner, it can be said that it is daunting enough for one to memorize and perfect the postures, concentrate on the basic importance of structure, execution, and body energy states. But, in order for one to properly grow into the form, all it's movements must be internalized. And as one's expertise progresses, it should not only become more-and-more apparent that the foundational qualities of Sung and hua are essential for long-term advancement, it becomes ever more obvious that fluid-like movement is principle to one's continued physical evolution.

An important distinction needs to be made at this juncture. Sung and Hua are not a type of movement. Instead, they are a quality of the practitioner, not characteristics of the movement; although the possession of these principles do directly influence the movement. In other words, Sung and Hua are what you are and not what you do. This decisive fact is why this book concentrates on these fundamental essences over the other potential avenues of exploration.

With that understanding, let us shift back to the movement itself. For the sake of this discussion, we will consider two types of body movement: segmented (a.k.a. robotic) and unitary (a.k.a. fluid). Unitary execution is the first order of business in Tai-Chi. Because it is so foundational, flowing, unsegmented dynamism is our first and last thought.

The development of this type of movement can be facilitated by affecting an archetype reminiscent of a more primordial time. A time before our own evolution, when amorphous creatures such as earthworms, snails, and slugs proliferated. Organisms that may predate extant exo and endo-skeletal beings. This is relevant because one should strive to develop the fluidity of movement which is displayed during the locomotion of these invertebrate animals. These inchoate organisms serve as a good example, when thinking of the body as one pliable unit. This unique physiology of the hydrostatic body type would exemplify Tai-Chi movement. Creatures such as this are possessed of a Fluid filled body cavity. Their hydrostatic "skeleton" produces a complimentary hydrostatic pressure that undulates unencumbered by osseous structures. This uninterrupted wave moves along synchronously through their entire body. In these creature, their architecture is altered by fluid pressure and muscular contraction and can change the actual shape of the organism.

In humans, this wave is replicated by conventional muscular action supported by an endo-skeleton, not hydrostatic pressure - only a vestigial reminder of how original lifeforms maneuvered through their environment. In an effort to replicate this type of flowing movement (often for offensive and defensive purposes), it may help the reader to build a mental picture of the dermis in the extremities as flexible tubing (almost) filled with liquid; one in which the liquid that can be sloshed around to aid in the potential energy of the movement. This mental aid exemplifies the expand and contract movements of the Tai-Chi player

Fun fact: The dermis is the largest organ in the human body.

This primitive amoeboid movement is reminiscent of when we ourselves were just a blob of protoplasm. Indeed, we are still mostly a bag of water, and, if suitably executed, can approximate hydrostatic movement with the proper squeeze/release contraction of our muscles. This unitary kinesis contributes to affects referenced in the afore mentioned chapter Voltage, where bioelectric activity such as the piezo-electric effect is induced by movement and conducted by bone and connective tissue.

Affecting this type of action also allows for the transfer of power from one body to another, via fluid mechanics. In accordance with the laws of fluid dynamics, while executing the posture "push" the fluids inside the body of the recipient flow in the direction of the "push", via hydrodynamic flow. In contrast, when the same form is executed with a ballistic delivery, the force is instead transmitted through the medium of the fluids of the internal organs, only via hydrostatic pressure.

Through hydrostatic pressure, the force travels through the fluids of the body, but does not cause the fluid to flow. This is an example of Pascal's law, which states that any pressure applied to a fluid is transmitted uniformly throughout the fluid. Employing this principal allows for the martial artist to effect the organs remotely by hydrostatic pressure, even though the impact may have been received entirely on the other side of the body. Put another way, the pressure on a fluid at rest is isotropic, which allows the fluids to transmit forces through the medium across distances, if desired.

In summation, distinct types of energy transfer are achieved by the manner in which the power is applied.

The above conditions are valid, and may indeed facilitate longevity and/or enhanced martial effectiveness. And as a real science, may also provide other tangible benefits. However, as a practical approach, needlessly fixating on sophisticated concepts may prove to be practically unnecessary; not only for the neophyte, but possibly for the advanced practitioner as well. When Tai-Chi people start beating M.M.A. fighters, or living 240 years, high level esoteric technique may prove to be more warranted. Until that time, investing one's time on such abstruse subjects will undoubtedly prove fruitless. That is why this book has chosen the subjects on which it expounds. They will unquestionably be of most benefit and provide a more than sufficient adjunct to any martial art or standard heath maintenance routine.

The End
UKUPHELA

In an attempt to answer some basic questions that most people have when contemplating Tai-Chi, I have created this book. It is a beginners guide and there are no in-depth examinations of the notable aspects of the art. There are, however, enough road signs to kick-start an inquiry into any of the topics introduced here. It is the intent of this volume to be a starting point and not a definitive authority. It is my understanding of the art, its applications, and benefits supported by some science and anecdotal empiricism. As a compilation of germane points presented throughout this book, in this last paragraph I will offer a summary.

Movement is essential. Mind, body and spirit work synergistic. Eat living foods. Stress is caustic. Relaxation allows the body to function optimally. The mind is powerful. compromise is laudable. Always seek peace. Be prepared for anything. The world is unpredictable. Follow the middle path. Extremism in anything is anathema. You may be wrong. The human body can generate tremendous power. Clear thinking in a crisis increases survivability. Trust your training. Never stop fighting. Be the tiger, be the dragon but leave an escape route. Most fights can be avoided. No one has anything to prove. There is a power in the universe. There is a spiritual world. Science is always still learning. No one knows anything for sure. You need friends. Life should be enjoyed, do it for all those poor bastards who can't. Treat your neighbor kindly, he is you. Understanding Yin and Yang can help in all endeavors. Love is not just the best thing, it is the only thing.

Epilogue

A friend and colleague, was the federal cop who literally put the cuffs on legendary criminal Manuel Noriega. After his retirement, he worked for me several times as an investigator and surveillance operative. Due to the nature of my clientele, often I would receive payments in cash. Once while I was counting out his remittance in currency, he commented; "how do you get all these big cases?" He interrupted himself by saying; "I know, it's because your honest."

For someone to function at a high level in any profession, integrity is paramount. Subterfuge and deception, soon catches up with the cunning and duplicitous, Lies and misrepresentations are eventually revealed, heralding an end to any enterprise.

In this volume, I have tried to disseminate this information in a factual manor. I know which questions people have regarding this subject, and have attempted to provide the answers understandably. Due to the esoteric nature of much of the subject matter, however, this can often prove problematic. Therefore, an anecdotal, narrative style, seemed prescriptive.

The real purpose of this book, then, is not to produce a manual detailing proper Tai-Chi execution; but rather, a compendium to proffer a receptive mindset. Preparing the neophyte mentally and placing them in a state ready to assimilate hypothesis and abstractions that may seem exotic and extra-local. To ensure that apperception is amenable to these ideas and concepts, the proper medium in which to germinate must be provided. A type of mental fertilizer if you will. This book is my opportunity to spread around some of my fertilizer.

In order to both articulate and make more palatable, procedure and modus are obscured with some science and tall tales. If nothing else, this book is a treatise on empiricism; my actuality of the capabilities of this subject matter. There is much more to be said, but I feel I have sufficiently expounded upon the mysteries of the cosmos; enough for today.

I would like to thank everyone who has helped make this book possible. The obvious patrons, but also those who have contributed over the years, including the unwitting and covert. I would like to thank the reader for taking the time to imbibe, and hopefully absorb, this information; while also indulging my ramblings and allowing me to share my perspective and experience. I hope my musing have proven worthy of your time and attention. My greatest reward would be to believe that someone, somewhere will be inspired by this endeavor to participate or persevere in the art.

PAX VOBISCUM

NEWTAOAIN PHYSICS

Throughout this tome, I have been seemingly critical of Sir Isaac Newton: presenting him as a nuts and bolts pragmatist. It is germane to his legacy, however, that his genius not be misrepresented by this source - or any other. At times in this writing, It proved helpful to my position to accentuate one particular aspect of this great man's work. It is a point of personal concern, that I too have emphasized his well known mechanistic view and deemphasized his organismic understanding. Therefore it is only equitable to present a more comprehensive discernment. To recognize, that when necessary, I have referenced the Newtonian era; wherein science embraced a more single minded world view. I have maintained this focus to purposely establish the dichotomy between cause and effect physics and Eastern ideas of interconnectedness. Newton serves as a convenient foil for this faction, during the embryonic era of science.

This, however, is was not the actual worldview of the renowned philosopher and alchemist who was much more aligned with enigmatic thought, and wrote over one million words on Alchemy. For a more accurate representation of the Newtonian worldview, it would prove worthwhile to peruse his scholarly translation of the emerald tablet. Sir Isaac Newton clearly embraced expansive ideas and held a hermetic understanding of the organic and mechanistic interconnections. Viz; a Western Tao.

Looking Forward

There is an old zen or Chan story about a seeker who endures a vary arduous journey in search of a sage. When at last he finds the old mans compound in the Forrest, he inquires of the sagacious servant boy how he might locate the sophic hermit.

I ASKED THE BOY BENEATH THE PINES

HE SAID THE MASTERS GONE ALONE

HERB GATHERING SOMEWHERE

ON THE MOUNT

CLOUD HIDDEN

WHEREABOUTS UNKNOWN

Index

- A -

Amplitude   28, 225, 243
An   149, 177, 397

- B -

Bai-Hui   70, 85, 266, 268
Boson   279, 321

- C -

Center of Gravity   16, 122, 267
Chen   11, 179
Chi   24, 25, 26, 27, 28, 40, 46, 80, 82, 141, 149, 150, 175, 291
Chi-Kung   11, 12, 16, 29, 30, 47, 49, 77, 82, 106, 150, 179, 227, 246, 291, 312
Chinese Medicine   11, 20, 58, 62, 79, 242, 349
Chin-Na   158, 160, 175, 176, 205

- D -

Dead-Hand   141, 142, 143, 145, 175, 176, 292
Dim-Mak   11, 165, 176, 204, 205, 206, 207, 303

- E -

Earth   123, 149, 230, 231, 233, 235, 244, 245, 291, 301, 306, 307, 314, 317, 325, 330, 393
Einstein   13, 60, 64, 65, 242, 301, 306, 307, 315, 334
Electron   38, 229, 278, 279, 286, 287, 305, 315, 316, 318, 319, 321, 331, 332
Energy Transfer   48, 49, 119, 141, 142, 143, 191, 226
Enthalpy   145
Essence   27, 144, 147, 148, 150, 193, 230, 278, 299, 394, 395

- F -

Fa-Jin   85, 118, 141, 145, 147, 150, 175, 176, 220, 303
Field   26, 28, 30, 40, 45, 64, 66, 74, 137, 227, 234, 246, 252, 255, 259, 279, 281, 286, 287, 295, 296, 300, 301, 315, 316, 318, 320, 322, 325, 332

- G -

Gluon   321
God   53, 88, 155, 164, 196, 230, 231, 237, 251, 260, 261, 264, 301, 302, 303, 310, 322, 325, 326, 327, 354, 393
Gravity   37, 62, 72, 121, 122, 177, 225, 236, 237, 238, 240, 242, 243, 244, 245, 246, 306, 307, 326
Gu-Chi   79

- H -

Hua   106, 122, 148, 149, 150, 174, 175, 177, 191, 395, 396, 397

- I -

Internal Energy   49, 59, 265, 267, 303
Ion   28, 38

- J -

Ji   149, 177, 397
Jin   147, 148, 149, 150
Jing   147, 176, 291, 292, 293

- K -

Karate   129, 131, 134, 141, 151, 162, 165, 166, 196, 203, 356, 365, 371, 374, 381, 387
Kenpo   9, 47, 150, 162, 167
Kinetic Energy   24, 26, 42, 72, 96, 118, 119, 121, 141, 142, 145, 148, 149, 176, 191, 359, 373
Kung-fu   12, 63, 118, 125, 133, 138, 150, 158, 159, 160, 166, 175, 191, 192, 193, 258

- L -

Lao Tzu   234, 300
Li   175
Liu   149, 177, 397
LUM   140

- M -

Maxwell   65, 66, 67
Meditation   31, 53, 137, 138, 261, 262, 263, 264, 266, 303, 315, 345

- N -

Neutrino   321
Neutron   229, 278, 305, 315, 331
Newton   65, 119, 159, 242, 277, 320, 321, 322

- P -

Pai-Lum   126, 259
Particle   278, 279, 286, 287, 307, 315, 320, 321
Peng   96, 148, 149, 174, 175, 177, 191, 397
PH   37, 38, 40, 48, 319
Photon   63, 321
Positron   305, 318
Proton   229, 278, 315, 331
Psychic Energy   26, 49, 141

- Q -

Quantum   26, 63, 64, 66, 227, 230, 232, 245, 252, 263, 278, 279, 285, 286, 287, 289, 294, 295, 297, 300, 301, 315, 318, 320, 321, 322, 325, 327, 331

Quark   229, 279, 321, 332

- S -

Schrodinger   77, 297
Shen   67, 291, 292, 293
Six Healing Breaths   69
Space   24, 88, 231, 237, 238, 239, 277, 278, 320, 321, 325

Space-Time   232, 238, 242, 244, 246, 306, 315
Sung   23, 57, 59, 70, 122, 123, 141, 143, 148, 149, 176, 266, 284, 292, 303, 333, 396, 397

- T -

Tai-Chi Diagram   147, 177, 231, 232, 248, 305, 308, 314, 316, 318, 331
Tao   28, 50, 72, 80, 155, 197, 201, 235, 276, 286, 303, 309, 325
TCM   62, 242, 349
Time   15, 24, 118, 236, 237, 238, 239, 240, 241, 244, 245, 333
Time-Gravity   236

- V -

Vibration   60, 61, 62, 63, 64, 72, 231, 315, 320
Voltage   27, 30, 32, 33, 37, 38, 40, 48, 244, 319

- W -

Wade / Giles   141, 147, 192
Wu-Chi   67, 106
Wu-Gi   284

- Y -

Yang   25, 63, 79, 100, 138, 141, 147, 148, 155, 177, 188, 190, 201, 202, 254, 263, 305, 306, 318
Yang Lu Shan   11, 12, 179
Yin   25, 63, 100, 147, 148, 155, 177, 180, 186, 190, 201, 202, 254, 263, 305, 306, 318
Yin/Yang Concept   14, 15, 18, 21, 25, 28, 37, 39, 50, 55, 58, 62, 67, 72, 74, 76, 85, 87, 88, 92, 104, 116, 119, 120, 122, 126, 129, 136, 138, 139, 140, 142, 144, 147, 149, 152, 154, 155, 156, 159, 175, 177, 194, 195, 200, 201, 202, 203, 225, 226, 230, 231, 235, 238, 242, 246, 248, 249, 251, 255, 258, 262, 272, 273, 276, 283, 284, 287, 289, 291, 294, 296, 298, 303, 305, 306, 308, 309, 312, 313, 314, 315, 316, 317, 318, 331, 333, 346, 376, 383, 387, 392, 393, 400
Yin/Yang Symbol   147, 177, 224, 231, 232, 248, 305, 308, 314, 316, 318, 331
Yoga   30, 49, 69, 82, 196, 261, 262, 322, 350, 392

- Z -

Zen   31, 66, 193, 195, 233, 259, 318, 364, 382, 403

Zhan   176, 177

Zong   149

Professorial elucidation may be

obtained by trans-continental cable

or by electronic mail at:

TheBookOnTaiChi@gmail.com

Gail Brubaker

Printed in Great Britain
by Amazon